Sexed Texts

Language, Gender and Sexuality

Paul Baker

LONDON   OAKVILLE

Published by
UK: Equinox Publishing Ltd., Unit 6, The Village, 101 Amies St.,
London SW11 2JW
USA: DBBC, 28 Main Street, Oakville, CT 06779
www.equinoxpub.com

First published 2008

British Library Cataloguing-in-Publication Data
A catalogue record for this book is available from the British Library.

ISBN-13   978 1 84553 074 7   (hardback)
            978 1 84553 075 4   (paperback)

Library of Congress Cataloging-in-Publication Data
Baker, Paul, 1972-
  Sexed texts : language, gender, and sexuality / Paul Baker.
     p. cm.
  Includes bibliographical references and index.
  ISBN-13: 978-1-84553-074-7 (hb)
  ISBN-13: 978-1-84553-075-4 (pb)
  1. Language and sex. I. Title.
  P120.S48B35 2008
  306.44--dc22
                                        2007019397

Typeset by Catchline, Milton Keynes (www.catchline.com)
Printed and bound in Great Britain and the USA

Sexed Texts

Contents

Acknowledgements   vii

1 Introduction   1
  'Some people get really angry about labels'   1
  Defining terms   3
  Why gender and sexuality?   7
  Identity, difference and power   10
  Language and identity   14
  Action research?   16
  Texts and methodologies   20
  Overview of the book   23

2 Accounting for difference   29
  Introduction   29
  Jespersen and Legman – deficit   29
  Second wave feminism – dominance   32
  Sexist language and political correctness   36
  Men are from Mars – difference   41
  Difference revisited – corpus approaches   45
  'Gay' language   50

3 Doing gender: community and performativity   63
  Community, contact and co-operation   63
  Gender as performance   72
  Conclusion   87

4 Constructing normality: gendered discourses and
    heteronormativity   91
  Gendered discourses   91
  Compulsory heterosexuality and heteronormativity   107
  Conclusion   118

5 Maintaining boundaries: hegemony and erasure   121
  Introduction   121
  Hegemonic masculinity   122
  Hegemonic femininity?   136
  Exaggerating binaries: the erasure of bisexuality   145
  Conclusion   152

6   Selling sex: commodification and marketisation   155
    Introduction   155
    A new, improved gender!   156
    Commodity feminism and the 'pink pound'   166
    The marketisation of the self: personal adverts   174
    Resisting commodification?   178
    Conclusion   182

7   Queering identity: the new tolerance (and its limits)   185
    Introduction   185
    Queer theory   186
    Queer straights   197
    Bachelors and husbands   203
    Conclusion   215

8   Exploring taboo: on and beyond the margins   219
    Introduction   219
    Vile perverts   220
    Doggers, feeders and swingers   227
    Straight to hell   240
    Conclusion   248

9   Conclusion   251

References   265

Index   289

Acknowledgements

I would like to thank Judith Baxter, John Heywood, Sally Johnson, Veronika Koller, Matthew Davies, Jane Sunderland and Joan Swann, who provided comments, suggestions (and proof-reading) on various parts of the book. Thanks also to my supportive publisher Equinox, and particularly Janet Joyce and Valerie Hall.

1   Introduction

'Some people get really angry about labels'

Recently, I stopped at a coffee shop on the way home to get a drink and a muffin. At the counter, I noticed that the range of muffins on display had been being labelled according to their 'gender', with the larger ones tagged 'male' and the smaller ones, 'female'. Normally, I would have chosen a small muffin as I wasn't very hungry. But I paused. I suddenly felt a bit 'girly' buying a small muffin, and, as a gay man, I didn't want to feel as if I was conforming to a stereotype of gay men as being like women or effeminate. So buying the large 'man'-sized muffin felt more appropriate. But I didn't really want a large muffin, and I didn't want to feel as if I was conforming to the expectation that men should eat larger muffins, or that I was somehow 'denying' my sexuality. Whatever choice I made, it seemed that I would be confirming someone else's expectations, that my behaviour could be predicted and explained – 'he bought the small muffin because he's trying to show he doesn't agree with stereotypes even though he confirms the 'gay' stereotype' or 'he bought the large muffin because he's a conformist with internalised homophobia'.

On the other hand, it was only a muffin and nobody was watching. So I wondered why I was so bothered.

I asked a shop assistant why the muffins had been labelled in this way and she made a vague reference to differences in male and female dietary requirements. She then turned to another assistant and said, 'Some people get really angry about the male and female labels'. They both looked nonplussed. I decided to order a non-labelled slice of carrot cake (presumably of ambiguous gender) instead.

I have described this event because it addresses some of the wider issues regarding language, gender and sexuality that will be discussed throughout this book. Why would male and female labels on muffins make people angry? And, consequently, why would some people not understand why it would make others angry? I will try to answer both questions. First, it could be argued that this 'gendering' of muffins is unnecessary. Most people already know if they want a large or a small portion. To assign food sizes on the basis of whether

1

you are male or female makes at least three assumptions: all men are roughly the same as other men; all women are roughly the same as other women; men and women are largely different from each other.[1] It emphasises what some academics have referred to as a 'discourse of gender differences'. There is also an element of implicit prescription at work, too. People may feel awkward if they want to choose the muffin that is not intended for their gender. It might imply that women ought to be more concerned about their weight than men, or encourage men who wish to lose weight to take a larger portion than they require.

Furthermore, a fixed association is made between size and gender, which is emphasised by labelling the muffins themselves as 'male' and 'female' (rather than say 'intended portion size for the average male (or female))'. We are invited to make comparisons between the sizes of the gendered muffins and the sizes of people. Men are supposed to be bigger than women – anything that does not fit this proposition could therefore be seen as abnormal. While, clearly, the average man *is* taller and heavier than the average woman, such statistics may problematise people who differ from the average. By only offering two sizes of muffins and linking size to sex, the range of different sizes of people is reduced to two categories: large-male and small-female. People who differ from the average could find their masculinity or femininity brought into question. Additionally, such a system requires people to make a choice. They either purchase the 'correct' muffin intended for their gender, and validate a system that has been imposed on them – conforming to the stereotype and perhaps feeling *more* of a man or woman for doing so. Or they purchase the 'incorrect' muffin – and then are required to explain why, at least to themselves (and in my case, the muffin labels raised a number of issues to do with negative stereotyping of gay people and internalised homophobia). I am not sure why food portions need to be labelled as 'appropriate for males or females' or, as in this case, 'male' and 'female' at all. Surely 'large' and 'small' would suffice. Or better still, why bother with *any* labels – it is obvious that the muffins are different sizes.[2]

On the other hand, does it really matter? The intention of muffin gendering is simply (a suggestion about) portion control, isn't it? Nobody was forcing anyone to choose a particular size. Some people would say that the larger Mr Muffin, sitting alongside Mrs (Miss? Ms?) Muffin on the shop counter, looked cute. If people complain about it, so what? Who gets hurt? There are far more important things going on in the world to get upset about. There is an element of truth in the stereotype of men being bigger than women anyway. And who cares which muffin anyone chooses? Nobody is going to notice except for the customer and the shop assistant, who is probably too busy to pay any attention.

The story about the male and female muffins is a single, small example of the way in which expectations about gender and sexual identity are continually encountered in our day-to-day existence, often through language use. In this case it was the written labels 'male' and 'female' which made me consider my own identity in relation to them. In the coffee shop I was faced with a very explicit choice which was so 'upfront' that it caused me to pause for thought. However, every day of our lives, we all engage in making small choices regarding the ways that our identities are constructed. For the most part, such decisions are instantaneous, ongoing and unconscious rather than deliberate. They are, to use a term popularised by Billig (1995) in his work on national identity, *banal*. In many cases we may not be aware that we have made a choice or even that a choice existed in the first place. Even if these decisions are pointed out, for many of us, they won't appear to be important. So did it really matter which muffin I chose? Did it matter that the muffins were labelled in the way they were? I would argue that in both cases the answer is 'yes, but in a small way'. Small things, however, are often connected to larger structures. They go unnoticed because it appears petty to challenge them. And ultimately, day after day, year after year, small things mount up, reflecting, contributing towards and impacting on much larger aspects of our lives.

Defining terms

This book is about the ways that language is used in relation to *gender* and *sexuality*. Over the course of this book I will try to explain what I (and others) mean by those terms, but to begin, it is useful to give a few short working definitions, to help get started.

The words *sex* and *gender* are slippery terms to define, not least because both terms have two primary meanings each, have sometimes been used interchangeably, and have also changed in meaning and usage over time. *Sex* can refer to sexual acts (for example, 'sexual intercourse', 'oral sex' etc.), but the word is also commonly used to define the biological distinction between males and females. So when a person is born, they are assigned a *sex* based on their reproductive organs (either male or female – although in a small number of cases, a child may be inter-sexed). In addition to reproductive organs there are other differences: men have one X and one Y chromosome, whereas women have two X chromosomes. This assignation of sex is determined by biology and is usually a binary assignation. We label a new baby by saying 'it's a boy' or 'it's a girl'. A baby is thus either one or the other, and for the vast majority of people, their sex will remain constant throughout their lives.

However, as babies grow up, they also develop a gender. Some writers have used the terms *gender* and *sex* interchangeably to refer to the same concept (as I did above when I wrote about muffins being labelled according to their gender – more accurately, they were labelled according to their supposed *sex*).

In some cases *gender* is used as a 'politer' euphemism for *sex* (perhaps because *sex* can refer to sexual acts as well as the biological distinction between males and females). So with a newly-born baby we could conceivably ask, 'What is the baby's gender?' and the reply would be 'a boy' or 'a girl'. Therefore *gender* can also refer to the biological distinction between males and females. However, most gender theorists use *gender* and *sex* differently.

This different understanding of *gender* was introduced by Money in 1955 who wrote, 'The term *gender role* is used to signify all those things that a person says or does to disclose himself or herself as having the status of boy or man, girl or woman, respectively'. So *gender* refers to differences between male and female behaviour that are agreed on by members of a particular society. The psychiatrist Robert Stoller noted the distinction between sex and gender in 1968, while feminist writers went on to develop the theory in the 1970s. One of the most famous of these was Rubin's 'sex gender system'. Rubin (1975: 165) theorised, 'a set of arrangements by which biological raw material of human sex and procreation is shaped by human, social intervention'.

While *sex* refers to a male/female binary, *gender* has been traditionally thought to operate as a masculine/feminine binary (although as we will see, some people have argued that this is an over-simplification of matters) linked to societal expectations and mores. Kimmel (2000: 5) writes that it is only in the last few decades that we have come to be aware that, 'gender is one of the central organising principles around which social life revolves'. Western society (along with many other societies) traditionally expects men (and boys) to behave and think in ways that are (currently) described as masculine: being assertive, active, aggressive or competitive, taking the lead, being the family 'breadwinner', being realistic, logical, pragmatic, not expressing emotions etc. On the other hand, women (and girls) are expected to behave in a set of ways that are labelled as feminine: being more passive or gentle, taking care of people, doing domestic work, being sentimental or emotional. Such sets of masculine and feminine behaviours and traits are set up in opposition to one another. So men are said to be rational whereas women are emotional. Men are supposed to be competitive whereas women are co-operative. Until the 1970s the terms *gender* and *sex* were often used inconsistently and were interchangeable. However, by the 1980s most feminist writers in academia had agreed to use *gender* to refer to socially-constructed traits, while *sex* referred to a person's 'born' biological status. Connell (1995: 69) explains a key way in understanding how gender and sex are different concepts: while we may define masculinity as 'what-men-empirically-are' this rules out the sense that we can refer to some women as masculine, or some men as feminine. Additionally, he notes that, 'The terms 'masculine' and 'feminine' point beyond categorical sex difference to the ways men differ among themselves and women differ among themselves, in matters of gender'. Clearly, not all men and women act and think in traditionally gendered (masculine and feminine) ways, which makes the idea of always linking sex to gender (e.g. male=masculine, female=feminine) erroneous. So, for example, the boxer Mike Tyson, the female impersonator RuPaul, the pianist Liberace, the American president George W. Bush and the actors Brad Pitt, Pee Wee Herman, Rock Hudson and Woody Allen all express(ed) their gender in different ways, though their sex was the same.

The list of men above raises another gender-related issue. Does RuPaul have the same gender when he is dressed as a woman and performing onstage compared to when he is at home and (presumably) without his wig, make-up and frock? Do actors like Pee Wee Herman and Rock Hudson also change their gender when they are performing? Do non-actors, for that matter, always have the same gender, all the time? While sex could be characterised as immutable (for most people), gender is now perceived as a much more fluid concept. Throughout their lives, individual people appear to change their gender, becoming more or less masculine or feminine over time. And societies can either gradually, or quite dramatically, alter the consensus about what constitutes masculine and feminine behaviour. So in western society, bar a few exceptions, wearing a dress has always been characterised as feminine behaviour, whereas, in the past, wearing trousers was always associated with masculinity. However, during the nineteenth and twentieth centuries, women began wearing trousers for work, fashion and general comfort. Specific nineteenth century cases include the Wigan pit brow girls who wore trousers for work in coal mines and the women who worked on ranches in the American West. In the twentieth century, many women who worked in factories during World War II wore trousers, and after the war, trousers became acceptable casual wear for women. Gradually, then, norms about what was acceptable feminine behaviour changed – arguably in a positive way, since women were less restricted in what they could wear. Interestingly, the reverse ('ordinary' men wearing dresses or skirts) is still viewed as problematic by many people, which suggests that masculine and feminine behaviours are not exact opposites of each other.

So two separate societies may have different notions about what constitutes masculinity and femininity. While *sex* is a fairly concrete concept, *gender* is far more malleable, subject to change across societies and within individuals. Also, while sex is (mostly) binary,[3] it is possible to characterise gender on a linear scale, with masculine at one end, feminine at the other and a 'grey' part towards the middle which comprises a mixture of both behaviours. Such a linear scale can only help us to make sense of gender up to a point (for example, what about people who embody qualities that are both very masculine and feminine? Or people who embody neither?) but for the moment, we will go along with it.

As well as being able to characterise people according to sex and gender, a third aspect of identity, *sexuality*, is related to both sex and gender. In many societies, one of the primary ways that acceptable masculine and feminine behaviour is constructed is to do with expectations and norms about sexuality. *Sexuality* refers to the ways that people conduct themselves as sexual beings. This covers an extremely wide range of phenomena: sexual *behaviour* (what people do), sexual *desire* (what they like and don't like to do and who they like to do it with) and sexual *identity* (how people express and view themselves as sexual beings). One important aspect of sexuality concerns a person's *sexual orientation* (sometimes referred to as *sexual preference*): the extent to which someone prefers opposite sex or same sex partners. In the nineteenth century people viewed sexual orientation as a binary (people were either heterosexual, which was viewed as 'normal', or homosexual, which was deviant). Later, scientists like Kinsey et al. (1948) proposed that sexual orientation operated on a linear scale, with people having varying degrees of attraction to both sexes, and most people falling somewhere in the middle. Kinsey (1948: 639) wrote, 'Males do not represent two discrete populations, heterosexual and homosexual. The world is not to be divided into sheep and goats. It is a fundamental of taxonomy that nature rarely deals with discrete categories… The living world is a continuum in each and every one of its aspects'. Kinsey suggested that there were seven points to his scale, although in reality, people could be placed between particular points, e.g. 3.22.

0 – Exclusively heterosexual

1 – Predominantly heterosexual, only incidentally homosexual

2 – Predominantly heterosexual, but more than incidentally homosexual

3 – Equally heterosexual and homosexual

4 – Predominantly homosexual, but more than incidentally heterosexual

5 – Predominantly homosexual, only incidentally heterosexual

6 – Exclusively homosexual

More complex reworkings of Kinsey's scale have been developed by Storms (1980) and Klein (1978, 1980, 1985). Storms (1980) created a scale based on a grid, with homosexuality on the *x* axis and heterosexuality on the *y* axis. A person who was placed at 0, 0 on the grid, would be classed as asexual (not having sexual desire towards anyone), whereas someone at 5, 5 would be strongly attracted towards both sexes. Klein developed an even more complex set of measures, based on the fact that people change throughout their lives and that there are different types of desire. He devised scales which represented people's past, present and future in terms of their sexual attraction, actual sexual behaviour, sexual fantasies, emotional preference, social preference, lifestyle preference, sexual identity and political identity. For example, someone may score 6 in terms of sexual attraction and sexual fantasies, but would be 0 in terms of sexual behaviour, emotional preference, political identity etc. Just like gender, then, sexuality is potentially a much more complex, variable and sophisticated aspect of our identities than we may at first realise.

Why gender and sexuality?

Weiss (2001:131) writes, 'Gender identity is different from sexual orientation in that it is considered so fundamental to personal identity that it is fixed and recorded by the government, and is required by law to be disclosed whenever personal identity is in question… Gender identity is also different in that its expression is composed of many immediately perceptible clues such as body shape, body styling, voice, gait, and attire. Sexual orientation can be denied; transsexuality is much more difficult to deny. Thus, gender identity is subject to scrutiny in a way which sexual identity is not'.

It could be argued, however, that sexuality and gender are intrinsically linked in a number of ways. For example, one way that people are expected to express their gender is through their sexual behaviours and desires. Men display traditional masculinity by being the person who does the pursuing in a relationship, whereas women are supposed to be more passive. In the past, men were expected to penetrate and be physically active during sexual intercourse, whereas women were penetrated, while, according to the famous saying, 'lying back and thinking of England' (or France, or America or wherever they live). In addition, the sorts of bodies and sexual identities that are considered to be most sexually desirable in (current western) society, are strongly linked to ideas about traditional masculinity and femininity. So an attractive man is tall and muscular, with broad shoulders and a defined chest. On the other hand, an attractive woman would be smaller and thinner, embodying adjectives like 'petite' or 'dainty'. Additionally, when people 'deny' their sexual orientation (as Weiss notes, above), it could be argued that a strong reason for doing so is because gender norms place expectations on people regarding the ways they should behave sexually – a 'real' man does not find other men desirable or allow himself to be penetrated, for example. As we will see throughout this book, there are many ways in which gender and sexuality are mutually dependent.

In the past there have been many interesting and informative books that have primarily focused on either gender or sexuality from a linguistic perspective. For example, Kramarae (1981), Coates and Cameron (1988), Graddol and Swann (1989), Spender (1990), Perry et al. (1992), Coates (1993, 2002), Tannen

(1993), Mills (1994, 1995a), Johnson and Meinhof (1997), Talbot (1997), Wodak (1997), Romaine (1999) and Litosseliti and Sunderland (2002), have all written about the relationship between language and gender from different perspectives. Similarly, Chesebro (1981), Leap (1995, 1996), Livia and Hall (1997), Baker (2002, 2005), Campbell-Kibler et al. (2002), Cameron and Kulick (2003, 2006) and Leap and Boellstroff (2003) have published similar work on language and sexuality (although many of these books concentrate mainly on homosexuality, for reasons that will be addressed later). Some of the books mentioned above are edited collections (consisting of distinct chapters written by different authors), and in those cases there is sometimes a more sexuality-based subject appearing in a book on gender or vice versa (for example, Heywood's (1997) chapter on 'homosexual' narratives which appears in Johnson and Meinhof's edited collection *Language and Masculinity*). However, on the whole, books on language and gender tend to have (nominally heterosexual) men and woman as their subject, whereas those on language and sexuality tend to be written about (nominally) gay men (and to a slightly lesser extent, lesbians).

There are perfectly good arguments for this state of affairs: gender and sexuality are both weighty topics and there is much worth in considering them singly. Gender and sexuality are components of a person's identity, along with many other components (age, social class, ethnicity, religion, health or ableness etc., see McClintock, 1995, and Skeggs, 1997). However, in this book I argue that while all these components interact in a variety of ever-changing ways to construct an individual's identity, the interaction between gender and sexuality is special – it has a saliency that is worth highlighting and investigating in detail. In more recent times, this relationship between sexuality and gender has been increasingly referred to by other researchers. For example, Remlinger (2005: 133), in her study of classroom ideologies writes that, 'ideologies of gender and sexuality are interdependent. How students believe, value and practice gender in their talk directly connects to how they believe, value and practice sexuality'. And in the edited collection *Talking Gender and Sexuality* (McIllvenny, 2002: 139) argues '...gender and sexuality cannot be separated out: doing gender produces heteronormativity, not only gender hierarchy. And 'doing' sexuality (or sexual harassment) may have a lot to do with reproducing gender hierarchy as well'. Cameron and Kulick (2003: 72) point out that 'there is a close relationship between gendered speech and the enactment of heterosexual identity – but also the relationship is more complicated than it might initially seem... a performance of heterosexuality must also be in some sense a performance of gender, because heterosexuality requires gender differentiation. There is no such thing as a generic, genderless heterosexual: rather there are male and female heterosexuals'. Speer and Potter (2002: 174) also acknowledge the strong link between gender and sexuality: 'heterosexist talk relies on and invokes normative notions of gender and sexuality, policing their boundaries, consequently telling us much about the construction of both'.

So gender norms are very strongly linked to sexuality norms. A masculine man is often expected (or required) to be heterosexual. A feminine man, on the other hand, is usually (though not necessarily correctly) regarded as homosexual, while the reverse is true for women: masculine women are usually regarded as lesbians. One of the goals of this book is to show how language is used in order to map sex, gender and sexuality onto each other, making them function as a triangle of connected identity components.

In western society, and many other societies, until relatively recently, the dichotomies of biological sex have provided a strong basis both for defining gender expectations *and* sexuality expectations (see also Parsons' (1955) model of the nuclear family). Relatively speaking, in Victorian times the ways that male and female roles, behaviours and desires were conceived were more predictable and narrow than they are in the present day. Men and women were expected to get married to a partner of the opposite sex, have children and live in a monogamous relationship (or at least keep up the appearance of one). Men were normally expected to be the main breadwinner of the family, whereas women were expected to look after children (and other relatives) and carry out domestic tasks at home, receiving no official payment, or sometimes working in a part-time, temporary capacity. Forms of sexual expression or behaviour which ran counter to the emergence and maintenance of a basic family unit (such as divorce, never marrying, promiscuity, homosexuality, prostitution, transsexualism, rape, paedophilia, bestiality, or even a young man marrying a much older woman who could not have children) were taboo to varying degrees. And to ensure that people did not deviate too much (at least publicly) from these rules, social institutions such as the church, the law and local communities ensured that rewards and punishments were meted out accordingly.

Obviously, this is a somewhat simplistic view of society: in individual families there could have been a great deal of variation regarding the division of tasks and the different kinds of power that people possessed. Social class also played a large part in determining how rigid these 'traditional' sex and gender roles were (the very wealthy were often able to break conventions, as could the very poor), and despite women 'staying at home', many of them would have possessed power in other ways, e.g. by being in control of how the husband's wage was spent (see also Marwick, 1996: 63–69). Also, although it was considered normal to marry and have children, other forms of sexual expression often occurred but were not talked about or considered less important, provided that people did not deviate too much from the expected family route. Gender and sexuality norms served to encourage *ideals* although divergence from these ideals did occur. Traditions were not static either, for example, in the UK, people living in the Restoration period had different ideas about sexuality and gender to the Victorians or people living in the 1950s. Yet despite these riders, we could still view the sexual and gender roles of the past as being somewhat traditional and restricted – at least when compared to the present day.

However, due to a number of advances (including those associated with technology and philosophy), traditional expectations about gender and sexuality were challenged during the twentieth century. For example, the feminist movements of the twentieth century argued, at different times (e.g. the Suffragettes of the early twentieth century, the 'women's libbers' of the 1960s), that women's status should be equal to men's. Additionally, movements in the second half of the twentieth century, started by gay men, lesbians and bisexuals (the Campaign for Homosexual Equality, Gay Liberation, Stonewall, Outrage, the Lesbian Avengers, Queer Nation) carried out political campaigns aimed at changing the status of gay men, lesbians, bisexuals and other 'sexual minorities', although, again, the aims of these groups and the methods they employed have differed widely.

Despite the successes of such movements, we should not assume that traditional conceptualisations of sexuality and gender have been (or even ever will be) completely over-turned. For example, as Eckert and McConnell-Ginet (2003: 39–40) point out, although many women now work, they have still tended to be employed in 'nurturing' contexts such as teachers of small children, nurses, secretaries and flight attendants. Additionally, some people who experience same-sex desire still take pains to conceal such desires, and verbal and physical violence towards people who identify themselves as gay or lesbian (or are suspected to hold those identities) still continues (see, for example, Plummer, 2001, King and McKeown, 2003, Kosciw, 2004).

One intention of this book is to examine what the consequences of these recent social changes have been on western society's definitions of gender and sexuality. What is now acceptable, and what is not, and how are these competing understandings of sexual and gendered identities played out, particularly through language?

Identity, difference and power

Having referred to the importance of *identity* several times now, it is useful to explain what is meant by it. Unfortunately, it is not easy to define. Gleason (1983: 918), in his review of the term, points out that *identity* is relatively new, emerging in social science literature in the 1950s and made popular by the psychoanalyst Erik Erikson in his works *The Problem of Ego Identity* (1956) and *Identity and the Life Cycle* (1959). For Gleason, most definitions of *identity* tend to fall into one of two opposing conceptions. In one sense, identity is 'intrapyschic' in that it comes from within, is fixed and stable and is what people speak of when they talk about 'who we really are'. But on the other hand identity can be 'acquired' in that it is an adoption of socially imposed, or socially-constructed roles – therefore, someone can be said to identify as *X* or *Y*. Such social identities are liable to change over time. Epstein (1998: 144) points out that Habermas's (1979: 74) discussion of ego identity is a mediation point between the two definitions. For Habermas (1979: 74), ego identity is a socialised sense of individuality, '...a growing child first of all integrates itself into a specific social system by appropriating symbolic generalities; it is later secured and developed through individuation, that is, precisely through a growing independence in relation to social systems'.

When I use the term *identity* in this book, I acknowledge that it has different meanings for different people, but I use it to refer mainly to socially-constructed identities that are subject to change throughout the course of our lives, although at any given point, such identities may feel solidified and reflect 'the real self'.

Although we often talk about identity in the singular, it could be said that we have *identities* made up of many different and interacting components. I have already discussed the concepts of sex, gender and sexuality. So individuals could be said to hold a sex identity, a gender identity and a sexual identity, as well as an ethnic identity, a national identity, a social class identity, an age identity, a religious identity, a work identity, a physical appearance or body identity etc. It is the sum of these identities that makes us who we are. That is not to say that we can change our identities at will. We are born with some identities, like our sex and ethnicity, and although we may try to deny or alter them, traces are still likely to remain. Other identities, such as social class, may change throughout our lives or they may stay constant. We may make a conscious effort to change social class – for example, by pursuing further education courses, getting a different type of job, altering our accent, making different friends etc. With other aspects of identity, the identity could change, but the process would be less self-conscious. For example, many people do not consciously try to adopt a particular gender as they grow from an infant to a child to an adult, rather it seems to be picked up unconsciously. However, some people may try, consciously, to alter their gender identities in different contexts. Similarly, a person may attempt to alter their sexual identity. Thus, a man who strongly experiences same-sex desire, may claim that he is heterosexual, marry a woman and have children, although it is unlikely that his attraction to men will disappear, rather it will be backgrounded. Finally, our age identity is constantly changing throughout our lives, and there is very little we can do to stop it changing. We have no choice in becoming a teenager, adult or old person (although we do have more control over the way we orient to and outwardly express those identities, for example, by attempting to hide our increasing years by wearing clothes normally worn by younger people). So we have varying amounts of control over, and consciousness of, the different types of identities that we possess.

A central component of identity theory is the concept of difference. The significance of identifying as a man, or masculine, or heterosexual, is linked to the relationship that these identities have with the possible identities that a person *could* hold, but does not. In other words, identities (like many other things) acquire meaning and value in societies because of what they are *not*. A man is not a woman. Masculine is not feminine. Heterosexual is not homosexual. So whilst social identities carry prescriptive rules about the ways that people should behave and think, there are also rules about the ways that they *mustn't* behave and think, lest they stray from a particular identity. The boundaries of some identities are more strictly policed than others (for example, it is unusual for men to wear skirts, but not unusual for women to wear trousers). And in addition to difference, not all identities hold equal power. Power is one of the driving forces behind the construction and maintenance of identities. With so many identities being characterised in terms of binary distinctions – black/white, man/woman, child/adult, heterosexual/homosexual – Derrida (1981a: 41) notes that there is often a power imbalance between the poles of these binaries. So, as Hall (1997: 235) suggests, we should really write **white**/black, or **man**/woman in order to capture this power dimension. Of course, as already suggested, these binary distinctions are simplifications of more complex relations. There are several ways in which the binary systems are reified (or made to appear 'real'). For example, people who can not be easily allocated an identity on one side of a binary (perhaps they occupy a position outside the binary or embody aspects of both sides) are often dealt with in ways that downplay their existence, as is examined in more detail in Chapter 5.

Another way of reifying the binary model of identities is by using stereotyping: exaggerating the differences between the binaries and reducing the behaviour, speech and other characteristics of all the members of the less powerful side of the binary to a few traits (which are often negative and/or humorous). For example, Hall's (1997: 223–79) discussion of the stereotyping of racial identity in the eighteenth and nineteenth centuries notes how black people were represented in terms of a few essential characteristics, or reduced to their supposed essence and naturalised: a strategy designed to fix difference and thus secure it forever: 'Laziness, simple fidelity, mindless 'cooning', trickery, childishness belonged to blacks as a race, as a species. There was nothing else to the kneeling slave but his servitude; nothing to Uncle Tom except his Christian forbearing; nothing to Mammy but her fidelity to the white household – and… her 'sho' nuff good cooking' (Hall, 1997: 245). My own research (Baker, 2005) on tabloid newspaper stereotypes of homosexuals found that they were frequently represented through a number of negative traits: having transient relationships, being sexually promiscuous, proselytising children, being politically strident and having their sexual identities characterised in terms of either secrecy and shame or obviousness and flamboyance.

Stereotyping deploys a strategy of splitting, by excluding or expelling everything which does not fit: '...boundaries...must be clearly delineated and so stereotypes, one of the mechanisms of boundary maintenance, are characteristically fixed, clear-cut, unalterable' (Dyer, 1977: 29). Stereotyping tends to occur where there are gross inequalities of power: 'in a classical philosophical opposition we are not dealing with the peaceful co-existence of a vis-à-vis, but rather with a violent hierarchy. One of the two terms governs the other (axiologically, logically, etc.) or has the upper hand' (Derrida, 1981a: 41).

But the many identities that we hold may not have equal importance to us at any given point in our lives. We may consider certain identities to define us more strongly at different times. And, typically, identities which are problematic in some way tend to be the ones that become focused on. Becker (1963: 33–4) suggests, 'One will be identified as a deviant first, before other identifications are made'. While for Goffman (1963: 14), it is not only outsiders who place a premium on stigmatised identities; those who are stigmatised must constantly 'manage' their identities on dichotomies such as excuse/confront and reveal/conceal. In some cases, identity management becomes the central tenet of a person's life. Epstein (1998: 145) echoes these points in his discussion of labelling theory, arguing that stigmatised or deviant identities are likely to subsume other aspects of identity – all behaviour of people with a stigmatised identity will therefore be seen by others as a product of that stigmatised identity.

However, because we hold so many different types of identity (which are prone to change), for most people, power is not a simple case of all or nothing. We can all utilise different types of power in different contexts and with different people. Due to the multiplicity of identities we hold, it is likely that we will possess at least one type of identity that is stigmatised or tends towards the more powerless half of a supposed binary (or, indeed, doesn't occur on either side of the binary). Additionally, it is perhaps simplistic always to view one side of the binary as holding all the power. Men are traditionally understood to hold power over women, for example, but that is not to say that we do not find instances of women holding power over men. The way that they realise this power might be more subtle or different from male power, but it is still there. Additionally, women can hold power over other women, and men can dominate other men. Such an understanding of power as complex, subtle, context-specific and also affected (to varying extents) by movements such as feminism, have led to newer forms of analysis becoming popular. As Brooks (1997: 2) notes, 'Postfeminism... occupies a 'critical' position in regard to earlier feminist frameworks at the same time as critically engaging with patriarchal and imperialist discourses. In doing so, it challenges hegemonic assumptions held by second wave feminist epistemologies that patriarchal and imperialist oppression was a universally experienced oppression'. So while this book addresses issues of identity and power, it also takes into account the fact that power is not necessarily mono-lithic and, in particular, recent social changes have resulted in the relationship between power and identity becoming much more complex, requiring more sophisticated forms of analysis that take this into account.

Language and identity

So, if people possess a number of different identities, how are they realised? How do we know that someone belongs to a particular identity group? One of the central tenets of this book is that language plays a large part in the construction of identities. As Weedon (1997: 21) notes, language is a site for the construction and contestation of social meanings. For the purposes of this book I differentiate *language* from *communication*, defining language as a system of expression involving agreed-upon symbols (mainly written and/or spoken, e.g. combinations of sounds produced by voices, written marks produced on paper or keyboard presses resulting in electronic symbols appearing on a screen) in order to intentionally transmit a message to another being. The agreed-upon symbols are also required to conform to a grammar or system of rules in order for them to be manipulated in various ways.

I use *communication* as a wider term, which would cover all forms of language, but also includes any process which involves the transmission of information, whether intentional or not (in an embarrassing situation, a person who blushes is likely to communicate their embarrassment whether they want to or not), or whether involving a recognised symbolic system (such as an alphabet) or one which does not involve human-engineered symbols (such as pheromones, which people react to unconsciously).

Coming somewhere between the concepts of agreed-upon language systems and other forms of communication that are less intentional or self-conscious, is a somewhat grey area consisting of phenomena such as the way we wear our hair, the clothes we wear, the way we sit, walk or drive, which are all likely to communicate messages, and therefore aspects of our identity, to others, although we would perhaps not traditionally refer to these things as linguistic. And, clearly, identities are not signified merely by words alone. Although the choice of words that we use may tell people something about our gender or sexual identities, the *way* that we say or write something may also reveal a great deal (e.g. our accent and tone of voice, or what our handwriting looks like and the colour pen that we choose), particularly when considered along with non-verbal communication (amount of eye contact, gestures, stance when talking, etc.). Such phenomena may signify unspoken yet agreed-upon meanings within different societies. So we might see a man walking in a particular way and think, 'He's walking like a woman', but we can only make this judgement because we are aware of how different types of men and women usually or stereotypically walk in our society.

Therefore we communicate our identities in a variety of ways, of which recognised language systems are just one admittedly important aspect. Although the focus of this book is on language (in its traditional spoken and written forms), it is worth acknowledging that identities are communicated in a range of other non-linguistic ways, in combination with language.

Additionally, as well as language being an important way that we communicate aspects of our sexual or gender identities, language is also the way in which ideas and ideals about gender and sexuality are circulated within society. So for example, imagine it is a hot day and you have been running. Some people might say they have been *sweating*, others may say they have been *perspiring*. Others may say something else. The choice of verb could be said to communicate something about gender, as the following conversation between two teachers (taken from the British National Corpus[4]) rather humorously demonstrates:

Jan:	I'm not, I don't sweat do I?
Richard:	Er, no, ladies always perspire
Jan:	No, ladies glow. Men perspire or sweat
Richard:	Oh, oh, oh right, mm.

British National Corpus File KDR

It could be argued that at the start of this excerpt Jan behaves in a stereotypically female or feminine way by worrying about sweating. The conversation, however, quickly turns into a game regarding the definition of words for sweating that are applicable for men and women. So while language can be used to communicate sexual and gender identities, it also provides the means through which our understandings about sexuality and gender are formed. How do we learn what it means to be male, female, heterosexual, gay, etc.? How do we learn which identities are viewed as better or worse than others? And how do we contribute towards this ongoing societal evaluation of sexual and gender identities? Again, language is the key process by which we develop accounts of sexuality and gender.

In the excerpt of the conversation above, both Jan and Richard use language to note that men and women are different: 'ladies always perspire', 'No, ladies glow. Men perspire or sweat'. And at the same time, the way they describe the difference between men and women is centred around the choice of verbs which refer to the physical process of sweating. In real terms, sweating is the same for men and women – but by labelling the process with different verbs (*sweat* vs. *perspire* vs. *glow*) which have different connotations, language is used to create a kind of social reality – the *appearance* of difference between men and women, where there is actually no physical difference. Richard says that ladies perspire rather than sweat, whereas Jan takes the distinction a step further, arguing that ladies actually glow. It is possible that the two participants are both joking, referring to the linguistic difference in order to make fun of it – the use of a more delicate or euphemistic verb like 'glow' suggests a belief that women do not or should not sweat (probably because of the association of sweating with physical labour). It positions women as delicate, fragrant and somewhat passive. See Ventola (1998) for further discussion of the *sweat/perspire/glow* distinction.

We might also notice that there is a difference in lexical choice regarding the gender labels assigned to the sexes. Richard refers to *ladies* rather than *women*, whereas Jan refers to *men* rather than *gentlemen*. By using a polite word for women, *ladies*, while using the standard word for adult human males, *men*, the difference between the sexes is exaggerated. The two speakers therefore co-construct shared knowledge about what it is to be male or female in society, echoing what I would call 'received wisdom'. Even though they may be drawing on such knowledge in order to make a joke about it (and therefore to possibly challenge it), this can only be achieved through the use of language. Language both communicates and constructs male and female identities. In the story about the muffins with which I began this chapter, it was again the use of language, in this case, the written labels 'male' and 'female', which presented a particular view of the world in terms of gender and the expectations regarding food choices that customers were supposed to make.

So we use language both to communicate our own gender and sexual identities and to demonstrate how such identities are understood in society. These two aspects of language are linked, as we will see. Language is therefore an important, if not a central aspect, of any study of gender or sexuality.

Action research?

One important question which concerns the study of language, gender and sexuality is 'What do researchers hope to achieve by doing this?' There are a number of possible responses. On a purely descriptive level we may simply be interested in outlining, as accurately as possible, the relationship between language, gender and sexuality, or by describing the ways in which language is used to communicate sexual and gender identities and ideologies. Such an approach has much in common with methodologies in the sciences and social sciences which have variously been referred to as empirical, positivist, quantita-tive or structuralist. In this sense, the researcher tends to be viewed as a 'neutral observer'. He or she reports or interprets results in as unbiased a way as possible, for example, by testing hypotheses (often under experimental conditions) and trying to remove bias by using equal sized samples that are representative of a population.

We could characterise a lot of 'hard' science in this way – for example, the categorisation of plants and animals, the observation of chemical or physical reactions, or the positions and trajectories of various stars, planets and comets in the night sky. Initially, when social scientists started studying human behaviour, they also used such methodologies (see Chapter 2 for further discussion). However, we could argue that it is more difficult to subject human behaviour and societies to the same rigorous, descriptive methods of categorisation that have been favoured in physics, medicine and biology, particularly when looking at subjects like identity and language. And in taking a dispassionate, 'neutral' perspective in the social sciences, there are a number of potentially negative consequences. For example, Hacking (1990) suggests that the scientists who produced a wealth of statistical data regarding humanity in the nineteenth century effectively created a form of social regulation. These statistics (coupled with various tables of averages) helped to define what was 'normal' behaviour, thereby creating deviants – people who did not fall within an accepted range. Other researchers have suggested that the notion of an unbiased researcher, par-ticularly when studying human subjects is problematic. So Cicourel (1964) has argued that quantitative researchers tend to fix meanings in ways that suit their own preconceptions. Similarly, social psychologists in the 1960s and early 1970s argued that the discipline was implicitly voicing the values of dominant groups (see Harré and Secord, 1972, Brown, 1973, and Armistead, 1974). Gergen (1973) has argued that all knowledge is historically and culturally-specific and that it is not possible to look for definitive accounts of people and society, because social life is continually changing. Baxter (2003: 6) refers to the *fictionalising* process of research: 'Fictionalising… means that all pursuits of enquiry are concerned with creating a world through language and hence research is itself constitutive or 'world-making'… No form of knowledge can be separated from the structures, conventions and conceptuality of language as described within discourses and texts'.

To give an example of such fictionalising in research, writers such as Easlea (1983), Keller (1985) and Harding (1991) have made links between gender and science, pointing out that natural science and technology is gendered as masculine in many different ways – its metaphors, impersonal discourse, power structures and participants all stem from the fact that men are dominant in society. Masculine discourse can also favour men in other ways. So Bowker

(2001) has demonstrated the existence of a male bias in scientific writing on infertility. She examined how the presence of antibodies (a medical condition which can cause infertility) is written about in relation to men and women. Male antibodies tend to be labeled as *auto-immunity* or *sperm antibodies*, whereas the word *hostility* is used to describe female antibodies. Women are referred to as having *incompetent cervixes*, whereas men have *retrograde ejaculation*: the adjective *incompetent* tends to have a more negative meaning in general language use than *retrograde*. Therefore, terms used in relation to women are more negative – suggesting that they may be at fault, whereas men are simply assumed to have a medical condition.

Because of these concerns, since the 1980s, an alternative set of methodologies has been popular in the social sciences. Such methodologies have not disregarded descriptive analyses, but have instead tended to use them as a springboard for more qualitative and involved forms of analysis. These methodologies are roughly based on the concept of post-modernism and can be referred to as social constructionist or post-structuralist. Baxter (2003: 22) writes that post-structuralist research practices consider knowledge to be 'constructed not discovered; contextual not foundational; singular, localised and perspectival rather than totalising or universal; and egalitarian rather than hierarchical'.

Post-structuralist researchers tend not to believe in the idea of completely unbiased research (because humans themselves are biased), nor do they think that unbiased research would necessarily be a good idea, even if it was possible. Instead, one important aspect of their research has been to deconstruct older ways of thinking. This may involve, for example, examining the social and historical factors behind the ways that categories like male/female or homosexual/heterosexual have been understood, how our understandings of such categories have not remained stable over time, and the consequences that such categorisations have had on society and individuals, particularly in relation to issues of power and inequality (see especially Chapters 4, 5 and 7).

One important aspect of this type of research, then, is to pave the way, inspire or set in motion some sort of social change. Such researchers are not 'unbiased' then, in the sense that they merely want to describe a particular social phenomena but not get involved in changing it. There is the belief that it is impossible to be uninvolved in any case. Therefore, these researchers want their work to act as a catalyst to trigger beneficial social changes. This kind of research did not start with post-structuralism – indeed, a lot of the feminist research on 'women's language' from the 1960s onwards (see Chapter 2) had the explicit goal of raising people's consciousness regarding inequalities between men and women, while researchers into gay and lesbian language were concerned with introducing sexuality as a worthwhile focus of academic study. Such research is sometimes referred to as 'action research' (Burr 1996:

162) because it has change and intervention, rather than just the discovery of facts, as its explicit aim. Many action researchers are concerned with addressing particular inequalities in society, and we could therefore characterise disciplines such as critical discourse analysis, feminist research and gay and lesbian or queer studies as different forms of action research. As Lazar (2005: 6) writes, 'A critical praxis-oriented research, therefore, cannot and does not pretend to adopt a neutral stance'. A lot of the research discussed in this book could be characterised as action research.

On the other hand, queer theory (see Chapter 7) and feminist post-structural discourse analysis (see Chapter 4) could be criticised because they reject an emancipatory agenda, and do not adhere to 'grand narratives'.[5] However, Baxter (2003: 54) indicates that such forms of analysis can still have the goal of empowering minority groups, by supporting 'small-scale, bottom-up social transformations, which are indeed of central importance to the erosion of grand narratives' and allowing us to make sense of 'the relative powerlessness or 'disadvantage' experienced by silenced groups of girls or women'.

We may want to raise a number of questions about action research – for example, how effective is it? In what ways does such research actually impact on the lives of everyday people? Sometimes social researchers can feel that they are working in an 'academic bubble' and that their findings will have little impact beyond others working in their field. Gilbert (2001: 252–53) writes of this when she says, 'I'm afraid that what was feminist criticism… [has] become another sector of the academic technocracy… Some of the leading gender theorists speak in the most arcane ways and are the least capable of addressing public political issues that continue to be centrally urgent in our culture… I want to feel that we have a social impact, that we make a difference in the world off campus. And it begins to feel sometimes that the world on campus isn't just a microcosm of the world off campus, it's a different universe – and that upsets me'.

However, theories and findings *can* be disseminated beyond academia through the media, and ideas that are developed through academic research can find their way around the world, resulting in change. We may also find that action research can be controversial at times – anything that seeks to change an existing situation has the potential to upset or threaten. And even if people broadly agree on what needs to be changed, they may disagree on how to go about it. Because action researchers can sometimes hold personal goals or 'vested interests', this may also lead to claims that they are being overly biased, or are simply pursuing their own agendas at the expense of others. Such issues are worth bearing in mind, but should certainly not preclude action research, particularly as there is a general consensus in academia to carry out such research with a moral and political sensitivity, aiming to ease oppression (Parker and Burman, 1993: 159), while maintaining strict ethical standards.

Texts and methodologies

Because this book is concerned with real-life ways that language is used in constructing gender and sexuality, it is necessary to examine cases of everyday language that occur in a range of different situations. Here, the concept of the *text*[6] is useful. The exact definition of the text is a source of some dispute. For example, Bernstein (1990: 17) refers to a text as, 'the form of the social relationship made visible, palpable, material' while Talbot (1995: 14) calls a text, 'the fabric in which discourses are manifested'. Barker and Galasinksi (2001: 5) position a text as, 'any phenomenon that generates meaning through signifying practices. Hence dress, television programmes, advertising images, sporting events, pop stars, etc., can all be read as texts'. My definition of texts is closer to that of Fairclough (1995a: 4), who argues against an understanding of text as *anything* that generates meaning. Instead he proposes that a text is an inherently linguistic event, and two fundamental processes, cognition and representation of the world, are materialised in texts (1995a: 6). For the purpose of this book, I mainly limit the conceptualisation of text to contexts which involve recognised language systems (as opposed to the wider sense of communication); so this could include an advertisement, story, poem, play, song, newspaper article, conversation or email. However, I would not define something like a hairstyle or football match as a text – although aspects of these things would be related to language, e.g. the name of a hairstyle, talk occurring about it, etc. But here it would be the talk about the hairstyle, rather than the hairstyle itself which would constitute the 'text'. Some researchers (e.g. Hodge and Kress, 1988, Caldas-Coulthard and van Leeuwen, 2002) *have* considered objects such as toys as texts and I touch on this approach in Chapter 4. And in some cases, texts contain visual images which can be 'read' or analysed in order to determine their meaning or message. For example, advertisements regularly combine written words with pictures, and the meaning of the advert can only be decoded by taking into account the relationship between these different parts. Additionally, as discussed earlier, typographic information such as font size, colour and style may also impact on gendered or sexed constructions within a text (see the discussion of use of the colour pink in advertising in Chapter 6, for example).

Another type of data I refer to in this book is corpus data. A corpus can be understood as an electronic body of data or a collection of texts – often taken from a range of sources and consisting of millions of words (McEnery and Wilson, 1996). Corpus data can be useful in providing a wider overview of the way that language operates in a society, providing evidence for linguistic trends and patterns (and so we can use corpora to examine frequencies or collocations[7]). Corpus data can also provide interesting individual examples that are illustrative of a particular point, as with the conversation from the British National Corpus examined above.

As well as text analysis, the related analysis of its context is also relevant. Context refers to the wide range of ways that a text is situated within society, for example, the process of production (who authored it, how many copies were made, how it was distributed, the type of audience for whom it was intended, how much money and effort went into its production, what the authors' goals were) and the process of reception (how many people saw, engaged with or read the text, where and in what ways they encountered it, who they were, how they interpreted it and what consequences (if any) resulted from the text's publication). At a few points in this book, I examine focus-group data – a form of meta-data (or a text about a text) where people discuss other texts or aspects of language in order for researchers to garner a better understanding of context. Texts can therefore be naturally-occurring or elicited for the specific purposes of research.

So in thinking about context, we also need to consider the ways that a text functions in relation to the society it appears in. Is it a new form of media? Is it challenging in some way? Is it unique? In what ways is it intertextual, referring to other texts that already exist? (See also Fairclough, 1989, and Wodak and Meyer, 2001). Contextual analysis often requires the researcher to step outside the text in order to consider additional types of information such as other texts or attitudinal, etymological or historical research. Although the focus of this book is the linguistic analysis of a range of different everyday texts, the importance of combining text analysis with contextual analysis should not be under-estimated. The combination of textual and contextual analyses is a central feature of one of the main approaches used in this book.

While I agree with a broadly action-based research model, one point that is clear about this approach to academic study is that there is no single agreed-upon method of carrying out analysis. Instead, researchers have approached the subjects of language, gender and sexuality from an array of methodological perspectives, employing conversation analysis, phonetics, ethnography, interviews, focus groups, visual analysis, content analysis, discourse analysis, critical discourse analysis, historical-socio analysis, corpus analysis and other forms of quantitative and qualitative analyses. Such approaches have also been combined in a variety of ways, resulting in more eclectic forms of analysis. Similarly, the data or texts used in these analyses have also been drawn from an equally wide range of sources, including writing, speech, Internet, non-verbal, visual, mediated and naturally-occurring texts. Some writers have focused solely on corpora, while others have carried out closer analyses of single texts. It could, perhaps, be argued that there is no need for any type of data or text at all – and instead we could achieve results using introspection. I would argue, however, that because gender and sexuality are such real-world social phenomena, it makes sense to study them in relation to real-life examples of language. Not only would a data-based analysis be grounded in the real world rather than the abstract, but it also allows us to test our theories in a way that introspective studies do not. Also, data at least give us a way of restricting some of our biases – we can't theorise *anything*, because we have to account for the existence of an actual text (be it a conversation, text message or novel) that humans created. Of course, the way that we choose to interpret such a text, and the texts that we choose to analyse, are potentially open to bias, but at least if we make that text available and explain why we chose it, then we make it easier for others to replicate our findings or suggest alternatives to them.

The method of text analysis is often dependent on two other phenomena: the nature of the text itself, and the research question(s) that are asked of it. For example, with the research discussed in Chapter 2, in the past people were often concerned with delineating linguistic differences between men and women (or gay and heterosexual people), which led researchers to record and transcribe naturally-occurring conversations and then carry out quantitative analyses based on counting and comparing sets of linguistic features across speakers. However, in later chapters which consider more recent research, the focus shifts to other questions – how do people construct themselves as men, women, etc.? How does language enable the construction of discourses, which in turn positions people in different ways? How do people make sense of their own gender and sexual identities? In what ways are different texts liberating and/or restrictive? Such questions require a more critical approach to text analysis – analysing linguistic features within texts in order to uncover more subtle clues about the text's meaning. This could involve the analysis of word choice – for example, when someone uses a word like *lady* (instead of *woman* or *girl*), what possible messages are they communicating and is this the same as the message they intended to communicate? In what other contexts do we normally find *lady* – what mental concepts does the word trigger for us? Here, reference to focus group or corpus data might be revealing. The analysis of a conversation or interview may focus on the significance of features like pauses or laughter, whereas the analysis of an advert could centre on the relationship between visual and written aspects of the text as well as ways in which the text accesses ideas about gender or sexuality in order to persuade readers to purchase its product.

The combination of so many different approaches and types of data is potentially liberating for researchers in that it does not force academics from a range of backgrounds to 'convert' to or learn a form of analysis that they are unfamiliar with, or may fundamentally disagree with. The fields of language, sexuality and gender cross many different disciplines in the arts, humanities and social sciences: linguistics, literature, cultural studies, media studies, sociology, women's studies, gender studies, queer studies, lesbian and gay studies, anthropology and philosophy, each of which has preferred and dispreferred ways of approaching research. By embracing an eclectic approach, a much wider range of voices may be heard. Additionally, exposure to different approaches may help to broaden the perspectives of individual researchers. It is not, therefore, the intention of this book to provide readers with a definitive list of ways that they can carry out the analysis of language in texts in order to investigate issues of gender and sexuality. Instead, I employ or refer to a (non-exhaustive) range of possible ways that text analysis can be carried out, acknowledging that students and other researchers may find that some of them are appropriate (or not) for use with their own texts. In using a range of different text types I hope, instead, to be able to illustrate how abstract theories relating to gender and sexuality can be both made comprehensible and tested in real-world contexts, while also indicating the enormous potential, both in terms of data and analytical methods that these fields can usefully exploit.

Finally, an additional point of saliency needs to be taken into account before the close of this section. 'Reality (the potential, the actual) cannot be reduced to our knowledge of reality which is contingent, shifting and partial. This applies to texts: we should not assume that the reality of texts is exhausted by our knowledge of texts. One consequence is that we should assume that no analysis of a text can tell us all there is to be said about it – there is no such thing as a complete and definitive analysis of a text' (Fairclough, 2003: 14). I do not offer an 'exhaustive' account of any text in this book, rather, I acknowledge that my own interpretations are likely to be biased, that multiple interpretations (reflecting other biases) are also possible and different ways of approaching analysis may yield different conclusions to those reached in this book. At times I have stressed this potential diversity of readings, but also indicate that there may be intended and unintended readings, those which are dominant or mainstream, and those which are secondary or more subversive – in such cases it is useful to take into account context, including methods of production and reception. This reflects the 'post-modern' stance, where it is acknowledged that multiple readings of texts are always possible.

Overview of the book

There are also potential drawbacks in entering a field where there are a range of ways of carrying out analysis. One is that people may find it difficult to engage with or agree on the analysis, because the methodology and the language used to delineate it are unfamiliar or even discredited in their subject discipline. For example, a potential conflict exists between quantitative and qualitative approaches. Also, differing theoretical perspectives are likely to underline the forms of analyses that are carried out, and subsequently the findings. So, for example, there have been points of disagreement between those who have written about the subject of a 'gay language' and those who have argued that such a thing does not exist. And, as with all disciplines, accepted theories and ways of study do not remain static; this seems to be particularly true of research into language, gender and sexuality, where methods of collecting and analysing data and the sorts of research questions that are asked have changed considerably over the course of the twentieth century (and are still changing). Potentially, this creates a somewhat disordered feel to the areas of language, gender and sexuality. Edited collections of chapters written by different individuals can sometimes be jolting experiences to read as each chapter dramatically shifts its methodological and/or theoretical approach. Also, the more these fields have developed, the more complex a task it becomes to engage with them, because a reasonable knowledge of what has gone before is required. This is one reason why I try to summarise some of the earlier findings in these fields in Chapter 2, which takes a somewhat historical overview, introducing and critiquing some of the most influential studies, as well as highlighting a few of the theoretical approaches that underpin the analyses in the remainder of the book. So Chapter 2 looks at what some researchers have referred to as 'the 3Ds': Deficit, Dominance and Difference – older perspectives on language and gender, which are viewed as necessary steps, yet are now regarded as incomplete standpoints. I examine early feminist responses to the issue of male *dominance* and sexist language, relating these to the concept of *political correctness*. I spend time relating difference theory to the concept of *essentialism* by reviewing studies using conversation analysis, content analysis and corpus analysis that have argued that men and women or gay and heterosexual people use language differently – for example, I consider the debate surrounding the questions of whether there such a thing as an essentially gay way of speaking or a 'gay language'? I also discuss the range of critical arguments against '*difference*' accounts.

Chapter 3 moves towards later perspectives which took the concepts of communities, contact and co-operation into account. Such perspectives were driven by an emphasis on diversity, the idea that men are different from other men and women are different from other women. The chapter also includes an account of *performativity theory*, which has proven to be a central concept in studies of language, gender and sexuality since the mid-1990s. The idea that gender can be linguistically performed (in different ways) explains why concepts like 'men's talk' and 'gay language' are so difficult to define.

The next few chapters take the reader on a journey from what is regarded as 'absolutely normal' in terms of gender and sexuality to what is regarded as 'absolutely tabooed'. Chapter 4 introduces the concept of *discourse*, by examining the ways that discourses are circulated through language in order to teach gender roles to children through nursery rhymes, stories and toys. I examine how terms like *man* and *woman* occur differently in corpus data, being indicative of gendered discourses and go on to introduce the concept of *heteronormativity*, showing how heterosexual identities and desires are constructed as normal, mundane and assumed in different media texts and in conversation.

Chapter 5 continues the theme of 'normal' sexuality and gender, by introducing the concept of *hegemonic masculinity* and demonstrating how language is used (often in ambivalent or paradoxical ways) in order to define and regulate masculine identities whilst subordinating and marginalising other identities in the process. I address the roles of humour, irony and story-telling as ways of maintaining hegemonic masculinity's status quo, as well as considering the related concept of 'hegemonic' or 'emphasised femininity'. The subject of *erasure* is addressed in the final part of the chapter, by showing how dominant identities require boundaries to be fixed and difference to be exaggerated: identities which threaten to blur the *us/them* distinction are therefore anathema to hegemonic systems. Corpus data shows that real-world references to the problematic 'in-between' category of bisexuality are rare, despite other research which suggests that bisexual potential exists in the majority of people. Additionally, where bisexuals are mentioned in different corpus texts, they are often the subject of denigration (from both mainstream heterosexual and the more marginalised gay standpoints).

Chapter 6 situates gender and sexuality within contemporary western capitalist society by investigating the ways that power relationships are played out through the *marketisation, commodification* and *consumption* of identities and desire. I identify how language is used to arouse desire in advertising through the creation of hegemonic identities. Gender can therefore be 'purchased' by the consumption of products, although, ultimately, we must engage in a process of reiteration – the promise of a 'perfect' gender constantly just out of our reach. I examine a number of ways that consumer identities are created in order to sell brands to specific groups – examples are the concepts of 'The Pink Pound' and 'commodity feminism'. I then explore the use of language in a situation where individual sexual and gender identities are marketed – personal advertisements designed to attract sexual or romantic relationships. And finally I consider whether consumers actually adhere to the 'mindless dupe' model which has driven the more critical consumer-based research, through an examination of focus groups based on men's magazines.

Moving away from 'normal' identities, the next two chapters consider types of people and practices which are tabooed or problematised in some way, taking a broadly queer perspective. Chapter 7 begins by showing how *queer theory* has been used to deconstruct or 'query' the binary and fixed distinction between *homosexual* and *heterosexual*, through etymological and historical analyses. I then go on to address how *queer* has been semantically widened as a non-specific term which can refer to anything which is against the 'normal', and the inherent paradoxes in attempting to work with a category which refuses to identify itself. I consider how *queer* can be an inclusive strategy in order to query problematised *heterosexual* identities, by examining the construction of sexual identities in a newspaper article about a divorced actress involved in a number of short-term relationships with younger men. I then use corpus data to explore discourses surrounding marriage – notably the oppositional terms *bachelor* and *husband*, in order to show how marriage is frequently depicted in a range of different text types as a preferred, normal state of being for adults, and how such discourses feed into gender norms and are strongly associated with the concept of monogamy.

Chapter 8 is perhaps the most challenging chapter in the book as it analyses language practices associated with identities, desires and behaviours which contemporary society would class as *deviant, marginalised* or *tabooed* in some way. I write about how such phenomena are constructed, demonised or alluded to in the media, examining the construction and maintenance of moral panics surrounding the tabooed identities of paedophiles and doggers (people who engage in outdoor, anonymous sex). Such texts reflect an ambivalent fascination with 'deviant' sexuality. I consider the extent to which queer theory can be effectively employed upon such sexual identities or practices which exist beyond the remit of the law or outside an 'informed consent'-based code of ethics. I also show how language is used as part of the maintenance of '*communities of practice*' based around particular sexual fetishes, and how language is important in redefining how people make sense of the world (Halliday's concept of anti-language is useful here), by using a case study involving the language use of the FA (Fat Admirers) and swingers communities via websites. Finally, I examine an aspect of the '*sex wars*' which took place in the late 1970s and early 1980s – the debate over pornography. I consider a pornographic narrative concerning sex between men, in order to show how such texts raise questions about the nature of sexual identity as stable as well as highlighting the ambivalent relationship between dominance and desire.

Finally, Chapter 9 serves as a conclusion, summarising the key points of the book, turning a more critical eye over the research findings, and, finally, making suggestions about possible future directions that the field is taking and some of the potential problems it may face.

This is a lot to cover, then. In terms of writing, I have tried to be as clear as possible. An unfortunate consequence of writing an academic book, is that many people (students, researchers and non-academics) can find that the language and terminology is impenetrable or difficult to follow. This denotes a failing because the ideas and concepts discussed in this field can be made more accessible, and therefore have greater impact, if they are expressed in a way which can be readily grasped. Ironically, a goal of many post-structuralist researchers is to challenge or 'deconstruct' existing power structures. Therefore, their work should be accessible to everybody. It would be a rather fruitless 'own goal' if such researchers created a new power binary based on an academic/non-academic distinction. A further goal in focusing on textual analysis is to show how theories about language and gender can be made clear, by basing them in real-world contexts.

Bearing this in mind, Chapter 2, therefore, starts 'at the beginning', by providing an account of some of the earlier ways in which research into language, gender and sexuality were conceptualised and carried out.

Notes

1   In other cases, such as packets of crisps, recommended calorie intakes are given for men and women on the packet, although these are described as based on averages and it is stated that individuals may have different requirements. Such cases therefore make more allowance for variation.

2   Muffins are not the only example of gendered products I am aware of. A supermarket near me sells 'male' and 'female' herbal tea – the male tea is packaged in a brown box, while the female tea comes in a pink box. And in a pub near where I live, I have been asked whether I would like my orange juice in a 'gentleman's glass' or a 'lady's glass' – the gentleman's glass is a traditional pint glass used for beer, while the lady's glass is a smaller, curved wine glass. Many people will have heard of 'man-sized' tissues. Are men really so much bigger than women that they require larger tissues?

3   The existence of small numbers of intersexed and transsexual people actually challenges the notion that sex is a male/female binary, although most people only perceive there to be two sexes.

4   The British National Corpus is a corpus of almost 100 million words of contemporary written and spoken British English, gathered from a wide range of contexts.

5   Queer theory, for example, is less concerned with achieving 'liberation' or 'acceptance' of gay or lesbian people because it argues that identity categories are socially constructed (in order to establish power hierarchies) and therefore unstable. Feminist post-structural discourse analysis does not start from an assumption that all women are oppressed by all men, all the time.

6   Sometimes texts can be short, consisting of a few sentences, or conceivably a single phrase, word, letter or number. In other cases, texts can be extremely long – an entire book could be a text, for example. Throughout this book I have quoted illustrative examples from a variety of texts, although, due to issues of space and

copyright, I have not always been able to include the whole text in full. Clearly, part of a text may result in part of an analysis, and in some cases I refer to additional parts of the text not quoted.

7   Collocations are systematic co-occurrences of words, which can often reveal something about connotations or hidden associations which are triggered when we encounter a particular word. For example, in the British National Corpus, the word *gay* tends to collocate with words which reference community or politics such as *rights*, *activists* and *communities*, whereas *homosexual* collocates with words which reference sexual behaviour or disease, including *acts*, *behaviour*, *seroconverted* and *hiv-1* (Baker, 2005: 243). An examination of such collocates could be used to argue that *gay* and *homosexual* are not synonyms, but represent very different ways of constructing same-sex desire.

2   Accounting for difference

Introduction

In Chapter 1, I mentioned that earlier studies into language and identities tended to separate gender and sexuality from each other, only focusing on one or the other. So studies which considered women's and men's language use tended to assume a nominally heterosexual subject, while early studies of gay language use tended to focus on gay men rather than lesbians. In order to understand current thinking about language, gender and sexuality, it is necessary to spend some time examining earlier work, to ascertain how such research was gradually built on, with newer theories reconfiguring or replacing old ones. It is also useful to relate these older studies to the social climate of their time: many of them reveal a great deal about the changing status and roles of men and women over the twentieth century.

Therefore, this chapter begins with a historical overview of some of the most important milestones in language, gender and sexuality research. More recently, some researchers have grouped earlier paradigms under one label, the '3 Ds', referring to the ways that male and female language use was characterised according to Deficit, Dominance or Difference models.

Jespersen and Legman – deficit

So where did the first D, Deficit come from? Most researchers cite Otto Jespersen, an early twentieth century Danish linguist whose speciality was English grammar. Jespersen was an influential linguist, helping to support and develop Esperanto as well as founding the International Phonetics Association with Paul Passey. His 1922 book, *Language: Its Nature, Development and Origin*, had a chapter on 'The woman', where Jespersen put forward a number of conjectures about the way that women use language. Although it has been rightly argued (Talbot, 1998: 37) that Jespersen assumed that women's language was somehow deviant from a male 'norm' (there was no separate chapter on men's language – perhaps because this was represented in the rest of the book), Jespersen at least made the ground-breaking acknowledgement that women were relevant to linguistic study, even if what he went on to say about them was questionable.

In his chapter on women, Jespersen set up a binary distinction between men's and women's language use. Women were characterised as helping to maintain the 'purity' of language, whereas men, on the other hand, were responsible for its innovation and creativity. The role of women in maintaining language purity had, according to Jespersen, very little to do with ensuring that nouns agreed with verbs; in fact, Jespersen was quite disparaging of their language use, claiming that women spoke without thinking, didn't know how to use intensifying adverbs, couldn't finish their sentences and had a limited vocabulary. Instead, this linguistic 'purity' was to do with the fact that women apparently, 'shrink… from coarse and vulgar expressions' and instead have a preference for, 'refined (and in certain spheres) veiled and indirect expressions' (1922: 246). To hammer home the point about the apparent superiority of men, Jespersen warned that without male creativity, language would, 'become languid and insipid'. In addition, although women had smaller vocabularies (which they didn't know how to use properly), they also had more to say than men – a sign that Jespersen thought that women talked *too much*.

Jespersen's views were mainly based on (non-scientific) observations. He also took evidence from unnamed observations of his acquaintances, 'others have told me that men will generally say 'It's very good of you,' where women will say 'It's very kind of you',' (1922: 245) as well as examples from fiction (written by men), including *The Gay Lord Quex* (1900) by Pinero, *The Pretty Lady* (1918) by Bennett and *Vanity Fair* (1848) by Thackeray; this last novel being almost 75 years old when Jespersen referred to it. How can we make sense of his findings then? They certainly represent a sexist 'male superiority' viewpoint that was typical of the first half of the twentieth century. On the other hand, perhaps Jespersen was doing his best to report on observations about the sorts of women he had met, even if this was biased – i.e. he remembered evidence that backed up pre-conceived ideas and disregarded the rest. During the 1920s, social expectations that women were supposed to act in 'refined' or 'insipid' ways were much stronger than they are now. Talbot (1998: 38) suggests that if women did have smaller vocabularies then it was likely to be because they hadn't had the same access to education as their male counterparts. Considering his status, Jespersen himself may have also been an intimidating figure to converse with, and this could explain why women had the supposed habit of not being able to finish a sentence around him. Or he may have surrounded himself with the sorts of women who confirmed his worldview. Whatever the reason for Jespersen's remarks, it is difficult to take them seriously: they are too generalising and stereotyping. Instead they tell us far more about Jespersen himself, his place in society, and what his society thought about women than about how women used language.

However, Jespersen did not present women in a completely inferior way. For example, he claimed (1922: 252–3) that they were more voluble than men, who had a 'slower intellect', evidenced by his observation that women were faster at reading than men and that if they used a pronoun like *he* or *she*, they may not be referring to the last person they mentioned, but to someone else. Women were also much closer to language norms, according to Jespersen, who claimed that males tended to be at the extremes of idiot or genius more often than females. Jespersen ended his chapter on women by attempting to explain the reasons for these differences, which he suggests were socially constructed due to the division of labour between the sexes – men, involved in war and hunting for food, allegedly had fewer opportunities for conversation, whereas women's domestic duties had not claimed so much energy or 'deep thought', allowing them to 'chatter' in company as they worked. Despite this rather questionable theory of the origins of linguistic differences between men and women, Jespersen at least notes (1922: 254) that social changes would be likely to, 'modify the linguistic relations between the two sexes'. However, we can characterise his theory as a Deficit Model, with women's language being a deficient approximation of men's. Unfortunately, it was a long time before anyone actively challenged this standpoint.

While we can assume that sexuality was not a subject that Jespersen cared to talk about, what research, if any, was carried out on language and sexuality? Cameron and Kulick (2003: 79) cite earlier writers such as Burgess (1949: 234) and Westwood (1952: 126) who asserted that a secret homosexual language had been established towards the beginning of the twentieth century. The most often-mentioned early work is a chapter entitled 'The Language of Homosexuality: An American Glossary' written by Gershon Legman and published in the book *Sex Variants* (Henry, 1941). Legman was a very different figure to Jespersen, not associated with 'respectable' linguistics, but instead residing on the edge of academia. He had worked for, and subsequently fallen out with, the sexologist Alfred Kinsey, and was closely involved with the journal *Maledicta*, which focused on 'bad language': swearing, taboo language and verbal aggression. Legman's chapter viewed the 'language of homosexuality' as consisting of a number of unique terms that were used by, 'homosexuals and their associates'. He listed several hundred such terms, many of which were sexual in nature, either concerned with the act of having sex or making sexual contacts, along with terms which described different sexual activities and types of people according to their personality or sexual preferences. Legman did not write about the language used by lesbians, suggesting instead that they had a practice of, 'gentlemanly restraint'. Oddly, then, Legman suggests that it is gay men who are the innovators of language, but lesbians are restrained, in a way similar to upper-class men. This has some similarities to Jespersen's views: men (whether heterosexual or gay) are innovators, but if Legmen's lesbians are supposedly *like* men, then one would imagine that they would have some trait of innovation, too.

Jespersen and Legman share the view that female language and gay male language are somehow marginalised from an imaginary, heterosexual, male 'norm'.

Second wave feminism – dominance

Some of Jespersen's claims about women's language were subsequently confirmed by variationist sociolinguists. For example, Labov (1966) and Trudgill (1972, 1978) consistently found that women used a more standard form of language than men, even when taking into account other factors such as social class, age or ethnicity.

The 1960s and 1970s are sometimes referred to as the period of Second Wave feminism. The First Wave, involving the Suffragette movements, took place earlier in the twentieth century, while the Third Wave could be treated as the 'post-modern' approach to feminism beginning in the 1990s and discussed in Chapter 3.[1] It was during the nominal period of Second Wave feminism that a more politically-focused theory of women's language in terms of male dominance started to present a serious challenge to the older 'deficit' model, beginning with the publication of Robin Lakoff's *Language and Woman's Place* in 1975. One important aspect of this book was that Lakoff pointed out that there were many asymmetries between supposedly *equivalent* male and female terms such as *master* and *mistress*, which embedded sexist attitudes. Like Jespersen, Lakoff assumed that men and women used language differently, but Lakoff wrote from a feminist perspective and wanted to outline the numerous ways in which she felt that men's use of language dominated women. Again, though, Lakoff started from a position of defining women's language use as somehow deviant from standard 'male' language, and she had no quantifiable evidence for her descriptions of gender-related language use, but instead based her claims on her own observations.

Lakoff claimed that women were politer than men and used a number of linguistic strategies which framed them as subservient. Their politeness was characterised by the use of forms like 'would you mind?' and 'I'd appreciate it if you'd…' They used 'empty' adjectives such as *divine* and *lovely*. They also made use of tag questions such as 'It's hot in here *isn't it?*' which were a way of seeking approval and confirmation, along with using a rising, questioning intonation in declarative statements. Women also supposedly employed hedges such as *perhaps* or *kind of*, making their statements appear less certain (and more easily challenged) than men's statements. Additionally (echoing Jespersen), Lakoff claimed that women used hyper-correct grammar and pronunciation, adhering closely to the rules of 'Standard English' (Lakoff was writing about English-speaking women, but we might assume that her theory could be transposed onto other languages, too). Women were also supposed to avoid slang and taboo words.

As with Legman's view that gay men have a special lexicon, Lakoff assumed that women used certain words that (heterosexual) men would not use. These included precise colour terms, particularly words which distinguished between subtle shades such as *mauve, ecru* and *lavender*. Lakoff noted that if a man were to say something like 'The wall is mauve' then 'one might well conclude that he was imitating a woman sarcastically or was a homosexual or an interior decorator' (1975: 43). Lakoff's linking of (assumedly heterosexual) women's speech with gay male speech is worth noting here.

As well as lexical features, there were other aspects of Lakoff's theory which suggested that women's language was somehow inferior to men's. Apparently women did not tell jokes very well or understand the punch-lines of jokes, and they were often interrupted by men, who talked more – and even when men didn't talk, they used silence as a form of power.

Lakoff, and others after her, interpreted these aspects of women's language as being due to childhood socialisation processes, where girls were encouraged to use a more 'elegant' form of language, whereas boys were expected to be more flexible and 'rough' (see also Goodwin, 1980; and Maltz and Borker, 1982).

Although Lakoff was one of the first to address the issue of gender and language from a political perspective, her work subsequently received a number of criticisms. As with Jespersen, the fact that she had based her theories on her own observations, or from examples she had encountered in the media, meant that their validity was questioned. Also, her research tended to reflect the language use of her peer group. To be fair to Lakoff, she did not try to hide this, writing, 'The data on which I am basing my claims have been gathered mainly by introspection... is the educated, white, middle-class group that the writer of this book identifies with less worthy of study than any other?' (1975: 40).

Many of the aspects of women's language that Lakoff talked about could be characterised as forms of talk that are associated with *any* type of person who is powerless – a useful criticism to make, suggesting that these language 'differences', even if they are found to exist, are not necessarily indicative of an essential element of being a woman, but are instead more due to the social context that women found themselves in. So men may also use these strategies in certain situations. We could reformulate a great deal of Lakoff's women's language in terms of Brown and Levinson's (1978) theory of negative politeness, whereby people adopt particular linguistic strategies in order to show respect for an interlocutor's rights and privileges, and try not to impose on him or her.

Despite these criticisms, a large number of people agreed with Lakoff's claim that men and women used language differently – particularly when additional studies that painstakingly recorded conversations and counted up linguistic features produced evidence which backed up a great deal of what Lakoff had said. For example, Zimmerman and West (1975) carried out an analysis of sex differences based on quantification, looking at conversations that took place in a college community. They established that when conversations were between people of the same sex, interruptions were distributed fairly evenly between participants. However, when the conversations occurred between men and women, on average, men were responsible for about 96 percent of the interruptions. Other quantitative studies, e.g. Eakins and Eakins' (1978) study of staff meetings, found that men enjoyed more frequent conversational turns, and spoke for greater lengths of time, interrupting more, and being interrupted less, than women. They also found evidence that women's language-use contained more 'empty' adjectives and adverbs which 'connote triviality or unimportance' such as *sweet, dreadful, precious* and *darling.* Soskin and John (1963), who looked at conversations between husbands and wives and Swacker (1975), who studied the lengths of time it took men and women to describe pictures, also found that, on the whole, men spoke for longer periods than women. Crosby and Nyquist (1977) reported that women used more tag questions than men (but only in two out of three of the different contexts that they examined) while Mulac et al. (1988) discovered that women used more hedges than men when in mixed-sex conversations. A larger set of studies also seemed to confirm that women are more likely than men to use questions as a form of affiliation (Fishman, 1978, Pearson, 1981, Beck, 1988, Lesch, 1994, Meyers et al., 1997). Such studies (of which only a small number are listed here) appear to confirm Lakoff's theories, at least in part.

Fishman's (1977, 1978, 1980, 1983) theory of 'interactional shitwork' can also be linked to (male) dominance theory. In her 1980 study, Fishman taped the conversations of three young heterosexual American couples and found that the women tended to ask questions about two and a half times more often than men, while they employed hedges five times more often. Fishman suggested that women use so many questions and hedges in order to force responses from men and facilitate the smooth flow of conversation. This 'interactional shitwork' that women engage in was a reflection of their inferior social position.

There are potential political consequences of accepting the 'Dominance' model. For example, it positions women as 'victims' of male power. Furthermore, some authors have suggested that if women wished to gain social power, they needed to learn how to talk 'like a man'. So a number of management books have advised women that if they want to succeed in the workplace, they need to think, act and talk in more stereotypically masculine ways. For example, Lois Frankel's (2004) book on management for women: *Nice Girls Don't Get The Corner Office*, advises that women should refrain from using 'touchy-feely' language, 'non-words' like 'I see', qualifiers like 'sort of', and apologies, explanations, and statements that are couched as questions. Frankel writes 'Observe how men sit at meetings. When they're speaking, confident men almost always lean in with their elbows and hands resting on the table… And what do *we* do? We… sit coyly with our hands folded in our laps' (2004: 206). A similar book *Play Like A Man, Win Like A Woman* (Evans, 2000) lists ten 'gender-bender vocabulary words' which mean different things to men and women, e.g. 'Women have been acculturated to believe that no means NO!… Men learn at a young age that no is a relative rather than an absolute term – a temporary rebuff rather than an outright rejection'. While both writers emphasise that the language differences here are culturally-determined rather than absolute, their advice on how to succeed at work involves accepting the status quo and behaving more 'like a man', rather than challenging existing workplace norms (see the discussion of complicity in Chapter 5).

While it is easy to criticise writers like Frankel and Evans, it should also be pointed out that they are in a double-bind. Women leaders who act in stereotypically 'feminine' ways are viewed as lacking the strength to succeed, while those who behave in more 'masculine' ways could be seen as acting inappropriately or being complicit. The problem stems from associating powerful and powerless forms of language with males and females respectively. Rather than advising that women ought to 'play like a man', we should perhaps advocate that powerful and powerless ways of speaking are de-gendered, while recognising that many managerial 'styles' can be successful, including those which are more nurturing. But, as Cameron and Kulick (2003: 58) argue, the same way of speaking can signify a professional identity *and* a gendered identity, and it can be difficult to separate the two because both are potentially relevant. Recent research suggests that context is relevant and that styles of talking can be used in more fluid and complex ways. For example, Holmes and Schnurr (2006) examined a number of different workplace interactions. While they found that in some workplaces typically 'masculine' or competitive ways of talking predominated, they also found other contexts where typically 'feminine' ways of speaking were reclaimed and reinterpreted positively. For example, Jill, a company director, used a range of speech strategies and drew on 'masculine' ways of talking, such as being direct and interrupting small talk to start a meeting. At other times she employed more polite, typically 'feminine' strategies, such as apologising or using facilitative and supportive strategies when running a meeting. And on other occasions she would use 'feminine' strategies in a self-aware and ironic fashion to exploit and parody gender stereotypes, for example, by self-deprecatingly referring to herself as a 'technical klutz'. Holmes and Schnurr (2006: 43) argue that Jill's humorous parody of such strategies, rather than reinforcing masculine workplace norms, troubles and contests the assumptions underlying them.

Dale Spender's book *Man Made Language* (1980) can also be regarded as a contribution to the 'Dominance' model of language and gender. Spender writes (1980: 6), 'language and material resources have been used by the dominant group to structure women's oppression... One cannot be formed without the other if women are to be liberated and patriarchy is to be prevented from persisting'. Spender began from a different position from Lakoff, suggesting that Lakoff assumed that men's language was superior and that women's language was a deviant version of it. Spender divides earlier language and gender research into two types: sexist research (which aims to show women's language as deficient) and feminist research (which aims to challenge this position). She focused on the construction of women's silence both in their use of language and in language itself. So women have, historically, been denied a voice – men tend to only assign importance to what other men say. And also, language itself reflects male dominance – through the use of phenomena like the generic male pronoun *he* and the naming of God as male (see Chapter 4). Spender concludes that the problem is, 'not the deficiency of women, but the deficiency of a social order, a symbolic system, in which they are not represented, in which they have been denied the means to produce and sanction' (1980: 231).

Sexist language and political correctness

Feminists and other writers did attempt to suggest or incorporate changes to language in order to redress some of the inequalities noted above. For example, *Ms* was suggested as an equivalent to *Mr*, rather than the older *Miss/Mrs* distinction which forces women to reveal their martial status. The use of inclusive hyphens or conjunctions: *him/her, her or his* offers a potential 'solution' to generic male pronouns, while gender-neutral terms like *chairperson* and *firefighter* and the avoidance or reclaiming of pejorative terms like *slag* and *bitch* have also been offered as alternative linguistic strategies, designed to address male bias in language.

These suggestions, along with those aimed at equalising or removing stigma from other identities (such as disabled people, gay men and lesbians or particular ethnic groups) have been broadly referred to as 'political correctness'. Hall (1994: 167) notes that, 'PC is… characteristic of the rise of 'identity politics' where shared social identity (as woman, Black, gay or lesbian)… is the mobilising factor. It reflects the spread of the political from the public to the private arena, the sphere of informal social interaction and the scenarios of everyday life. The feminist slogan 'The personal is political' captures these shifts'. Gott (1993: 8) argues, however, that PC was more of a concept than an official movement, claiming that it is, 'a notional construct put together by the Right to create a non-existent monster on the Left that it can then attack. For although everyone knows the idiocies uttered in the name of PC, it is hard to find anyone who has actually heard them in person or even encountered them seriously in print…' Cameron (1994: 17) agrees that 'conservatives have deliberately set out to redefine the term 'political correctness''. This redefinition was achieved through the media's circulation of myths, for example, left-wing local councils banning terms like 'black coffee' on the grounds that the term could be racist and cause offence. Furthermore, right-wing pundits invented new PC terms as hypothetical examples, designed to show how the argument could be taken to extremes. Such terms were then taken out of context and held up as further examples of 'political correctness gone mad'.

While conservatives have redefined PC so that they can attack it, others have also raised points of concern, which are perhaps more valid. Dunant (1994: xi-xii) warns that censorship does not bring freedom and argues that positive discrimination is still discrimination, pointing out that terms like *whitewash* could potentially discriminate against white people. Furthermore, PC thinking can assume that minority groups are a homogenous entity: not all members of minority group want to be referred to in the same way. Pinker (1994) and Ehrenreich (1992) have questioned the relationship between language and thought. Pinker suggests that applications of PC can result in a euphemism treadmill, whereby new terms continually need to be replaced as older ones acquire negative meanings: *crippled, handicapped, disabled, differently abled*, leading to confusion and uncertainty. And Ehrenreich (1992: 335) argues that, 'If you outlaw the term 'girl' instead of 'woman' you're not going to do a thing about the sexist attitudes underneath'. However, Cameron (1994: 24–33) presents a strong defence of PC, arguing that language and thought are related, 'Radicals of my generation… attach more importance to linguistic and other representations than their predecessors did… we regard words and images as useful material with which to work for social change' (1994: 24). She also notes that, 'The verbal hygiene movement for so-called politically correct language does not threaten our freedom to speak as we choose… It threatens only our freedom to imagine that our linguistic choices are inconsequential, or to suppose that any one group of people has an inalienable right to prescribe them' (Cameron, 1994: 33).

Despite its criticisms, the political correctness movement (if it can be called a movement) does appear to have had some impact on actual language use. Table 2.1 shows standardised frequencies of some so-called PC and non-PC terms in the written section (approximately 90 million words) of the British National Corpus over three time periods. Overall, there appears to have been a small increase in the usage of terms we would recognise as PC between 1960 and 1993 and an overall reduction in the more sexist terms. Yet despite actual changes, Cameron (1995b: 123) notes that, 'PC now has such negative connotations for so many people that the mere invocation of the phrase can move those so labeled to elaborate disclaimers or reduce them to silence.'

Table 2.1. Frequencies of sexist and non-sexist terms in the written section of the British National Corpus over time (numbers are given as standardised occurrences per million words of data)

	1960–1974	1975–1984	1985–1993
Sexist terms			
mankind	15.5	23.06	7.39
Miss (term of address)	173.4	156.35	71.75
lady doctor/novelist/ gardener/golfer[2]	1.14	0.21	0.35
male nurse/stripper/ prostitute/model[3]	0.57	0.21	0.78
ladylike	0.57	1.06	0.48
early man	0	0.28	1.06
Non-sexist terms			
him or her	2.87	2.75	4.06
he or she	12.63	11.43	17.81
Ms	0.57	9.52	16.98
chairperson	0	1.27	1.63
firefighter	0	0	0.28
police officer	0.57	2.33	5.35

Schwarz (2006) took another approach to the issue of non-sexist language, by conducting focus groups[4] among women of different ages and academic backgrounds in order to ascertain the different interpretative repertoires[5] (Gilbert and Mulkay, 1984) that were accessed, regarding the topic. Collectively, her subjects accessed a range of interpretative repertoires, some of which were conflicting. For example, in the excerpt below, Chris, Anne, Maggie, Barbara and Lorraine, who were all female students aged over 50, talk about understandings of the word *girl*, in response to the moderator's question, 'how old is a girl?'

1 Anne:	ooh anywhere from 2 minutes to 92
2 Barbara:	yeah, I'm a girl
3 Lorraine:	you're always a girl
4 Chris:	it depends who I'm with at the moment we are all girls [all: yes] but when I'm at home I'm not a girl [laugh]
5 Maggie:	it's the same with *boys* (.) it's the same with *boys* though (.) isn't it (.) It's the same with *boys* though (.) isn't it when the boys go out (.) boys (.) boys night out yeah but er (.) actually (.) that's the only derogatory one [Barabara: is it] yeah (.) because (.) you can say (.) you can say (.) oh yeah (.) boys night out (.) oh yeah (.) you know (.) and you know (.) darn well they're stupidly drunk [Barbara laughs]
6 Chris	that is a derogatory one [laughter]
7 Maggie:	that's great (.) we've found one (.) whereas they would not see it as derogatory (.) though
8 Chris:	don't you think *girl* is a bit derogatory as well (.) though
9 Anne:	when you apply (.) *boy* to a grown man (.) it's displaying only one characteristic of male and that is (..) immature
10 Maggie:	yeah (.) that's true and the same with if you apply *girl* to a woman
11 Lorraine:	no (.) it's not the same because when you say (.) us girls (.) you just mean young inside (.) and you=
12 Maggie:	=ha ha ha (.) you're kidding yourself if anyone used *girl* about me (.) I would think they were being a bit derogatory
13 Lorraine:	it's obviously a personal thing (.) isn't it it depends who said it
14 Chris:	I just see it as (.) we women being light hearted=
15 Lorraine:	=yeah (.) that's how see it=
16 Chris	=we women being (.) not being serious

(.)	pause
[..]	interruptions and laughter
=	overlapping speech

Adapted from Schwarz (2006: 193)

The women do not initially view *girl* as problematic, joking that the term can be used by females of all ages (lines 1–3). Chris, however, restricts this interpretative repertoire: it does not depend on the referent's age, but on who they are with at any given time, saying that she would not be known as a girl at home (line 4). After Maggie argues that *boy* is derogatory, Chris asks whether *girl* is derogatory too (line 8). Maggie agrees that it is, whereas Lorraine contests this by drawing on a different repertoire, saying that *girl* symbolises being young inside, a point which is eventually supported by Chris (lines 14, 16). There are a number of possible positions expressed here: Maggie's negative conceptualisation of *girl* when applied to an adult female as derogatory, Lorraine's more positive attitude that *girl* means 'young inside' and Chris's shifting position from *girl* being 'a bit derogatory' to 'not being serious'. The exchange therefore shows the important of context; the term is only viewed as sexist in some situations.

A further example from Schwarz's focus-group research, regarding discussion of the generic pronoun *he* and the alternatives, *he or she* and *s/he*, shows how other concerns can also impact on the use (or non-use) of non-sexist language.

1 Maggie:	but (.) isn't that a precision thing I mean (.) you don't want to say just *he* (.) because you don't mean just *he* you mean (.) *he or she* (.) so (.) to be precise (.) you would use *he or she*	
2: Chris	it's less distracting (.) we (.) would you reading a text (.) and (.) if you reading a text you want to be informed (.) to keep on coming across (.) *he or she* or (.) *s* (.) slash (.) *he*	
3 Anne:	=it's messy (.) it's messy	
4 Maggie:	I agree with that	
5 Chris:	it's distracting	
6 Maggie:	I agree *s* (.) slash (.) *he* is distracting (.) why is *he or she* distracting (.) I mean (.) that's (.) that's preci (.) that's precise (.) isn't it	
7 Chris:	it is (.) perhaps it's because I do lump it together with *s* slash *he* think (.) I think (.) I'm quite content=	
8 Maggie:	if anyone caught me using that (.) I could be hung drawn and quartered (.) I mean that really is appalling but (.) but (.) *he or she* (.) but I wouldn't (.) I would never use *she or he*	

Adapted from Schwarz (2006: 205–6)

Here, a range of interpretative repertoires are accessed regarding non-sexist alternatives to the generic *he*. Maggie evaluates *he or she* positively, drawing on a 'precision language' interpretative repertoire, judging *he* as wrong – 'you don't just mean he' (line 1 and later line 6). However, Chris views *he* as less distracting (line 2), which Anne and Maggie agree with, calling *s/he* messy (lines 3–4). Although Maggie is initially very positive about inclusive pronouns, challenging Chris's negative evaluation; in line 8 she appears to distance herself from them, saying she would never use *she or he*. Therefore, the participants of the group seem to be explicitly focused on whether generic pronouns offer the reader precision or accuracy, or whether they distract the reader from the flow of the text. The 'precision' interpretative repertoire could be interpreted as containing a feminist standpoint, e.g. generic *he* is wrong because *he* does not include *she*, although this point is not openly referred to.

The focus group discussions on *girl* and the generic *he* therefore suggest that responses to non-sexist language use are complex and sometimes contradictory, being context-dependent and also subject to other considerations such as how distracting a term is. Also, attitudes towards a term may be in conflict with actual linguistic practices, so people may argue that a word or phrase is non-sexist, but then claim never to use it themselves (despite sometimes using it). Choices regarding the use of a sexist word or non-sexist alternative are not necessarily straightforward or consistent over time (see also Mills, 1998). In some cases, therefore, dividing language into binary 'sexist' and 'non-sexist' categories is perhaps an over-simplification of matters.

Returning, however, to Spender's dominance model of language and gender, Talbot (1998: 45–49) acknowledges the importance of Spender's approach in that it took feminist arguments beyond the women's movement to a much wider audience, and promoted awareness of some of the more deep-rooted sexist aspects of English language use. However, she notes that some of Spender's uses of key terms were either too rigid or vague. For example, Talbot points out that if language was as monolithic and as influential on thought as Spender claims, then Spender could never have written her book – she would have been constrained by the limitations of sexism. Even though it is true that men have compiled dictionaries and therefore controlled official or standard usages, language is owned by the people who use it, which includes men *and* women. And as Segal (1994: 29) argues, Spender's view of male power as monolithic – that all men are in a position to dominate all women, is somewhat reductive. Segal instead notes that, 'we could do better to study how particular groups of people are able to control the specific institutions which construct dominant frameworks of meaning'.

Men are from Mars – difference

Eckert and McConnell-Ginet (2003: 1) point out that Lakoff's *Language and Woman's Place* resulted in a separation of academic opinion which was concerned with explaining the reasons why the perceived difference between male and female language-use existed. Some academics, like Spender, believed that it was to do with men's dominance of women; others claimed the difference was connected to the fact that men and women just *are* different (although there was some disagreement over whether the difference was due to social factors such as upbringing, societal expectations and roles, or essential factors, such as genetics, the brain or different amounts of chemicals present in the body, or a combination of both).[6]

For example, Aries and Johnson (1983) and Seidler (1989) found evidence to suggest that men and women tend to discuss different topics – men talk about sport, politics and cars, and women talk about child-rearing and personal relationships. Maltz and Borker (1982), who looked at children's playground interactions, found that boys and girls tend to have different norms during segregated play. Boys usually play in large hierarchical groups where a competitive style of speech dominates, whereas girls play in smaller groups of 'best friends', where they use a more supportive speech style. These peer cultures, which develop while young, result in a form of 'cross-cultural' miscommunication between males and females, echoing Gumperz's (1982) work on ethnically-distinct subcultures. The theory of cross-cultural miscommunication was later developed and popularised by Deborah Tannen (1990) in her book *You Just Don't Understand: Men and Women in Conversation*. Tannen wrote about the different conversational rules that men and women adhere to, arguing that men grow up in a world where conversation is a contest, but for women it is a way to exchange confirmation and support. So a woman would use a word like *let's* as a suggestion or proposal in order to obtain agreement, whereas a man would misinterpret this word as an indirect command and be annoyed.

Tannen's approach was influential, resulting in the release of many other relationship guide books (mainly aimed at women), such as Gray's *Men are From Mars, Women are from Venus* (1992), where women are described as wanting to talk about problems, whereas men 'retreat into their cave'. Similar 'difference' books included *Why Men Don't Listen and Women Can't Read Maps* (Pease and Pease, 2001), *Men Are Like Fish: What Every Woman Needs To Know About Catching A Man* (Nakamoto, 2002) and *He's Just Not That Into You: The No-Excuses Guide To Understanding Guys* (Behrendt et al., 2004). While Tannen (1990: 16) warns of the danger of generalisations, she holds that we ought not ignore what she calls *real difference*, 'Denying real differences can only compound the confusion that is already widespread in this era of shifting and re-forming relationships between women and men'.

Tannen takes her examples from a variety of sources. She tells anecdotes, and quotes conversations between individual men and women which she recorded herself (although some of these conversations may have been 'tided up' or simplified as they do not contain many false starts or hesitations which are usual in naturally-occurring talk). She also uses the transcriptions of other researchers such as West and Zimmerman (1985), Erikson (1990) and Sheldon (1990). Like Jespersen, she relies on fiction, quoting from the Jules Feiffer play *Grown Ups*, the Celia Fremlin novel *The Jealous One* and the Alice Mattison story *Sleeping Giant*. The criticisms of using such data types are obvious. First, it is difficult to extrapolate from phenomena that occur in a small number of conversations in order to conclude, then, that such differences are representative of the wider population. Even a larger, more quantitative study which revealed clear patterns of sex difference in language would have to acknowledge that it was based on a sample that was specific to the population and time period from which it was collected (e.g. white, middle-class Americans sampled in 1990). Secondly, it is difficult to draw conclusions about actual speech from works of fiction. That is not to say that fictional texts are not helpful in revealing gendered discourses (something which will be explored in later chapters), but an analysis of fiction only tells us about how the author wished to represent the world, not how it actually is. And again, even if the fictional events which an author writes about *were* based on personal experience, they are only drawn from a small sample, and it could be argued that such events were chosen because they were dramatically interesting, and not perhaps representative of ordinary conversation.

Tannen has very little to say about gay men and lesbians in her book, so we may want to assume that her claims about sex differences can only be applied to heterosexual people. She does mention gay men and lesbians twice (1990: 147–148, 292), although not in direct reference to language use, and both times she quotes research by Blumstein and Schwartz (1984) which claims that lesbians have sex less than gay men, because amongst gay men at least one partner takes the role of initiator, whereas amongst lesbians neither partner tends to enjoy being the initiator, because they don't want to be perceived as making demands. Also, when lesbians earn power, it is apparently to avoid dependence rather than to be dominating in a relationship, whereas for gay male couples, one partner feels more successful if his earning power is higher. So Tannen uses these two examples in order to suggest further evidence of difference between men and women – characterising a gay relationship as consisting of two dominant males and a lesbian one as having two passive females.

While Tannen appears to argue from a position that men and women simply have different *genderlects* (1990: 42) a term coined using a similar derivational process to the word *dialect*), it is possible to see how both men and women could feel rather limited and stereotyped regarding the ways they are represented. Women are somewhat positively described as desiring connection and intimacy, with a focus on co-operation and consideration towards others in conversation. They give praise rather than information (p. 69), prefer private speaking or 'rapport talk' (p. 76), small-talk (p. 102) or gossip (p. 104), make suggestions or proposals (pp. 152–4), act as peacemakers (p. 167) and adapt to male norms (p. 235). Men on the other hand, are said to desire independence and status (p. 42), which can be linguistically manifested by their giving orders (p. 44), problem solving (p. 52), engaging in more public speaking or 'report talk' (p. 76), talking about themselves (p. 126), telling jokes (pp. 139–40) and using conflict as a means of affiliation (pp. 162–5).

Tannen points out that the genderlects in themselves are not necessarily a problem, rather, expectations that one must conform to their genderlect is likely to restrict both men and women in different situations (1990: 181), and not being aware of the opposite sex's genderlect will result in communicative stalemates that spiral out of control (1990: 298). So she cites awareness as a key, rather than explicitly suggesting that people ought to change their styles or that society's expectations about male and female language-use ought to be changed.

She illustrates her 'miscommunication' argument with a number of transcripts from recorded conversations. For example:

HE: I'm really tired. I didn't sleep well last night.
SHE: I didn't sleep well either. I never do.
HE: Why are you trying to belittle me?
SHE: I'm not! I'm just trying to show that I understand.

Tannen (1990:51)

In the case above, Tannen suggests that conflict arose because women tend to respond to hearing the troubles of others by offering matching troubles, while men take offence at such responses, because they feel that the uniqueness of their experience has been denied. So the female speaker was attempting to establish a connection, through voicing a shared experience, whereas the male speaker wanted to preserve his independence. A number of Tannen's excerpts centred on married couples – a different interpretation may be that people in close relationships often get on each other's nerves!

Critics of Tannen's position, e.g. Troemel-Plotz (1991), have argued that it is a 'non-engaged and apolitical stance' which aims at 'the cementation of patriarchy'. Another criticism of the 'Difference' model is that it over-accentuates differences, while ignoring similarities between males and females. Difference was re-evaluated by Janet Holmes (1995), who examined politeness strategies (including compliments, apologies and hedges) among a larger sample of men and women in New Zealand. In her data, she concluded that in general, there *were* sex differences, for example, women tended to perceive and use compliments as positively-affective speech acts and expressions of solidarity, whereas men were more ambivalent about them (1995: 152). Although Holmes points out that there are plenty of counter-examples, she also notes that 'the overall patterns are compelling', arguing that it is males who define appropriate behaviour in public and formal domains so that women's polite patterns of interaction are unlikely to predominate in such contexts (1995: 227–8).

However, a number of meta-analyses, which examined large numbers of studies on male and female linguistic differences (Wilkins and Anderson, 1991, Dindia and Allen, 1992, Canary and Hause, 1993) have found little evidence for sex differences in language use. Dindia and Allen, who focused on self-disclosure, advised that, 'it is time to stop perpetuating the myth that there are large sex differences in men and women's self disclosure' (1992: 188), while Canary and Hause (1993: 140) conclude that, 'The hundreds of studies represented in the meta-analyses indicate that sex differences in social interaction are small and inconsistent; that is, about one percent of the variance is accounted for and these effects are moderated by other variables'. Finally, Hyde (2005), who reviewed 46 meta-analyses on sex variation comprising 20 years of data, argued that on most psychological characteristics, males and females were more alike than different. She argues that the inflation of differences can result in a self-fulfilling prophecy that can be potentially damaging, for example, the belief that men are better at maths or make better leaders than women may discourage women from attempting to enter particular fields of expertise.

Difference revisited – corpus approaches

There have also been attempts to analyse social differences in language use, including gender, from a corpus-based perspective. According to McEnery & Wilson (1996: 1) *corpus linguistics* is, 'the study of language based on examples of real life language use'. However, unlike purely qualitative approaches to research, corpus linguistics utilises bodies of electronically encoded text, implementing a more quantitative methodology, for example, by using frequency information about occurrences of particular linguistic phenomena. An advantage of using a corpus-based approach is that the data sample used is often extremely large, consisting of millions of words. Therefore any findings are more likely to be generalisable to a wider population (although, even then, care must be taken when making conclusions). Secondly, because computers count and sort the language data, as well as performing statistical tests of significance on them, it is less easy to criticise researchers for picking out single examples which confirm their initial suspicions or biases. Even so, it is still the task of human researchers to decide what to look for in a corpus, then interpret the results and provide explanations for them.

A number of researchers have used language corpora in combination with speaker-annotated data in order to ask questions about usage. Rayson et al. (1997) examined the spoken demographic section (about four million words) of the British National Corpus in order to explore sex variation. They found that the female speakers in the corpus tended to take more turns and talk for longer than male speakers. Looking at words which occurred statistically more often in male speech when compared to female speech, they reported that males used more taboo words (*fucking, fuck, shit, hell, crap*) and numbers (*one, two, three, four, hundred*). They also made use of more colloquial language (*guy, quid, mate*) and more informal interjections (*yeah, okay, right, ah, aye*). On the other hand, females used more first person pronouns (*I, me, my, mine*) and family terms (*mother, father, sister, brother*). Finally, males used more common nouns, while females favoured personal pronouns, verbs and proper nouns (although this only related to personal names like *Jim* – males used more proper nouns referring to geographical places like *London*). To an extent, therefore, Rayson et al.'s research confirms Tannen's (1990) hypothesis of male and female difference, in that male speech is more factual and concerned with reporting information, whereas female speech is more interactive and concerned with establishing and maintaining relationships (the male 'report' versus female 'rapport' distinction discussed in the previous section).

Taking a grammatical rather than a lexical approach, Schmid and Fauth (2003) identified 45 linguistic features from various grammatical domains and retrieved their occurrences from same-sex conversations taken from the International Corpus of English (ICE). They found that four features correlated with female speech: use of third person pronouns, indefinite pronouns, predicative adjectives and intensive adverbs. On the other hand, male speech was characterised by the use of definite articles, nominalisations and noun phrase post-modifications realised by *of-* prepositional phrases. Their analysis allowed them to predict the sex of speakers in same-sex conversations with a probability of 88.10 percent for females and 85.80 percent for males.

A note of caution is sounded by Harrington (2006), who examined a small corpus of conversations between men and women in order to examine the extent which people used traditionally 'gendered' language. She looked specifically at cases of reported speech, and while she found, overall, that women tended to engage more often in reporting the speech of others, when compared to men, it was also useful to go beyond reports of simple frequencies, by examining the speech of individuals in the corpus. A small number of female speakers were found to be responsible for the overall high rate of reported speech among women, while many of the other female speakers had similar levels of reported speech to males in the corpus. Harrington's study indicates the dangers of assuming that 'averages' are representative of the whole sample (or can be generalised to an entire population), when small numbers of speakers may actually skew the sample.

Table 2.2 shows some frequency data for males and female speakers taken from the whole spoken section (10 million words) of British National Corpus. I have grouped the words into categories which have, in the past, been said to suggest some of the most distinctive differences between male and female speech: empty adjectives, hedges, taboo words and precise colour terms.

Table 2.2. Frequencies of 'gendered' words and phrases in the spoken component of the British National Corpus

	Males		Females	
	total	frequency per million words	total	frequency per million words
lovely	665	135.14	1428	437.04
nice	2194	445.87	3262	998.33
fabulous	15	3.05	22	6.73
super	177	35.97	72	22.04
terrific	64	13.01	34	10.41
fantastic	70	14.23	56	17.14
fuck	336	68.28	107	32.75
shit	314	63.81	262	80.19
piss	64	13.01	59	18.06
cunt	55	11.18	18	5.51
cock	27	5.48	10	3.06
bastard	118	23.98	52	15.91
hell	566	115.02	479	146.6
perhaps	2273	461.92	1096	335.43
maybe	1497	304.22	926	283.4
possibly	530	107.71	174	53.25
sort of	5737	1165.88	3522	1077.91
kind of	1464	297.52	577	176.59
ecru	0	0	0	0
beige	9	1.83	9	2.75
maroon	3	0.61	11	3.37
mauve	2	0.41	11	3.37
chartreuse	1	0.2	0	0
cyan	0	0	1	0.31

What does the table reveal? First of all, it should be noted that this is extremely generalised data. It does not reveal, say, differences between young, middle-aged and old women and men, and we do not know the social class, ethnicity or sexuality of the speakers, either. Nor does the table account for the possibility (as Harrington (2006) found) that a small number of unusual speakers may have skewed the results by over-using certain terms. Additionally, the terms examined for each linguistic category are not exhaustive, so other results may be obtained if other terms were examined. Bearing these points in mind, we can compare the numbers to see whether the suggested differences hold true for this corpus (which is one of the largest bodies of spoken data ever collected). It is more helpful to compare the columns marked frequency per million words, as they give a standardised figure – the raw frequencies are not so helpful to compare, as there were not equal numbers of male and female utterances in the corpus.

For empty adjectives, it appears that women do use *lovely* and *nice* more than men. But for other adjectives, which, equally, could be classed as empty, *super* and *terrific*, males are more frequent users. Most of the results show that differences are not particularly marked in either direction. So, while we may conclude that women use certain empty adjectives more than males, it is not the case that they are the only users.

In terms of swearing, males use *fuck, cunt, cock* and *bastard* more than females but the opposite is true of *shit, piss* and *hell*. Again, the corpus data does not always directly correspond to theories or small-scale observations about gendered language use. Not only do women swear, but there are some swear words where they apparently *exceed* male usage.

For the hedges *perhaps, maybe, possibly, sort of* and *kind of*, we have an even more unexpected result: the male speakers in the corpus tended to use these terms more than women. Once again, these are not enormous differences, and, of course, it is not the case that women avoid these terms, but that men appear to use them more. How can we reconcile this with earlier difference and dominance theories of language use? We should bear in mind that Lakoff was writing from 1970s America, while the BNC spoken data was collected in the 1990s in the UK. Furthermore, it may have been that Lakoff simply noticed more cases of female hedging than male hedging, and this confirmed her initial suspicions.

Finally, as regards precise colour terms, perhaps the most useful thing we could note is that these are very rare. The figures are so small for both males and females that any differences are very unlikely to be statistically significant. And, again, use of precise colour terms is not exclusive to females.

One problem with Table 2.2 is that it takes cases out of context – so it would be helpful to know in what situations men and women use rare colour terms, taboo words, hedges and empty adjectives and what they are using them to achieve. For example, are they being used in order to offer praise to the hearer (e.g. 'that's a lovely dress'), to boast about a personal possession (e.g. 'My car is fantastic'), or to refute something (e.g. 'That's not nice'). Regarding precise colour terms, an analysis of context reveals that men seemed to be using them to talk about car colours, men's suits or in workplace situations where subtle colour distinctions were relevant. Women tended to use these colours in discussions about clothing or interior decorating, which goes some way towards confirming Lakoff's difference hypothesis – although the overall frequencies are still too small to draw any real conclusions here.

Schmid (2003) carried out a more exhaustive examination of semantic domains of language use in the male and female spoken data in the BNC, arguing that that there were some statistically significant differences: women were more likely to use words connected to the semantic domains of basic colours, home, food and drink, body and health and people. On the other hand, men more frequently used words from the domains of work, computing, sports and public affairs. However, Schmid (2003: 212- 213) argues that his findings do not demonstrate any essentially different concerns and interests between men and women, but are more likely to be the result of the social roles of the men and women whose conversations were recorded for inclusion in the corpus e.g. more women staying at home to bring up children. In societies where roles are distributed differently, we would not expect to find the same results.

Corpus analysis is useful in helping to confirm or refute theories of gendered language use, by allowing us to identify trends within a wider population, rather than simply making claims based on introspection or the examination of a limited number of speakers. However, as Rayson et al. (1997) point out, care needs to be taken with the interpretation of these results – and one finding which corpus-based approaches almost always reveal is that differences are rarely absolute but are more often based on gradients. As Schmid (2003: 219) concludes 'to a very large extent, these two 'cultures' overlap' (my quotes). So, for example, while male speakers use more taboo words overall, they are by no means absent from female speech. The 'Difference' model tends to background the existence of similarity – creating the erroneous notion of two gendered 'species' of language user. Corpus linguistics research or other large scale meta-analyses can therefore usefully rein in this view. While we may argue that it is important not to over-generalise differences, I agree with Sunderland (2004: 16–7): 'I do not (have not been able to) abandon the idea of gender as premised on 'difference', nor do I wish to, since it is important not to lose sight of the ways in which *notions of gender* can adversely affect women's access to important linguistic resources and possibilities of expression…' (my emphasis). Sunderland's point is not, then, that men and women are intrinsically different, but that society's belief in, and acceptance of, gender difference impacts on everybody's lives. I shall discuss this in more detail in Chapter 4.

'Gay' language

While researchers who worked on language and gender grappled with Difference and Dominance models in relation to (mainly) heterosexual men and women, a small number of other researchers focused on sexuality. However, just as in the past, work on women's language was seen as deviating from a male norm, in terms of sexuality, it was the language of gay men (and to a lesser extent, lesbians), rather than heterosexual people which received the most attention.

The early research on gay male lexicons, begun by Legman, Burgess and Westwood, continued into the 1960s and 1970s, with attempts to outline the language use of the American gay male subculture.

Cory (1965) published a 40-word lexicon, noting two uses of homosexual slang – pejorative slang used by unfriendly heterosexuals, and secret 'insider' slang used by gay men in order to protect, strengthen and affirm membership to the 'despised in-group'. He argued that such words are often stinging in their critical content, reflecting the two-sided feelings of gay people towards themselves (hardly surprising, considering mainstream society's taboos on homosexuality). *The Queen's Vernacular* by Bruce Rodgers, published in 1972, was the largest lexicon of gay language ever produced, containing over 7,000 entries (although estimates tended to put it at 12,000). The thinking behind the book was to produce a dictionary of 'homosexual cant' – as the data were derived from participant observation and ethnography, the author had a claim to authenticity which he argued was lacking in most other gay glossaries. The collection is a result of years of interviews with hundreds of informants whom Rodgers sought out in bars, steam baths, dance halls, public rest rooms and on street corners, on the basis that this is a work which charts spoken, rather than written language.

Following Rodger's lexicon, there have been several studies of smaller lexica which attempt to discover patterns or impose some kind of linguistic or social theory on their sample. For example, Stanley (1972) bases her study of gay slang on three assumptions: first, that a homosexual subculture exists in America, and that such a subculture is homogeneous; secondly, that vocabulary items will cut across other social boundaries such as class, race, profession or religion (but not gender); and, thirdly, that increasing tolerance of homosexuality would be result in 'outsiders' becoming knowledgeable about homosexual slang. Stanley noted the existence of a core and fringe slang vocabulary – the core vocabulary containing few words known to many, and the fringe vocabulary containing many words known to few. Finally, she cited six methods of word formation – compounds (*closet queen, chicken queen, trick towel*), rhyme compounds (*kiki, chichi*), exclamation (*Mary!, For days!*), puns (*Give him the clap*), blends (*bluff*), and truncations (*bi, homo,*

Table 2.3. Gay slang terms adapted from Rodgers (1972)

Word	Meaning
abdicate	v. to leave a public toilet because of interrogation by the police
aging actress	n. older gay man who hogs the limelight
amyl queen	n. a gay man who inhales the recreational drug amyl nitrate
ass hound	n. someone who lusts after backsides
auntie	n. old prostitute
back stage	adj. wicked, uncouth, unrehearsed
ball gown	n. a man's suit
banana	n. penis
beads	n. the inner awareness of being gay
beat the meat	v. to masturbate
beefcake	n. muscular attractive man used in erotica
bitch	v. to complain n. an unpleasant gay man (or woman)
blue boys	n. the police
blue stockings	adj. strange, odd
(to) brown one	v. to anally penetrate
buttercup	n. an effeminate gay man
bull dyke	n. a masculine lesbian
charm a snake	v. to masturbate
closet case	n. someone who keeps his/her sexuality a secret
cookie crumbs	n. semen stains on a man's trouser leg
curtain calls	n. multiple sexual activity
daddy	n. an older gay man who showers affection on a younger one
daisy chain	n. an orgy
dethroned	adj. forced to leave, by the police
dinge palace	n. a gay bar frequented by black homosexuals
doff the tiara	v. to be gay
drag king	n. a female who wears male clothing
dragon lady	n. an aggressive gay man
easy meat	n. someone easily persuaded to have gay sex
fairy godmother	n. a homosexual mentor/protector
fairy pants	n. an evening gown
feature a matinee	v. to have sex in the afternoon
fish-tank jewelry	n. tacky inexpensive jewelry
flamingo	n. an opulent dresser
head cheese	n. smegma on a man's penis
gay chick	n. a lesbian
hung like a field mouse	adj. having a small penis

hetero). In a paper on gay lexical items, Farrell (1972) claims that, '...the major function of the homosexual argot seems to be that of ordering and classifying experience within the homosexual community, particularly those interests and problems which are of focal concern to the homosexual' (1972: 98).

What else can lists of slang reveal about gay male uses of language? Table 2.3 shows some of the words described in Rodger's *Queen's Vernacular*. One way to consider these words collectively, is in terms of metaphor. For example, there are words relating to royalty (*abdicate, amyl queen, dethroned, dinge palace, doff the tiara, drag king*), the theatre (*back stage, aging actress, curtain calls, feature a matinee*), food (*banana, beat the meat, beefcake, cookie crumbs, easy meat, head cheese*) and animals (*ass hound, bitch, bull dyke, charm a snake, dragon lady, fish tank jewellery, gay chick*). The metaphor 'Sex is Food' is found in many other forms of slang and may, therefore, reveal something about the ways in which sexual desire is generally conceptualised; some of the other metaphorical categories are more telling about the ways which the gay men who Rodgers examined understood and interacted with the world, for example, by casting themselves as royalty or film stars. Furthermore, we can see how sets of words can be classed semantically, e.g. sexual activities, preferences and body parts, types of people and clothing. It may be that the subculture needed to invent terms to name certain concepts because they were absent from 'mainstream' language, but they simultaneously reveal some of the main preoccupations of the gay subculture who developed the slang. We could characterise the gay men who Rodgers studied as creative and humorous, but they also focused on sexuality and physical appearances – the lexicon seems to conform to a stereotype of gay men as bitchy, feminising and obsessed with sex.

However, lists of words are a limited resource in that they provide only the briefest outline of the language use of a particular identity group. So while a lexicon may tell us about the preoccupations or taboos of a particular group, taken out of context they do not reveal much about the ways in which identities are constructed, and to an extent they serve to exoticise the group, again focusing on the ways that its members differ from 'mainstream' society.

For example, the lack of context in Rodger's dictionary was later exploited by right-wing and religious writers who argued that gay men were paedophiles and amoral, e.g. 'The lexicon contains over 12,000 entries most of which are not fit for decent conversation. *The Queen's Vernacular* reinforces Jude's description of homosexuals as 'filthy dreamers' (Jude 1: 7,8). It also confirms the fact that homosexuals do seduce and molest youth. Such acts are written into homosexual figures of speech, e.g., chicken freak, chicken hawk, ladder, vampire etc.' (Noebel et al., 1977). While terms which implied paedophilia *did* exist in the book, they almost certainly referred to a minority of men and did not necessarily equate with actual child abuse; they could have simply been used as insults (so a 35-year old man in a relationship with a 22-year old man could have been sarcastically referred to as a *chicken freak*). Additionally, the lexicon was decontextualised from the society that it occurred in. Rodgers did not reveal much about the context of what it was like to be gay in America in the 1950s, 1960s and 1970s – a period of enormous social change, but also one in which gay people remained on the margins of society. Long-term gay relationships were not recognised and gay people were discriminated against in professional, public and private contexts. An awareness of this discrimination was only beginning to emerge, but it would make sense that a stigmatised group, who were not encouraged to form long-term same-sex relationships but instead had to find short-term partners through cruising or going to bars, used a coded form of language with each other in an ambivalent way.

A later approach, which did consider gay male language use from a context-based perspective, was developed by Hayes (1976, reprinted 1981). Moving away from lexicon collecting, Hayes attempted to make sense of the functions of gay male speech, which he called GaySpeak. His theory took into account the fact that people, including gay men, modify their behaviour (and language) according to the social context in which they find themselves at any given time. Thus, for Hayes (1981: 46), GaySpeak had three distinct branches, according to whether a gay man was in a *secret* setting, a *social* setting, or a *radical-activist* setting. Each setting required a different use of language, for example, in public places, gay men would modify their use of language, speaking in agreed-upon codes (such as pronoun switching or euphemisms) so that strangers in the same vicinity would not be able to identify them as gay – Secret GaySpeak. The social setting is where the large gay lexicon established by Rodgers, Cory and Stanley is more likely to be heard, with language used humorously and theatrically as a way of establishing cama-raderie. Hayes points out that Social GaySpeak was a form of acting within acting – a language of irony where gossip and trivia were lampooned and exaggerated for comic effect. Finally, Radical-Activist GaySpeak was a more politicised use of language which Hayes (1981: 51) described as the 'rhetoric of gay liberation'. This use of language is more politically aware, influenced by the political correctness movements described earlier in this chapter. So speakers would avoid the feminising kinship terms of Social GaySpeak like *mother* and *auntie*, which were viewed as elitist and sexist. This third use of language is seen as a natural progression from the first two – liberation can only be achieved once networks have been established and solidified through Secret and Social GaySpeak.

Hayes' theory was criticised by Darsey (1981: 63), who argued that, 'Hayes fails to provide us with any words or word patterns that have a constant function and usage across settings which might indeed illuminate something uniquely and universally gay'. Darsey's main contention was that the types of language use that Hayes had described could also be used by other types of people in different circumstances – Secret GaySpeak, for example, was dismissed as 'lying', similar to heterosexual college students who wanted to hide a relationship from their parents. Darsey referred to Social Gayspeak as 'camp' and Radical-Activist Gayspeak as a version of radical revolutionary theory.

More recent perspectives of language and identity recognise that there is no such thing as a form of language that is uniquely and universally gay, just as there is no distinct 'women's language'. Instead, language use is specific to time and place, and identities such as *gay man* or *woman* are not cast in stone, but, rather, subject to change, influenced by society and also diverse: gay men are not a homogenous, indistinguishable mass. So Hayes' findings may have constituted a reasonable description of how (some) gay men were using language in the mid-1970s in America, but it was unwise, even pointless, to attempt to generalise his findings beyond that. Cameron and Kulick (2003: 88) write that research which tries to postulate something like GaySpeak faces two main problems: first, documenting that gay men and lesbians use language in empirically delineable ways, and, secondly, answering the question, 'In what sense is that language gay?' Ultimately, then, the underlying issue is, 'What does *gay* (or *straight*) actually mean?' If we conceptualise sexuality as being an essential aspect of identity then we could propose a binary distinction between homosexual and heterosexual, and chart the differences between these two sexual identities. However, as later chapters in this book will show, sexuality is not a simple matter of binaries. Many people have the potential to experience sexual desire for both men and women, whether such potential is acted on or not. Other people may have same-sex or opposite-sex partners at different times and for different reasons. Furthermore, the way that we understand same-sex or opposite-sex desire can change according to the society and time period that we live in. Sexual identity is also dependent on other aspects of identity such as an individual's age and personal circumstances, or their social groups. So just as gender was divided into an exaggerated masculine/feminine either/or binary, sexuality was equally divided into two extreme states which appeared to be fixed. Hence, researchers trying to outline such a thing as 'gay language' faced similar criticisms to those who attempted to demarcate 'women's language' – it was an impossible task because the model of gender or sexuality they were starting from made incorrect assumptions, was over-simplified and, therefore, ultimately inaccurate.

It is understandable, however, that some researchers in the 1970s and 1980s did assume that there was such a thing as a universal gay identity. They were working within a society where conceptualisations of homosexuality had changed from regarding it as a deficient mental condition or perversion (see Chapter 7) to an essential aspect of identity. In many ways, it was necessary for gay identity to be essentialised – liberationist politics required that people were united behind the identity of 'gay' in order to fight for a common cause. So with this in mind, as well as the continuing interest in lexical items and phrases specific to the gay subculture, research on other *features* of 'gay language' became popular in the 1970s and 1980s.

For example, Humphreys (1970) and Ponte (1974) carried out ethnographic research in gay cruising areas, looking at non-verbal behaviour in such settings. Humphreys spent several months as a 'watch-queen', observing how sexual encounters and roles between men were negotiated in public lavatories in America, whereas Ponte examined the socialising and pickup activities of men in a California beach car park. Humphreys characterises sexual activity as a game, with players taking different roles and engaging in a number of discrete 'moves', which are usually communicated by non-linguistic or paralinguistic means. For example, he describes an early move in the 'game', *approaching*, in the following way, 'From the viewpoint of those already in the restroom, the action of the man outside may communicate a great deal about his availability for the game. Straights do not wait; they stop, enter, urinate and leave. A man who remains in his car while a number of others come and go – then starts for the facility as soon as a relatively handsome young fellow approaches – may be revealing his preferences and his unwillingness to engage in action with anyone "substandard"' (1970: 61).

Webbink (1981) examined gaze and posture, whereas other studies of gay communication looked at code-switching (Lumby, 1976), stress patterns (Moonwomon, 1985) and intonation (Goodwin, 1989, Moran, 1991, Gaudio, 1994). Chesebro (1981) addressed rhetoric, communication and media portrayals of gay men and lesbians whereas Zeve (1993) examined metaphor in the speech of gay men. The political vocabulary of homosexuality was reassessed by White (1980), while Taub and Leger (1984) looked at how language created social types in the gay bar culture.

Echoing Darsey's requisite of providing, 'patterns that have a constant function and usage across settings which might indeed illuminate something uniquely and universally gay', in the 1990s a notable amount of work was carried out by phoneticians attempting to chart features of the so-called 'gay voice'. Gaudio (1994) hypothesised that gay and straight men would demonstrate differences in pitch when speaking. He asked eight gay-identified and eight straight-identified men to read two passages into a tape recorder. One was from an accounting volume, the other from a play about gay life by Harvey Fierstein. Gaudio found neither pitch range nor pitch variability correlated with the sexual identity of the speakers. Other researchers *did* uncover some evidence to suggest phonetic differences. Crist (1997) noted that for five out of six speakers whom he examined, the segments /s/ and /l/ were longer in stereotypically gay speech, while Rogers et al. (2000) obtained similar results, finding that the sibilants /s/ and /z/ and the lateral approximant /l/ were longer in the language use of gay men.

A study by Podesva et al. (2002) attempted to address the issue of context in relation to the 'gay voice'. They examined the speech of two men during a political discussion on gay rights in a radio programme: Speaker A who identified as gay and Speaker B who did not. They focused on the presence or absence of features found in earlier studies of the 'gay voice' and concluded that, 'Speaker A is not exploiting pitch or the duration of /l/ to produce a gay speech style, even though these features have been linked to stereotypically gay speech... Speaker A is performing a non-stereotypical gay identity, and his performance illustrates that linguistic styles – including gay styles – are as diverse as the individuals and communities using them' (2002: 187). Earlier in the paper, Podesva et al. suggest that the context of the speech production is likely to have had an impact on language use, 'Gay identity is highly salient for representatives of gay political organisations, especially in public discussions. But at the same time, participants are frequently warned against sounding 'too gay'' (2002: 181).

A related aspect of work attempting to uncover the existence (or not) of the so-called 'gay voice' takes a slightly different approach. Rather than attempting to compare features of a small number of gay and heterosexual speakers, instead the researcher asks people to judge whether someone *sounds* gay. For example, Jacobs et al. (1999) found that listeners were more likely to identify speakers as gay if they had large pitch ranges, regardless of their sexual identity. Gaudio's (1994) study contained a similar finding: even though pitch didn't appear to be a factor in differentiating gay and straight speakers, most of the 13 judges who listened to the voices were able to correctly identify their sexuality. Zwicky (1997: 31) polled linguists for phonetic characteristics associated with gay speakers. He received a wide range of suggestions, such as wide pitch range, frequent fluctuation in pitch, use of high rising-falling pitch pattern, concentration on pitches towards the high end of a speaker's range, large falls in pitch at the end of phrases, breathiness, lengthening of fricatives (particularly /s/ and /z/) and affrication of /t/ and /d/. However, other linguists suggested that a gay voice would utilise dentalisation of alveolar /t/, /d/, /s/, /z/ and /n/ which Zwicky argues is associated with white working class communities in American cities and is therefore likely to be a marker of (stereotypical heterosexual) masculinity. He notes *ib id* that, 'It is entirely possible that everyone is right – but for different speakers, in different places, on different occasions'.

Moonwomon (1985) also asked judges (who were students) to identify lesbian speakers, and found that they were not very successful (about half of the judgements were correct). She gives a number of possible reasons for this: the age of the judges and the fact that they may not have been exposed to different kinds of people, as well as their unwillingness to label people as lesbians, possibly due to an assumption that everyone is heterosexual (see Chapter 4). However, the reason she found most convincing was an unwillingness to acknowledge lesbian presence as it goes against enforced invisibility.[7] The media has played a large part in perpetuating the stereotype of the gay voice – with gay male celebrities like Paul Lynde, John Inman, Larry Grayson, Kenneth Williams and Julian Clary becoming well-known for their humorously camp ways of speaking. Therefore, it appears that people possess some sort of shared understanding of what constitutes a 'gay voice' (although not necessarily a 'lesbian voice'), based on features used by some gay men, but not all of them, and also used by some heterosexual men. As Cameron and Kulick (2003: 90) point out, 'Not all gay men have 'the voice' and not everyone who has 'the voice' is gay'. Furthermore, as the research by Podvesa et al. (2002) suggests, 'the voice' can come and go in different contexts.[8]

So, while the focus on 'gay linguistics' steered away from collecting lists of slang, a good deal of the research until the 1990s attempted to describe quantifiable features of 'gay language' through what could be treated as a constructionist approach – listing all the ways that 'gay language' was different to a supposed heterosexual norm.[9] Such research, therefore, although separate from research into language and gender per se, mirrored the work that was done in this area. So gender research focused on women's language, whereas sexuality research emphasised gay men's language, but both were concerned with charting the ways that these two groups differed in relation to a male heterosexual norm. A notable aspect of much of this early research, however, is that it sometimes ignored, and in most cases backgrounded, the speech of the supposed male heterosexual norm. So research into gender did not look at male uses of language, except when it was being compared to women's language, and research into sexuality did not consider the language of heterosexuals (Chapters 4 and 5 address research which does focus on heterosexuals and men). The lack of research into lesbian language use is also notable – lesbians, being women *and* homosexual, were doubly stigmatised since they possessed two marginalised identities – and researchers were considered daring for just considering one. Finally, as we have seen, both gender and sexuality researchers often assumed that the groups they were studying were relatively homogenous, that people used language in a certain way *because* they were female or gay. As we will see in the following chapter, this thinking would eventually be radically contested. A key difference between the two approaches, however, is that there was a strong feminist component to gender research, characterised in the work of Lakoff and Spender, where men were broadly viewed as oppressive, and research into language and gender had the political goals of raising awareness and challenging the patriarchal status quo. Until the 1990s, for the most part, research into the language use of gay men was rather less politically focused. Researchers may have wanted to raise awareness of the existence of gay people or had the underlying goals of tolerance or acceptance of a minority group, and some work was carried out on pejorative terms (e.g. Cory, 1965), but there was little research on other ways that language was used to oppress gay people or normalise particular types of sexual identities at the expense of others. As with language and gender research, the focus on gay men's language use was rooted in approaches which assumed an essential, generalisable difference which aimed to define a minority sexual subculture.

This chapter therefore ends with a somewhat unsatisfactory account of language use as it relates to gender and sexuality. If there are differences in the ways that men and women use language, then they are not necessarily the same differences that were postulated by early researchers, and they are not absolute or even large differences, nor are they applicable to all men and all women. They are, though, context-dependent and subject to change. There is a general feeling that the underlying premises which fueled early research were flawed, with researchers falling into a trap of reifying identity categories, assuming that there *were* essential or generalisable differences in language use that could be mapped onto gender and sexuality and focusing on one side of the supposed binary distinctions (gay people or women) at the expense of the 'normal' other (heterosexuals, men).

Although it is possible to criticise such pioneering studies, it is important to note that they were necessary steps: the fact that people wrote about concepts such as male dominance or homosexuality was challenging in itself. As Cameron (1995a: 39) notes of the Dominance and Difference models, 'both… represented particular moments in feminism: dominance was the moment of feminist outrage, of bearing witness to oppression in all aspects of women's lives, while difference was the moment of feminist celebration, reclaiming and revaluing women's distinctive cultural traditions'.

In Chapter 3, I shall move on to consider more recently-published research, where paradigms shifted away from Difference and Dominance models, to focus on other concepts which provided a more complex and sophisticated approach to understanding the relationship between language, gender and sexuality.

Notes

1 Cameron (2005: 483–4) gives a critical discussion of the problems surrounding definitions of different 'waves' of feminism, along with the distinction between 'modern' and 'post-modern'.

2 The plurals of these terms were also examined, with the same process carried out for male nurse/stripper/prostitute/model.

3 In fact, frequencies of these terms rose slightly over time, but this may be because concepts like the male stripper were largely unthinkable in mainstream western society for most of the twentieth century.

4 Focus group discussions as a research method were developed by Robert Merton and colleagues in the 1940s (Merton and Kendall, 1946, Merton et al., 1956), becoming widespread in market research from the 1950s onwards. They were used in media research from the 1980s and became popular as a social science research method in the 1990s. They usually consist of about 6–12 participants who have certain characteristics in common (such as age or gender). Focus groups are normally facilitated by a moderator who leads the group through a discussion which follows a warm-up exercise such as a playing a game or watching a video. They are not necessarily intended to be representative of a particular population but are instead indicative (Litosseliti, 2003: 22). Kitzinger (1995: 299) argues that data from focus groups can help to highlight respondents' attitudes, priorities, language and frameworks of understanding, and can make it possible to identify group norms and cultural values that are co-constructed between multiple participants.

5 Edley (2001: 98) writes that interpretative repertoires are, 'relatively coherent ways of talking about objects and events in the world. In discourse analytical terms, they are the 'building blocks of conversations', a range of linguistic resources that can be drawn upon and utilised in the course of everyday social interaction. Interpretative repertoires are part and parcel of any community's common sense, providing a basis for shared social understanding'.

6 Cameron (2005: 486) argues that the difference and dominance approaches to language and gender had a great deal in common: they both looked for differences between men and women, pointing to differences in gender, rather than sex, due to early socialisation. Furthermore, both concentrated on white, heterosexual, middle-class speakers as a kind of mainstream prototype, assuming that differences were well-defined and homogenous.

7 Zwicky hypothesises that the 'gay' voice develops because of the way that gender roles are acquired, suggesting that people model their own behaviour on those around them by choosing people they believe themselves to be like, or wish to be like. At the same time they avoid the behaviours associated with people they do not believe themselves to be like or do not wish to be like. Furthermore, social groups maintain norms by rewarding conformity and punishing nonconformity, either

openly or covertly. Therefore, Zwicky suggests that gay men perform their identities by distancing themselves from heterosexual men, whereas lesbians identity with other women. So, one reason why people are less successful at identifying a 'lesbian voice' may be that lesbians do not try to distance themselves from heterosexual women in the same way that gay men distance themselves from heterosexual men. Such a point is demonstrated by Harris (1997: 8–9) who writes that, as a child growing up in Appalachia, he developed a British accent, derived from identifying with 'cultured' Hollywood actresses like Katharine Hepburn, Bette Davis and Tallulah Bankhead: 'This strange act of ventriloquism… is the direct outcome of my perception in my youth that, as a homosexual, I did not belong in the community in which I lived, that I was different, a castaway from somewhere else, somewhere better, more elegant, more refined'. However, even if a gay man marks himself as gay by not speaking like heterosexual men (assuming that we can reach a consensus on what heterosexual male speech sounds like), then there would, potentially, be many ways to do this, and this means that it is difficult to make generalisations on what constitutes a 'gay voice'. This could explain why gay men don't sound the same either. Additionally, not all gay men may want to disassociate themselves with heterosexual male speech styles – particularly as a heterosexual identity tends to be associated with stereotyped masculinity and so is viewed as sexually desirable by many gay men (see Chapters 5 and 7).

8   And as with some of the work on 'women's language', a further methodological problem with these studies is that they have tended to gather relatively small data samples from equally small sets of speakers (often white and middle-class) in order to make extrapolations about the language use of an entire identity group, which is not homogenous in any case.

9   A small number of non-linguistic studies have proposed that there *are* 'essential' biological differences between gay men and heterosexual men. Studies carried out in the early- to mid-1990s claimed to pinpoint a specific genetic marker on the X chromosome linked to male homosexuality. Hamer et al. (1993) found that in 40 pairs of gay brothers, 33 had the same set of DNA sequences in a region of the Xq28 chromosome. A follow-up study (Hu et al., 1995) reported similar findings. However, a more recent study by Rice (1999) which looked at 52 pairs of gay brothers found that their Xq28 sequences were no more similar than what would be expected by chance. It may be the case the 'gay gene' exists elsewhere, or that many genes are involved in homosexuality, or that non-biological factors (for example, society) are more important. Other researchers have focused on differences in the brain between gay and heterosexual people. LeVay (1991) found that a tiny section of the hypothalamus in the brain was smaller in gay men than in straight men. Allen and Gorski (1992) found that a section of the fibres connecting the right and left hemispheres of the brain is one-third larger in gay men than straight men. Such findings are open to challenges, e.g. critics have noted that LeVay's findings may be due to the fact that the 'gay brains' belonged to men who died of AIDS, whose nuclei might have been shrunk by their medications. More recently, Wilson and Rahman (2005) argue that there is no single gay gene, but that genes make a contribution, along with the effect of sex hormones to which foetuses are exposed in the womb. They suspect that some male foetuses absorb low amounts of testosterone in certain parts of the brain, which means

that this part of the brain follows an index development route which is 'female'. They have also noted something called 'the big brother effect' – the more older brothers a man has, the more likely he is to be gay, due to the possibility that maternal antibodies developed in early pregnancies may cross the placenta in later pregnancies to disrupt testosterone absorption. However, their research does not explain why some people may appear to change their sexuality, nor does it give a detailed account of male bisexuality. Additionally, brain and gene-based studies tend to deal in 'probabilities' that someone will be gay or heterosexual – they do not offer full explanations or completely accurate predictions. And, importantly, they do not take into account the relationship between the individual and society's changing conceptualisations of sexuality and sexual categories.

3   Doing gender: community and performativity

Community, contact and co-operation

If the three 'D' models discussed in Chapter 2 offered an incomplete or problematic set of ways of understanding the relationship between language, gender and sexuality, then what other ways of approaching the subject are available, building on the research that has gone before? Swann (2002: 44) reports that more recently, language and gender researchers have refocused their work on the concept of *diversity*, emphasising differences amongst women and amongst men, rather than differences between women and men. This has also resulted in a greater need to take context into account, viewing language and its meaning as context dependent, while gender is seen as a contextualised social practice. Similarly, more recent corpus-based work (e.g. Harrington, 2006) has been useful in revealing how putting people into groups can produce 'flat' averages whilst overlooking the linguistic 'spikes' of individuals. Not all men are the same as each other. Nor are all women the same. More likely, some men and women exist at extreme ends of a gendered continuum, producing stereotypically gendered language, while there are others whose speech is less stereotyped, or even conforms slightly or a great deal to the opposite sex stereotype. Furthermore, at different times, people are likely to use language in different ways, depending on who else is present, the mood that they are in, the sort of persona they wish to project, the setting (workplace or home, etc.) and dozens of other variables. And as Talbot (1998: 50) points out, 'We need to shift from itemization of linguistic features to an examination of the dynamics of interaction'.

As described in Chapter 1, a potential problem with using empirical methods to measure human behaviour is that human societies are constantly changing. If we measure the composition of a metal alloy, the orbit of the Moon around the Earth or the temperature required to boil water, there is relatively little or no variation over time. However, because humans and human societies are in continuous development, many research findings are only valid for the point in time and place at which they were taken. This observation should not undermine the importance of such research, but highlights the need for the context of research to be acknowledged. So studies which examined the language of white, middle-class women from English-speaking countries in the 1970s should not be assumed to be representative of all women who have ever lived or those yet to be born.

Therefore, later studies have moved away from making generalisations about male and female uses of language and have instead focused on research of a more qualitative nature, which examined a much wider range of language use occurring in specific contexts. The view of gender as simply one component of identity, inter-related with many others, was also popularised, for example, by Eckert and McConnell-Ginet (1998: 488–89): 'Gender can be thought of a sex-based way of experiencing other social attributes like class, ethnicity, or age (and also less obviously social qualities like ambition, athleticism and musicality). To examine gender independently as if it were just 'added on' to such other aspects of identity is to miss its significance and force'.

Not all research has rejected quantitative paradigms, though. Jenny Cheshire (1982) developed Milroy's (1980) social network theory, in which it is claimed that members of a speech community are connected to each other in social networks which help to reinforce vernacular norms. Cheshire counted use of non-standard linguistic features amongst boys and girls in Reading, England, concluding that there were differences in language use between male and female speakers, as well as differences between individual males and females. For example, the non-standard use of the word *come*, as in, 'I come down here yesterday', was always used by all the boys in her study. However, a group of girls whom she classed as 'good girls', only used non-standard *come* 30.77 percent of the time, whereas a group referred to as 'other girls' used non-standard *come* 90.63 percent of the time. Cheshire found that social networks were organised around sex differences, which helped to explain why boys and girls used non-standard features differently.

Eckert (1998) studied phonological variation at a Detroit high school, focusing on two groups of students: 'jocks' who were enthusiastic participants in organised school culture and 'burn-outs' who rejected school activities. She found that gender *and* social class were interacting factors in determining language use. Female jocks were the most conservative speakers, using fewer non-standard phonological variables, whereas female burn-outs used more vernacular forms than anyone else. Eckert argued that the relatively extreme speech styles of females could be accounted for by the fact that females were marginalised in the linguistic marketplace (drawing on Bordieu and Boltanski's (1975) notion of a symbolic market): they had to work harder than males in order to be seen as good jocks or good burnouts. Eckert's study is, therefore, important because it acknowledges that gender interacts with other aspects of identity, but it also points to the fact that different gender identities are awarded varying degrees of status in societies.

Eckert and McConnell-Ginet (1998) adopted Lave and Wenger's (1991) concept of *communities of practice* in order to explain how gender is produced and reproduced in differential forms of participation. A community of practice is based on an, 'aggregate of people who come together around mutual engagement in some common endeavour' (1998: 490). 'Speakers develop linguistic patterns as they engage in activity in the various communities in which they participate' (1998: 492). Communities of practice can be gendered, as in, for example, male or female sports teams, and can occur instantaneously and be short-lived, e.g. after a family meal, the women may team up to serve and clear away food, whereas men may watch a sports game on the television. People belong to multiple communities of practice, operating in different capacities within them. Eckert and McConnell-Ginet's theory allows for continuous change, '…although the identity of both the individual and the individual community of practice is experienced as persistent, in fact they both change constantly. We continue to adopt new ways of talking and discard some old ways, to adopt new ways of being women and men, gays and lesbians and heterosexuals, even changing our ways of being feminists or being lovers or being mothers or being sisters' (1998: 492).

A community-based position was also taken by Queen (1997), who drew on the idea of *imagined communities* – a term coined by Anderson (1983) who used it to explain how the concept of nationhood is socially constructed. Anderson theorised that communities are, 'imagined because the members of even the smallest nation will never know most of their fellow-members, meet them, or even hear of them, yet in the minds of each lives the image of their communion' (1983: 6). Queen (1997: 233, 254) wrote that lesbian identities were constructed from a number of such imagined communities:

> The few studies that exist on lesbian language either centre on lexical or topic issues… or come to the conclusion that there are no unique linguistic features used by lesbians… The characterization of lesbian language does not revolve around a simple binary choice: Either we speak like women or we speak like men. Instead lesbians have a rather broad range from which to draw their linguistic choices. Elements of these choices incorporate the construction and enactment of a lesbian identity, a queer identity, a female identity, an ethnic identity and a class identity, in addition to a variety of other kinds of identity… I propose that it is through the combination of the linguistic resources available from each of the 'imagined' communities to which lesbians 'belong' that we get a lesbian speech style. Through taking such a contact-based perspective, we may begin to accommodate the vast social and individual ways that lesbians use language as indexical markers of identity.

Similarly, Barrett (1997) employs Pratt's notion of *linguistics of contact* in order to theorise issues of sexual orientation and gender identification. One problem with traditional community-based approaches to language, according to Pratt, is that they tend to assume that speakers are monolingual, even monodialectal – so that the focus is on homogenous communities, with linguistic idiosyncrasies being passed down from one member to another as kind of 'inheritance'. However, Pratt argues that communities do not work in this way: people can belong to numerous communities at any given time, particularly because identities are multiple and changing. 'Imagine, then a linguistics that decentered community, that placed at its centre the operation of language across lines of social differentiation, a linguistics that focused on modes and zones of contact between dominant and dominated groups, between persons of different and multiple identities, speakers of different languages… Let us call this enterprise a linguistics of contact' (Pratt, 1987: 60).

Pratt's contact framework was applied by Barrett in his study of Texas 'bar queens'. Barrett noted that the bar queens in his study used a variety of linguistic features such as lexical items from Lakoff's 'women's' language' including precise colour terms, empty adjectives, a wider range of intonational contours, lexical items specific to gay subcultures (such as those noted by Rodgers and Stanley, described in Chapter 2) and hyper-correct pronunciation. Barrett argues that it is possible to view gay men's use of these features as cases of 'borrowing' from one community by another – i.e. gay men are borrowing stereotypical features of women's language or African American Vernacular English when using phrases like *work it, girlfriend* or *Miss Thang* (see also Barrett's (1995) study of African American drag queens). However, Barrett (1997: 194) argues that such cases should not be regarded as traditional borrowings, but cites that linguistics of contact theory, 'in which community boundaries are not assumed to be static and rigid, allows for an analysis in which bar queen speech may be composed from the speech of a variety of individuals (or groups of individuals) with different linguistic backgrounds who participate in mutual acts of identity (Le Page and Tabouret-Keller, 1985) to create shared linguistic markers of social identity… In a situation where gay men from various backgrounds come together in the setting of a bar, stereotypes of effeminate linguistic behaviour from white English and African American English, as well as from other ethnic and regional varieties, come together to create a unified stereotype of what constitutes gay English'.

The concepts of community and contact were also referenced in my (2002) study of Polari (also spelt Palari or Palare), a variety of language spoken mainly by British, working-class gay men, lesbians and drag queens (see also Partridge, 1950, Hancock, 1984, Green, 1987, and Lucas, 1997). Using interviews, Polari texts and a semantic analysis of its lexicon, I traced Polari's growth in popularity and its eventual decline across the twentieth century, relating it to the development of gay communities in the UK. At first, Polari was a secret code used for the identification of other gay people, but it became useful during the oppressive social climate of the 1950s, allowing speakers to gossip about other people while on public transport or in nominally gay pubs or cafes. Its lexicon developed from gay men's contact with numerous communities of practice: sailors, prostitutes, theatrical performers, fairground and market workers, beggars and drug-users as well as Italian, Yiddish and East End London communities. It was never a fully-developed language in that its limited lexicon and grammar meant that speakers also had to rely on English, and it functioned best in contexts where other people's physical appearances were being described and evaluated. However, the more fluent speakers (for example, 'sea queens' or gay sailors) improvised and developed Polari so it appeared unintelligible to outsiders or those with only a basic knowledge:

> The sea queen would accentuate or elaborate a lot more on the Polari. If you were going to say 'Look at that guy standing next to me,' the shore-side Polari part would be 'Vada the omee standing next to me'. A sea queen would say 'Vada the schwawarly on me jaxys way out'. They just elaborated on it, because it was meant to sway people, so they didn't understand what you were talking about. Even with the sea queens not wanting a shore side West End queen to understand what she's saying. You'd be standing there and you'd say 'Oh vada that naff queen. What a coddy kaffall dear. Oh vada the shnozzle on it dear.' And you'd be doing all this Polari, they'd understand the basics. They understood bona and camp and cod and riah and things like that, but the sea queens would really go to town.

David McKenna, *Summers Out* Channel 4, 1993, quoted in Baker (2002: 71)

Polari's popularity (and eventual demise) can be linked to the political and social context of twentieth century Britain. So, changes in the legal status of gay men impacted on the way that Polari was conceived and used as a form of gay expression. From being an underground subcultural language before the 1960s, it was eventually popularised in the British media, where a simplified, somewhat sanitised version of it was used in a popular BBC Radio comedy programme *Round The Horne* in the late 1960s. The well-received appearance of Polari speakers in the mainstream media reflected the fact that society's attitudes to homosexuality were becoming more positive, and this allowed further social acceptance. However, the exposure of the secret, together with the decriminalisation of homosexuality in 1967 and the onset of Gay Liberation, made gay communities re-evaluate Polari's usefulness, as Raban (1973: 17) points out, 'a language of body parts and fucking… isn't it time for everyone to tidy their toys away… and to take a few bricks out of the ghetto'. The use of Polari went into decline in the 1970s, when it was associated with unfashionably camp or unattractive 'old queen' stereotypes, and was regarded as a symbol of earlier oppression. However, by the 1990s, gay communities revived interest in (but not regular use of) Polari, reframing it as an important aspect of 'gay history' and a testament to the ingenuity of gay men and lesbians who had lived through difficult times. Research on Polari confirms that communities of practice are not stable entities, and the way that they use language changes over time.

The 1990s also saw the emergence of 'lavender linguistics' as an academic field, with the first Lavender Languages conference held in Washington DC in 1993 (the first Berkeley Women and Language Conference had been held in 1985). Leap's edited collection *Beyond the Lavender Lexicon*, published in 1995, brought together a wide-ranging set of papers which aimed to go beyond the field as it currently stood in a number of significant ways. First, Leap wanted to focus on specific texts and their contexts, rather than looking at lexica or other aspects of language taken out of context. Secondly, the authors in the book acknowledged their own positions in the communities that they were researching, making no attempt to conceal their subjectivity but instead using their involvement in order to make insights. Thirdly, Leap characterised gay and lesbian language use as consisting of *languages* rather than a secret code or argot. Fourthly, the authors assumed the existence of gay and lesbian cultures rather than considering gay and lesbian life as a, 'marginal, imperfect imitation of heterosexual life' (1995: x). And, finally, the book attempted to give equal coverage to both gay and lesbian uses of language, rather than simply focusing on men. Leap writes, 'If there is no lesbian/gay language, there is no reason for this book. What the authors present in these chapters is a celebration of lesbian and gay experience as revealed and displayed through the practice of spoken and written communication. All of us assume that there is something unique about this discourse' (1995: xiv). The book covered a wide range of uses of language in different contexts, looking at language used by and about gay and lesbian people. This was, therefore, an approach which differed from earlier studies which had focused on gay men involved in negotiating anonymous sexual encounters or examining words for exotic sexual practices or ways of evaluating and insulting others, '…a gay linguistics which focuses only on erotic discourse may promote an unbalanced image of gay men's experience' (Leap, 1995: xvii). Instead, the concepts of community and co-operation were emphasised. For example, Morgan and Wood (1995) tape recorded a group of lesbian friends and quoted a number of examples from their conversation which showed what they called the co-construction of lesbian identity:

Tonya:	Remember those bubble umbrellas (laugh)… came out like mushrooms… Those were big back then.
Mandy:	Our moms used to make us wear those big old rain boots you know.
Linda:	Galoshes.
Mandy:	Yeah, galoshes on the way to school. So we always, you know, got a block down the street, took 'em off and then stomped through the puddles and…
Sandy:	mmhmm.
Kathy:	get home, put 'em back on.

Morgan and Wood (1995: 244)

In order to show how this conversation constitutes the construction of a shared narrative, Morgan and Wood rewrite it as a single paragraph:

> Remember those bubble umbrellas (laugh)… came out like mushrooms… Those were big back then. Our moms used to make us wear those big old rain boots you know. Galoshes. Yeah, galoshes on the way to school. So we always, you know, got a block down the street, took 'em off and then stomped through the puddles and… mmhmm… get home, put 'em back on.

Of these sorts of exchanges, Morgan and Wood (1995: 245) observe that, 'The co-construction of a narrative binds us together in a sort of temporary conversational community, for the purpose of creating solidarity, tying us to a collective past as well as to each other within this conversation… This unrehearsed, rhythmic collusion was another tool, which worked to connect us as lesbians to a perceived, shared past'.

This argument was, however, reformulated by Cameron and Kulick (2003: 95) who write of one of the excerpts which Morgan and Wood analysed, 'Confronted only with this transcript, an analyst might be hard pressed to identify its specific lesbian content. However, because Morgan and Wood know the participants to be lesbians, they interpret this conversation as specifically *lesbian talk*… Because the ones doing this conversational colluding are lesbians, the authors also see this kind of conversation as 'challeng[ing] the 'hegemonic discourse' of heterosexuality'.

A related point is raised by Swann (2002: 49) who addresses the issue of *warrants*. She points out that across a range of studies, researchers have adopted varying decision-making procedures that justify the interpretation of data (such as a linguistic construction), as in some ways gendered. Such warrants range from patterns found in quantitative comparative studies (such as corpus data of male and female conversation), indirect reliance on quantitative or general patterns, 'participants' orientations' as evident in the text, participants' solicited interpretations, analyst intuition or the simple fact that the speakers are male/female (or whatever). Swann (2002: 62) suggests that, '…researchers need to be more flexible and 'open' in their approach to models of language and gender… [they] may, then, legitimately be viewed from different perspectives: a pragmatic combination of methods and approaches, along with an acknowledgment of their possibilities and limitations'.

Morgan and Wood's approach to 'lesbian language' was similar to the stance taken by Leap, who characterised the language used by gay men as 'Gay English'. Leap viewed Gay English as a, 'distinctive gendered approach… to oral, written and signed text making. [These] texts may include a specialized vocabulary or may be rich in male homoerotic content, but fluency in Gay English involves more than a personal familiarity with those words and phrases' (1996: xii).

While Leap's initial goal was to define Gay English in terms of isolating a list of linguistic features, he found that it was more useful to concentrate on how such features related to social practices – those which define gay experience. Two aspects of Gay English which Leap focused on were the ways it was used as a form of co-operative discourse and as a language of risk. By analysing a series of exchanges between gay men, he noted how features such as turn-taking, pauses and metaphor were employed in order to ensure a form of co-operative discourse. Drawing on Goodwin's theory of the double subjectivity of interpretation (1989: 12) – whereby meaning must be doubly subjective, that is, both the sender and receiver must be relied on for parts of the content of a message to be received – Leap examined a number of cases where strangers successfully or unsuccessfully attempted to establish a common ground with 'suspect gays'. By broadening the scope of his research to explore how gay men use language in situations where they are uncertain about the sexuality of another man, Leap notes how ambiguity is negotiated. In the following example, taken from a conversation between two male customers (who are in a relationship) and a male assistant, the three participants co-operate with each other in order to disclose, gradually, their sexual identities:

1 Assistant: May I help you?
2 Customer 1:   [*Presents item to be charged; says nothing*]
3 Assistant   [*Looks at merchandise*] Was this on sale? [*Customers 1 and 2 say nothing.*] Let me check the amount of the discount. [*Leaves counter, checks, returns and begins transaction.*] Do you need gift boxes for these?
4 Customer 2:   No. We don't believe in Santa Claus.
5 Assistant: You didn't see that movie last night? With Kate Jackson? About Santa Claus and orphans. That'd make you believe in Santa Claus.

6 Customer 1:   Sounds thrilling.

7 Assistant: Yes, I enjoyed watching it. But my roommate fell asleep.

8 Customer 1:   [*Said to Assistant but half-directed at Customer 2*] Sounds like our house.

9 Customer 2:   We sit in front of the TV and I fall asleep.

10 Assistant: Like at our house.

11 Customer 2: That's why we always go to bed so early.

12 Assistant: Old age is not for sissies, just like Bette Davis said. [*Pause*]. Here's your purchases. I hope you'll come again.

Adapted from Leap (1996: 53)

Leap suggests that gay-centred codes and meanings are encoded in every segment of this exchange, for example, the dismissal of Santa Claus, a primary icon for family-oriented heterosexual lifestyle (line 4), the reference to actresses Kate Jackson and Bette Davis (lines 5 and 12), the use of the euphemism *roommate* (line 7) and the shift in pronouns, from the singular person *I* and *my* (line 7), to the plural *our* and *we* (lines 9, 10 and 11).

Again, Leap's work is contextually specific and his examples were gathered from personal observations, including conversations in which he was one of the participants. He was, therefore, in a good position to make insights into the subtleties and ambiguities of the interactions. However, it is important not to generalise his research – so it is not possible to claim that all gay men incorporate aspects of co-operation in this way.

Cameron and Kulick (2003: 94) point out that the studies of gay language which occurred in the 1980s and the first half of 1990s abandoned 'bitchy queens', while 'argumentative dykes never appear… Instead what appears to be foregrounded is consensus and co-operation'. Taking into account the social context of this period, there were perhaps justifiable reasons for this approach. Many responses to the HIV virus in western countries, which had initially arisen among gay male communities, were not positive and resulted in further discrimination against gay people. Right wing governments and the media had also reacted with apathy or antipathy.[1] Such negative responses helped to galvanise gay and lesbian activism. It is therefore understandable that research findings were reported which constructed gay men and lesbians as possessing a distinct, united and proud identity, focusing on gay and lesbian speakers as co-operating with each other in order to strengthen communities which were under attack in a range of ways. As with all research, the paradigms used, and the way that the data for analysis is chosen, analysed and interpreted, tell us a great deal about the social and political context in which the research was conducted.

Gender as performance

For the remainder of this chapter, I would like to consider how a shift in our understanding of knowledge-making has resulted in a significant change in the way that we understand the relationship between language, gender and sexuality. Before the 1980s much early research in linguistics had a structuralist approach to knowledge-making. However, as mentioned in Chapter 1, the 1990s saw a significant change in the way that a great deal of research was carried out in the social sciences and humanities. The overlapping concepts of *social constructionism*, *post-structuralism* and *post-modernism* became central to new ways of understanding the world. Although the term *post* implies 'after', these new approaches actually added to what had gone before, rather than rejecting earlier approaches outright. Two important figures who influenced this shift were Roland Barthes and Jacques Derrida. Barthe's essay *Death of the Author* (1968, translated into English in 1977) asserted that literary texts were not restricted by the meaning that the author originally intended; rather, a range of interpretations from different readers were possible and valid. Derrida (1974, 1978, 1981a,b) approached the notion of meaning from a slightly different perspective, building on sign theory which had been advocated by the structuralist linguist de Saussure (1974).

Within sign theory, Saussure had claimed that signs (things which people refer to, talk to others about, think about, etc.) consisted of two parts: a *signifier* (which refers to the sound made when a word is spoken or the marks made on paper when it is written down), and a *signified* (which is the mental concept of the thing that is being referred to). Saussure claimed that the relationship between the signified and the signifier was arbitrary. So, for example, there is no reason why the signifier *dog* is used to represent that which is signified – the mental concept of a dog. When talking to a child, for example, we might use a different signifier like *doggie* or *woof-woof*, and if we were speaking French the signifier would be *chien*. All signs, however, have to be agreed on by members of a society or group in order for them to acquire meaning.

However, Saussure also claimed that once established, the relationship between the signified and the signifier was fixed. Derrida disagreed with this, arguing that meanings of words can change over time and are dependent on context. Therefore, a central tenet of post-structuralism is that meanings are not fixed – they change from person to person and over time. As Burr (1995: 41) points out, '…rather than language being a system of signs with fixed meanings upon which everyone agrees… it is a site of variability, disagreement and potential conflict. And when we talk about conflict, we are inevitably dealing in power relations'.

In terms of the influence of post-structuralist studies on language as related to gender and sexuality, the work which has probably had the greatest impact on the field is Judith Butler's *Gender Trouble* (1990), followed by *Bodies that Matter* (1993). Butler introduced the theory of gender as performance, developing Austin (1962) and Searle's (1969, 1979, 1983, 1989) theory of speech acts. Austin had noted that illocutions such as 'I promise' or 'I christen you...' were 'performatives' in that they brought a state of affairs into being, rather than described something that already existed (which he termed 'constatives'). Such performatives cause changes in the world. Looking at statements like 'I now pronounce you man and wife' and 'It's a girl!' (on assigning the sex of a newborn baby), Butler argued that language can be used in order to *construct* gender. Furthermore, though, gender itself is performative – a socially constructed and never-ending process, a 'work-in-progress and in-practice', which we are continuously engaged in. Gender therefore becomes something that we do, rather than who we are: 'Gender is the repeated stylization of the body, a set of repeated acts within a highly rigid regulatory frame that congeal over time to produce the appearance of substance of a natural sort of being' (Butler, 1990: 33).

This conceptualisation of gender extends earlier feminist theory (e.g. Simone de Beauvoir 1969) that one is not born but becomes a woman. According to Butler (1990: 33), becoming a woman is, 'a term in process, a beginning, a *constructing* that cannot rightfully be said to originate or to end' (my italics). As Cameron (1997: 48) points out, Butler completely changed perspectives on language and gender: in the past, sociolinguists took as given that people spoke in certain ways because of who they were – an underlying assumption of much of the research discussed in Chapter 2. But Butler reversed this thinking, instead arguing that people constructed identities for themselves, based on the ways that they spoke. Language use was only one (central) aspect of gender performance, however. The way a person stands, the way they style their hair, their clothing, their gaze, their walk, etc., would all contribute towards an overall gender performance. For example, Bornstein (1995) and Kulick (1999) examined aspects of change that male-to-female transsexuals undergo, in terms of 'feminising' their behaviour and language use. Kulick notes that transsexuals are advised to produce the features of Lakoff's 'women's language' in their own speech (see Chapter 2), while Bornstein, herself a male-to-female transsexual, describes how her own experiences of 'passing' as a woman highlighted the fact that gender must be constantly constructed. After having surgery and changing her name from Al to Kate, Bornstein learned how to change her voice, the way she made eye contact and even the way she exited lifts so that she could communicate her femininity to the outside world. In Bell (1997: 12)

Bornstein describes how she was taught to speak in a high-pitched, breathy, sing-song voice, add tag questions to the end of sentences and smile while talking, her teachers making use of supposed stereotyped features of 'women's language'. Bornstein's writing demonstrates that gender is not necessarily fixed to sex, nor is sex itself necessarily fixed (although the bodies we are born with entail restrictions for most people) and that gender work is never finished but is ongoing. Butler also considered people who change their gender by focusing on female impersonators or drag queens – men who 'perform' being women by adopting or copying stereotypical female behaviours. These gendered performances can be viewed as subversive because they question the supposed 'essential' link between sex and gender. Although such examples are 'extreme' in that most people do not have sex change operations, and most men do not become female impersonators, it could still be argued that if some men can appear to be women, then *everyone* has the potential to engage in a wide range of alternative gender performances.

Thinking in terms of the claims that earlier researchers had made about male, female, gay and heterosexual uses of language, we can see how performativity theory helps to explain some of the apparent (but not absolute) differences that were found or suggested. Some women may use a more co-operative form of language, employing, say, hedges or empty adjectives, in order to perform a feminine gender, because they see such forms of language as stereotypically associated with feminine (and ultimately female) ways of interacting. One set of questions which performativity theory raises, however, is how, when and why did certain linguistic (and other) features become associated with gender? And how did certain gender performances become associated with (biological) sex? When did empty adjectives (Lakoff, 1975), for example, become associated with 'female' ways of speaking? Butler (1991: 21) implies that the relationship is circular and continuous, 'Gender is a kind of imitation for which there is no original; in fact, it is a kind of imitation that produces the very notion of the original as an effect and consequence of the imitation itself'. So, as with accents, ways of performing gender have developed gradually over time as power relationships between people in societies developed. Equally, Ochs (1991) posits that linguistic resources are not directly related to social categories of identity but instead tend to bear pragmatic information about different situations, e.g. 'tag questions may index a stance of uncertainty as well as the act of requesting confirmation/clarification/feedback' (Ochs, 1991: 335). Over time, then, speakers acquire an understanding about how such linguistic resources are used in different contexts, and develop, 'norms, preferences, and expectations regarding the distribution of this work vis-à-vis particular social identities of speakers, referents and addressees' (Ochs, 1991: 342). So, gradually, certain speech styles become associated with particular contexts or (stereo)types of identities – resources indirectly indexing social categories. The fact that such 'indexes' of identity can shift over time could be partly due to linguistic innovators within social networks, e.g. people who use specific types of language in certain ways, which are then replicated by others (Milroy and Milroy, 1985). In *Bodies that Matter* (1993) Butler cited Derrida's theory of iterability, arguing that gender is a form of citationality: we ventriloquise or attempt to copy the acts of other speakers.

Cameron and Kulick (2003: 128–29) note that gender performances have the capacity to fail and also to be forged. They compare a gender performance to signing your signature or entering a pin number. The way that such actions are carried out are always going to be slightly different (we may push the buttons faster or softer than before, for example), and, at the same time, others may appropriate our signature or pin number for themselves. As Lloyd (1999: 200) notes, the construction and maintenance of gender is always 'repetition with a difference'. In the same way, gendered behaviours (such as language) are appropriated. So a female impersonator or drag queen may appropriate uses of language that are considered to constitute a feminine gender performance (calling people *honey* or using adjectives like *gorgeous* or *fabulous*, for example). But a 'real' biological woman is also performing a feminine gender when she uses such words – she is consciously (or more often unconsciously) replicating the performance of other women that she has seen and heard, who in turn have replicated other women, creating a seemingly endless series of reflections, stretching back over time, yet differing from each other in minor ways. As Butler (1990: 31) notes, 'The parodic repetition of 'the original'... reveals the original to be nothing other than a parody of the idea of the natural and the original'.

There is a strong political argument within Butler's writing. She rejects the concept of gender identity, 'There is no gender identity behind the expressions of gender... identity is performatively constituted by the very 'expressions' that are said to be its results' (1990: 25). Therefore, Butler also rejects the idea of viewing women (and subsequently any group based on gender) as a unified group, 'The very subject of women is no longer understood in stable or abiding terms' (1990: 1). The effect of such a classification, according to Butler, has been detrimental to feminism. If women and men are seen as different and separate (either due to essential biological factors or because this difference is socially enshrined in culture), then equality is impossible because there is little room for choice. Butler also argues that the idea of there being two distinct 'genders' is dependent on heterosexuality, referring to a 'heterosexual matrix' (1990: 5). Butler outlines the relationship between sex, gender and sexuality as follows, '...for bodies to cohere and make sense there must be a stable sex expressed through a stable gender (masculine expresses male, feminine expresses female) that is oppositionally and hierarchically defined through the compulsory practice of heterosexuality'

(1990: 151). Sexuality, gender and biological sex are therefore mapped onto each other, fixed, and the relationship between the three phenomena is made to appear somehow 'natural', unchanging and having been that way forever.

As well as developing ideas from Austin and Searle, Butler was inspired by the psychoanalysts Sigmund Freud, Jacques Lacan and Luce Irigaray, as well as the French post-structuralist philosophers Jacques Derrida and Michel Foucault. Expanding on Foucault's work she suggests that certain cultural expressions of gender have become naturalised in society, seizing a hegemonic hold. Everyone engages in gender performance, whether traditional or not, therefore the issue is not whether we *do* gender performance (we always will), but the form that it takes. Butler argues that the current 'privileging' of certain gender performances over others does not have to continue indefinitely, calling for subversive action or 'gender trouble': in other words, 'the mobilization, subversive confusion, and proliferation of precisely those constitutive categories that seek to keep gender in its place by posturing as the foundational illusions of identity' (1990: 34). Butler therefore proposes a deconstruction of gender, a break-down of the traditional and limiting roles which lie at the root of the inequality of the sexes, 'If identities were no longer fixed as the premises of a political syllogism, and politics no longer understood as a set of practices derived from the alleged interests that belong to a set of ready-made subjects, a new configuration of politics would surely emerge from the ruins of the old' (1990: 149).

Butler's theories have raised a number of questions and criticisms. First, some researchers found her early writing style unnecessarily difficult to follow. For example, Nussbaum (1999) accused Butler of wilful obscurantism. She points out that it is, 'obvious that Butler's work is not directed at a non-academic audience eager to grapple with actual injustices. Such an audience would simply be baffled by the thick soup of Butler's prose, by its air of in-group knowingness, by its extremely high ratio of names to explanations'. On a related point, Butler has also been criticised for basing her theories on abstractions, made-up or decontextualised examples that are, 'lacking in social specificity' (McNay, 1999: 176). Speer and Potter (2002: 158) argue, 'While Butler talks about discourse, citation and iterability, her theorization of the processes underpinning the reiteration of gender is an abstract one, separated from features of interaction in specific contexts. Consequently, since Butler does not analyse 'real-life' accounts, there is no sense of a peopled world in which participants interact and speak with one another'. Grant (1993), Kotthoff and Wodak (1997) and Hekman (1999) have also criticised Butler for locating everything in discourse while overlooking experiential and material aspects of identity and power relations, while Lazar (2005: 12–13) notes that Butler's cross-dressing example is actually problematic from certain feminist perspectives, i.e. such acts arguably help to reinforce gender structures, rather than (or as well as) radically subverting them.

And in rejecting the idea of unified political movements based on disadvantaged groups, perhaps Butler does not give enough credit to the fact that there have been tremendous political advantages to identity groups such as women and gay men uniting in a common cause. For example, the mass collective pressure brought about by the suffragists and suffragettes contributed largely to women obtaining the vote, and gay rights movements such as the Mattachine Society, the Gay Liberation Front and the Campaign for Homosexual Equality helped to inspire legal and social changes which benefitted gay men and lesbians. Some feminists might argue that it is difficult to see how individuals can engage in 'gender trouble' in order to contribute towards an overall deconstruction of gender, and what might be more useful would be improved childcare or legislation helping more women to work outside the home and enter politics. Butler's proposed suggestions for change seem rather abstract and small-scale by comparison. As Nussbaum (1999) notes, '[Butler] doesn't envisage mass movements or resistance or campaigns for political reform, only personal acts carried out by a small number of knowing actors. Just as actors with a bad script can subvert it by delivering the lines oddly, so too with gender, the script remains bad, but the actors have a tiny bit of freedom. Thus we have the basis for what… Butler calls 'an ironic hopefulness''. And it is difficult to see how such subversions could be carried out in societies where 'gender trouble' might incur strong negative reactions or punishments.

In *Bodies that Matter* (1993) Butler addressed criticisms of *Gender Trouble* which interpreted her theory of gender performativity as a voluntary, daily choice. And in Glover and Kaplan (2000: xxvii) she is quoted as saying, 'The bad reading [of gender performance theory] goes something like this: I can get up in the morning, look in my closet and decide which gender I want to be today. I can take out a piece of clothing and change my gender… and then that evening I can change it again and be something radically other, so that what you get is something like the commodification of gender, and the understanding of taking on a gender as a kind of consumerism'. Such an interpretation incorrectly assumes that people are at liberty to 'try on' any type of gender that they like, whenever they like. Glover and Kaplan (2000: xxvii) observe that, 'gender underpins our capacity to make decisions and act on them, while constantly slipping out of our control and ensnaring us in complex webs of meaning that no individual can ever hope to master'. Additionally, Livia and Hall (1997: 12) note, '…it is discourse that produces the speaker, and not the other way round, because the performance will be intelligible, only if it 'emerges in the context of binding conventions'. Even activities like gender impersonation are reiterative, because the impersonator must invoke the very essence of these 'binding conventions' in order for the performance to be comprehensible'.

Despite its criticisms, Butler's theories have been tremendously influential, changing the focus of academic research in the mid-1990s, particularly in terms of language and sexuality research as well as post-structuralist or post-modern approaches. In the collection of articles on language and sexuality, *Queerly Phrased* (Livia and Hall, 1997), the editors pay tribute to Butler. Thus, two goals of post-modern theorists of language and gender are the examination of the ways that people use linguistic resources in order to produce gender differentiation, and the analysis of the norms or boundaries that define which types of language are possible for performing particular types of gender. The concept of Queer Theory, which became popular in the 1990s (see Chapter 7) is also strongly indebted to Butler.

Taking into account Speer and Potter's (2002: 158) point about the importance of providing real-life accounts of gender performativity, I want to examine how the theory can be used in order to understand the relationship between language, gender and sexuality in everyday life. In order to achieve this I shall refer to a number of examples.

The following example demonstrates how gender identity can be performed through the use of computer-mediated communication. Bornstein (1998: 206–7) has written on the liberating power of the internet to allow its users to alter their gender identities, 'One of the truly wonderful things about cyberspace is that it hasn't been around long enough to fall utter prey to the two-gender system… When I first went online in 1990, I was astounded by the freedom it gave me. I didn't need physical cues to pass! I felt I could finally participate in discussions *as a woman*'. The sense of disembodiment that the Internet provides temporarily frees people from gendered restrictions resulting from inhabiting a particular body (where biological sex, age, size, ethnicity, etc., are difficult to hide or alter). Therefore, sexual or gender identity is constructed online through language alone. Because interaction on the Internet does not have to involve face-to-face communication it is a useful epistemological site for the study of how language creates identities. Reid (1993: 63) claims that, '[gender's assumed] fixity, and the common equation of gender with sex, becomes problematic when gender reassignment can be effected by a few touches at a keyboard'. This freedom of such gender reconstruction, Reid notes, has the capacity to delight or overwhelm its users.

Other researchers have critiqued the liberating potential of 'cyber-identities'. Robins (2000: 80) writes, 'New identities, mobile identities, exploratory identities – but, it seems, also banal identities. Only the technology is new: in the games and encounters in cyberspace, it seems there is little that is new or surprising'. Some early studies of the Internet reported that the sorts of gendered power-relationships found between men and women in the 'real world' were simply being replicated online, for example, Herring (1993) reported that men tended to lead conversations and control discussion on an academic mailing list. Kramarae and Taylor (1993) also noted that male control of computer-mediated communication had extended to women-related and women-only bulletin boards. Rodino's (1997) study of gender constructions in IRC (Internet relay chat) was more optimistic, concluding that while some gender performances conformed to binary categories, others broke out of these categories. So while computer-mediated communication offers the potential for people to perform a variety of virtual gender or sexed identities, the way that such identities will be related to by others may involve the same sorts of expectations that are held in the real world – gendered stereotypes, roles and restrictions can still perpetuate.

An example of the Internet's dual capacity for allowing people to perform alternative models of gender while at the same time reinforcing society's prescriptive gender roles involves a multi-player online environment called *Second Life*. In Second Life, players (or 'residents', as they are referred to) experience and interact with a virtual world by creating an avatar who represents their identity in the game. The avatar is humanoid in shape, but can be customised by having its gender, hair style, size, build and skin colour altered. Clothing or objects can be attached to avatars to customise them yet further, so they can potentially look like animals, robots or aliens. Avatars are able to move around the three-dimensional virtual environment and interact with others by having the (human) player type text into a chat box. Anyone in the immediate vicinity is able to overhear this chat and respond accordingly. Avatars are also able to interact with each other in other ways, for example, if a resident clicks on a dance floor, the avatar will be animated to dance. There are a number of player-created places in Second Life where avatars can 'have sex' with each other, by clicking on small icons which animate them into joint positions or repetitive actions that depict different sexual acts. The use of 'chat' during these bouts of sexual activities is used to create and maintain an erotically-charged atmosphere. One way that this is achieved is by using language performatively, to construct gendered participants who are considered to be sexually desirable – although this requires a shared understanding of what *is* a sexually desirable gender performance.

The following excerpt (spelling is as per the original) is taken from a chat which took place between two male avatars who were engaged in sexual activity. The activity occurred in a public place and other avatars were also engaged in other (unrelated) conversations at the same time, which I have removed from the transcript for the sake of making the chat more readable. The names of the two avatars have been anonymised as AV1 and AV2. In order for such online interactions to succeed, the players involved have to reference a shared knowledge of what constitutes a desirable sexual and gender identity to gay men, using written language in order to perform that identity.

1 AV1:   Reamin your nice tight ass real good
2 AV2:   Yeah breed me
3 AV1:   Gonna shoot me thick wad inside ya. You like that?
4 AV2:   Oh yeah, feels so good mate. Can't wait to cum.
5 AV1:   Yeah, take my thick cock. All 8 inches.
6 AV2:   Ready to shoot
7 AV1:   Mmmmmm
8 AV2:   Aaaaaaaaaaahhhhh! Fuck!!!

Example 1: Second Life

While these avatars were engaged in 'sex' with each other, they avoided using language which research has suggested is stereotypically associated with gay men (see for example, Hayes, 1976, or Harvey, 2000). Instead, they used forms of language which index a more masculine (or even hyper-masculine) gender performance. Examples include direct, unhedged imperatives (*breed me, take my thick cock*), non-standard language (*reamin, real good, yeah, ya, gonna*) and reference to high impact verbs (*ream, shoot*). The use of the term 'breed me' frames the sexual act within a heterosexual context – which is interesting considering that it is impossible for a man to 'breed' another man.[2] However, this is not a sexual exchange where one man (the inserter or 'top') acts masculine while the other (the insertee or 'bottom') acts feminine – instead *both* men use language to perform masculinity in a similar way: the 'passive' partner using an imperative 'breed me' to direct and control the interaction in a similar way to the 'active' partner's 'take my thick cock'. The physical appearance of the avatars also contributed towards their hyper-masculine performance. Both had been customised to appear tall, heavily muscular, with cropped hairstyles and hairy chests.

Within many societies, stereotyped gender performances are conceptualised as 'normal' and sexually desirable. Also, stereotypical masculinity tends to be associated with heterosexuality, whereas mainstream society has tended to associate homosexuality with effeminacy (and vice versa). It is perhaps unsurprising, then, that some gay men have responded to these associations by fetishising male heterosexuality (see also the discussion of Heywood (1997) in Chapter 8). The owners of the two avatars both claimed to identify as gay men in 'the real world'. However, although they were engaged in an ostensibly 'gay' virtual sexual act, it could be argued that the act appears to be idealised as sex between two hyper-masculine (even ostensibly heterosexual) men. O'Brien (1999: 87) notes that the construction of hyper-gendered stereotypes in online communication is likely, as participants tend to draw on existing cultural gender codes. We might more accurately describe AV1 and AV2 as performing

MSM identities (men having sex with men) rather than gay identities.[3] The key here is that the MSM identity is considered to be attractive to some men who identify more straightforwardly as gay in real life. For these men, there are motivations for them to perform their gender identity somewhat differently: as heterosexual men who engage in sex with other heterosexual men. The desirability of this hyper-masculine gender identity is also consistent with the fact that it is a powerful one in most societies (see Chapter 5). The gender performances of the two avatars are therefore likely to be inter-textual repetitions, perhaps indexing linguistic conventions acquired from pornography and fiction marketed to gay men, as well as from earlier sexual encounters the participants nay have witnessed or experienced in Second Life or in non-computer mediated situations.

Le Page et al. (1974) hypothesise that people use language as a means of accommodation in order to, 'resemble as closely as possible those of the group or groups with which from time to time we [speakers] wish to identify' – a theory which bears some similarity to Butler's. Le Page et al. give 'four riders' to their hypothesis: our linguistic behaviour is restrained by:

a) the extent to which we are able to identify our model group

b) the extent to which we have sufficient access to [the model groups] and sufficient analytical ability to work out the rules of their behaviour

c) the strength of various (possibly conflicting) motivations towards one or another model, and towards retaining our own sense of our unique identity, and

d) our ability to modify our behaviour.

Equally, people may not always have the ability to 'carry off' a particular gendered performance successfully. All the riders may have implications for a person's gender performance, for example, we may not have the analytical ability to work out the rules of typically masculine or feminine behaviour, there may be conflicting motivations to perform gender in different ways, or we may want to perform a certain gender, but simply not have the ability to do so. We can see then, how the computer-mediated communicative context of Second Life facilitates a 'successful' gender performance – only knowledge of the linguistic conventions for stereotypical masculinity are required in order for the performance to be successful, and the participants do not have to actively perform masculinity in real-time, using their own voices. They only have to type the words and can think about what to type in advance. This increases the likelihood that their gender performance (in this admittedly limited context) will be effective. The performance must also be understood in relation to social conventions and expectations about what are acceptable and unacceptable types of performances for particular types of people.

However, an important point about gender performance is that it is *always* performance. When the two participants in Second Life switch off their computers and interact with others in a face-to-face context, they will also be performing their gender; it will be a different gender performance from Second Life and they might argue that, face-to-face, there is no performance, rather, they are simply being 'the real me'. However, post-structuralist theorists would argue that there is no essential 'real me' and that all (gender) performances are socially constructed and subject to change over time. We only think that our usual, everyday gender performance is not a performance because it has been instilled in us from birth – that this *is* the way we are, the way we ought to be and the *only* way of being. Clearly, though, that is not necessarily the case – people do have the ability to recognise that the way they 'perform' gender is based on copying, filtered through society's norms. And under various circumstances, people are able consciously to change their performances, rejecting or subverting norms at different points.

The use of language in Second Life to perform (or forge) a desirable gender/sexual identity is similar to Kira Hall's (1995) study of Adult-messages services. Hall interviewed a number of women and one man who worked for a telephone chatline service aimed at heterosexual men which offered 'live conversation with a personal touch' or 'dial-a-porn'. She notes (1995: 190) that because the participants in each conversation did not know each other, they did not have access to the usual shared allusions, jointly created metaphors and telegraphic messages that usually defines private discourse. The callers could not see each other either, again resulting in a form of disembodiment, where language becomes the sole means of gender performance. The operators created a feeling of intimacy by evoking a frame of reference which the majority of the male callers would understand, using largely shared cultural perceptions of the 'ideal woman'. Hall (1995: 192) quotes the following recorded message from a national fantasy line that advertises 'girls, girls, girls':

> oo::f:: i'm so ((in breathy voice)) ex<u>ci</u>ted – i just got a hot new job. (0.8) well,
> – ((in a slight southern accent)) i've been bored a lot lately .. hh – i live in a
> small town and my husband travels a lot, (0.5) i have lots of time on my hands
> – .hhh of course, i've always managed to stay busy (0.4) lots of girlfriends, you
> know, – ((whispered)) i love to <u>shop</u>, i ((laugh)) ^pract^ically live at the mall it
> seems

The operator uses various techniques to project an idealised female identity – the use of the breathy voice and whispers, references to emotions as well as typically 'female' interests like shopping and malls, the intensifier *so* and hedges (*practically*, *it seems*). Similar techniques were used by the male operator, Andy, who posed as a number of heterosexual women from different ethnic backgrounds: Emily, Belle, Fong Su and Winona. Andy used different linguistic strategies for each persona. For example, in becoming Emily (a Euro-American women), he would alter his voice to make it sound 'soft and quiet'. For Belle he would affect a southern accent with elongated vowels. Hall (1995: 201) describes how callers placed a great deal of value on hearing the stereotyped language features of particular identities, which, ironically, at times over-rode the 'true' identities of the women they spoke to. One participant, Sheila said:

> 'Most of the guys who call are white… and for them talking to someone of a different race is exotic and a fetish… They have this stereotypical ideal of how, like, a Black woman should sound… So frequently, we'd have women who were actually Black and we'd hook them up, and they wouldn't believe the woman, that she was Black, because she didn't <u>sound</u> like the stereotype…there was this one women who did calls and she had this sort of Black persona she would do, which was like the total stereotype… And the guys loved it! They <u>really</u> thought that this is what a Black women was.'

We can therefore see how in both of Hall's examples, and with the Second Life avatars, stereotypes about language were drawn on in order to perform 'idealised' gender identities that were viewed as desirable. Returning to Second Life, interestingly, on other occasions AV1 used language to perform a different type of identity. In Example 2, which was a non-sexual chat between AV1 and AV3, the avatars commented on the state of the (virtual) room they were in – a dungeon area which had been designed in order to appear grim and dirty.

1 AV1:   filthy in here
2 AV3:   i knoww
3 AV1:   could do with someone getting the Jif out
4 AV3:   or a glade plug-in
5 AV1:   lol
6 AV1:   its like your feet stick to the floor when you walk
7 AV3:   well you know why that is
8 AV1:   dirty bitches what come in here

Example 2: Second Life

In this exchange the two participants used language to perform a 'camp' gay identity – disapproving of the state of the dungeon and referring to domestic products (Jif, Glade Plug In) designed to clean or freshen rooms. This is a more humorous use of language, intended to be entertaining rather than erotic (in line 5, AV1 writes 'lol' which stands for 'laughs out loud'). Here the players construct their avatars as having a more stereotypically feminine or effeminate identity – showing concern with cleaning and appearances. In the final part of the exchange, the participants obliquely refer to the fact that other avatars have sex in the room (hence the apparently sticky floors), labelling them with a feminising and disapproving 'dirty bitches'. AV1 therefore engages in different types of gender performance in different contexts in Second Life – a masculine, overtly sexualised MSM identity and a camp (see Harvey, 2000), humorous, 'prissy' gay identity. Both gender performances rely on the use of different sorts of language in order to be effective.

In the two excerpts there is an obvious gap between the player sitting at home, typing into a textbox on a screen, and his (or her) avatar. Many Second Life players may or may not directly identify with their avatars, but instead may simply be 'role-playing' within the context of the game, e.g. trying on an alternative identity (or series of identities) in a relatively anonymous and safe context. But whilst online environments like Second Life present us with a valid way of understanding how language can be used performatively to construct gender (or other aspects of identity), they are not exactly the same as face-to-face cases of gender performance, where we often have less time to think about what we are going to say or how to say it. Also, just as Lippi-Green (1997: 49) argues that the majority of people would find it difficult to 'put on' a different accent from the one they usually speak for long periods of time, most of us would also find it difficult to carry out a prolonged gender performance in a way that is radically different from the way we usually perform our gender. Although we may have the tools at our disposal in the form of knowledge about what constitutes a particular gender performance and the ability to enact it, there is a difference between the mainly unthinking performances that map gender onto sex – the ones that society expects us to engage in during our everyday lives and any self-conscious 'alternative' performance which we have to think about more carefully. One of Butler's arguments was that for the majority of the time gender performance is *not* usually a conscious or controlled phenomenon, although in realising that gender is always performance, we possess the potential to change our performances in order to break down the 'heterosexual matrix' or the way that sexuality, gender and biological sex have been prescriptively linked in society. Similarly, with Hall's analysis of operators on telephone sex lines, the gender performances which occur within this context are extremely self-conscious and designed for the specific purpose of making money (see also Chapter 6). Most people do not have such goals in mind when performing gender on an everyday basis. Kitzinger (2005: 223) suggests that the identities of Hall's operators are 'worked up' and actively displayed rather than 'given off'.

We should not assume though, that our 'everyday', 'usual' gender performance is more 'real' than any other: the point is that they are all equally real, or equally unreal for that matter.

With those points in mind, the following example considers gender performance in terms of being 'given off' rather than 'worked up'.

Jemma: aged 22 unemployed Home Counties
Gill: aged 21 waitress, Home Counties

1 Gill	That's a really lovely jumper, is it new?
2 Jemma	Erm
3 Gill	Have I seen it before? (pause) I don't think I have.
4 Jemma	I got it in the summer (pause) erm but then for some reason I decided I didn't like it. I– it's nice but it's a bit, it's a bit erm impractical, it looks, it look– it's not as thick as it looks (unclear)
5 Gill	Oh really?
6 Jemma	I mean
7 Gill	It looks very thick.
8 Jemma	Well feel it, it's not. (pause)
9 Gill	Oh it's cos it's this new velvety stuff isn't it?
10 Jemma	Yeah.
11 Gill	(laughing) Oh this new velvety stuff (pause)
12	(a couple of minutes of talk deleted)
13 Gill	He's fucking mad, Simon, he always makes people think and talk about these mad things that they probably wouldn't talk about that often.
14 Jemma	Yeah. He's fucking excellent, he sparked me off (unclear) (pause) erm (pause) shit what was I saying? (unclear)
15 Gill	Oh I don't know, I can't really remember.

Adapted from the British National Corpus, file KC7

This excerpt is of a private conversation between two young women, taken from the British National Corpus. The female speakers are aged in their early 20s; one works as a waitress, but the other is unemployed. The conversation is an everyday discussion about Jemma's 'lovely jumper', which then moves onto a mutual friend, Simon, who is not present.

In terms of gender performativity, it could be argued that in the first part of this excerpt, the two women are using language to perform femininity in a somewhat stereotypical way – for example, Gill gives Jemma a compliment about her jumper (line 1), using the empty adjective *lovely*, and an intensifer *really*. Jemma uses a strategy of modesty, downplaying the compliment (line 4) 'it's nice... but it's a bit... impractical...it's not as thick as it looks'. Both Herbert

(1990) and Holmes (1995) have noted that women tend to reject compliments more than men, a possible reason being, 'the influence of social pressure to be modest' (Holmes, 1995: 42). Gill also uses a tag question (line 9) *isn't it*. There are three uses of *oh* during lines 5–11. Biber et al. (1999: 1083) note that the core function of *oh*, 'appears to be to convey some degree of surprise, unexpectedness or emotional arousal'. As Harvey (2000: 241) points out, 'exclamations are identified as 'feminine' because they are essentially *reactive*'.

However, in lines 13–15, Gill and Jemma begin to use more taboo forms of language that are *not* associated with a stereotyped feminine gender performance: intensifiers (line 13 *fucking mad*, line 14 *fucking excellent*) and a general expletive (line 14) *shit*). However, Jemma's agreement (line 14) with Gill and repetition of Gill's use of *fucking* could also be interpreted as co-operative, person-focused, 'rapport' speech. It is also worth noting that *shit* is used more by females than males in the BNC (see Table 2.2) so although taboo language is generally thought of as being 'male', the use of 'shit' actually suggests that Jemma is *conforming* to a gender norm.

This exchange, although short and mundane, reveals how participants, often un-self-consciously, draw on a range of linguistic phenomena, which construct their genders in different ways at different points. People are (consciously or not) aware that different types of language index different gender identities, and are able to draw on this knowledge when speaking or writing. Some people may be relatively consistent or narrow in terms of the range of linguistic strategies that they incorporate into their own gender performance, while others may use a much wider range of strategies. Some may remain consistent within a single conversation, but differ widely from conversation to conversation, depending on whom they are with, while others may draw on different strategies from minute to minute. As expectations about what it means to be a man or a woman change in societies, so too do the ways in which people feel able to express themselves. The example above also indicates how difficult it can be to 'fix' the notion of gender performance: within a single utterance a person may use different types of language which positions them as both masculine and feminine. Furthermore, our own understandings of what constitutes stereotypically 'male' or 'female' language are likely to differ from each other, with beliefs sometimes running counter to actual practices.

The examples considered so far also reveal that gender is only one aspect of identity. At the same time that we are performing gender, we may also be performing other aspects of identity: ethnicity, age and class. In Example 1 from Second Life it is difficult to separate the concept of gender identity from sexual identity as the two are so closely linked: a masculine performance is also constructed as potentially heterosexual (despite the fact that, paradoxically, the male participants are engaged in sex with each other). And it could be argued that one way in which an 'authentic' masculine identity is constructed here is by using forms of language more traditionally associated with working-class men (such as reduced forms – *reamin* rather than *reaming* and non-standard forms – *yeah* rather than *yes*). Such reduced forms are consistent with studies that have shown that working class men in some communities tend to pronounce words in this way, whereas women are more likely to use 'hyper-correct' forms (Labov, 1966). Also, AV2's use of the term of address *mate* suggests he is performing a British identity (many of the participants in Second Life are American, and might be more likely to refer to each other using different terms like *man, bro'* or *dude*). In Hall's examples of sex-work on telephone chat-lines, Andy and other workers also produced different national or regional identities (the voice for Belle was different for that of Fong Su). And in the conversation between Jemma and Gill, we may say that their use of swearing in lines 15–16 could also reflect an age or social-class performance.

The point made earlier about people being able to change gender performances depending on who is present, means that we also need to take into account the fact that performativity implies an audience. Leap (1996: 160) notes that a performative effect requires listener as well as speaker involvement, which he calls *co-operative discourse*. Post-structuralist theory allows for multiple interpretations of meaning, including performances. So a gender performance will be successful (for the performer) if a person is able adequately to perform an approximation of the gender he or she is aiming to reproduce *and* if the audience present are able to decipher the behaviours as belonging to a particular gender. This may explain why some people are unable to identify the 'gay voice' (Chapter 2): they may not be aware that certain stereotyped features to do with intonation or pronunciation have been characterised by wider society as 'gay' (even though research does not usually support this), or may not be aware that gay identities exist (for example, depending on their age or their cultural background). They may interpret a stereotyped 'gay voice' as different in some way, but they would not automatically associate it with homosexuality. On a related point, Leap (1996: 49–73), describes a number of incidents involving gay speakers talking to either non-gay or 'suspect' gay speakers, where confusion results because the participants make incorrect assumptions about the sexual identities of each other.

Conclusion

The performance of gender as a continuous imitation of itself implies that gender performances, and our understanding of what types of performance constitute gender, can change, because imitations are rarely exactly the same as the original. We also need to understand gender performance in the context of the value systems of particular societies. It could be argued that those who are powerful in society have the ability to influence what are viewed as acceptable and unacceptable gender performances for various types of people, through the use of explicit and implicit rewards and punishments.

As discussed earlier, societies have mapped gender, sex and sexuality onto each other in particular ways (out of a range of possible configurations), and this mapping determines which performances are acceptable and which are not. So, for example, men are 'required' to perform their gender in ways associated with stereotypical masculinity, whereas women are allotted behaviours considered to be stereotypically feminine. While such a model applies to heterosexual people, homosexual people are often constructed in reverse – so that gay men are defined as effeminate while lesbians are seen as masculine. Such identities are viewed as inferior to heterosexual ones because the gender/sexuality mapping is 'incorrect', and heterosexual men and women who do not or cannot perform their gender identities according to this biological sex mapping are also stigmatised.

It is normally in the interest of powerful groups that the status quo is maintained. However, power does not remain in the hands of the same people indefinitely: leaders eventually die or stand down, governments can be overthrown, and laws and social values can change. In the same way, ideas about what constitutes powerful, acceptable or taboo gender performances can also change. Our 'everyday' gender performances do not appear like performances because they have the appearance of being natural and society validates them in dozens of different ways. However, it is by studying people who do *not* conform to society's expectations of the way gender should 'correctly' be performed (such as Butler's drag artistes) that we can ascertain that all gender is performative. So how are certain gender performances sanctioned as appropriate and others not? The following chapter considers one of the most important ways through which gender performances are legitimised or tabooed: *discourses*.

Notes

1   For example, in the US on 6 May 1983, a doctor on ABC's *Good Morning America* told viewers that although AIDS is 'still confined to male homosexuals, Haitians, and haemophiliacs', it could soon spread to 'normal people'. In the same year state legislators in Austin Texas claimed that 'the diseases now being transmitted by homosexuals... threaten to destroy the public health of the state of Texas' and attempted to recriminalise homosexual acts between consenting adults as well as banning homosexuals from taking jobs in teaching, food-handling or 'any other position of public leadership or responsibility' (Rutledge, 1989: 20). In the UK in 1988, Margaret Thatcher's conservative government produced legislation which banned the 'promotion of homosexuality' by local education authorities, while British tabloid newspapers referred to AIDS as a 'gay plague'.

2   The use of the term *breed* has also been cited as barebacking slang. Barebacking is the practice of engaging in sex without a condom. As well as allowing users to create 'fantasy' or idealised selves, Second Life offers people the opportunity to virtually act out tabooed sexual practices.

3   Davies et al. (1990) describe the origins of the term *MSM*. Researchers working on Project Sigma (designed to address the impact of HIV and AIDS), among others, had found that large numbers of men who had sex with other men did not identify as gay – many of them were married and maintained a heterosexual identity. The term therefore addresses the potential difference between claiming a gay identity and engaging in male-male sexual behaviour.

4 Constructing normality: gendered discourses and heteronormativity

Gendered discourses

At the end of the previous chapter I wrote that it is in the best interests of powerful groups in society to ensure that the status quo is maintained in terms of gender and sexuality (and other aspects of identity such as social class and ethnicity for that matter). So how is this achieved? We can point to legislation which ensures that people adhere to prescribed gender or sexual performances. For example, marriage laws in the past have usually sanctioned only relationships between two people of the opposite sex, while before the twentieth century, women were denied the ability to vote. Within western societies, in the past, institutions such as parliament, law courts, the medical and teaching professions also tended to be populated by the powerful (white, heterosexual, middle-class men) and there were various subtle and obvious mechanisms in place for ensuring that such people continued to populate those institutions, to the exclusion of others.

As well as laws and institutions, though, another (related) way in which gender and sexuality have been regulated is through reference to what we might call 'common sense' beliefs or traditions: the values, mores and taboos of society. Such ideas can be collectively referred to as *discourses*, and research by Foucault (1972, 1976), Holloway (1984), Fairclough (1989, 1995a,b), Parker (1992), Van Dijk (1991, 1993) Mills (1997), Sunderland (2004) and many others have been instrumental in furthering our understanding of the relationship between language and discourse. Lazar (2005: 9) notes that in modern societies, discursive power is 'pervasive and insidious', referring to it as 'subtle and seemingly innocuous'.

Discourse is a rather awkward term to define as it is used in social and linguistic research in a number of inter-related yet different ways. In traditional linguistics it is defined as either, 'language above the sentence or above the clause' (Stubbs, 1983: 1), or 'language in use' (Brown and Yule, 1983). We can also refer to the discourse structure of particular texts. For example, a recipe will usually begin with the name of the meal to be prepared, then give a list of ingredients, then describe the act of preparation. There may be variants to this, but on the whole we are able to recognise the discourse structure of a text like a recipe fairly easily. We would expect certain lexical items or grammatical structures to appear at particular places (for example, numbers and measurements would appear near the beginning of the text, in the list of ingredients '4 15ml spoons of olive oil', whereas imperative sentences would appear in the latter half 'Slice each potato lengthwise'). Discourse is also sometimes applied to different types of language use or topics, for example, we can talk about political discourse (Chilton, 2004), colonial discourse (Williams and Chrisman, 1993), media discourse (Fairclough, 1995b) and environmental discourse (Hajer, 1997). This is a conceptualisation of discourse which is linked to genre, style or text type.

However, discourse can also be defined as, 'practices which systematically form the objects of which they speak' (Foucault, 1972: 49). It is this meaning of discourse which I intend to focus on in this book, though it is, in practice, difficult to consider this meaning without taking into account other meanings, too, and Foucault's understanding of discourse entails the other conceptualisations of the term.

To expand on Foucault's definition, discourse is a, 'system of statements which constructs an object' (Parker, 1992: 5), 'ways of seeing the world, often with reference to relations of power' (Sunderland, 2004: 6) or 'language-in-action' (Blommaert, 2005: 2). Discourse is further defined by Burr (1995: 48) as, 'a set of meanings, metaphors, representations, images, stories, statements and so on that in some way together produce a particular version of events... Surrounding any one object, event, person etc., there may be a variety of different discourses, each with a different story to tell about the world, a different way of representing it to the world'. Foucault's notion of *practices* leads us to view discourse as countable: *discourses* (Cameron, 2001: 15). Burr (1995: 71) says that discourses give people a framework for their everyday experience and act as a form of social control – although this process is not always recognised as such. For example, 'Discourses such as 'education as a meritocracy' and career success as 'survival of the fittest' serve to justify the greater wealth and opportunity of the (relatively powerful) middle class by representing education and capitalism as unbiased, egalitarian institutions' (Burr, 1995: 55). One way that discourses are controlled and made legitimate is through publication. As Spender (1985: 313) points out, 'The power to decree what is good and what is not, to decide what will be published and become part of a reservoir of knowledge, is significant power. It is the power of the gatekeepers'.

It is possible to give names or labels to discourses. For example, Sunderland (2004: 50) lists specific discourses such as 'permissive discourse', 'equal opportunities discourse' and 'God's will discourse'. Furthermore, Sunderland (2004: 49) notes that discourses can be categorised in terms of their function, e.g. damaging, liberating, resistant, subversive, conservative, etc., as well as being labelled in relation to other discourses (e.g. as competing, dominant, mutually supporting, coexisting, alternative, etc.).

However, discourses are not 'set in stone': it is likely that there are multiple ways of constructing discourse around any given object, concept or practice, reflecting the fact that humans are diverse creatures; indeed, we tend to perceive aspects of the world in different ways, depending on a range of factors. Also, discourses allow for people to be internally inconsistent – they help to explain why people contradict themselves, change position or appear to have ambiguous or conflicting views on the same subject (Potter and Wetherell, 1987). We can view cases like this in terms of people articulating competing discourses. It is possible to conceptualise discourses as *ideologies* and the terms seem to be used in ways which suggest they share similar meanings. Sunderland (2004: 6) suggests that, 'Ideology can... be seen as the cultural materialist antecendent of the post-structuralist use of discourse, and... discourse can be seen as carrying ideology'.[1]

Discourses are also similar to *interpretative repertories* (see Chapter 2), in that both can be used as, 'distinctive ways of talking about objects and events in the world' (Edley, 2001: 202). Potter and Wetherell (1995) note that interpretative repertoires were developed in order to do some of the same explanatory work as discourses. Perhaps the most significant difference between the two concepts, according to Edley (2001), is that interpretative repertoires are employed more in studies where human agency is emphasised, in order to show how people 'choose' from a pool of available repertories. Discourses, on the other hand, tend to highlight inegalitarian power relationships and show how individuals are constructed in relation to them. Obviously, there is a fine line between the two concepts and the distinctions may often be blurred – not all discourses are 'damaging' to use Sunderland's (2004: 191) term. And the extent to which people are free to 'choose' from a range of repertories is dependent on a range of factors, some of which may be beyond their control. Furthermore, as Talbot (1998) points out, the view of gender as performance helps us to avoid a position where we assume that people are passively 'put together' by discourse alone. With that said, we also need to bear in mind that performance and agency are always constrained, due to 'the regulatory practices of gender coherence' (Butler, 1990: 24).

So how can discourses be defined or analysed? As Sunderland (2004) points out, there is no 'dictionary of discourses'. And returning to one of the central tenets of post-structuralist theory, which is that multiple interpretations of a sign are possible in different contexts, similarly, any act of naming or defining a discourse is going to be an interpretative one. Where I see one discourse, you may see a different discourse or no discourse at all. Our identification of particular discourses is going to be based on the discourses that we already (often unconsciously) live with. As Foucault (1972: 146) notes, 'it is not possible for us to describe our own archive, since it is from within these rules that we speak'. Butler (1990: 31) is more hopeful, asking, 'Even if heterosexist constructs circulate as the available sites of power/discourse from which to do gender at all, the question remains: What possibilities of recirculation exist? Which possibilities of doing gender repeat and displace through hyperbole, dissonance, internal confusion and proliferation the very constructs by which they are mobilized?'

Conceptualising language use in terms of discourse has therefore opened up the potential for studies of language, gender and sexuality to consider a much wider range of texts. So it is possible to view the language used in a novel, newspaper article, letter, conversation, advertisement, political speech, pop song, email, etc., both in terms of its telling us about how the author uses language to perform a gendered or sexualised identity, and also to reveal the gendered discourses that they are accessing. Such a perspective also helps us to interpret earlier academic research in a different light. For example, as we saw in Chapter 2, Jespersen's work on 'The Woman' contained many citations from novels which he used as bona fide examples to support his arguments about how women supposedly used language. By using such fictional examples, Jespersen was inadvertently referring to and reproducing the gendered discourses of his society and time, and it can be argued that by reproducing such discourses in an academic setting he was actually strengthening them. As Cameron (2003: 449) writes of Jespersen, 'As well as telling us something about historical understandings of gender, this tells something about historical understandings of language'.

Examining the use of language in fiction is, therefore, useful in the context of helping us to understand discourse, both in terms of what particular discourses *are* and how they are subsequently presented, accepted, contested or altered. But such fictional uses should not be used as evidence of ways that people actually speak. In being critical of Jespersen, we need to understand his research within the context of the discourses that were available to him at the time. Obviously, people are not completely 'trapped' by mainstream discourses, otherwise nothing would ever change; but discourses are still a powerful force, and at times, change can be so gradual that it is difficult to perceive. As society changes, discourses will alter (and vice versa), and academic approaches to language, sexuality and gender are likely to develop accordingly.

As with Butler's idea of gender performativity, discourses can be made to appear fixed or naturalised because they are reiterated through language use.

With reference to the media, Fairclough (1989: 54) observes, 'The hidden power of media discourse and the capacity of… power-holders to exercise this power depend on systematic tendencies in news reporting and other media activities. A single text on its own is quite insignificant: the effects of media power are cumulative, working through the repetition of particular ways of handling causality and agency, particular ways of positioning the reader, and so forth'. Mills (1997: 17) suggests that we can 'detect a discursive structure' due to 'the systematicity of the ideas, opinions, concepts, ways of thinking and behaviours which are formed within a particular context'. And as Stubbs notes (2001: 215), 'Repeated patterns show that evaluative meanings are not merely personal and idiosyncratic, but widely shared in a discourse community. A word, phrase or construction may trigger a cultural stereotype'. All of these writers stress the same point: in order to be powerful, discourses often require repetition.[2]

So what is the relationship between language and discourse? Are they the same? Sunderland (2004: 28) argues not, stating that, 'People do not… recognise a discourse… in any straightforward way… Not only is it not identified or named, and is not self-evident or visible as a discrete chunk of a given text, it can never be 'there' in its entirety. What is there are certain linguistic features: 'marks on a page', words spoken or even people's memories of previous conversations… which – if sufficient and coherent – may suggest that they are 'traces' of a particular discourse'.

So language is a central way that discourses are constructed and circulated, and it is through the analysis of 'linguistic traces' (Talbot, 1998) in texts that we can start to identify particular discourses – whilst, of course, bearing in mind that identification is a matter of subjective interpretation. One goal of discourse analysts, then, is to try to identify the range of possible discourses in a particular text, by examining linguistic traces. Such a goal involves carrying out an analysis of the text on several levels. For example, Fairclough (1989, 1995a) characterises discourse on three main levels, consisting of (a) a language text, (b) discourse practice and (c) sociocultural practice. An analysis at the first level, language text, could consider the range of linguistic structures in the text, examining features such as metaphor, agency, pronoun use, nominalisation, passivisation, lexical choice and collocation, etc. At the second level, discourse practice, we could consider processes of text production and reception – why was the text produced and by whom? Who is the (ideal, real or potential) audience of the text and how was it received? Finally, at the third level, sociocultural practice, we would try to explain how the text is made sense of and relates to the context of wider society. We might consider how the text references other texts (intertextuality) and how it is positioned historically.

In her analysis of gendered discourses, Sunderland (2004: 32) focuses on social actors and social action – examining verb types, verb phrases and activisation/passivisation, as well as examining collocations (the systematic co-occurrence of words in particular patterns, which can act as triggers for each other), multi-functionality of forms and content words and absences as well as presences – what is *not* written or said can be as revealing as what is. Baxter (2003: 76), in her examination of classroom talk, looks at non-verbal language (eye contact, gestures, seating positions), verbal language, particularly repetitions of keywords and phrases and meta-language (language used in interviews relating to participants' own descriptions of their behaviours). Other researchers have focused on the analysis of modality and transitivity choices, semantic relationships between words or patterns over sentences. A potential problem with this methodological approach is that it can be difficult to know which linguistic features to examine, and at times some aspects of a text may be more obvious or easy to identify and analyse than others (the identification of potential absence, for example, can be extremely difficult, although comparing one text to another text or a larger sample may help to reveal this). However, the analysis of discourse (and its related paradigms) allows for a great deal of researcher freedom. As stated in Chapter 1, it is not the intention of this book to provide a 'how to do text analysis' because different text types will require different types of analysis, but, rather, to show how different types of text analysis help to illuminate aspects of gender and sexuality theory.

Discourses are pervasive – they help to position or construct us even before we are old enough to understand language. For example, the fact that infants are often dressed in blue if they are boys and pink if they are girls, suggests that a discourse of 'gender differences' is one of the most important distinctions in western society (Sunderland, 2004: 69, refers to this as an over-arching or 'higher-order' discourse.) We could argue that there is nothing essentially male about the colour blue or female about the colour pink (see also Chapter 6), but the colours act as signs, interpreted according to the norms of society. So encounters with discourses occur from the moment we are born, although it is only when we begin to acquire language that we are likely to internalise them. The fact that children are exposed to gendered discourses is one of the reasons why they continue to be so influential: they are learnt from an early age, when we tend to be uncritical and more readily accept 'the way things are'.

An important means by which children in some societies are initially exposed to discourses is through nursery rhymes – short, rhythmic poems or songs which can be learnt and repeated, long before the child understands the meaning of what he or she is saying.[3]

One of the most obvious discourses of gender is evident in the following rhyme:

What are little girls made of? Sugar and spice and all things nice. That's what little girls are made of.

What are little boys made of? Frogs and snails and puppy dog's tails. That's what little boys are made of.

This nursery rhyme focuses explicitly on difference but it also suggests specific ways in which boys and girls are supposed to differ: girls are made of sweet or 'nice' things, whereas boys are made of less pleasant things. The discourses within this rhyme might, for example, be used to explain, predict or even condone the naughty behaviour of boys, while at the same time placing greater restrictions on, or expressing expectations of, the behaviour of girls. Sunderland (2004: 58) has observed the existence of a 'boys will be boys' discourse, which has links to greater tolerance for boys' transgressions in classrooms (see also Sadker and Sadker, 1985, Epstein et al., 1998). While this rhyme is extremely clear in its gender differences discourse, other rhymes are more subtle. Compare some of the actions that different people carry out in various rhymes:

Polly put the kettle on…
The Queen of Hearts, she made some tarts…
There was an old woman who lived in a shoe, she had so many children she didn't know what to do…
Little Polly Flinders sat among the cinders, warming her pretty little toes. Her mother came and caught her and whipped her little daughter for spoiling her nice new clothes.
Little Miss Muffet sat on a tuffet eating some curds and whey. Along came a spider who sat down beside her and frightened Miss Muffet away.
Old Mother Hubbard went to the cupboard, to fetch her poor dog a bone…
Mary Mary quite contrary, how does your garden grow? With silver bells and cockle shells and pretty maids all in a row.

Michael row the boat ashore. Sister help to trim the sail.
Wee Willie Winkie runs through the town upstairs and downstairs in his nightgown.
Georgy Porgy pudding and pie, kissed the girls and made them cry. When the boys come out to play, Georgy Porgy ran away.
Little boy blue come blow your horn. The sheep's in the meadow, the cow's in the corn.
Ding dong bell, pussy's in the well. Who put her in? Little Johnny Green. Who pulled her out? Little Johnny Stout…
This is the house that Jack built…
Jack be nimble, Jack be quick, Jack jump over the candlestick.

Although this is a small sample (and no doubt there are exceptions to these cases), it is possible to notice patterns of repetition which articulate particular gendered discourses in these traditional nursery rhymes. Female characters in rhymes are more likely to be associated with domestic duties and settings (putting the kettle on, making tarts, caring for animals, having children, etc.). They seem likely to be passive recipients (even victims) of the actions of other characters – Polly is whipped by her mother, Miss Muffet is frightened by a spider and the girls in Georgy Porgy cry when they are kissed. As well as being passive, girls are constructed as somewhat squeamish. When Polly Flinders is whipped for spoiling her clothes, it indicates a way in which her gender transgression is explicitly punished – girls are supposed to care about their appearances and keep themselves clean. Along similar lines, Polly's feet are described as 'pretty', as are the maids in 'Mary Mary'. While Michael rows the boat ashore, the female character in the rhyme, his sister, *helps* to trim the sail, rather than carrying out the task by herself.

On the other hand, males are represented as having more agency, as well as being more active or physical: running, jumping, rowing and building houses. Boys are also more heroic or villainous – Georgy Porgy and Johnny Green are trouble-makers, Johnny Stout rescues a kitten. Georgy Porgy is only made to run away by the presence or threat of other boys. Quickness is also referenced in the rhymes: both Wee Willie Winkie and Georgy Porgy are described as 'running', whereas in the last rhyme, Jack is instructed to be 'nimble' and 'quick'. While female characters are described in terms of how they *look*, male characters are described in terms of how they *move*.

Even in a rhyme in which male and female characters appear to be *equally* represented, it is possible to note ways in which they are positioned differently:

> Jack and Jill went up the hill to fetch a pail or water. Jack fell down and broke
> his crown and Jill came tumbling after.

Note here the ordering of the two characters in the rhyme. Jack is referred to first – he is foregrounded and given more attention. Jill only comes 'tumbling after', suggesting a discourse of 'male firstness'. And the second verse of this rhyme (not shown here) refers only to Jack; Jill is not mentioned at all. Researchers have noticed that attention is one of the ways in which power is awarded in society, for example, studies of classrooms have found that in mixed-sex classrooms, boys tend to receive more attention from teachers than girls (Kelly, 1988, Jule, 2001).

In most nursery rhymes, if we examine them alone, we cannot say that there is an obvious discourse of gender differences, because many rhymes only refer to one character, e.g. 'Jack be Nimble' is just about one person, Jack. So although such rhymes do contain gendered discourses – they tell us about the ways that males or females are represented, the sort of things that they do and how they respond to particular situations – it is difficult to contrast them with how people of the opposite sex would act, unless we view their absence as a form of difference, e.g. if Jack is nimble, Jill is *not* nimble due to her absence from the rhyme. But when taken collectively, the rhymes *are* more indicative of a 'gender differences' discourse. Because children's rhymes are often centuries old, referring to famous historical figures and historical incidents, and originally written at a time where male power over women was more categorical, it is hardly surprising that males are represented in these rhymes as more active or dominant in a range of ways. However, the unthinking acceptance and reiteration of such rhymes, often as ways of teaching language to children, is also likely to result in the residual transference and survival of older sexist discourses to the present day.

Similar stereotyped gender differences have been found in the design and descriptions of children's toys. Caldas-Coulthard and van Leeuwen (2002) examined toys like Barbie, Ken and Action Man, which they argue are representations of social actors, conditioned through the contexts and ideologies of the time of production. Hodge and Kress (1988: 6) point out that toys can be read as texts, where 'by texts, in an extended semiotic sense, we mean the concrete material object produced in discourse, the structure of messages which has a socially ascribed unity'. So the shape, clothing, facial expressions, range of movements and accessories of toys can all indicate gendered discourses. Caldas-Coulthard and van Leeuwen (2002: 98) observe that Action Man, for example, can stand up by himself, can be made to hold objects, and his head can move sideways (but not up or down) and his legs can open. He has a muscular body and powerful hands. Barbie, on the other hand cannot stand up by herself or hold anything in her hands. Her head can move in any direction, meaning that she can be placed in a submissive position, with her head down. Written descriptions of the dolls found on the manufacturers' websites, and quoted by Caldas-Coulthard and van Leeuwen (2002:104), also reveal gendered discourses:

Action Man Bungee

Action Man is the greatest hero of them all! Action Man leaps into the unknown with his fabulous bungee jumping kit, which includes a two-stage harness, grappling hook and super-cool sunglasses.

Blushing Orchid Bride™ Barbie©

Blushing Orchid Bride Barbie doll is the third Limited Edition porcelain doll in the Wedding Flower Collection.

> Celebrating the beauty and meaning of the orchid in the wedding ceremony, she wears a soft, blush satin bridal gown with train and layers of sparkling tulle edged with ribbon. Iridescent lace covers the bodice, which dramatically tapers into long petals simulating an orchid. Her delicate hand-painted face is framed by a blush veil, which flows in two layers from a double circle of simulated pearls, matching her jewellery and even the tiny simulated pearls on her gloves and in her bouquet.

Action Man is described in terms of action – he 'leaps into the unknown', he is the main actor in the material processes described, in control of his actions. The adjectives used to describe him refer to social judgements: *greatest, fabulous, super-cool*. However, Barbie is simply described in terms of what she is wearing rather than what she does, with aesthetic adjectives: *blushing*[4], *soft, sparkling, iridescent, delicate*, and *tiny*. The worlds that the two dolls inhabit (action and adventure vs. a dream wedding) also indicate the different sets of social values that are attributed to males and females. As Caldas-Coulthard and van Leeuwen (2002: 106) conclude, 'If boys and girls are exposed to such a different version of the world from very early on, their identities might also be constructed (although in different ways) on the basis of this difference'.

The Action Man and Barbie dolls (and the texts about them) access a higher-level 'gender differences' discourse, as well as more specific discourses such as 'privileging of appearance (in women)', 'active man/passive woman' and 'boy as adventurer' (see Sunderland, 2004: 91, 144, 151). However, an important aspect of discourse theory is that discourses always have the potential to be transgressed or subverted. An example of such subversion relating to Barbie involves an organisation called the Barbie Liberation Organisation (BLO), who, in 1989, entered toy shops and absconded with several hundred Teen Talk Barbie and Talking Duke GI Joe dolls. The BLO swapped the circuit boards which made the dolls talk, before returning the dolls to shops, where they were unwittingly sold to children. As a result, the Teen Talk Barbie dolls uttered normatively 'masculine' phrases like 'Vengeance is mine' and 'Dead men tell no lies', while the GI Joes indexed stereotypically 'feminine' speech, saying 'Math is hard!', 'I love shopping' and 'Will we ever have enough clothes?' The BLO effectively ensured that the two dolls carried out alternative 'gender perform-ances' to their usual, expected performances. And in altering the dolls' voices, the BLO drew attention to the fact that the 'gender differences' discourse is often unthinkingly accepted, yet is only one possible configuration of gender roles. As well as being a humorous example of discourse subversion or 'gender trouble', the BLO had a political message to make about the effects of gender stereotyping on children.

Gendered discourses are also widely evident in children's fiction: see Hillman (1974), Petersen and Lach (1990), Adler (1992), Stephens (1992),

Kortenhaus and Demarest (1993), Turner-Bowker (1996), Levorato (2003) and Sunderland (2004). Stephens (1992: 5) notes that, 'it is through language that the subject and the world are represented in literature, and through language that literature seeks to define the relationships between child and culture'. For example, in fairy tales, male characters are often represented as more active than females, who are characterised as passive and unadventurous, waiting for rescue from a prince or other male hero. Powerful female characters tend to be either supernatural entities such as fairies or witches, which girls may find it difficult to identify with, or evil step-mothers, which girls are unlikely to want to identify with.

The following example is taken from the children's adventure story *Five Get into Trouble*, written in 1949 by Enid Blyton, and still sold in bookshops. Blyton was a prolific British writer of children's fiction, writing 700 books which were translated into more than forty languages, selling in excess of 400 million copies.

> 'Good old Anne. Look she's got all the food ready. Proper little housewife aren't you Anne?'
>
> 'You are silly Dick' said Anne. 'You ought to be glad I like messing about with food and getting it ready for you.'
>
> Enid Blyton, *Five Get Into Trouble* (1949: 28–9)

Although this excerpt is only about two children, the way that their gender identities and roles are represented is very different. Dick half-mocks Anne for being a 'proper little housewife', while Anne acknowledges that she is happy 'messing about with food and getting it ready'. Anne could therefore be characterised as accepting her subordinate 'service-providing' place in a gendered hierarchy. A trace discourse of 'women as domestic' (Sunderland, 2004: 144) could therefore be identified through language use in the text.

But as seen with the example of the BLO above, discourses are open to subversion or change. In 1982, a new television channel, Channel 4, was launched in the UK. It was initially intended to offer a more contemporary representation of the UK, with newer forms of documentary, social commentary and comedy. A comedy programme called *Five Go Mad in Dorset* was shown on the first night, which parodied the Famous Five novels written by Blyton. In the programme, Dick was shown telling Anne that she was a proper little housewife and that it must be awful for her to be a girl. Anne replies that it would be nice to do some of the exciting things that boys do, but she doesn't mind being dominated, because at least she is quiet and pretty, not like Georgina, the other female character.

By the early 1980s, the view of women as passive housewives, in the West at least, was regarded by many as outdated and sexist (even though many women *were* housewives in the early 1980s). *Five Go Mad in Dorset* was an early example of British 'alternative comedy', which was espoused by younger British comedians who had become frustrated by the sexist, homophobic and racist comedy characteristic of earlier decades. This use of parody reveals another way that discourses can be challenged. In *Five Go Mad in Dorset*, the 'women as domestic' discourse is critically exaggerated and made more explicit so that it can be ridiculed.

'Gender trouble' and parody are not the only ways in which discourses can be subverted or altered. Many critics directly attacked Blyton's books for their sexism, and Rudd (2000) describes how they were banned in some libraries, while certain aspects of Blyton's writing were altered (see also the description of the political correctness movement in Chapter 2). This suggests a more extreme form of change, whereby traces of discourses are erased. More recently, the sexism of the Blyton books could be categorised as being a reflection of its time or historically relevant: the books can be regarded as instructional in revealing something about gender relations in earlier decades, and could be used as educational tools in order to encourage children to engage critically with gender stereotyping.

As I have argued before (Baker, 2005, 2006), a potential problem with analysing single texts (fiction, newspaper articles, conversations, etc.) in order to find evidence of discourses, is that we may tend to focus on what we find interesting or that which confirms our suspicions. There is worth in critiquing texts that contain obviously damaging (sexist or homophobic) discourses; by drawing attention to such texts we would hope to increase awareness about their potential harm. However, Widdowson (1995: 169) has criticised critical discourse analysis for biased interpretation in a dual sense: first, the researcher is prejudiced due to having an ideological commitment and, secondly, the researcher will choose texts which support his or her preferred interpretation. In response to this criticism, Fairclough (1996) points out that critical discourse analysts are at least explicit about their positions and that one of the key principles of CDA is that results should be open-ended, allowing for multiple interpretations.

Clearly we should not discard texts just because they confirm our hypotheses – all forms of language are worth examining and as long as the text is considered in the context of its wider impact on society, this should not present too much of a problem. However, we may ignore other aspects of the text, or similar texts, which might suggest the presence of different discourses. Therefore, it is sometimes helpful to take a more quantitative perspective so as to produce a more balanced picture and to ascertain the cumulative effect of discourse. We will obtain stronger evidence for a mainstream discourse if we can see particular uses of language, occurring across a range of texts in similar ways. This is where corpora (see also Chapter 2), can be effective sources of data for analysts of discourse: rather than examining individual texts, we can examine the use of particular linguistic items (e.g. gender-relevant terms) across many texts in order to ascertain their frequencies as well as identifying patterns or themes which emerge in terms of the way such terms are written or talked about.

The majority of corpus studies which have examined language and gender have concerned themselves with studies of sexism. Some studies have compared corpora gathered from different points in time or from different countries. Kjellmer (1986), for example, used the American Brown and British LOB corpora (each consisting of a million words of general English from the early 1960s) to examine frequencies of male and female pronouns and the items *man/men* and *woman/women*. The frequencies of the female items were much lower than those of the male items in both corpora, suggesting an overall bias towards males in general language use. Similarly, Biber et al. (1999: 312–16) report that words which refer to males tend to occur more frequently than those which refer to females. In the Longman Spoken and Written English Corpus there are 620 nouns ending in –*man* and only 38 which end in –*woman*. Romaine (2001) examined supposedly male and female sets of terms in the British National Corpus, showing that there were differences in usage and frequency; for example, *lady of the house* is not matched in meaning by the equivalent *gentleman of the house*, while *man of the world* is more frequent than *woman of the world*. She points out that *Mr* occurs more than *Mrs*, *Ms* and *Miss* taken together, while *chairman* and *spokesman* continue to prevail. In another study, Sigley and Holmes (2002) examined sexism in corpus data gathered in America, Britain and New Zealand, concluding that, in many ways, proscriptions of sexist uses appeared to have been largely successful between the 1960s and the end of the twentieth century, with reductions in the use of sexist suffixes such as –*ess* and –*ette*, the 'psuedo-polite' *lady/ladies* and the pseudo-generic *man*. They found weaker uptake of positive prescriptions of specific recommended forms such as *Ms* or –*person* (e.g. *chairperson*, see also Table 2.1 in Chapter 2). Collectively, though, such frequency differences in general language use point to male bias which reflects male dominance in society.

Table 4.1 shows the frequencies of *man* and *woman* in different genres of writing in the British National Corpus (about 90 million words collectively). Figures are given as occurrences per million words. So the first figure in the table means that the word *man* occurs 295.7 times in every million words in the 'Social Sciences' genre.

Table 4.1. Standardised frequencies of *man* and *woman* in the British National Corpus

	man	*woman*	**ratio**
Social science	295.7	193.37	1.5
Imaginative	1434.9	589.63	2.4
Arts	775.08	290.16	2.6
Belief and thought	965.34	341.51	2.8
World affairs	503.97	155.85	3.2
Leisure	604.33	162.49	3.7
Natural and pure sciences	165.69	39.11	4.2
Applied science	169.47	37.02	4.5
Commerce and finance	164.24	33.76	4.8
Average across all written genres	625.58	235.74	2.6

The table shows that *man* is more frequent across all genres of writing in British English, although, perhaps unsurprisingly, this is more marked for the tradition-ally male bastions of Commerce and Finance, Applied Science and the Natural and Pure Sciences. Interestingly, the ratio is smallest in the Social Sciences genre, although even here there is bias towards *man*. However, frequency is a somewhat raw indicator of bias – the context of use is perhaps equally or even more important. Sigley and Holmes (2002) examined the use of the terms *girl* and *boy* in detail, in a number of similar-sized corpora of English. They found that age and even gender were not always fixed when people used these terms (for example, 'old boy' does not refer to a male child, while anyone joining a medical team might be referred to as 'the new boy'). Overall, though, *girl* was three times more likely than *boy* to refer to an adult. And while both *boy* and *girl* were usually used with positive effect, a woman who was referred to as a *girl* was often characterised as possessing youthful beauty, domestic skills and a dependent status in a relationship. Such findings suggest that women are still often represented through discourses which position them as subordinate to men (although see also the discussion of Schwarz's research in Chapter 2). Returning to the BNC, some of the uses of *man* in the corpus are generic, indicating an erasure (see also Chapter 5) of *woman* from language:

- It's one of the most dangerous substances **known to man**.

- They suffer; and they wrestle with the big themes of good and evil, heroism and betrayal, **man and God**.

- The real cause of war and strife is not religion, but man's **inhumanity to man**.

- Whether **man or beast**, we are all of the same essence, we all have a soul.

- Of course **primitive man** was a sun worshipper.

Other, non-generic uses of *man* in the BNC are clearly suggestive of male power and independence.

- He was the **man of the house**, you see, since my father was dead, and he became very strict when I was around fourteen or fifteen.

- Dave is very much **his own man** – young and impulsive and finally the arbiter of his own convictions.

- Bach speaks of such things with the passion of a **self-made man** who has beaten personal adversity.

- Our **man of the moment** is 32 year old Russell Sherwood, a tool maker from Mansfield.

- So his wicked sister's vanished and now he's **big man on campus**.

- 'After an hour I realized that if I didn't go after her, I'd **never be a man**.'

- 'I know what you're saying is right, Eve, but I'm not sure I'm **man enough** to do what you suggest.'

- 'And Lilian is my **right-hand man**. I don't know what we'd have done without her in those dark years.'[5]

- 'Oh, and by the way, Mum,' went on Violet, 'Philippa rang and said could you **man** the Bric-à-Brac Stall on Saturday.'[6]

This is not to say that phrases like *woman of the house* or *woman of the moment* do not exist in the BNC or other corpora, but where they do exist, they either tend to be less frequent and/or have different meanings – so a phrase like 'the man of the house' occurs ten times in the BNC and often implies a position of familial power, whereas 'the woman of the house' occurs three times and is used in reference to a woman performing domestic chores.

Another approach to examining gendered discourses in relation to language use is to consider the ways that men and women are *represented* as using language, rather than their actual uses of language. Johnson and Ensslin (2007) analysed a corpus of British newspaper articles, focusing on the phrases 'his language' and 'her language'. They found that, overall, such phrases tended to refer to four different themes surrounding language use: aesthetic value, being plain talking, transgression of norms and language skills. A further analysis of these themes revealed that there were differences regarding expectations and evaluations in terms of how gendered speakers were represented. So male language use was more often referred to in terms of its aesthetic value (usually positively). Furthermore, while both men and women were described as being 'plain-talking' or 'saying what they mean', this was seen as a positive, normal aspect of male language, while there was an implication in some articles that women should *not* be forceful or strong in their language use. Men were also represented more often as using language transgressively or breaking norms (for example, by swearing), but when women were represented in this way, it was seen as exceptional or unusual. Male language skills were often characterised in terms of being competent regarding foreign languages, enabling men to be employed in high profile or dangerous careers, whereas female language skills were more likely to be referred to in relation to jobs such as 'personal assistant' or in terms of female personal development or 'rapport talk'. Taken collectively, the newspaper articles indexed a discourse of traditional gender differences, not too far away from the stances of supposed male and female differences outlined by Jespersen or Lakoff (see Chapter 2).

Perhaps one of the most powerful ways in which gendered discourses have been legitimised in societies is through religion. The following excerpt is taken from Genesis in the King James Bible.

[18]And the LORD God said, *It is* not good that the man should be alone; I will make him an help meet for him.

[19]And out of the ground the LORD God formed every beast of the field, and every fowl of the air; and brought *them* unto Adam to see what he would call them: and whatsoever Adam called every living creature, that *was* the name thereof.

[20]And Adam gave names to all cattle, and to the fowl of the air, and to every beast of the field; but for Adam there was not found an help meet for him.

[21]And the LORD God caused a deep sleep to fall upon Adam and he slept: and he took one of his ribs, and closed up the flesh instead thereof;

[22]And the rib, which the LORD God had taken from man, made he a woman, and brought her unto the man.

[23]And Adam said, This *is* now bone of my bones, and flesh of my flesh: she shall be called Woman, because she was taken out of Man.

[24]Therefore shall a man leave his father and his mother, and shall cleave unto his wife: and they shall be one flesh.

²⁵And they were both naked, the man and his wife, and were not ashamed.

King James Bible, Genesis 2

This passage, in which God's creation of the first woman is described, establishes the status of women as inferior and secondary to men through the differential positioning of the characters. For example, the creator of the universe, God, is constructed as male rather than genderless or female: being referred to with the male pronoun *he* (verses 21, 22) and given the male title *Lord* (verses 18, 19, 21, 22). God decides that the function of women is to provide company for men, in the form of a 'help meet'. The first woman is created from one of Adam's ribs, suggesting that woman is nothing more than part of a man, not an entity in her own right – more of an after-thought, created second. The woman is passive in this excerpt: she is 'brought... unto the man' and is named 'woman' by Adam. In order for man to be whole again, it is implied that he needs to be with a woman, 'shall cleave to his wife and they shall be one flesh'. In verse 25, the couple are referred to as 'the man and his wife'. The woman then is only referenced in terms of her (married) relationship to a man – she is constructed as a possession of the man through the use of the possessive pronoun *his*. The man is not referred to in similar terms – he is not a 'husband' which would reference his relationship to a woman, but simply a man in his own right. Later in Genesis, the first woman, Eve, is responsible for feeding Adam fruit from the tree of knowledge which results in their being cast out of Paradise (although the Bible states that only Adam is cast out, we may assume that Eve suffers the same fate). Men and women are therefore characterised as different but complementary to each other, with men firmly positioned as the primary, dominant and superior part of the pair (see also Innes-Parker, 1999). Heterosexuality is also strongly prescribed in this passage of the Bible, 'a man... shall cleave unto his wife'. Therefore, discourses of gender difference tend to work with a further discourse which we will consider in the following section: compulsory heterosexuality.

Compulsory heterosexuality and heteronormativity

The analysis of discourse in relation to language, gender and sexuality is a relatively recent focus in the two fields, although it could be argued that it has always been an integral, if implicit, part of scholarly work in these areas. One of the most influential works on studies of discourse (although not mentioning the term) is Adrienne Rich's 1980 essay 'Compulsory Heterosexuality and Lesbian Existence'. Rich implies that because women are primary carers of children, a young female will first experience caring and nurturing from her mother – another woman. She writes that it is then logical to ask, 'why in fact women would ever redirect that search' (1980: 637).

Rich's reason is that, 'Heterosexuality has been both forcibly and subliminally imposed on women' (1980: 653) in order for men to wield power over women. She cites and expands on Kathleen Gough's essay 'The Origin of the Family', which lists a number of ways in which men are powerful – denying women their own sexuality, forcing male sexuality on women, using the institutions of marriage and motherhood as unpaid labour, controlling or robbing women's children, confining women physically, using them as objects in male transactions, cramping women's creativity and withholding them from large areas of society's knowledge and cultural attainments. In critiquing four books (all which are written from a feminist perspective), she notes that in none of them, 'the question is raised, whether in a different context, or other things been equal, women would choose heterosexual coupling and marriage' (1980: 633). Rich therefore argues that heterosexuality 'needs to be recognized and studied as a *political institution*' (1980: 637, emphasis as original).

Rich (1980: 659) concludes by warning that, 'in the absence of choice, women will remain dependent on the chance or luck of particular relationships and will have no collective power to determine the meaning and place of sexuality in their lives'. One of the reasons why lesbian experience is either largely unacknowledged or tabooed by mainstream society, is that it would give women an alternative choice, which would decrease male power over women. She therefore calls for a greater understanding of lesbian experience, which is seen as an extension of feminism. Rich characterises a *lesbian continuum*, which goes beyond that of erotic experience. Instead it consists of, 'a range – through each woman's life and throughout history – of woman-identified experience; not simply the fact that a woman has had or consciously desired genital sexual experience with another woman. If we expand it to embrace many more forms of primary intensity between and among women, including the sharing of a rich inner life, the bonding against male tyranny, the giving and receiving of practical and political support...' (1980: 648–49).

It is possible to critique Rich's thesis in a number of ways. Her descriptions of male power include a number of extreme cases (infanticide, pimping, clitoridectomy) which may be beyond the experiences of her readers. She does little to acknowledge that power is rarely absolute and that in some situations women have access to power, too. More recent feminist thinking has conceptualised power as flowing omni-directionally in a net or web-like fashion, suggesting that powerlessness is no longer experienced by all women all of the time; instead it may pertain to many women some of the time or to a minority of women most of the time (Baxter, 2003: 5). Rich's work has also been described as having an 'anti-sex' attitude (see Rubin, 1984). However, in naming compulsory heterosexuality, Rich provides a useful identification and analysis of one of the most powerful discourses in many societies.

While 'compulsory heterosexuality' has been regarded as a gendered discourse (see Sunderland, 2004: 39–40), it might also be characterised as a *discourse of sexuality*. References to *discourses of gender* or *gendered discourses* often occur within academic literature, while *discourses of sexuality* or *sexed/sexualised discourses* are rarer. However, the terms clearly reference over-lapping concepts – most gendered discourses require that assumptions are made about sexuality in order to be recognised, and vice versa. Various aspects of the 'gender differences' discourse discussed earlier in this chapter only make sense if we assume that they refer to heterosexual men and women, and that gay men and lesbians, if we consider them at all, are exceptional in some way, again indicating the 'special' relationship between gender and sexuality. I refer to *gendered discourses* at various points in this book, because most of the research on discourse has examined the interface between language and gender. However, it should be acknowledged that gendered discourses are often discourses of sexuality, too.

A concept related to compulsory heterosexuality is that of *heteronormativity*, a term coined by Warner (1993) and developed by Chambers (2003). Warner defines heteronormativity as the organisation of all patterns of thought, awareness and belief around the presumption of universal heterosexual desire, behaviour and identity. In Nagel's (2003: 49–50) words it is, 'the assumption that everyone is heterosexual and the recognition that all social institutions… are built around a heterosexual model of male/female social relations'.

Heteronormativity therefore covers a range of beliefs – that human beings fall into two (different but complementary) categories: male and female, and that sexual relations are normal *only* when they occur between two people of the opposite sex. One of the main heteronormative arguments in society is that because a woman and a man are (normally) required for procreation, heterosexuality is normal. The term is most often used in a critical sense, to question or disrupt the ways in which social institutions and policies are seen to reinforce such beliefs. Heteronormativity therefore involves the recognition of a number of social practices – those which assume that everyone is automatically heterosexual and those which attempt to erase, regulate, taboo, punish or silence anything that is not heterosexual. Such social practices can be overt, covert or implied. For example, the anti-gay religious aphorism 'God made Adam and Eve, not Adam and Steve' is an extremely overt example of heteronormative (and homophobic) thinking, whereas the (admittedly ironic) opening sentence of Jane Austen's *Pride and Prejudice* (1831), 'It is a truth universally acknowledged that a single man in possession of a good fortune must be in want of a wife' is more covert in that same-sex relationships are not acknowledged.

Heteronormativity is such a pervasive part of society that people will often find that they are assumed to be heterosexual, whether they are or not . I can provide a couple of examples from my own experience. As a student at university I found that platonic friendships I made with female classmates were often interpreted by others as my showing a romantic interest in them, and on several occasions I was accused of 'checking out' women because I was perceived to be sexually attracted to them. A more recent example involves a stay at a hotel I had with my (male) partner. We ordered room-service for breakfast. I answered the door while my partner remained in bed. A waiter delivered the food to our room and said, 'good morning madam' to my partner, without looking at him. The waiter presumably assumed that any couple sharing a bed in a hotel room would consist of a man and a woman.

So how is the discourse of compulsory heterosexuality realised through language in society? For the remainder of this chapter I want to examine the language use of a number of 'everyday' texts, in order to demonstrate the banality of the compulsory heterosexuality discourse. As Billig (1995: 8) notes of *banal nationalism*, 'In so many little ways, the citizenry are daily reminded of their national place in a world of nations. However, this reminding is so familiar, so continual, that it is not consciously registered as reminding. The metonymic image of banal nationalism is not a flag which is being consciously waved with fervent passion; it is the flag hanging unnoticed on the public building'. It is easy to see how this description of nationalism as familiar and continual – banal in other words, echoes both Butler's idea of gender performance as a set of behaviours which are repeated in everyday life and the concept of gendered discourses. The more overtly homophobic examples of heteronormativity (such as the 'God made Adam and Eve...' statement) are more easily open to contestation; in liberal-leaning societies most people do not like to be seen as openly oppressive. Banal uses, on the other hand, tend to 'slip by' people, almost unnoticed, and yet they are extremely influential, expecting (and often receiving) continuous conformity.

Although discourse positions can sometimes be presented in an unequivo-cal, explicit way (for example, I remember my grandmother telling me, 'Stop crying, be a brave soldier, *boys don't cry!*' after I hurt myself at her house when I was six), they are most often encountered as being subtle and banal – part of our everyday existence and requiring an almost unconscious decoding of society's norms in order to be internalised. In order to demonstrate this, I want to refer to a short example taken from a British magazine for young girls, called, appropriately, *Girl*.

Girl Gossip

WILLAMINA BALLERINA

We've heard it all now – the singing sensation that is Will Young has revealed he's a bit of an Angelina Ballerina on the quiet! The Willster reportedly goes to ballet classes several times a week to keep toned and taut! Well, we can't argue with the results, can we?!

Girl (May 2006 no. 98, page 4)

What does this short text tell us about gendered and sexualised discourses? The magazine is aimed at girls. Although the target age range of the magazine is unclear, clues can be gleaned from looking at the picture of the girl on the front cover, the language used and the topics covered. It is likely to be aimed at girls aged about 8 to 13 years old. Visually, the magazine is colourful, making strong use of 'feminine' pinks throughout. The font size is large and a range of 'fun' font styles are used. As with most magazines, there is also a very high ratio of pictures to text.

It is important to take the context of this article into account. The article is about a British pop singer, Will Young, who won a televised talent competition in 2002 and afterwards came out in the media as gay (see below). The article does not openly refer to Will's sexuality, although it could be argued that it is alluded to through reference to his gender 'deviance'. For example, the fact that his attendance at ballet classes is reported as newsworthy 'we've heard it all now', and the female nicknames which are given to him 'Willamina Ballerina' and 'Angelina Ballerina' serve to feminise his identity. The phrase 'on the quiet' also implies secrecy about his ballet classes, referring, perhaps, to his supposed shame over deviating from typical masculine roles, but also, in terms of inter-textuality, by implicitly referring to his previously closeted sexual status which had been the subject of media focus.

Furthermore, Will's motivation for going to classes, 'to keep toned and taut', suggests a feminine fascination with physical appearance. Two pictures accompany this article. The first is a drawing of a mouse, ballet dancing in a pink tutu – again indicative of the mocking, feminising construction of Will's identity. The mouse is a further intertextual reference to Angelina Ballerina – a character from a popular series of children's books by Helen Craig and Katherine Holabird, while the labelling of Will as Willamina Ballerina also draws on the same reference.

The second picture is a photograph of Will, shirtless. The final line of the text, 'Well, we can't argue with the results, can we?' refers to this picture, offering Will's toned chest for the reader's inspection. Will's 'feminine' hobby is therefore condoned by the narrative voice of the article, because it produces 'results', e.g. an attractive 'masculine' body.

The article therefore draws on a number of discourses relating to gender and sexuality. The 'gender differences' discourse is present, in that the writer of the article suggests that it is unusual for men to engage in activities that society considers feminine. If they do, it is likely to be a secret worthy of 'gossip' and a warrant for light ridicule which acts as a form of social control. The audience of the article (mainly young girls) should be borne in mind here: so here, the continued dissemination of the discourse(s) in the article is most likely to involve girls remarking on the behaviour of boys – which is not to say that boys do not learn such discourses in numerous other ways.

Secondly, the 'compulsory heterosexuality' discourse is present. Girls are directed to find Will's body attractive, '…we can't argue with the results, can we?' Note how the plural first person pronoun *we* is used ambiguously. Does it refer to the production team of the magazine, or does it refer to an attitude shared by the reader and the writer(s)? The article therefore suggests a number of assumptions regarding 'girl sexuality': that girls are sexually aware enough to be able to make judgements about what constitutes an attractive male, that possessing a 'toned and taut' body like Will Young's *is* sexually attractive, and that the object of desire for girls should be male – i.e. an assumption that the reader is heterosexual (or, at the least, bisexual). This is a potentially damaging stance to take, because we can not be certain that all *Girl's* readers will pursue heterosexual relationships when they are older. Also, many readers may not yet have considered men's bodies in terms of whether they are attractive or not. The article therefore erases the possibility of lesbian identities, super-imposing an expected heterosexual identity onto female children, which could be confusing or worrying for girls who currently do not (or never will) find Will's body attractive.

This is not the only article in the magazine which assumes the heterosexuality of its readers or encourages them to consider adult males in terms of relationship/sexual potential. On the same page, an article about another male celebrity, Declan Donnelly, tells us that he is, 'searching furiously for Miss Right – so form an orderly queue girls!' Here, the discourse of compulsory heterosexuality is encoded within a directive, 'form an orderly queue girls', rather than an evaluative, 'we can't argue with the results, can we?'

Taking a post-structuralist approach, Baxter (2003: 8) warns that we should not view discourses as isolated, but instead reminds us that within any given context there are always plural and competing discourses constituting power relations, 'Such discourses do not operate in discrete isolation from each other but are always intertextually linked, that is, each discourse is likely to be interconnected with and infused by traces of others'. It is possible to see this multiplicity of discourses within the *Girl* article. For example, the 'traditional' discourses of compulsory heterosexuality and gender differences described above mutually support each other.

But we could also argue that by making Will Young the subject of celebrity gossip and reporting on him in a way that constructs him as desirable (helping to sell records in the process and so perpetuate his career), there is an implicit liberal 'discourse of sexual tolerance' at work in the magazine. Perhaps by not focusing on the singer's sexuality, the article refrains from a potentially reductive position of constructing Will Young as a 'gay' singer and nothing more. Yet in *not* explicitly referencing Will's homosexuality, it could be argued that there is an implication that the writers regard homosexuality as an inappropriate topic for young girls – what we might call a discourse of 'childhood innocence'.

In terms of constructing the sexuality of the *Girl* audience, by presenting Will Young as a sexual object, girls are placed in a potentially powerful position – being able to pass judgements on others – a reversal of Berger's (1972: 47) 'male gaze': 'Men look at women. Women watch themselves being looked at'. This could constitute a discourse of 'empowering girls'. Yet, from another perspective, the language in the article could entail a discourse of '(hetero)sexualising girls' at an age which is perhaps not appropriate (and also in conflict with the discourse which constructs children as innocent and needing to be protected from overt sexuality, see also Chapter 8). Clearly, Will Young is unlikely ever to reciprocate any sexual feelings experienced by his young female fans, given that he is a pop star *and* gay. Perhaps the unattainable status of the object of desire will alleviate concerns that girls are being sexualised because nothing can come of it. Yet, girls are still encouraged to experience desire, which could have consequences in other contexts.

The discourses in the article can therefore be summarised as:

- Gender differences
- Compulsory heterosexuality
- Sexual tolerance
- Childhood innocence
- Empowering girls

- (Hetero)sexualising girls

This is not a 'complete' analysis: it can never be complete in the sense that others may disagree with the discourses I have listed, or spot others that I have missed. However, it shows how even within a short text which appears to be cohesive, co-existing discourses have the potential to be in direct conflict. This 'multiple' discourses perspective therefore acknowledges that power is rarely absolute – a text may position a person in a range of ways, some powerful, some powerless. As Foucault (1984: 100) points out, 'We must not imagine a world of discourse divided between accepted discourse and excluded discourse, or between the dominant discourse and the dominated one; but as a multiplicity of discursive elements that come into play in various strategies'.[7]

Kitzinger (2005), using techniques of Conversation Analysis, examined a number of conversations between people in different contexts where the heterosexuality of the speakers was referred to in a number of different ways. She points out that the speech of heterosexuals has tended to receive much less attention than the speech of more marginalised groups like homosexuals, and she advocates treating, 'the language through which heterosexuality is displayed with the same 'outsiders'' curiosity that has animated the analysis of the subcultural argot of pickpockets... drug addicts... or dance musicians' (2005: 224). Kitzinger's analysis reveals a number of strategies which are used by heterosexuals in order to reinforce the presumption of universal heterosexuality. For example, people engage in sexual joking, banter, reports of (hetero)sexual activity and innuendo. They regularly use terms like *husband, wife* and *in-law*, or talk about other heterosexual relationships. What is interesting about these conversations is that heterosexuality is routinely deployed as a taken-for-granted resource: '...nowhere in the data is heterosexuality itself treated as problematic: Instead, even in the course of complaining about it, the difference-sex definition of marriage is underwritten and reinscribed simply through being treated as taken-for-granted' (2005: 231).

In the example below (Kitzinger, 2005: 238), Mrs Mears has telephoned the owner of a house she would like to rent.

```
01 Own:    I'll continue to try to get the tenant: and see:
02         'n let her know that someone wants to see it.
03         .hhh Do you mind giving me you:r na:me.
04 Mea:    mm We:;ll my na:me is Missus Mears. My husband
05         is Doctor Mears
06 Own:    Uh tha- How do you spell that.
```

Kitzinger argues that the participants in these interactions are not actively 'doing being heterosexual', they are simply getting on with their lives and their hetero- sexuality is displayed incidentally. The owner of the house in the example above simply accepts Mrs Mears' casual disclosure that she is married (and most likely heterosexual) without further comment, and continues with the conversation. Although only a small number of cases in Kitzinger's paper dealt with gay or lesbian speakers, the ways that participants in those conversations orient to the disclosure of a gay or lesbian sexual orientation is much more marked. In one case (2005: 234) a woman refers to her partner using the pronoun *she* during a dinner party, after which the woman next to her abandons their conversation completely and does not address her again for an hour. In another conversation (a call to a suicide prevention centre), the caller gives his sexual orientation as the reason for the call, and so it becomes a topic of discussion. These different orientations to the disclosure of homosexuality show how gay identities are not taken for granted – in one case, the disclosure possibly acts as a conversation killer, while in the other, it is the focus of the conversation.

Chirrey (2003) has also examined the ways in which homosexual identity is related to – although her study examined the case of a more public 'coming out', which occurred in the media, that of Will Young (see above). She argues that a range of different strategies of media representation were used. For example, the liberal broadsheet newspaper *The Guardian* wrote that Young had 'disclosed he is gay', which framed Young's action in terms of a neutral act of revelation that was to be viewed in a non-judgmental way. On the other hand, the *Daily Express* wrote, 'Will admits he's gay', while the *Daily Mail* wrote of Will's 'frank admission' and 'his secret'. *The Mirror* claimed that Young was, 'in hiding yesterday after telling the world he is gay'. Chirrey (2003: 32) sug- gests that the choice of lexis in these newspapers, 'resonates with a sense of acknowledging criminality, sinfulness and blame, while phrases such as "his secret" and "in hiding" suggest that being gay is characterized by clandestine activity, presumably due to its supposedly shameful nature'. My own research (Baker, 2005) found that while British tabloid newspapers regularly used a 'shame and secrecy' discourse in relation to homosexuality, on the other hand, they also employed a reverse discourse of 'shamelessness' which was used in reference to a set of people who did not appear to be ashamed of their sexual- ity. In such cases, these people 'don't *confess* their sexuality, but they *declare* or *proclaim* it, like a town-crier with a piece of important news. Such people are *infamous*, *visible* and *famously* homosexual. Their sexuality is *well-known* by everyone and prefaced by adverbs that suggest that the person being talked about purposefully seeks attention. Such people have no compunction not just in being *openly* gay but *flagrantly*, *flamboyantly*, *outrageously* or *unbelievably* gay… phrases like *proudly gay, happily gay* or *assuredly gay* never occur in the tabloid corpus. The emphasis on these types of people is not to do with pride, but to do with showing off' (Baker, 2005: 79). Such a discourse is, therefore, forced to acknowledge a conflicting position: not everyone is ashamed of being gay. However, by representing such people as occupying the opposite extreme, the media is still able to retain its negative view of homosexuality by characterising openly gay people as attention-seeking while implying that it should be normal for them to be ashamed and secretive. Taken together, then, the discourses of gay shame and gay shamelessness reinforce one other, continuing to problematise homosexuality and thereby contributing to the overarching 'compulsory heterosexuality' discourse.

However, 'compulsory heterosexuality', while still a dominant discourse, is perhaps not as monolithic as it once was. While Chirrey and Baker's research on the media suggests that mainstream society is prepared to acknowledge the existence of gay people, in terms of being newsworthy (exotic and against the normal), in other quarters, more measured steps are being taken to counter heterosexual bias in language. The example below is taken from a set of guidelines on inclusive language use at Lancaster University. The use of gender-specific terms such as 'the opposite sex', 'husbands' or 'boyfriends' is not recommended, with more ambiguous alternatives 'other people' and 'partners' being suggested instead.

Here are examples of everyday language which exclude lesbians, gay men and bisexuals. Alternatives are also suggested.

'There'll be lots of chances to meet the opposite sex at the party.'

Not much chance there for anyone who prefers people of the same sex! What about just saying 'There'll be lots of chances to meet other people at the party?'

'Any husbands or boyfriends are welcome to come too.'

Be careful with such words, if you are speaking to a group of women. Lesbians obviously do not have boyfriends. 'Partners are welcome to come too' is a good solution.

From Social Diversity and Inclusive Language at Lancaster University http://www.lancs.ac.uk/depts/equalopp/lang.htm

A few short examples taken from British newspapers demonstrate how writers negotiate the discourse of 'compulsory heterosexuality', taking into account the fact that there are exceptions to the rule.

Nine thousand women and a smattering of red-faced men go berserk, yelling, crying and jumping up and down. (*Daily Mail*, 24 April 2006, from an article concerning the reunion of Boy Band 'Take That')

How torn was your husband on Wednesday night, when the Champions League Final clashed with The Line of Beauty? In 1977, two televisions would have solved this problem in any household. In 2006, women (and gay men) suffered a profound and visible agony of choice. (*The Observer*, 21 May 2006)

No Big Brother house would be complete without a bit of eye candy. And this year is no exception. Former Miss Wales Imogen Thomas, 23, and buxom blonde Nikki Grahame, 24, will keep the straight blokes in the house as well as red-blooded male viewers very happy. (*The Daily Star*, 22 May 2006)

Although these three articles make attempts to counter the discourse of compulsory heterosexuality in different ways, there are still aspects of heteronormative discourse at work in all of them, again pointing to the 'multiplicity' of discourses in any text. In the first article, the fact that there are a 'smattering' of men who are 'red-faced' (possibly implying that they are embarrassed), serves to normalise the overtly heterosexual nature of the Take That concert, where it is mainly women who are supposed to be excited by the presence of the male performers.

The second article, while trying to be more inclusive, 'women (and gay men)', marginalises gay men to a parenthical afterthought. *The Line of Beauty* was a drama series which showed attractive men having sex with each other. An assumption is, therefore, made on the part of the writer, that women (who are all presumably heterosexual) and gay men would want to watch this programme. Lesbians might also want to watch the series, but the positioning of the ideal reader of the article as a married woman, 'How torn was your husband', negates the possibility of a lesbian addressee. Also, there is no acknowledgement that bisexual men may also want to watch *The Line of Beauty*: recognition of the existence of bisexuality is problematic for heteronormative discourse in a number of ways, a point that is addressed in more detail in Chapter 5.

The third article acknowledges that it is only 'straight blokes' who will be pleased by the presence of attractive females in the Big Brother house. But it does not also say that lesbians or bisexual men and women may be attracted to these women. It also refers to 'red blooded male viewers' (who are presumably equivalent to the 'straight blokes' referred to earlier), implying figuratively that gay men do not have red blood, and are therefore not normal. Or we may understand the term *red-blooded* as an allusion to masculinity, strength, robustness, good health, etc. – which again associates heterosexuality with normality, leaving a question mark over gay identities.

So while such articles at least acknowledge homosexuality, it still appears that traces of older, more conservative discourses are at work in them, co-existing alongside more inclusive discourses in subtle ways.

Conclusion

In the previous chapter we saw how Butler's theory of gender performativity highlights the fact that gender is socially constructed, a potentially fluid phenomenon mapped onto sex and sexuality, and requiring constant repetition in order to appear stable. Butler's theory offers a way out of restrictive gender roles: once we realise that gender is not fixed, there is the capacity for change. But at the same time, our gender performances have not become fixed in random ways – it is difficult to decide to change them and then implement such a change. Their mapping to sex and sexuality is constituted, strongly or loosely, by discourses, which reflect norms and taboos. Just as gender must be constantly performed, the discourses which determine the supposed right and wrong ways of doing gender for different people also require continual repetition and circulation in order to appear fixed and natural. The two concepts work together, reinforcing each other – and are, ultimately, linked to power relations. They are also strongly linked to language – gender performance is realised linguistically – by what we say (or write) and how we say it: the words we use, the way our voice sounds, the subjects we talk about. Furthermore, discourses are transmitted through language in an enormous variety of ways: pop songs which prime us to 'fall' in love with an opposite-sex partner, war movies where 'a man's gotta do what a man's gotta do', wedding, fashion and parenting magazines, religious stories, beauty pageants, laws, sports contests, soap operas, gossip columns, business news, science journals, a trip to the hairdressers, pornography, children's fiction, toy shops, holiday brochures, family meals, muffin labels... the list goes on and on.

That is not to say that discourses can not be challenged. I hope that this chapter has shown some of the ways that discourses surrounding gender and sexuality are in flux, and that, within a single text, elements of competing discourses may reside, suggesting that discourses always have the potential to be countered, subverted or transgressed. In order for us to understand why certain discourses exist, we need to relate them to the hierarchical gender and sexuality system that exists in our society. In the following chapter I sharpen the focus to consider how one particular configuration of gender has come to take precedence over the others, resulting in its boundaries needing to be fiercely policed and its power continually reiterated: hegemonic masculinity.

Notes

1   Sunderland's approach is strongly influenced by critical discourse analysis (Fairclough, 1995, Wodak and Meyer, 2001). Although Cameron (1998) indicates that critical discourse analysis is marginal to language and gender research, more recently, writers such as Lazar (2005: 5) have conceptualised *feminist critical discourse analysis* – a form of analysis whose central concern 'is with critiquing discourses which sustain a patriarchal social order: that is, relations of power that systematically privilege men as a social group and disadvantage, exclude and disempower women as a social group'. Also, Baxter (2003) offers a different approach to the study of discourse, with feminist post-structuralist discourse analysis. Both approaches combine feminist theories with discourse-based methods of analysis.

2   Repetition is not the only requisite of a powerful discourse: the articulation of a new discourse, produced by a powerful speaker or writer, may also be extremely influential. Furthermore, a discourse which is accessed by large numbers of people may also gain precedence. So methods of text production and reception are also important in terms of examining the impact of discourses.

3   Although many rhymes were published in Kate Greenaway's *Mother Goose, or the Old Nursery Rhymes* in 1881, they do not appear to be attributed to a particular author. Nursery rhymes can often be traced to specific people or events that were often gruesome, e.g. 'Ring a Ring of Roses' is said to refer to the Great Plague of London in 1665 (although this may an urban myth because the song did not appear in print until 1881). 'Jack and Jill' may refer to Louis XVI of France and Queen Marie Antoinette, who were beheaded in 1793, whereas 'Mary, Mary, Quite Contrary' apparently refers to Mary Tudor, a staunch Catholic who had religious dissenters executed. However, despite these origins, the vast majority of people who sing nursery rhymes are unaware that they may have referred to specific people or events.

4   We might also want to ask why Barbie is described as blushing – in corpus data the adjective regularly occurs as part of the collocational fixed pair 'blushing bride'. We rarely find references to 'blushing grooms' in naturally-occurring language use, suggesting that women are more likely to be characterised as blushing (signifying embarrassment) than men. Is this because women are expected to be more introverted and uncomfortable with being the centre of attention than men, or does the embarrassment refer to expectations of their 'wedding night'?

5   This example listed is of note, not only because the term 'right-hand man' is a positive term, indexing competence, but because this label is ascribed to a female.

A similar point can be made about the last example, where a woman is asked to 'man' the Bric-a-Brac stall.

6   The use of *man* as a verb is interesting, *woman* does not have the same grammatical function.

7   It may be easier to apply the post-structuralist approach to discourse analysis in certain situations. For example, in the excerpt from the Bible and in the nursery rhymes quoted in this chapter, it is more difficult to identify a range of conflicting discourses. Baxter's approach is based on identifying discourses within (current) spoken conversations, and it may be that texts that are decades or centuries old may more straightforwardly reflect the traditional 'sexist' discourses that were prevalent of their time. That is not to say that there were no competing discourses in existence before the twentieth century, just that they may have been more repressed and less easily observed in individual texts. A more thorough examination of the particular historical and cultural contexts regarding such texts and others like them would therefore be required.

5 Maintaining boundaries: hegemony and erasure

Introduction

In earlier chapters we have seen how various models of male and female language use have been popular at different times. One aspect that most of these models have had in common, however, is an underlying focus on difference in one form or another. In this chapter I want to examine more closely the reasons for the longevity of the Difference model (Chapter 2), and argue that the creation of difference is one of the most important ways that we make sense of the world and establish our position within it. Both Douglas (1966) and Levi-Strauss (1970) have claimed that our obsession with difference is an attempt to impose sense on a disordered world, 'ideas about separating, purifying, demarcating and punishing transgressions have as their main function to impose system on an inherently untidy experience. It is only by exaggerating the difference between within and without, above and below, male and female, for and against that a semblance of order is created' (Douglas, 166: 4). So a key way that we make sense of something is by casting it in relationship to something else, for example, we understand the concept of Sunday by comparing it to and differentiating it from other days in the week (Douglas, 1966: 64). Therefore, we understand X in terms of what is *not* X – a binary distinction in other words. Derrida (1981a) argues that there is a power imbalance between the two positions: one is considered preferable to the other. Equally, Cixous (1975) has theorised that within these dualisms, one state is usually considered to be the 'norm', while the other is viewed as deviant or outside. Cixous (1975: 90) stresses that many binary oppositions are gendered: men are associated with activity, culture, the head and rationality, whereas women are associated with passivity, nature, the heart and emotionality. Irigaray (1985) suggests that it is through these dualisms that women are constructed as 'the other' – they are what men are not. In terms of sexuality, opposite-sex attraction (heterosexuality) is viewed as normal or right, whereas same-sex attraction (homosexuality) has been constructed as deviant or wrong at various points in time and in various societies. Such classifications are not restricted to gender and sexuality, for example, Tajfel and Turner (1979) have examined racial classifications, finding similar good/bad normal/abnormal distinctions.

As we saw in the previous chapter, we invoke and adhere to discourses in order to establish a shared understanding of our different ways of classifying things and types of people in terms of powerful/not powerful, good/bad, normal/not normal, etc. So, in order for us to be able to identify 'normal', it is imperative that we demarcate what is *not* normal. And as with the discussion of gender performativity and discourses, Derrida (1981a) has argued that many binary oppositions only *appear* to be fixed, but in fact are fluid and uncertain, with no real point of closure. Binaries and their meanings can, therefore, be changed or subverted. In this chapter, then, I want to examine some of the ways in which normal or powerful identities are constructed, by focusing on discourses and practices which could be said to be regulatory or repressive of particular types of gendered or sexed identities, while privileging others.

Hegemonic masculinity

So far we have considered how society tends to model gender as a masculine/ feminine binary, or in some cases, a linear continuum with an infinite number of possible positions within it. However, Bornstein (1998) and Weiss (2001) conceptualise gender differently – as a kind of caste system or hierarchy, with certain types of gendered identities at the top, and others below. For Weiss, the caste system privileges non-transsexuals over transsexuals, while for Bornstein, gender is a pyramid of power, with the most 'perfectly gendered' people (white, male, American, middle-aged, wealthy, heterosexual) at the top and other identities occupying the lower parts. Bornstein's model is useful in reminding us that gender is not the only component of identity but instead interacts with many other elements, resulting in a wide range of ways that people can be seen as powerful or powerless in different circumstances. In terms of the pyramid model, people who perform a very masculine *or* a very feminine gender would appear near the top. As I will argue later in this chapter, while typically masculine men are afforded a great deal of power in society, very feminine women can also be relatively powerful, although the way in which their power is exercised may be dependent on their indirect influence on others. In the past (and, to a lesser extent, now), by embodying qualities of passivity and helplessness while possessing a 'Barbie doll' appearance (see Chapter 4) or by having children, being a good carer, homemaker or sexual services provider, typically feminine women can appeal to powerful males to provide for them, and they are afforded a higher status than less 'feminine' women. Such female power is precarious, though: it is both dependent on male power and requires women to play a role which subordinates them to men.

Despite women's potential to possess power, in patriarchal societies it is stereotyped masculinity which is normally recognised as the most powerful gender in society. And because stereotyped masculinity is positioned at the top of the gender pyramid, it is the expression of gender which is most inordinately concerned with power and the policing of its own boundaries – those who occupy the higher positions of the gender pyramid have further to fall, and potentially more power to lose. So, the discourses regarding what constitutes an acceptable masculine gender performance are strict, with harsh penalties imposed, traditionally, on those who are seen to transgress (such as gay men who are often characterised as effeminate or sexually receptive). Masculinity must therefore be strongly articulated against what it is not.

However, the term *masculinity* is misleading because it implies that there is only one way of being masculine. As Johnson (1997: 19–20) points out, 'Work within pro-feminist approaches to masculinity has explored men in terms of "multiple subjectivities", and this has led writers to abandon the idea of "masculinity" in the singular, in preference for the pluralized "masculinities"'. The idea of plural *masculinities* is in keeping with the Diversity model of gender, which postulates that there are differences between men (or between women). It also helps us to disconnect gender from sex – so we could consider the idea of masculinities being applied to women (or femininities to men).

Connell (1995) notes that there are four main typologies which help us to explain the relationship between different masculinities. The first (and main concept) is *hegemonic masculinity* or a, 'correspondence between cultural ideal and institutional power' (Connell, 1995: 77). Hegemony is a concept popularised by Gramsci (1971, 1985), who theorised that it involves the exercise of power, whereby everybody in a society acquiesces in one way or another to a dominant person or social group. Perhaps the less powerful people are not fully aware of their true status in the hierarchy (or even that a hierarchy exists), or they may choose to allow others to wield power because there are benefits to themselves (they, in turn, may be awarded small amounts of power over others). Gramsci applied the concept of hegemony to early twentieth century politics, in order to explain why a socialist revolution, predicted by Marxism, had not occurred. He suggested that it was because power was maintained, not just through physical and economic coercion, but through ideology: the values of the bourgeoisie (the powerful class) had become established in wider society as common-sense values, applicable to everybody. Therefore, a culture of consensus had developed, whereby even people who belonged to the lower classes helped to maintain the status quo because they also identified with bourgeois values.

Connell's concept of hegemonic masculinity focuses on gender rather than social class relations, although the two are linked. Hegemonic masculinity therefore has dominance not only over femininity (or more rightly, femininities), but over non-hegemonic masculinities. Yet again, it is ideology, embodied in social structures, which forms the basis of hegemonic masculinity. 'Ascendancy of one group of men over another achieved at the point of a gun, or by the threat of unemployment is not hegemony. Ascendancy which is embedded in religious doctrine and practice, mass media content, wage structures, the design of housing, welfare/taxation policies and so forth is' (Connell, 1987: 184). It is discourse (see Chapter 4) which informs and regulates the articulation of hegemonic masculinity: as Talbot (1998: 192) points out in her discussion of masculinity, 'Bringing in the family wage is deeply entrenched as masculine in a wide range of discourses. Work is part of being a 'real man''. And, in a similar way to Gramsci's bourgeoisie, everyone in society is implicitly educated or expected to view the values and traits associated with hegemonic, stereotyped masculinity as 'commonsense' or the way things should be, always have been and always will be. An example would be the popularity of 'action' films like the Die Hard, Indiana Jones, Rambo and James Bond series which feature physically strong, resourceful, dominant and virile men who always triumph against adversity. By having action heroes as protagonists we are invited to identify with and/or desire such constructions of masculinity, thereby fuelling the expectation that their worldview, goals and ways of behaving will influence us – even though we ourselves are not action heroes, we are encouraged to accept this version of masculinity as the primary, perfect one.

Connell (1995: 77, 79) argues that the, 'most visible bearers of hegemonic masculinity' are not always the most powerful people in society, and the number of men who actually rigorously practice hegemonic masculinity can be quite small – yet the majority of men benefit from it, as the overall gain is the general subordination of women. This leads to the second typology of masculinity, *subordination*: 'specific gender relations of dominance and subordination between groups of men' (1995: 78). So as well as thinking of male subordination of women, we can also conceive of the, 'the dominance of heterosexual men and the subordination of homosexual men' (1995: 78). Male homosexuality is a subordinated identity, with its subordination achieved through a range of different strategies: the casual positioning of everyone as heterosexual through heteronormative practices, negative representations of homosexuals, e.g. as 'pansies', 'sissies', 'perverts', 'child molesters', etc., laws which have criminalised or tabooed same-sex relationships in various contexts and homophobic abuse and violence.

Another example of a subordinate masculinity would be what Connell identifies as 'protest masculinity' (1995: 110), associated with, 'violence, school resistance, minor crime, heavy drug/alcohol use, manual labour, motorbikes or cars, short heterosexual liaisons'. Pujolar (1997) also describes a similar type of subordinate masculinity, cultivated by young working-class men who have poor job prospects and inadequate housing. Messerschmidt (1993) argues that criminal behaviour or violence can be used as a resource for accomplishing masculinity when other resources (such as a 'good' job or a stable family life) are unavailable. A further type of subordinate masculinity would be a 'wimp', 'geek' or 'nerd': any male who is seen as weak, overly academic, quiet or socially inept (see the discussion of Edley and Wetherell's study below).[1]

The third typology of masculinity, which is necessary for hegemonic masculinity to maintain its power, is *complicity*: 'Masculinities constructed in ways that realize the patriarchal dividend, without the tensions or risks of being the frontline troops of patriarchy, are complicit in this sense' (Connell, 1995:79). Complicity can involve agreement or lack of disagreement, e.g. silence. So, for example, when a heterosexual couple have a child and everyone (men *and* women) expects and accepts that the female partner will have a break from her career for a few years (forgoing promotions), there is complicity of hegemonic masculinity. When a woman is required to talk and behave 'like a man' in order to be successful at work, this might also be regarded as complicity. And when a gay man says he dislikes gay men who are 'camp' and prefers the company of 'straight-acting' men that could also be complicity. In many cases people are unthinkingly complicit: the discourses they hold have been internalised, even though they do not always benefit from them. In other cases, complicity can involve a degree of compromise and, to an extent, realism – we recognise what the world is like, we might not like it, but in order to attain personal success we play by the rules, rather than trying to change them or refusing to play at all. However, in adhering to the system, we ensure that the 'winners' will continue to be those who display hegemonic masculinity.

Connell's final typology is *marginalisation* – referring to those who are different from hegemonic or subordinated masculinities as they are outside the, 'relations internal to the gender order' (1995: 80). So for example, while black sporting stars in America may be exemplars of hegemonic masculinity, being rich and physically fit, their power does not trickle down to other black men in America, who are marginalised rather than authorised by hegemonic masculinity. Lesbians could also be viewed as marginalised within society's system of gender relations – being women and homosexual. And people or groups who do not 'fit' into binary systems of identity are also often marginalised, as discussed towards the end of this chapter. Therefore, another power afforded to holders of hegemonic masculinity is that they get to decide which groups are authorised, subordinated or marginalised.

I would now like to examine a few texts taken from real-life situations which demonstrate how language is used in relation to hegemonic masculinity, subordination, complicity and marginalisation. Some of the examples below consist of naturally-occurring conversations, while others are 'elicited texts' containing talk about or around the subject of masculinity, obtained thorough interviews or focus groups. Furthermore, 'mediated' texts, such as adverts or novels, similarly attest to the ways in which hegemonic masculinity pervades society.

The first example involves a narrative adapted from Coates (2002: 122–23) which takes place during a conversation between seven male friends in their mid-twenties. The narrator's name is Gary. Interruptions to the narrative from the other participants are shown with italics.

1   I went to this customer's house the other day with um-
2   I was told to go there basically by um the corporate sales director for the Dixons
3   Stores group [*yeah*] he phoned me up and he said 'You've got to go to this
4   customer cos she's been like trying to write letters to Sidney Smith [*=the*
5   *managing director*] and stuff like this' [*yeah*]
6   so I get round there and there's like nothing wrong with her computer at all
7   whinging bitch
8   it was quite funny when I was walking out though
9   cos I was walking out –
10   the computer's in her bedroom
11   I was just sort of looking around
12   looked down on the floor under her bedri- bedside cabinet
13   and there was this fucking great vibrator
14   [LAUGHTER]
15   I sort of looked at her and she looked at me and she was like 'oh fuck'
16   [LAUGHTER]
17   *it's not the sort of thing you leave about when you get the engineers coming to do*
18   *the PC is it?*
19   she had kids as well though
20   fucking kids walking around
21   bloody great vibrator with a sucking cap on the end of it
22   *was she very nice looking?*
23   no she's a big fat pig [*oh*]

Coates argues that this narrative constitutes a performance of hegemonic masculinity. The narrator's self-presentation here is complex. On the one hand he constructs himself as a reliable employee who carries out the orders of an important senior male (lines 2–5) and someone who is aware of (and agrees with) society's moral standards (lines 19–20) but in other parts of the narrative he presents himself as a patriarchal male with contempt for women (lines 7 and 23) and as a sexually experienced man, who recognises vibrators and knows what they are used for (lines 13, 21). Hegemonic masculinity is achieved by the subordination of the female character in the story through negative stereotypes: 'whinging bitch', 'big fat pig' as well as the implication that she is immoral because she owns a vibrator when there are children in the house. Gary also implies that the woman is technically incompetent, 'there's like nothing wrong with her computer at all' (line 6). So while Gary presents himself in a range of positive ways, the female character in the story is described in more simplistic and negative terms. The other men's laughter at the story (lines 14 and 16) and the comments in lines 17–18 and 22 establish group complicity of Gary's hegemonic masculinity. Line 22 'was she very nice looking?' also positions the men as heterosexual, where the physical attractiveness of the woman is viewed as a relevant detail. Although no women were present to hear Gary's narrative, it also serves as an indirect way of regulating female sexuality, informing the other men present that a woman who owns a vibrator is noteworthy and 'funny' (line 8). The potentially threatening nature of female sexual desire existing outside male-female sexual relations is therefore defused by framing the story as humorous and the central character as immoral, ugly and whinging.

Coates (2002) gives a number of examples of such narratives where women are either denigrated or occur as peripheral characters in stories as wives or mothers. Using a quantitative analysis to back up her qualitative findings, she notes (2002: 121) that in the men's stories she analysed, 96 percent of the protagonists and 72 percent of the other characters were male, a finding which was not replicated with female stories where 86 percent included both men and women as central characters. Coates concludes that this absence of women from the 'storyworld of men's stories is a disturbing aspect of all-male narrative. These narratives do important ideological work, maintaining a discourse position where men are all-important and women are invisible' (2002: 121–22). Women are therefore marginalised as well as subordinated.

The subordination of women is not the only way in which hegemonic masculinity is established. Kiesling's research (1997, 2002) shows how hegemonic masculinities are negotiated in relation to other masculinities. Men position themselves as superior to other types of men, by policing the limits of what constitutes acceptable *masculine* behaviour. Kiesling recorded conversations between American students who belonged to fraternities (Greek-letter societies). He notes that, 'in interaction, men metaphorically represent other men as women in order to claim dominance over that man (even in play)' for example, by saying 'Honey I'm home' or referring to each other as 'bitch' (2002: 265). Like Coates, Kiesling found that story-telling played a significant role in the construction of hegemonic masculinities and heterosexual identity, with 'fuck stories' – tales about the sexual conquest of women – being a common narrative genre. He concludes that, 'male domination in heterosexual displays is about men displaying power over other men (and women) to other men. The stories and other forms of heterosexual display therefore represent same-sex status competition in which heterosexual gender differentiation and dominance is not the goal, but one strategy with which to construct a hegemonic masculinity' (2002: 266).

The examples above have both focused on the subordination of women in different ways. The following conversation, which took place in the changing room of a gym which I regularly attend, demonstrates another form of subordination. (Names have been changed to protect the identities of the participants.)

Batman and Robin
Mark and Tom are both males in their early 20s.

```
 1 Mark:  so are you going to Becky's party?
 2 Tom:   party?
 3 Mark:  yeah (.) I'm trying to rope John into coming with me (.) We've got a costume
 4        worked out
 5 Tom:   What are you going as?
 6 Mark:  I was going to be (.) Batman and John's got a Robin costume
 7 Tom:   riiiight
 8 Mark:  Except his costume is just this green lycra thing (.) He's going to look like a
 9        complete tit
10 Tom:   (laughing) What's yours?
11 Mark:  Mine's like this red body suit and it's got these foam muscles down the front
12        (.) So at least I'm not going to look *completely* gay
```

The two men in this conversation obliquely orient themselves to hegemonic masculinity in a number of ways. First, we should consider the context in which the conversation took place – a changing room where men undress in front of each other. This is a potentially face-threatening situation: the two participants must avoid looking directly at each other's bodies as this may imply sexual interest in each other. The topic and direction of the conversation may also be perceived as a possible compromise of Tom's and Mark's masculinity, particularly as Mark is referring to going to a fancy dress party with another man (which may indicate possible homosexuality) and talking about what they are going to wear – clothing choices being a stereotypically 'feminine' topic of conversation (lines 3–12).

The costume itself is also potentially problematic: Batman and Robin are fictional 'superhero' friends who appeared in a camp (by today's standards) 1960s television series of the same name; consequently, the choice of costume may also lead to speculation about Mark's sexuality. Tom's drawn-out response (line 7) *riiiight* was spoken sarcastically or quizzically, suggesting that he had acknowledged the potential compromise of masculinity and was orientating himself to it in a humorous way. But Tom's utterance also functions as both a warning and a form of implicit judgement. Mark is required to accommodate Tom's *riiiight* for the remainder of the exchange, working to defuse the question mark that has built up over his masculinity in order to re-establish his heterosexual/masculine credentials.

So Mark's disavowal of his friend's costume (lines 8–9), 'He's going to look like a complete tit', allows him to construct John as occupying a subordinate (and possibly feminine) position to himself – the word *tit* can be used as a colloquial term for a female breast. Also, Mark's description of his own costume (lines 11–12) contains an acknowledgement of the compromising nature of the costume, along with a disclaimer, 'at least I'm not going to look *completely* gay'. The conversation therefore contains a casual subordination of homosexuality. The presence of 'muscles down the front' of the costume (line 11) is given as the reason for protecting Mark's sexuality/gender identity – an association between heterosexuality, masculinity and muscularity. However, talk of men's muscles is also a potentially 'dangerous' subject: while the muscles in Mark's suit rescue him from being seen as 'completely gay', his acknowledgement that muscles constitute a preferred manifestation of masculinity could be interpreted as *his* finding muscles attractive.

It should also be noted that Mark's use of *gay* (line 12) is ambiguous. As well as being used to refer to homosexuality, the meaning of the term has shifted for some users to refer to anything that is pathetic or useless. However, this new meaning still draws on a conceptualisation of gay as something bad and is more likely to be due to polysemy rather than the two meanings being accidental homonyms, for example, those who characterised gay people as pathetic probably extended the term to refer to *anything* that is pathetic. Or it may have been that younger people heard older people using *gay* with negative intent and engaged in semantic over-extension of the word, not realising that it only referred to sexuality.[2]

Mark's negative use of *gay* in a public space, with other people listening, is open to a range of interpretations. He may have made the heteronormative assumption that everyone around him is heterosexual and holds similar opinions. Or he may have been suspicious of the sexuality of the other people present and wanted to signal to them that he is *not* gay. Another possibility is that he did not directly connect his use of *gay* to homosexuality. A less likely (but plausible) option is that he wanted to bring up the subject of homosexuality, perhaps to see what sort of response it would evoke, but the only way he could do so as a supposedly heterosexual man, was by disavowal.[3] Therefore, Mark constructs his own gender identity by engaging in the subordination of other identities: 'completely gay' and 'a right tit'. Complicity is shown through Tom's laughter (line 10) and the silence of the other men who were present in the changing room. Mark's rather homophobic remark in line 12 went unchallenged – his conceptualisation of masculinity legitimised.

Ambiguous uses of *gay* are also observed by Cameron (1997), who examined a number of conversations between (nominally heterosexual) male college students where they criticised other male students who were not present as being gay. She notes that, oddly, it was unclear whether the students being talked about *were* actually gay. For example, in one case, the men talked about 'four homos' who were continually 'hitting on' (making sexual overtures) one of the women who was described as 'the ugliest-ass bitch in the history of the world'. Clearly, men who 'hit on' women are not engaging in stereotypically homosexual behaviour, yet none of the speakers noted this apparent irony. Cameron (1997: 52–3) suggests that the contradiction can be resolved if the term *gay* is understood not in terms of sexual deviance but gender deviance for these speakers. The four male students who hit on the 'ugliest-ass bitch' were failing to live up to gender norms: hegemonic masculinity requires the object of desire not just to be female but also to be physically attractive. In the same way, Tom's discussion of his Batman costume as not looking 'completely gay' could also be read as his referring to gender rather than sexuality. The important point here is that for the maintenance of hegemonic masculinity, sexuality and gender must be conflated so as to appear indistinguishable. For men, masculinity must equate with heterosexuality and vice versa. If gender and sexuality are framed as separate and independent entities then we could conceive of the existence of a masculine gay man, or an effeminate heterosexual man. Such people would potentially confuse and threaten the status quo and blur the hard boundaries between the hegemonic in-group, and the subordinate and marginalised out-groups.

As Coates (2002: 196) writes of her analysis of a large number of male conversations, 'In most of the conversations most of the time, it is evident that male speakers are acting in a way that aligns them with these dominant norms, norms which prescribe 'acceptable' maleness'. And as Frosh et al. (2002: 75–6) point out, the dominant mode of 'being a man' is typically associated with, 'heterosexuality, toughness, power and authority, competitiveness and the subordination of gay men'.

While homophobic discourses are one way of ensuring that men maintain their powerful masculine/heterosexual identities, social changes in western societies have meant that such overt rejections of homosexuality are now often interpreted as a form of oppression, with homophobia viewed as an unacceptable form of intolerance. Competing discourses are therefore at work – with the older more established discourses of compulsory heterosexuality and hegemonic masculinity clashing with newer discourses of equality, tolerance or 'vive la différence'. The following example, taken from Speer and Potter (2002: 168–69) show how such conflicting discourses are carefully negotiated by a male who identifies as heterosexual. In this excerpt, Sue interviews Ben, a male friend in his mid-20s. Before the excerpt quoted, Sue has asked Ben if he has ever been to a gay club. Ben describes a time he went to one with his girlfriend and was 'chatted up' by a man there.

```
1 Sue:    Was he attractive?
2         (0.6)
3 Ben:    Phh.
4         (1.8)
5         I s'pose he was reasonably well looking,
6         Yeah.
7         (1.6)
8         But you know it doesn't interest me,
9         (.)
10        I'm definitely (0.8)
11        Not interest(h)ed(h) in(h) men)(h)
12 Sue:   hhh.
13        (0.8)
14 Ben:   You know, I think,
15        Yeah some men as- as,
16        I'm sure it's the same for women (0.6)
17        find (.) other men-
18        think that other men-
19        'he looks really good'.
20        (0.4) That's definite.
21        You know
22        some men will deny that
23 Sue:   Mm
24 Ben:   but I know people who I think
```

25   'bloody-hell he's absolutely awesome (.)
26   figure, awesome'.
27   You know.
28   Looks cool.
29   Totally and utterly.
30   Because I know I don't.
31   You know the- the- the Adonis type=
32 Sue: =Mm=
33 Ben: =physique and
34   (.)
35   whatever you know
36 Sue: Mm

Speer and Potter (2002: 169–71) show how Ben uses his talk to produce a response to Sue's question (line 1), which takes into account the potential conflict between discourses. Given that Sue has asked a yes/no question 'Was he attractive?' Ben's response is notable due to its length. His multiple short utterances and frequent pauses suggest that this is a carefully-worded response to a problematic topic. If Ben were to answer 'yes, I found him attractive' then he may construct himself as gay, but if he says 'no, I didn't', he may position himself as homophobic. Therefore, Ben needs to answer in a way which allows him to present himself as heterosexual yet non-heterosexist. Initially, his response is vague (line 5) 'I s'pose he was reasonably well looking', but then he gives a series of denials (lines 8–11) 'it doesn't interest me, I'm definitely not interested in men'. Having established that he is not gay, Ben then works to deflect the possibility that his earlier remarks may be interpreted as homophobic. 'I'm sure it's the same for women' (line 16), 'other men think that other men 'he looks really good'' (lines 17–19). In other words, he suggests that it is normal for both women and men to notice when a person of the same sex is physically attractive, although 'some men will deny that' (line 22). Ben therefore shows awareness of the competing discourses in society and negotiates a path between them where he is able to maintain a heterosexual identity without characterising homosexuality as problematic. We may also want to consider context again – Ben is aware that his remarks are being tape-recorded and he is talking to a female researcher in the social sciences. In other, less formal contexts, heterosexual males may not always feel required to give such a qualified response.

The examples above have concentrated on men performing hegemonic masculinity. But what about men who do not want to, or are not able to, engage in that gender performance? Speer and Potter's research suggests that some men are aware of, and negotiate, conflicting gendered discourse positions, while Edley and Wetherell (1997) were similarly interested in the more sensitive 'new man' identity and the ways in which males negotiated existing discourses of masculinity with respect to particular rhetorical or micro-political contexts. They carried out interviews with small groups of male sixth form students (aged 17–18) at a single-sex independent school in the UK. Their analysis focused on the talk of one group, who were considered to be 'subordinate' males, when compared to a dominant group, who were referred to as 'rugby players' or 'hard lads'. The rugby players were physically stronger than the other students, would take over communal space with boisterous games and had their dominant status supported by formal structures within the school. So the 'honours' system recognised sporting achievement in a more explicit way than academic success and positions of authority in the student body (such as the head boy and prefect positions) tended to be filled by the rugby players, personally selected by the school's staff.

There was antipathy between the two groups, with the subordinate males referring to the 'hard lads' as 'a complete bunch of wankers' and claiming to 'hate their guts'. Edley and Wetherell were interested in how the non-rugby playing group constructed alternative, counter-hegemonic identities for themselves. They noted that the non-rugby playing group often defined themselves in relationship to the hegemonic group, using a number of (sometimes conflicting) strategies. Below, I quote from one of the members, Neil.

Extract 1

Neil: Oh <u>yeah</u> (1.0) because (2.0) I've got this theory that erm (1.0) I'm ss(.) I don't do anything (.) I'm scared of getting hurt (.) I mean I suppose everybody is but er (1.0) <u>yeah</u> I do I mean er if a wimp (1.0) a wimp (2.0) if a wimp's somebody who'll <u>back</u> down from a <u>fight</u> or won't get into them (.) and is seen as being (.) you know (.) physically less able (.) then that's fine (.) I'm happy with that

Extract 2

Neil: Actually (.) just thinking like that I think you know a wimp is probably not just physically (.) I think people who are mentally weak as well (.) and I don't think I'm mentally weak as in I can't stand up for myself verbally or you know (.) or perhaps a wimp's someone's who's timid and shy as well […] I mean we could probably strike a balance between you know (.) talking about what they talk (.) talking about you know probably we'd class as the other people's talk because I mean they talk about all sorts you know (.) there's this lad Kelner who'll talk about nuclear physics or something you know spiel on for hours and the other lot'll talk about how did United do at the weekend and did you see that gorgeous bit of tot or whatever (1.0) so I think we probably (.) you know we talk about some interesting things including some bits in the middle.

Extract 3

Neil: I mean you could probably draw a list up (.) of what the qualities that make you
eligible for [the hard group] (.) I mean (.) you've probably got to be attractive (.)
handsome (.) good at sport (.) physically strong and I'd probably say mentally
<u>weak</u> to go along with them [laughter] but I mean you've got to be (.) probably
pretty sheepish follow the herd to do that whereas I doubt if one of them would
stand out and say something against their whole group whereas one of us lot
wouldn't think twice about it

(.)   Short pause of less than 1 second
[…]   Material omitted
<u>Text</u>   Word(s) emphasised
[text]   Clarificatory information

Adapted from Edley and Wetherell (1997: 210–11)

In these three extracts, Neil orientates himself to the discredited 'wimp' identity
in different ways. In extract 1, he defines a 'wimp' as someone who backs down
from a fight and is physically less able. He then accepts possession of the wimp
identity: 'I'm happy with that'. Such a strategy suggests a form of appropriation,
in the same way that words like *bitch*, *queer*, *slut* and *nigger* have been appropriated or 'reclaimed' by different groups. However, in extract 2, Neil produces
a different version of 'wimp' which he then goes on to distance himself from.
Here, a wimp is someone who is 'mentally weak', which he says he is not. Edley
and Wetherell (1997: 211) suggest that there is a kind of complicity occurring
here in Neil's talk: he admits to not having the physical strength of the rugby
players, but claims to at least possess *some* kind of strength – so his identity here
is still dependent on some level of proximity to the 'hard' group, with strength
being the key factor. And he views himself as being closer to this group than
someone like Kelner, who talks about nuclear physics for hours. Neil therefore
positions his group as existing between two states – the sport-and-sex obsessed
hard lads and boys who are obsessed with science.

Complicity appears to continue in extract 3 where Neil draws up a compli-
mentary list of traits that are required to belong to the hard group: handsome,
good at sport, strong. However, he again contrasts physical strength with
mental strength, suggesting that members of the hard group are conformists
who are unable or afraid to go against the herd. So Neil again represents both
groups as being strong *and* weak, but in different ways. In a later section of the
interview (not shown here), Neil and other members of his group construct
the 'hard group' as being unsophisticated, unable to control their aggression
in civilised ways and frequently resorting to violence, suggesting that the 'hard

group' feel the need to 'prove' their masculinity because they are insecure. In this way, Neil's group 'turns the tables' on the hegemonic group, claiming that it is their group which is actually more masculine, because they are more secure in their gendered selves. Edley and Wetherell's research shows that subordinated masculinities experience a complex and ambivalent relationship with hegemonic masculinity – acknowledging hegemony, defining themselves in relation to what they are not, complicit with but at the same time opposed to and scornful of those at the top of the gender hierarchy.

Hegemonic masculinity is not restricted to spoken conversations between groups of men. Its importance in society ensures that it is displayed through gender performance or discourse in a wide range of contexts. For example, Talbot (1997a) examined heterosexual masculinity in an article about sexual harassment in *The Sun* newspaper (a British tabloid). She noted that the article contained a combination of different discourses: reference to a 'male sexual drive' discourse (the belief that men have a biological need to have regular sex – discussed later in this chapter) and the objectification of women. But the article also contained a feminist counter-discourse, whose presence, Talbot suggests, is in response to social changes brought about by feminism. She concludes that, 'the capacity to blend such seemingly contradictory discourses… might enable hegemonic masculinity to withstand the risk of larger, more disruptive structural changes' (1997: 186). Similarly, Benwell (2002), in examining men's lifestyle magazines like *FHM*, *Maxim* and *Loaded* notes that they are written from a position which, 'primarily defines itself in hierarchical contrast to subordinate groups of constructs e.g. femininity, women, gay men, hippies. In addition, this masculinity embraces qualities of physicality, violence, autonomy, wit and irony' (2002: 158). The following example is from a description of bottled water in another men's magazine, *GQ*.

> Water for Men: This isn't some fancy, foreign water, full of poncy minerals. This extra-butch bottled water contains just one mineral: salt, and plenty of it. And because it's oestrogen-free it won't turn you into a eunuch like tap water does.
>
> *GQ* June 1997: 29 (quoted in Benwell, 2002: 164)

The description of the bottled water is meant to be humorous, countering a presupposition that drinking bottled water is unmanly, by pointing out that this particular brand is not *fancy* or *foreign* (denigrating a kind of upper-class, cultured masculinity) or full of *poncy* minerals (*ponce* is an abusive colloquialism for a number of socially tabooed sexual identities: pimps, homosexuals, effeminates, paedophiles). It points out that this water is actually better (in terms of masculinity) than tap water (which, it is claimed, contains oestrogen). The article therefore makes fun of male concerns about appearing effeminate by its use of exaggeration 'extra-butch' and over-justification of the masculinity of the bottled water. However, there is ambiguity here: although the irony and humour serve to place distance between the surface meaning and the intended meaning of the article, Benwell suggests that the surface meaning is not cancelled out – a trace remains. Irony preserves both the literal and non-literal meanings simultaneously, so that the writer can maintain traditional, masculine values and appear to be making fun of them at the same time. Therefore, in these magazines irony is used as a defence against the possibility of gender or sexual ambiguity – overcoming the potential problem of men being seen to be overly concerned with traditionally 'female' topics like fashion, diet and skin care, as well as disavowing the possibility of homosexual desire because the magazines display attractive male bodies to be looked at by other men. Benwell concludes that irony is another way in which hegemonic masculinity is able to accommodate social change. Rather than playing a subversive role (as shown in the BLO and *Five Go Mad in Dorset* examples in Chapter 4), irony and humour can also serve the more reactionary, conservative function of maintaining the status quo of hegemonic masculinity and compulsory heterosexuality (Benwell, 2002: 170). A derogatory remark, made at the expense of women or gay men, is more difficult to counter if it is couched as a joke.

Hegemonic femininity?

The focus on masculinities, and in particular the positioning of masculinities in relationship to hegemonic masculinity suggests that, to an extent, the Dominance model of male language (see Chapter 2) survives, although now in a more complex guise: men are preoccupied by establishing dominance over everyone – women and other men – by positioning themselves on a hierarchy. But we should not always conclude that marginalisation, subordination and complicity only occur with heterosexual males (traditionally those most closely associated with hegemonic masculinity). Rowe (2000), for example, identifies hegemonic homosexualities, discussed in more detailed in Chapter 6.

By the same token the Diversity model discussed at the beginning of Chapter 3 (which focuses on differences between men and between women) suggests that not all men engage in dominance-establishing hegemonic masculinity, and that not all women are co-operative all the time. Some writers have focused on women's communication in terms of its being friendly and co-operative. For example Coates (1996: 27) in her examination of women's talk, notes that 'women find conflict scary' although 'like any intimate relationship, friendship between women has its sticky moments'. Coates concentrates on the range of techniques that women use to *resolve* conflict, such as negotiation through talk, compromise, change in attitudes, anger and hostility. And, on the whole, she is very positive about the way that women's friendships are achieved through talk, concluding that her book is a, 'celebration of its richness and power, complexity and creativity' (1995: 286). This is in sharp contrast to the conclusion of her book on men's talk (2003: 200–201), which she views as more contradictory, inexpressive and sociable (on a rather superficial 'having a laugh' level) rather than intimate. Men's talk is therefore constrained by hegemonic masculinity – fears of appearing weak or effeminate – whereas women's conversation has the capacity to be more intimate.

While it is difficult to disagree with Coates' interpretations of the dozens of conversations she examined, we should not generalise to the point where all women are seen as constantly co-operative and afraid of conflict. Counter-examples are provided by Simmons (2002) and Wiseman (2002) who studied cliques of girls in American high-schools, noting that power hierarchies are established among girls, but often in more subtle and sophisticated ways than among boys. Wiseman's chapter titles include 'Uninvited: The Sixth Grade Birthday Party' and 'Even 11-year-olds Will Accuse Each Other of Acting like Sluts'. She describes compliment-giving among girl cliques as a complex ritual of negative politeness, where in order to maintain social status, girls must give compliments to other girls on their physical appearance, while at the same time denigrating themselves. Roles within cliques are also arranged in terms of a power structure, with Wiseman identifying social roles such as 'queen bees', 'wannabes', 'messengers', 'bankers' and 'targets'. Such emphasis on subtle competition and hierarchies suggests a gender performance which combines aspects of hegemonic masculinity with femininity.

Somewhat differently, however, the concept of *hegemonic femininity* (Bordo, 1993: 316) 'has a strong emphasis on appearance with the dominant notion of an ideal feminine body as thin and toned', and is identified as having strong associations with heterosexual sex and romance and whiteness. Choi (2000) and Krane (2001) write about sportswomen who are expected to per-form hegemonic femininity (e.g. wearing pink) while distancing themselves from behaviour seen as masculine – a difficult feat, as in order to be successful athletes they must develop characteristics that are stereotypically associ-ated with masculinity such as strength, independence and competitiveness. Holmes and Schnurr (2006) examined the speech of two senior women in the workplace, finding that they employed a range of different interactional strategies in various contexts when appropriate, which included drawing on normative masculine *and* feminine ways of talking, as well as parodying femininity in some circumstances (see also Chapter 2). They conclude that, 'As women who are secure in their professional identities, it seems that they do not to need to downplay the fact that they are female or minimise gender differences in aspects of their behaviour in order to ensure they are taken seriously' (Holmes and Schnurr, 2006: 44). Yet they also found that in some workplaces, typically feminine ways of interacting would attract negative comment or derision.

Similarly, Baxter (2003: 32) notes that her post-structuralist feminist analysis reveals, 'substantive examples of women/girls not only resisting positions of powerlessness but also taking up more active subject positions relative to men/boys... Theories of females as universal victims of patriarchy no longer *do*'. However, she also notes (2003: 32) that, 'This does not mean that feminist post-structuralism considers males and females to be equivalently positioned in terms of the ways in which power is negotiated through gender relations. Its focus is on the *pervasiveness* of dominant discourses of gender differentiation which often interact with other discourses to 'fix' women/girls in positions of relative powerlessness, despite 'breakthrough' moments of resistance and empowerment'.

Connell (1987: 183) argues that, 'there is no femininity that is hegemonic in the sense that the dominant form of masculinity is hegemonic amongst men'. Connell (1987: 183) therefore prefers the term 'emphasised femininity' as it positions *all* femininity as subordinate. Such a point is made clear by examining some of Wiseman's data, as in the following interview with a teenage girl:

> When I was in junior high, there was this new girl that a bunch of guys liked. Two girls in the grade went around with a petition they made all the boys sign that said 'I will never go out with the megawhore, Lori Shore.' After a while, one of her best friends told her about the petition. One of the girls flat out said 'Yeah, I did it and what are you going to do about it?' The other girl was a really good friend of Lori's and kept denying it and pretending to be her friend.
>
> Hope 17, from Wiseman (2002: 135)

At a first glance, it looks as if this is a case of female subordination of other females *and* males – after all, it is girls who are making other boys sign a petition against another girl. However, it could be argued that with Wiseman and Simmon's female cliques, girls adhere to traditional male double-standards in order to impose power over one another – for example, by calling each other *megawhore*. Additionally, emphasised femininity is achieved through *male* approval and attention. The new girl threatens to disrupt the established power hierarchy among other girls because she is liked by 'a bunch of guys'.

By characterising the new girl as promiscuous, she is constructed as 'cheating' by failing to conform to gender norms which prescribe that females should withhold sex or at least play 'hard to get'. The petition effectively takes away any potential power that the new girl may obtain from male attention. So male hegemony is maintained through female complicity – it is girls who carry out the policing of other girls. It is notable that no evaluation or commentary occurs regarding *male* promiscuous behaviour, perhaps because such behaviour is considered to be more acceptable. And, ironically, being a 'slut' may be a negative identity, but it does afford girls a relatively small amount of power as another of Wiseman's interviewees, Sasha (aged 14), is quoted as saying: 'Boys may call me a slut, but at least they call' (Wiseman, 2002: 134). Yet the regulation of girls who are labelled 'sluts' invalidates most of the potential power that comes with such an identity.

As Simmons (2002) points out, the use of more subtle forms of aggression, which she refers to as being catty, crafty or cunning, can also be seen as playing to male rules: women are tabooed from engaging in physical aggression or more fragrant displays of power – which are punished with social rejection.

In order to demonstrate that terms that denigrate women are not used exclusively by men, Table 5.1 shows frequencies of such terms in the spoken section of the British National Corpus. The contexts of words were investigated so that occurrences which were not used in an abusive manner and directed towards another person were not counted.

Table 5.1. Male and female frequencies of abusive terms towards women in the spoken section of the BNC. Numbers in brackets show standardised frequencies per million words of data

	Male frequency	Female frequency
bitch	36 (7.3)	53 (16.22)
slag	5 (1.01)	4 (1.22)
whore	3 (0.60)	7 (1.42)
cunt	55 (11.11)	17 (5.20)
tart	7 (1.42)	13 (3.97)
hussy	0 (0)	5 (1.53)

Bearing in mind that there is more male speech in the BNC than female speech (about 4.9 million words vs. 3.3 million words respectively), the standardised frequencies in brackets above suggest that, comparatively, although these terms are rare, females used all the above words slightly more often than males except for *cunt*. The following is an excerpt of a female use of *slag* in the corpus:

Unidentified speaker:	The rumour's going around that erm Dave and <pause> yeah <unclear>
Kath:	Well Pete <anonymised> walked in on them and apparently they were butt naked and shagging away <pause> and it was a load of crap ....
Unidentified speaker:	Who? Georgia and Dave.
Kath:	Though she's such a slag, I'm sorry but she…

British National Corpus: File KPH, lines 964–69

Kath constructs Georgia as subordinate by labelling her with an insult, 'such a slag', but at the same time, she positions herself as complicit within a hegemonic structure where male values determine the hierarchy. As Talbot (1998: 217) notes, 'what is the male equivalent of a nymphomaniac or a slut? There is none'. Clearly, though, the meanings of such terms are never fixed; in other conversations in the BNC, women refer to men as slags, and in one conversation a female jokingly refers to herself as a 'big slag'. The term *bitch* has been reclaimed by some women as a positive concept, whereas Easton and Lizst (1997: 4) have reclaimed and degendered the word *slut*, to mean 'a person of any gender who has the courage to lead life according to the radical proposition that sex is nice and pleasure is good for you'.

Writers like Levy (2005) have suggested that another way in which some women have achieved a kind of power over others is by becoming what she calls *female chauvinist pigs*. Levy suggests that a number of practices which could be described as demeaning or compromising women in various ways: going to strip clubs which feature female performers, wearing clothes with the Playboy logo, being interested in porn, working for men's magazines like *Maxim*, having breast implants, taking pole-dancing lessons, getting Brazilian waxes, 'being like a man' etc., have started to become popular with some women, who view them as sexy, fun, liberating and rebellious. Levy argues that such women are becoming complicit exploiters of other women and themselves. By showing approval of the dominant male hegemonic structure, they are awarded some power. However, this power comes at the expense of other women (see also Chapter 6).

Another way in which hegemonic masculinity maintains its ascendancy is through its association with desirability and, particularly, sexual desire. The following excerpt demonstrates the relationship between hegemonic masculinity and 'hegemonic' or emphasised femininity. It is taken from a Mills and Boon romance novel called *A Real McCoy*. According to their UK website[4], Mills and Boon cover almost 75 percent of the UK romance novel market, and 200 million books are sold worldwide each year – one sale every 6.6 seconds.

There are 3.2 million regular readers in the UK, of which the vast majority are women. About 57 percent of these readers spend three hours a week or more reading Mills and Boon's books. The books are, therefore, broadly popular and the discourses found within them have the potential to influence a large number of women.

Although Mills and Boon books may seem to be an 'easy target', I decided to investigate a recently published story, which at a first glance appeared to have taken feminist discourses into account. In earlier decades, Mills and Boon romance novels focused on women in stereotypically 'supportive' roles such as nurses, secretaries and air stewardesses. However, *A Real McCoy* was published in 2006 and its main protagonist is a female criminal defence lawyer called Kat Buckingham who is described, according to the summary on the back cover, as someone who 'could handle just about anything'. Rather than being constructed as a passive 'Barbie doll', reliant on male approval, Kat instead appears to be an independent and competent professional.

In the novel, Kat discovers she is adopted, is wrongfully arrested for the murder of her fiancé, and is then carried off into protective custody by a 'sexy, secretive stranger'. The main narrative of the novel therefore constructs Kat as someone who is overwhelmed by events that are beyond her control. And in the excerpt below, she begins a sexual encounter with Harry, the sexy, secretive stranger, which similarly focuses on her loss of control.

1   She'd never done anything so impulsive before. Not with James, not with anybody.
2   Everything had been perfectly timed. Third date, kiss good night. Fifth date, a little
3   scratch and tickle. Seventh date, they'd made their way to the bedroom. Not in a
4   flash of passion, but instead as an almost detached natural progression, like she'd said
5   'Okay, I like him, he likes me, let's go to the next stage.'
6   This unexpected mouth watering need she wasn't sure what to do with.
7   Her eyes began drifting closed and her heart hammered a thick rhythm in her chest.
8   Heat, sure and swift, surged to her delicate parts. At some point she'd lifted her right
9   hand and her fingers splayed against the side of his face, the stubble there scratching
10 the sensitized skin of her palm. He gently coaxed her lips open and she allowed him
11 access to her mouth, exploring his with the same lazy strokes, the sensations
12 hardening her nipples, making her underpants feel suddenly damp.
13 She heard a groan and realized Harry had made the low, guttural sound. He slid
14 sideways on the couch, his arms going around her, shifting her until she lay almost
15 completely flush against him. His fingers burned a path across her shoulders, down
16 to cup her bottom, then tunnelled under the back of her T-shirt and pressed her too
17 hot skin.
18 Kat gave an involuntary shiver, loving the feeling of his hands on her, his mouth
19 kissing her. It somehow seemed…right. She found herself moving until his thick,

20 hard length pressed against her lower belly, shooting fresh pangs of want and need
21 bulleting through her as she sought even closer contact.
22 The hands at her back unhooked her bra and then skimmed up her sides. She lifted
23 her shoulders slightly to give him access and just like that his hands caressed her bare
24 breasts. Kat moaned and the intensity of their kiss increased… She'd never felt so…
25 unable to control her own actions. So much at the mercy of her own desires.
26 She slid her fingers down his chest to his stomach and then lower still until she cupped
27 his length in her palm through his jeans.
28 Harry abruptly pulled away, looking like a kid who'd got caught with his hand in the
29 cookie jar. Although it was her who had her hand in a naughty place.
30 'Whoa,' he said, practically leaping from the couch.

Tori Carrington (2006) *A Real McCoy* pp. 121–23

The excerpt accesses a number of discourses of gender and sexuality. As with the vast majority – if not all – of the Mills and Boon novels, there is a heteronormative discourse in evidence: women are meant to find men physically desirable and vice versa. The excerpt does not contain a detailed description of Harry, but we are given three details: he takes control (lines 10–17, 22, 28–30), he has stubble on his face (line 9) and he makes a 'low guttural sound' (line 13) when aroused. All three details suggest a stereotyped, masculine gender performance in terms of Harry's behaviour, his physical appearance and his voice. In this way, discourses of desire are connected to particular stereotyped gender performances. As Talbot (1997b: 106) notes of male heroes in Mills and Boon novels, '…they are physically perfect, powerful and dominating. They are embodiments of hegemonic masculinity, presented as desirable, highly eroticised and utterly irresistible'.

At the same time, though, the excerpt contains discourses about the ways that women should behave in the context of a romantic relationship. The beginning of the excerpt (lines 1–5) reveals information about Kat's sexual history – that she is sexually experienced, but doesn't normally have sex with a man until the seventh date. This establishes Kat's credentials as the heroine of the book – a rather prescriptive 'nice girls aren't easy' discourse is referenced (echoing the story about the 'megawhore' petition, above), whereby women are expected to withhold sex within a relationship for a time, so they do not appear promiscuous. It could be argued that this discourse creates expectations about men too – an implicit aspect of this being that men are (mainly) interested in sex (a reference to the 'male sexual drive' discourse) and will lose interest in a woman if they obtain sex too early; they need to be held back, in order to get to know the woman first.

The bulk of the excerpt is taken up with a description of the physical contact between Kat and Harry. Although the narrative is written from Kat's perspective, she is relatively passive during most of this description. For example, lines 10–11: 'He gently coaxed her lips open and *she allowed him access* to her mouth'. Lines 14–15: 'his arms going around her, *shifting her* until she lay almost completely flush against him'. Lines 22–24: 'The hands at her back unhooked her bra and then skimmed up her sides. *She lifted her shoulders slightly to give him access* and just like that his hands caressed her bare breasts'. Kat's early actions in the narrative are framed in terms of her allowing Harry to have 'access' to her body: she needs to be 'gently coaxed' like an animal or a child. At various points, Harry's contact with Kat is described with verbs which suggest pain rather than pleasure: lines 8–9, 'the stubble there *scratching* the sensitized skin of her palm'; and line 15, 'His fingers *burned* a path across her shoulders'. In lines 19–21, the need that Kat feels in response to Harry's 'thick hard length' results in 'shooting' pangs 'bulleting' through her – contact with Harry's penis therefore causes a sensation more akin to contact with a gun, framing the sexual relationship in a metaphor of aggressor/victim.

When Kat does take a more active lead in the sexual activity, it is described as unusual for her, and in terms of her losing control: line 6, 'This *unexpected* mouth watering need *she wasn't sure what to do with*'; lines 8–9, '*At some point* she'd lifted her right hand' (suggesting she is so distracted that she is not aware of when exactly she lifted her hand); line 18, 'Kat gave an *involuntary* shiver'; lines 24–25, 'She'd never felt so… *unable to control her own actions. So much at the mercy of her own desires*'. There is a discourse here of sexual desire as uncontrolled. As noted earlier in this chapter, Holloway (1984: 223) has pointed out that this understanding of sexuality is normally associated with men, referring to it as 'male sexual drive'. Sunderland (2004: 59–60) points out that the men whom Holloway interviewed regarded themselves as not being the agents of their sexuality, and that the 'male sexual drive' discourse may play an important legitimising role (for example, by justifying male attacks on women). It is notable here, therefore, that the 'sexual drive' discourse is afforded to a woman, although the fact that it is described as unusual tends to confirm the sexual drive discourse as normally relating to males. Kat's sexual response is therefore coded as male.

The problematic nature of Kat's 'masculine' sexual drive is emphasised towards the end of the extract, when she needs to be brought back under control by the male character. In lines 28–30, Harry responds to Kat's touching of his penis (through his jeans) by abruptly pulling back and saying 'Whoa', showing that it is he who expects to be able to control the rate and amount of sexual activity that occurs. The word 'whoa' is interesting: it implies that Harry is 'holding the reins' and positions Kat as little more than an animal who is being driven or ridden. It is therefore acceptable for Harry to undress and fondle Kat (lines 15–17, 22–24), but she must remain passive. Kat is punished for her 'transgression' (acting like a man) by having the sexual encounter terminated by Harry. So while the excerpt suggests that women can also have a 'sexual drive', they are still expected to take a passive sexual role, letting men control the interaction. A 'male dominance' or 'male as active/female as passive' discourse is accessed.

As well as the roles of the two participants, the way that sexual activity is described in the excerpt is also of interest in terms of gendered discourses. Sexual body parts are sometimes referred to coyly through euphemisms: line 8, 'her delicate parts'; lines 20 and 27 'his length'; and line 29, 'a naughty place'. The usual target audience of Mills and Boon novels is women, and this suggests another way that the audience are positioned in relation to the text – sexual terms should not be presented too explicitly. Instead, women should be more interested in how people *feel* during sex rather than reading about explicit descriptions of body parts. So instead there are references to mouth watering need (line 6), Kat's heartbeat (line 7), dampness (line 12), feelings of heat or burning (lines 8, 15 and 16) and pangs of want and need (line 20).

The term 'naughty place' is interesting – 'naughty' being an adjective often associated with children (in the British National Corpus, *naughty* strongly co-occurs or collocates with the words, *boy*, *girl*, *child* and their plurals). Furthermore, the reference to 'the kid who'd had his hand caught in the cookie jar' (lines 28–29) compares sexual activity to a childish indiscretion. But sex is only naughty when Kat initiates it.

The excerpt then reveals numerous ways in which discourses of gender, sexuality and desire are inter-connected as well as how they are orientated to hegemonic masculinity. Romantic fiction generally describes 'idealised' sexual encounters – those which readers are expected to recognise as perfect. The excerpt tells the reader how women should ideally experience perfect sexual desire and who the ideal object of desire should be. In this case, the perfect encounter is ruined by Kat's transgression in attempting to take a more domi-nant role. Such a description may serve to inform or warn (female) readers about acceptable and unacceptable behaviours for men and women.

As the heroine of a Mills and Boon romance, Kat could be said to embody many of the characteristics of hegemonic or emphasised femininity – hetero-sexual, white and physically attractive. In addition, she is a 'career-woman', independent from men, suggesting that her character combines different types of femininity. However, the more dominant aspects of Kat's identity are constructed as problematic during the sexual encounter – her taking the lead during sex is viewed as so transgressive that her male partner takes control and ends their encounter. As Talbot (1997b: 118) observes, 'Romantic fiction does not offer an emancipatory discourse… It offers women participation in successful heterosexuality and a kind of triumph for femininity – and all without transgressing society's expectations concerning gender identity'. So within the novel, dominance is constructed as desirable – further legitimising hegemonic masculinity; at the same time, though, dominance is only sexy in the novel when it is in the hands of a man – women are not afforded the same rights to be dominant: ultimately, hegemonic masculinity is required to triumph.

Exaggerating binaries: the erasure of bisexuality

As stated at the beginning of this chapter, writers like Douglas, Derrida, Irigaray and Cixous have argued that we make sense of the world by imposing categories onto things – such categories often work as binaries – something is X or it is not, and we often define X by what it isn't. Furthermore, we apply hierarchies or preferences to these binary categories, so X is valued as superior or preferable to what is not X. When it comes to categories of human identity, we have tended to over-simplify the relationship between certain categories, for example by conflating gender and sex (so male=masculine), and by conflating gender and sexuality (so for men, masculine=heterosexual and feminine=homosexual, whilst the reverse is true of women). Writers like Butler, Foucault, Derrida and Connell have argued in different ways that power is a driving force behind the construction and maintenance of these categories.

In order for binary systems to be successful, X and 'not X' must be con-structed in ways that emphasise their differences while underplaying any simi-larities. For example, men must be constructed as different from women, and heterosexuals different from homosexuals. However, a potential problem for the maintenance of binary identity systems is that sometimes there are people who do not fit easily into one category or the other, but rather fall somewhere in between or outside the system.

So anything that crosses the boundaries between the two states can not be classified easily and is, therefore, problematic (Stallybrass and White, 1986). People who do not fit easily into an identity serve as awkward reminders that binary categories of identity are rarely closed, but instead exist in more complex ways, often with the possibility of varying degrees of membership, which are themselves subject to change over time. These people may therefore threaten group solidarity, which is often based on defining oneself as belonging to a group which is different from other groups. Such people are difficult to classify and recognise. They may also present threats to the current power system, disrupting the status quo. So how are such people dealt with by mainstream, hegemonic society? How are they constructed in discourse?

In the final section of this chapter I would like to focus on the ways that the category of bisexuality is constructed through discourse in society. The term *bisexual* is itself problematic, being open to a number of interpretations. For example, there is the view that bisexuality occurs in terms of biological sex – so male nipples and female facial hair may be viewed as signs of bisexuality. A second view, argued by Freud, is that it refers to masculinity and femininity in a psychological sense so that the same person can possess masculine and feminine traits. The third view, which is more popular today, is that bisexuality refers to sexual orientation. Even here, there are different ways that bisexuality can be understood – as a position that occurs in between homosexuality and heterosexuality, and either exactly in between the two, or closer to one than the other. Some writers use it to refer to sexual desire, while others relate it to sexual behaviour and others still to sexual identity (see Storr, 1999: 3–12, for a more detailed discussion). I use the term in this chapter to refer simply to people who are able to be sexually and/or romantically attracted to both males and females. The extent to which bisexuality is seen as a separate category from homosexuality and heterosexuality, or as a mixture of both is discussed by both Murphy (1997: 38) and Storr (1999: 4).

According to Kinsey (1948, 1953), who developed a scale of sexual orientation, most people have the capacity to be attracted to either sex, although usually one sex is preferred over the other.[5] If we are to accept Kinsey's findings, then we might, naively, expect that bisexuality would be a well-discussed phenomenon, being a 'majority' form of sexuality. Clearly though, this is not the case. Murphy (1997: 41) argues that the concept of bisexuality, 'challenges many popular understandings of sexual identity and related strategies for self-conceptualization. Particularly, acknowledging bisexuality challenges the notions that same-sex orientation is biologically determined and immutable'. Connell (1995: 154) writes of contemporary European/American society, 'At this time and place there is no positive social category of the bisexual, no well-defined intermediate identity that… men can take up. Rather bisexuality is experienced as an alternation between heterosexual and homosexual connections, or as a standing arrangement that fits them together by subordinating one to the other'.

In order to demonstrate the problem that bisexuality presents to mainstream society's sexual classification scheme, I wish to examine some corpus data. An analysis of the frequencies and the discourse categories of words pertaining to bisexuality ought to afford evidence of the extent and form of society's problematic view of bisexual identities. Table 5.2 indicates the frequencies of some terms relating to different sexual identities in a range of general reference corpora. In some cases the frequencies have been adjusted to take into account meaning, for example, there are 129 cases of *bi* in the British National Corpus, but instead of referring to sexuality, they all refer to scientific formula or are false-starts in conversation. Similarly, only uses of *gay* which refer to sexuality have been included. Data from the first release of the American National Corpus (10 million words) is included here, although at the time of writing, only the frequency information was available so in this case I have not given frequencies for *gay*, *bi* and *straight* as these words do not always refer to sexuality.

Table 5.2. Frequencies of sexuality terms in British (LOB, Flob, BNC) and American (Brown, Frown, ANC) reference corpora[6]

	Brown	LOB	Frown	FLOB	BNC	ANC	Totals
gay	0	0	66	21	1565	n/a	1652
homosexual	2	8	14	19	821	90	954
lesbian	1	0	9	0	705	78	793
homosexuality	0	5	20	7	609	98	739
heterosexual	0	2	13	10	377	27	429
lesbians	1	0	14	0	361	27	403
homosexuals	3	0	18	13	253	61	348
gays	0	0	7	8	170	129	314
lesbianism	0	1	0	0	90	5	96
bisexual	0	0	1	1	81	12	95
heterosexuals	0	0	1	2	73	13	89
heterosexuality	0	0	1	0	83	3	87
straight	0	0	3	0	32	n/a	35
homo	0	0	0	0	5	21	26
bisexuality	0	0	0	0	25	0	25
hetero	0	0	0	1	9	2	12
straights	0	0	0	0	5	7	12
bisexuals	0	0	0	1	5	1	7
bi	0	0	0	0	0	n/a	0

The table is useful in revealing the level of preoccupation that British and American societies have had regarding different types of sexual identities. . The most frequently-occurring categories of words are those to do with homosexuality: *gay* and *homosexual* are the most common terms overall. The term *lesbian* is also relatively frequent – but not as frequent as *gay* or *homosexual*. As a whole, words relating to heterosexuality occur less often. However, collectively, the lowest frequency words are those which refer to bisexuality: there are just over 100 instances in the six corpora (which together contain about 114 million words). Bisexuals are, therefore, mentioned less than once in every one million words! It is notable, then, that a form of sexuality which researchers like Kinsey have suggested is relatively common, is rarely referred to in general language use. For other examples of this *erasure* (see below) of bisexuality, see Hall and Pramaggiore (1996), Storr (1999), Angelides (2001) and Garber (2000).

Putting the matter of relative frequency aside for the moment, when bisexuality *is* referred to, how is it characterised? Of the 81 cases of *bisexual* in the British National Corpus, 19 of them are used in phrases like 'gay and bisexual'. This suggests that bisexuality is significantly referred to as a kind of tag-on 'after-thought' identity group that is both secondary and linked to gay identities. Tellingly, there are no cases of *bisexual* occurring as a tag-on in phrases like 'heterosexual and bisexual': it is more firmly associated then with the deviant (homosexual) part of the binary, rather than the mainstream (heterosexual).

An analysis of other cases of *bisexual* in the BNC suggests that the term tends to occur within a number of categories of discourse.

Bisexuals as at risk from or carriers/transmitters of HIV

1. Tom has in turn infected Mary and Sam – he's bisexual.
2. Bisexual women (who have sex with both women and men) may be putting themselves at risk if they have unsafe sex with male partners.
3. Last night, film director Michael Winner said: When I heard he was ill my first thought was of AIDS because he was an active bisexual.

Bisexuals as having potentially problematic relationships

4. Time and again he fell in love with young men who had nothing effeminate about them and who, though temporarily involved in a bisexual life, did not share Minton's inversion and could not on any long-term basis return his love.
5. To learn that he is bisexual is enough to plunge his wife into an abyss of torment, anger, pain and fear.
6. Some bisexual relationships work perfectly well as long as everyone knows the score.

Bisexuality as a compromise or code for 'gay'

7. Still, he was 'absolutely very aware' that 'bisexual' is often taken as some strange pop-code for 'gay' and is keen to point out that, as it happens, he is indeed bisexual.

8. David Bowie, announced his career in January 1972 with a public statement of his homosexuality, but, characteristically, hedged his bets as a 'bisexual'.

Bisexuals as promiscuous or liking group sex

9. Essentially, the bisexual Bessie was the Madonna of her day, the Queen Of The Blues, the Empress Of Erotica, her 'Empty Bed Blues' providing a catalogue of lovers who had satisfied her sexually
10. Bisexual couple for gleesome threesomes?
11. She says he was an enthusiastic bisexual who involved J Edgar Hoover in sexual orgies just as the Kennedys were trying to make him take action against the Mob.

Bisexuality as scandal/secret/newsworthy

12. I wondered what would have happened if I had told him that I was bisexual or that I liked little girls.
13. IT WAS WHILE 'I'M TOO SEXY' was enjoying its long stay at number two beneath Bryan Adams that Richard Fm told the Sun that he was bisexual.
14. Was he, too, after all, as I half suspected, a bisexual?

Bisexuality and negative stereotyping/misunderstanding

15. The transvestite serial killer in Silence of the Lambs, or the bisexual anti-heroine of Basic Instinct, are both examples of homophobia; of negative stereotyping.
16. Eszterhas' notorious $3 million script came under scrutiny due to the portrayal of Sharon Stone's character; a bisexual killer with a fondness for ice picks and her fratricidal psychologist lover.
17. There's a lot of misunderstanding about what being bisexual is.

A number of these categories are orientated to what Hutchins and Ka'ahumanu (1990) and Tucker (1995) refer to as *biphobia*. Bisexuals are the subject of scandal and secrecy; they are characterised as promiscuous and as having problematic relationships. In example 12, bisexuality is equated with paedophilia, and in examples 1–3 bisexuals are discussed with reference to sexually transmitted diseases. Similar discourses have been found to refer often to homosexual identities (Baker, 2005), again showing how bisexuality (on the rare occasions when it is discussed) is constructed as being more similar to homosexuality than heterosexuality. The last category refers more explicitly to the existence of biphobia, although it is interesting that in example 15, the 'bisexual anti-heroine' is referred to as an example of homophobia rather than biphobia – once again suggesting that bisexuality is often subsumed under homosexuality.

The categories found in the BNC also point to another relevant concept relating to the way in which bisexuals are characterised in discourse: that of *erasure*, a term discussed by Namaste (2000: 51–2) that has a number of inter-related meanings. It can refer to the reduction of an identity group to the merely figural, meaning that such identities become unthinkable. It also refers to the ways that identities are made invisible or left unrecognised by society (signified by their relative infrequency in language use). And it can refer to the nullification of an identity, rendering it impossible. Irvine and Gal's (2000: 58) model of semiotic processes by which social meanings become encoded relates erasure to two other processes: *iconisation*, whereby essentialist status is assigned to linguistic and social phenomena, and *fractal recursivity*, or the projection of binary oppositions. Erasure is, therefore, the process by which any facts or behaviour which are inconsistent with iconisation and fractal recursivity are ignored or explained away.

Erasure of bisexuality is therefore a powerful strategy for maintaining the illusion of the binary system of homosexuality/heterosexuality. The fact that bisexuality is referred to so infrequently in language use, as compared with other sexual identities, or is regularly 'tagged on' to *gay* or thought to mean the same thing as *gay*, all point to its erasure in different ways. Examples 7 and 8 also suggest forms of erasure – an acknowledgment that bisexual is a code for 'gay' and the suggestion that David Bowie's bisexuality is a form of 'hedging his bets'. Erasure suggests an extreme form of marginalisation – a way in which identities which threaten the established gender hierarchy (often because they blur boundaries or are difficult to classify) are overlooked or 'unsaid'.

But it should not be assumed that bisexuality is only erased by mainstream, hegemonic society. Hemmings (1999: 195) argues that it, 'is occasionally mentioned within queer and postmodern theories, but never engaged with in a serious theoretical way... The role of the bisexual in Britain and the US has been similarly marginalised, partly because many of the meetings have taken place in Lesbian and Gay Centres that do not extend access to bisexuals'.

Within gay and lesbian communities, bisexual people can be treated with suspicion, accused of using bisexuality as a way of obtaining heterosexual privilege, 'the benefits of basic civil rights and familial recognition that heterosexuals accord themselves as the norm' (Hutchins and Ka'ahumanu, 1990: 369) while enjoying the political, social and cultural cachet of an alternative identity (see also Wilkinson, 1996). The following quotes, illustrative of this, are taken from an online gay and lesbian bulletin board (OUTEverywhere.com) under a discussion with the title, 'Do bisexuals have the worst of both worlds?'

- Nope they do not have the worst, but they are greedy, they have their cake and eat it.

- To paraphrase a line from Torch Song Trilogy: I'll believe in bisexuals when a man cheats on his long term live-in boyfriend with a woman.

- Where I DO think they have the worst of both worlds is that they are much more likely to be accused of lying or covering things up. Gay and straight people will say that they are only saying bisexual because they can't go the whole hog and say gay. So even if it is a 50/50 split few people will believe that.

- Gay people are often pretty shitty about them, you only have to read some of the threads on here, and I have doubts about how many women would feel about them too.

- There is undoubtedly a sneering attitude, to put it at best, about bisexuals on here.

Quotes taken from www.outeverywhere.com (accessed 15 September 2006)

The first two quotes, which occurred early in the discussion, could be characterised as biphobic – the belief that bisexuals are either greedy: 'have their cake and eat it' or that they don't actually exist. The underlying belief is that bisexuals are really covert homosexuals – a form of erasure.

However, the last three quotes, which occurred later in the discussion, are also orientated to biphobia – pointing out that bisexual people do get accused of lying and that there is a 'shitty' or 'sneering' attitude to them on the online forum. Garber (2000: 89) argues that biphobia is a by-product of homophobia, 'There would be no biphobia against a (presumed) minority within a minority unless that minority, the gay and lesbian community were oppressed by hostile and fearful heterosexuals often overly anxious or complacent about their own sexual identities'. Sinfield (quoted in Garber, 2000: 85) claims that although there is a political suspicion of bisexuals among lesbians and gays, the climate is changing, with bisexuals less likely to be seen as reluctant gays or lesbians. However, according to Sinfield, a more difficult problem is the sense that bisexuality threatens identity politics and undermines the gains of gay and lesbian liberation (see also Chapter 7).

Bisexuality is by no means the only identity in terms of gender or sexuality which is erased by both mainstream and marginalised/subordinated groups. As Lazar (2005: 10) writes, 'systems of heterosexism and gender combine to produce normative gender identities that are implicitly heterosexist, which affords relatively more privilege to heterosexual women than their homosexual sisters. Lesbians, in fact may experience greater discrimination in that not only are they marginalised by the hetero-gendered order, they are made further invisible as 'women' even in the gay community'. And the category of transgendered people (an umbrella term which can cover cross-dressers, drag queens and transsexuals) is also subject to erasure.

Stone (1991: 295) claims that, 'the transsexual currently occupies a position which is nowhere, which is outside the binary oppositions of gendered discourse,' and that, 'for a transsexual, as a transsexual, to generate a true, effective and representative counterdiscourse is to speak from the boundaries of gender'. Namaste (2000: 10–11) points out, for example, that drag queens are only tolerated by gay communities if they appear on stage – they would not be accepted in other gay spaces, such as cruising areas. She argues that queer theory (see Chapter 7), 'must be challenged because it exhibits a remarkable insensitivity to the substantive issues of transgendered people's everyday lives' (2000: 23). In terms of the mainstream erasure of transsexuality she demonstrates that the lack of social policy in social service networks for transgendered people has resulted in their not being catered for in terms of shelters for homeless people. As a result, transgendered people are forced to make their own arrangements for housing, and this results in a cycle of reinforcement because staff at homeless shelters have no familiarity with transgendered issues, and they do not recognise the inadequacy of their training to handle such people. Ross argues (1995) that the words *men* and *women* constitute a form of erasure as they undermine the possibility of a transgendered or transsexual position. Cromwell (1999) describes a number of ways in which female-bodied transpeople are signified as invisible – through medical, historical, psychological and popular discourses which deny their existence or treat them as artificial or unreal to different extents. By erasing the concept of transgender, the categories of male and female are crystallised as distinct and immutable.

Conclusion

This chapter has focused on the ways in which gender/sexuality identity categories are constructed linguistically and discursively as distinct sets of binaries – binaries that are separate although, as we have seen, not equal. So that the most powerful identity category (hegemonic masculinity) is maintained, its boundaries must be carefully policed: its so-called oppositional categories (femininity, homosexuality) must be constantly identified as subordinate, while identities which threaten to pollute or disrupt the boundaries, such as bisexuality and transsexuality are erased or marginalised. However, the theory of hegemonic masculinity also enables us to consider identities as existing within more complex configurations than binaries – there are many types of masculinity reflecting diversity within sexes, although to different extents, all men (and some women) may gain some sort of power from hegemonic masculinity through complicity.

The following chapter examines the social construction of categories from a related, yet different perspective, focusing on the ways in which the socio-economic system of capitalism uses discourses in order to encourage sexual and gendered identities to be purchased or consumed, creating further distinctions in the gender hierarchy.

Notes

1   Nerds can sometimes become exemplars of hegemonic masculinity e.g. Bill Gates. A distinction should therefore be made between men who exercise economic or political power, such as a CEO or President of a country, and those who are possess physical capital, such as an action hero or someone who regularly does manual labour – clearly, there are different ways in which hegemonic masculinity can be performed. A 25-year old, physically fit man may hold hegemonic power over say, his family or among his friends but he is unlikely to be able to match the kind of social power wielded by a 70-year old billionaire.

2   In 2006, the British radio presenter Chris Moyles caused controversy by dismissing a mobile telephone ring tone on his Radio 1 breakfast programme, saying 'I don't want that one, it's gay'. A listener complained that Moyle's use of gay was homophobic. However, the programme complaints committee noted 'the word 'gay' in addition to being used to mean 'homosexual' or 'carefree' was often now used to mean 'lame' or 'rubbish'. This is a widespread current usage amongst young people'. http://www.timesonline.co.uk/article/0,,2–2212170,00.html

3   Difference can lead a social group to attempt to expel or denigrate anything that is viewed as impure and abnormal – but alternatively, a group first requires something to be constructed as impure and abnormal, in order to define itself as different and superior. However, paradoxically, difference can also become powerful and attractive, exactly because it is unknown, forbidden, tabooed and threatening to cultural order. 'What is socially peripheral is often symbolically centred' (Babcock, 1978: 32). Difference is therefore *ambivalent*, being positive and negative, threatening and fascinating. Connell remarks that '…gay men have also noticed a fascination with homosexuality on the part of straight men. Some have seen homophobia as the expression of a secret desire, driven out of consciousness and converted into hatred… Others have noticed a curious willingness for straight men to be seduced given the right time and a secluded place; or have noted how widespread homosexual sex becomes in all-male institutions… It points to the widespread but mostly unspoken sexualisation of men's social worlds, rarely acknowledged in academic research' Connell (1995:40). Cameron (2005: 496) notes that 'some of the most striking linguistic performances of heterosexuality are put on not to negotiate heterosexual relationships with women, but to further homosocial relations with men'. It may also suggest that the hard lines between heterosexuality and homosexuality are not as fixed as many people would imagine (see the section on erasure of bisexuality towards the end of this chapter, as well as Mieli (1980) and Connell, Davis and Dowsett (1993).

4   http://www.millsandboon.co.uk/cgi-bin/millsandboon.storefront/EN/Catalog

5   An interesting way of understanding sexuality would be to compare it to a trait like right- or left-handedness. It could be argued that the majority of people have the potential to be ambidextrous, with a few people being either solely right- or left-handed. However, because right-handedness tends to be institutionalised in most societies, many people who have the potential to be ambidextrous, find it easy to be right-handed most of the time. In the same way, because society favours heterosexuality, many people who have the potential to be bisexual, mainly identify as heterosexual. Such a view suggests that both 'nature' and 'nurture' have complementary roles to play in the way that sexual identities manifest themselves in society.

6   The Brown Corpus consists of a million words of American English, collected in the early 1960s. Similarly, the LOB (Lancaster Oslo-Brown Corpus) contains a million words of early 1960s British English. The Frown and FLOB corpora are 1990s equivalents respectively.

6   Selling sex: commodification and marketisation

Introduction

In previous chapters we have explored the ways in which gendered and sexed identities, desires and discourses are constructed through language. We have seen how the concepts of heteronormativity and hegemonic masculinity help us to understand how certain identities and discourses are privileged while others are subordinated or marginalised. In this chapter, however, I want to look more closely at the way in which gendered and sexed discourses and identities are embedded within the western socio-economic system and how this system contributes towards the maintenance or development of existing discourses, identities and desires. Contemporary western capitalist society, or late modernity as Giddens (1991) calls it, varies from country to country, but there are a number of features which appear to be fairly consistent: mass production of goods, consumer-choice and a free-market economy resulting in a 'survival of the fittest' approach to business and commerce.

Pleasance (1991: 70–71) points out that advertising is a central text of popular culture, adverts being a cultural product that, 'construct a closed and fixed story of social cohesion'. As Goldman (1992: 2) observes, 'Advertising is the key social and economic institution in producing and reproducing the material and ideological supremacy of commodity relations'. The association of products with desirable identities or the promise of sex are techniques that many advertisers have employed. Advertising links gender identity and sexual desire with almost any product that may be purchased: cars, cigarettes, food, holidays, insurance, sports and hobbies, clothing, furniture, film. Sex itself has become, 'an aid to sell everything from the automobile to soap flakes as images of female sexuality proliferate in ever more explicit forms' (Weeks, 1985: 24). In the past, advertisers exploited the sexual desires of men (who were assumed to be breadwinners and heterosexual). Female and gay sexual desire went largely unacknowledged by advertisers until the onset of women's and gay liberation movements in the 1960s and 1970s. Then, 'as the 1980s got under way, the commercial exploitation of men-as-sex-objects became very big business. The voyeuristic sexualisation of the female body, its packaging as visual erotica, was now transferred to the male body with the same purpose in mind – to sell, sell, sell' (Benyon, 2000: 103). Furthermore, just as advertisers began to treat (heterosexual) female consumers like men, they also realised that the opposite was possible – they could target male consumers in the same way as women. Male spending power on fashion, grooming, diet and style had been relatively untapped. But during the 1960s and 1970s, what had been a fairly uniform youth culture was disintegrated, replaced with proliferating expressions of young masculinities – Old Spice Man, Bitter Beer Man, Safari Man, Hair Spray Man, Lad Fop, etc. (Hunt, 1998). Nixon (1996) notes that the proliferation of clothing outlets and style magazines for men were linked to new visual representations of masculinities as narcissistic. By the 1980s and 1990s, grooming products and cosmetic surgery were being marketed to men (see later in this chapter), who were encouraged to subject their bodies to the same sorts of anxious scrutiny as women.

However, as well as attempting to embody consumer objects with sexual qualities, sex and sexual desire is also something which is a commodity in itself: we can purchase sex for its own sake. As Weeks (1985: 23) notes, 'Sex had long been something you were. By the 1950s it was also something you could buy, not just in the traditional form (for men) of prostitution, but in the form of glossily marketed fantasy… Playboy and the like were the respectable side of a sexual coin that went into ever more dizzying circulation by the 1960s and 1970s, producing on its offside the multi-billion growth industry of the post-war world, pornography' (see also Chapter 8). The concept of desire is marketed and consumed in other ways in societies – through romance novels and films (from *Pride and Prejudice* to *Bridget Jones's Diary* to *Mills and Boon*), which are often aimed at women and propagate a discourse of 'romantic love' (see Talbot, 1997b). And as Hall (1995) has shown, language is a key component in the performance of sexually desirable identities through sex chat lines. But in order for customers to hear and interact with these idealised, fantasy sexual identities, they must give their credit card details: the interaction is strictly transactional (see Chapter 3).

A new, improved gender!

A key aspect of capitalist society is consumption (Featherstone, 1991), which, Giddens has argued, allows people to 'buy' a lifestyle by making decisions about how to live, how to behave, what to wear and what to eat. He suggests that this shows the penetration of commercial practices into people's self-hood. In contemporary society, a person's identity tends to be involved less in traditional roles and structures, and more in market-place decisions. 'To a greater or lesser degree, the project of the self becomes translated into one of the possession of desired goods and the pursuit of artificially framed styles of life' (Giddens, 1991: 196).

Benwell and Stokoe (2006: 167) point out that goods are not simply made in order to *fulfil* needs, but rather needs must first be *stimulated* by producers and advertisers through appeals to identity and lifestyle. A pessimistic view of this would be that these are *false needs* which are 'superimposed upon the individual by particular social interests in his [sic] repression: the needs which perpetuate toil, aggressiveness, misery, and injustice... The result then is euphoria in unhappiness. Most of the prevailing needs to relax, have fun, to behave and consume in accordance with advertisements, to love and hate what others love and hate, belong to this category of false needs' (Marcuse, 1964: 406).

A contemporary articulation of the stimulation of 'false needs' is argued by Benwell and Stokoe (2006: 176) who write, 'One of the key imperatives of consumer femininity is that 'problems' are ultimately insoluble'. They suggest that the use of phrases in advertising which focus on the *appearance* of solutions is a key way in which this insolubility is perpetuated, for example, 'deep lines look lifted away', 'looks flawlessly natural', 'smoother looking skin'. The skin is not actually made smoother – it just *looks* smoother. As Corrigan (1997) explains, in order for modern capitalist societies to flourish, people must be encouraged to engage in a never-ending quest for new identities, characterised by desires that can never really be fulfilled: 'an endless discontent'. Advertising, therefore, offers the promise of a perfect identity or lifestyle, that can be achieved if a product is purchased; at the same time, it must never deliver on this promise or, if it does, a newer, better product must offer an even more improved lifestyle. A sense of final attainment must always be kept out of reach. The quest for a commodified identity is thus similar in some ways to Butler's concept of gender performance – both must involve continuous repetition in order to create the appearance of substance: just as a gender performance is a never-ending performance, so too is our engagement with commodified identity.

A number of writers have shown how advertisers draw on traditional gendered discourses as a way of making a product appear more desirable – although the relationship is two-way: advertising reproduces and thus strengthens existing gendered discourses at the same time as drawing on them. So, the product becomes associated with the hegemonic gender order through the way it is marketed. Thornborrow (1998) examined car advertising, which frequently uses sex and gender to sell. An advertisement for the Korando represents the car metaphorically as a living being 'a new breed of 4X4' with a 'stunning muscle-flexed body'; the product is therefore linked to hegemonic masculinity by its suggestion of physical strength. But it is also described as 'hard-nosed and playing hard to get until 23/08/97'. The phrase 'hard-to-get' implies that something is unavailable, but also, therefore, likely to be in control. On the other hand, Thornborrow describes a television advertisement for the Vauxhall Corsa, a small hatchback car, which featured Ruby Wax, a chat show host and comedian, putting a large quantity of shopping into the car boot, and then filling the car up with men. Again, a personification metaphor is used: 'the little car with the big personality', which could be seen as reference to Wax herself. The car is therefore associated with the woman – the size and 'personality' of both are viewed as equivalent. Wax's shopping behaviour also reinforces a stereotype of women as performing domestic chores, while a link is made between consumption and desire: the men in the advert are equated with shopping bags – something else that can be picked up, put in the car and taken home. There is humour and irony in both adverts, with the image of Wax 'consuming' men suggesting a feminist or post-feminist message which places emphasis on women's agency and sexual desire. However, ultimately, Thornborrow (1998: 271) concludes that, '[Car] Adverts targeting women tend to draw on the linguistic devices that signify smallness; while those targeting men are associated with the large… In the adverts for larger cars, the metaphors relating to desirability and sexual experience are built on predominantly masculine ground, a domain where speed, power and control are represented primarily as desirable physical experiences for men'.

The more recent theorising of gender as a potentially unfixed entity unexpectedly coincides with capitalist goals in some ways: gender can be altered… at a price. However, capitalist systems also require the existence of a more structured gendered hierarchy so that gender itself is regarded as a form of capital – its alteration or 'improvement' achieved by the purchase of specific products or procedures. The marketing of such products must, then, be tied into discourses of hegemonic gender, so there is value in purchasing products which alter a person (or their self-image) in some way so that their gender approximates hegemonic ideals. For example, masculinity is often associated with large muscles, leading some men (not specifically restricted to any sexual identity group) to purchase gym memberships or even use anabolic steroids in order to make their bodies larger. As Burroughs (2004: 231) observed of the gay community in Manhattan: 'I started to notice that every gay man in the city seemed to be getting larger. At the gym where I'd gone for years, guys who had previously been as skinny as me had ballooned into Mayflower moving men. There were now men walking the streets of New York with breasts that Pamela Anderson would envy. Overnight, it seemed, biceps were in. But where had they come from?'

Another way in which gendered identities can be 'enhanced' in line with hegemonic ideals is through the purchase of 'plastic' or cosmetic surgery.

Initially the province of women, such surgery is increasingly targetted at men. The following two excerpts are taken from a promotional brochure (which I obtained in 2006) produced by the Harley Medical Group, who specialise in elective surgical procedures. The brochure is produced on expensive, glossy paper and its text is illustrated with pictures of attractive male and female models.

1 **Men**
2 Men can be just as concerned about their looks as women, and for too long the
3 expectation has been for men to accept their lot and suffer in silence, though now, more
4 than ever before, there is increasing pressure on men to look good. External pressures,
5 such as an increasingly competitive workplace, mean that men need to look good – and
6 stay that way – to have the edge.

7 Thankfully, things are changing. Looking after your appearance is no longer considered
8 solely the domain of females…

9 …we understand that wanting to look good doesn't mean you want to give up your
10 masculinity. Our procedures will help give you the look you want on the outside, and
11 feel more virile on the inside.

12 **Chin Implants**
13 Traditionally, a face with a chiselled look, relatively large chin and solid, angular
14 profile has been regarded as an embodiment of masculinity. If a receding chin means
15 that your profile is not as masculine as you would like… chin implants are an effective
16 solution.

17 **Tummy Tuck (abdominoplasty)**
18 Lack of exercise, advancing age and years of business entertaining can all contribute
19 to increasing weight over the years.

The Harley Medical Group

20 **Women**
21 Your face is what you greet the world with and it's the first thing that people judge
22 you by when they meet you… You might be self-conscious about a feature such as a
23 receding chin or large nose, which makes your face look unbalanced, or maybe
24 Mother Nature simply didn't give you quite what you wanted. You might be unhappy
25 with the way that passing years have changed your appearance, or external pressures
26 may mean you would just prefer to look younger.

27 **Breast Surgery**
28 For many women, breasts are the essence of their womanhood, so it's no wonder that
29 they are conscious about their size and shape. Breast augmentation can make you feel
30 more feminine by not only increasing the size of your breasts, but also adjusting their
31 shape to produce a better symmetry.

32 **Breast Reduction**
33 Overly large breasts can be a source of physical discomfort, such as back and breast
34 pain, and can often lead to bad posture. Not only that, many women feel that their
35 breasts attract unwanted attention, making them self-conscious about their appearance.
36 Breast reduction can restore proportion to your body and give you more self-
37 confidence and freedom to lead the life you want to live.

The Harley Medical Group

The two excerpts show part of the text from the men's and women's sections of the brochure. In order to avoid giving precedence to one section over the other, the brochure has two fronts and no back. One front page shows a woman, but if the brochure is turned upside down and back to front, the alternative front page shows a picture of a man. The layout of the brochure therefore references the 'gender differences' discourse. Clearly, men's and women's bodies *are* different in some ways, and certain types of surgery for men would be inappropriate for women and vice versa. However, sex-specific surgery comprises only a small part of the procedures on offer – many of them are available to both men and women (tummy tucks, eye bag removal, isolagen, botox, etc.), yet are still described separately, resulting in some repetition, but also some interesting differences. For example, if the two sections of the brochure on eye bag removal are compared, the men's section refers to 'the stress of a pressurised life and lack of sleep'. There is no equivalent phrase in the women's section on eye bag removal. And although the brochure appears to target men and women equally, by having two 'fronts', the amount of space devoted to men and women is different. The women's section consists of thirty three pages; the men's, nineteen.

There are a number of other differences in the two extracts regarding the ways that language is used to market idealised gendered identities. In terms of gender, the brochure suggests a range of different procedures that can help to increase a person's feeling of masculinity or femininity. For men, features such as 'a face with a chiselled look, relatively large chin and solid, angular profile' (lines 13–14) are described as an 'embodiment of masculinity'. On the other hand, for women, the size of their breasts is linked to their femininity. According to Ritzer (1998: 13), in order to make a body consumable it needs to be 'rediscovered narcissistically'. Mills (1995b) describes the act of bodily consumption through fragmentation, whereby body parts are categorised as separate from each other: 'First, the body is depersonalized, objectified, reduced to its parts. Second, since the female protagonist is not represented as a unified conscious physical being, the scene cannot be focalized from her perspective – effectively, her experience is written out of the text' (Mills, 1995: 171–72). In a similar way, body parts in the cosmetic surgery brochure are dissociated from the human being, and are instead described under separate subheadings: chin implant, tummy tuck, breast reduction, etc.

The brochure creates desire for cosmetic surgery among its readers by the use of what Hoey (1983) calls a 'problem-solution pattern'. Such a pattern gives a series of propositions, linking them through conjunctions such as *but, so* and *therefore*, which create an implication of contrast, justification or causality. In this way, something is defined as a problem and a solution is suggested – the solution here being the consumable product. Propositions can be related to each in other in different ways: cause-consequence or situation-problem-solution, as in the case below (the co-ordinating conjunction *then* which occurs between the problem and solution is elided in this example, lines 14–16).

(situation) If a receding chin means
(conjunction) that
(problem) your profile is not as masculine as you would like
(conjunction) then (elided)
(solution) chin implants are an effective solution.

In other cases, the problem-solution pattern is achieved over multiple sentences (lines 34–37):

(situation) many women feel that their breasts attract unwanted attention,
(problem) making them self-conscious about their appearance.
(solution) Breast reduction can restore proportion to your body and give you more self-confidence and freedom to live the life you want to live.

In order to make sense of problem-solution patterns, the reader is required to decode the implicatures contained within them. As well as the way that conjunctions are used to suggest causality, the choice of lexis is also informative. The word *receding*, for example generally does not have a positive semantic prosody. We are likely to have encountered the word many times in a negative way and subconsciously internalised its meaning as something bad (its occurrence in the British National Corpus, for example, shows that it tends to appear in contexts like *receding hairline* – and that descriptions of people with receding chins or hairlines are not positive). On the other hand, a word like *masculine* (which occurs as part of the problem of *not* being masculine) has a much more positive semantic prosody (collocating in the BNC with *virile, tough* and *power*). The reader, then, is likely to infer that chin implants are the 'effective solution' to a receding chin, which therefore must be a problem. The use of problem-solution patterns does not so much help the consumer to fulfil a need, but creates the need in the first place.

Both men and women are presented as possessing a number of motivations for considering surgery. However, these motivations differ and in some cases are suggestive of competing discourses. In order to persuade men to have cosmetic surgery, the brochure must sell both the surgery and the gender identity it claims to enhance as being desirable. It also needs to navigate a way between two sets of competing discourses. The more established, traditional discourses of hegemonic masculinity and gender differences view male concern about physical appearance as vain and unmanly: women are expected to be concerned about their looks so that men will find them attractive, but the reverse is not the case – echoing Berger's (1972) 'men look, women are looked at' theory of the gaze and supported by a study by Dull and West (1991) which confirms that cosmetic surgery is considered natural for women, but not for men. In the cosmetic surgery brochure this discourse is addressed and critiqued by the expression 'for too long the expectation has been for men to accept their lot and suffer in silence' (lines 2–3). Agency is absent here – note the nominalisation of the verb *expect*. Who is expecting men to suffer in silence? Other men? Society as a whole? Further down, the word 'Traditionally...' (line 13) also suggests vagueness in the attribution of social beliefs. Such opacity is used in order to legitimise the discourse position, constructing it as a 'lifeworld' discourse (Fairclough, 1995b: 164), in other words, a discourse of ordinary life and ordinary experience, relevant to and understood by everyone.

However, this discourse is stated in order to counter it with another one – 'gender equality now achieved' (Sunderland, 2004: 44, 46), with an assertion that times have changed: 'Looking after your appearance is no longer considered solely the domain of females' (lines 7–8). Again, we are not told who regards 'looking after your appearance' as no longer 'solely the domain of females' – the lack of an agent suggests it is simply a worldwide view. The text also employs a relatively weak modal verb *can*: 'Men can be just as concerned about their looks as women' (line 2). *Can* is a deontic modal verb, in that it gives permission ('Okay, you can go out if you want'), but is also an epistemic modal verb, referencing truth or certainty ('That can be the case at times'). In the cosmetic surgery text, *can* operates in an ambiguous way, functioning potentially as deontic and as epistemic. It both gives permission for men to be concerned about their looks and asserts that (sometimes) they already are.

'Masculinity' is treated as something separate from 'wanting to look good', although the authors reassure the reader that the two are not mutually exclusive.

The text attempts, therefore, to accept the validity of being masculine and wanting to look good, despite the fact that the two states are set up in opposition to each other. One way of doing this is by suggesting that elective surgery will help give men the look they want on the outside, but also make them feel more 'virile on the inside' (line 11). Here the surface change is only considered to be a part of the process, countered by, or justified by, how such a procedure will make one feel inside. Such an argument also refers to received wisdom where 'what's inside is what counts, not shallow surface things'. Men are therefore encouraged to view the procedure as having a 'deeper' impact on their masculinity, rather than viewing it just in terms of how it will make them look. And in suggesting that cosmetic procedures will help a man 'feel' more virile, the reader is required to deduce that this is a good thing. So, a discourse of hegemonic masculinity is obliquely adhered to: the more masculine you are, the better.

There is further evidence that hegemonic masculinity is upheld when a more traditional construction of masculinity is referenced: the male breadwinner. As in the example on eye bag surgery noted above, which refers to 'the stress of a pressurised life' the reader of the 'Men' text is positioned as a busy working man: 'External pressures, such as an increasingly competitive workplace, mean that men need to look good – and stay that way – to have the edge' (lines 4–6). The presupposition underlying this text is that the reader or ideal male buyer of cosmetic surgery holds a reasonably powerful job. Clearly, not all workplaces are 'increasingly competitive' or require men 'to look good to have the edge'. The phrase 'years of business entertaining' (line 18) positions the male reader as working for a business (rather than, say, on a building site) which requires him to 'entertain' clients. We are asked to read between the lines here, imagining a man who regularly eats at restaurants and is perhaps, due to his highly demanding career, too busy to engage in regular exercise or count calories. No fault is attributed here – the reader is simply fulfilling his male role of working for a wage. However, the text implies a paradox: having to 'entertain clients' is likely to result in an increased waist-line, which could ultimately *undermine* business success. Use of modality is strong – 'Men *need* to look good' (line 5). Such a justification for having surgery – to get ahead at work – is used to limit concerns about male vanity, acting as a loophole which allows the potentially problematic (in this context) discourses of 'gender equality', 'gender differences' and hegemonic masculinity to co-exist. Note also the categorical use of *men* here, not 'some men' or 'men who work in business'; the potentially narrow subset of professional working men alluded to by their 'competitive workplace' and 'years of business entertaining' is taken to stand for *men* as a whole.

The text of the brochure therefore engages in a persuasive discourse whereby men are required to 'look good' (where 'good' is defined by the brochure as consisting of the cosmetic procedures it offers) for other men (business colleagues or superiors), not so they will be found physically attractive by women. This allows the (perceived) retention of hegemonic masculinity – and the possibility that men may be judged by women on how they look is left unstated. However, in needing to look good for other men, the brochure must also avert another potential threat to hegemonic masculinity – that of suspected homosexuality. This is achieved by simply obscuring the gender of the person or people that the male client of cosmetic surgery is supposed to look good for. The reference is to the 'competitive workplace' (line 5), where a genderless institution stands in for a more specified identity. Rather than focusing on their sexual or romantic relationships, men are positioned as career-oriented.

So, the text for men not only reproduces certain gendered discourses, but it also has to relate to men in a number of ways, particularly in countering the threat to hegemonic masculinity that the consumption of cosmetic surgery might suggest, in terms of repositioning men as requiring female *or* male approval. Also, the text must reconcile the potentially conflicting discourses of hegemonic masculinity and gender equality, showing how *both* can be used to justify surgery.

By contrast, the text for women does not need to present such a tortured negotiation through different discourse positions. According to prevailing conceptions of femininity, women *should already* be concerned about their appearance in order to present themselves as sexually-desirable commodities to men. While male clients are assumed to be a growing minority, women are assumed to be the 'default customers' who do not need to be excused for their interest in cosmetic surgery. The fact that the women's section of the brochure is longer than the men's section also suggests this – the number of procedures available to them is greater and well established.

There are no clear references in the text to women requiring cosmetic surgery due to their participation in the workplace – unlike men, women are not represented as being in paid work. Instead, the text focuses on how women are judged by others, 'it's the first thing that people judge you by when they meet you' (lines 21–22). There is a vague reference to 'external pressures' (line 25) in relation to women wanting to look younger, which could refer to the workplace, but could also refer to the desires of a partner. However, aesthetic reasons are also given: a receding chin or large nose may make the 'face look unbalanced' (line 23) whereas surgery can be carried out to adjust the shape of one's breasts 'to produce a better symmetry' (line 31). References to *balance*, *symmetry* and *proportion* firmly place female reasons for cosmetic surgery in terms of wanting to look beautiful. Furthermore, the use of the term 'balance' helps to reify the concept, naturalising society's standards of beauty – but what constitutes a 'large nose'? (and by whose standards?) and how can a 'large' nose unbalance the face?

Breast surgery is particularly related to gender – breasts being described as the 'essence of womanhood' (line 28). Another strategy of legitimisation, the phrase 'For many women' (line 28), is used in order to imply that what is being said is the popular, ergo *correct* stance, without requiring further elaboration or proof (e.g. attitude surveys). It is suggested that increasing the size of a woman's breasts can make her feel 'more feminine' (lines 29–30). However, in the section on breast reduction we are told 'many women feel that their breasts attract unwanted attention' (line 34–35). Again, the brochure uses 'many' to refer to popular thinking. Agency is obscured here to avoid attributing blame. Also, we are not told who gives women unwanted attention (although we could assume that it is likely to be heterosexual men). However, in suggesting a solution to a problem (breast reduction), the issue of unwanted attention is placed at the feet of women, rather than, say, suggesting that a less expensive and painful solution might be a change in society's values so that it became less acceptable for men to give women unwanted attention.

The brochure shows how different discourses of gender are utilised and/ or negotiated in sex-specific ways in order to sell procedures which alter the body. The marketisation of identity also indicates that social class becomes an increasingly important factor in terms of achieving gender 'perfection' – cosmetic surgery procedures are relatively expensive, usually regarded as a luxury rather than a necessity, and so are more likely to be taken up by wealthy people. That is not to say that people with less money can not be persuaded to purchase products which 'improve' their gender – instead, less expensive products, such as clothing or make-up will be marketed to them.

While it could be argued that the purchase of particular types of clothing etc. is an expression of a person's gender, I would argue that the reverse is also true: consumption is another way in which gender can be performed or constructed. The process becomes cyclical, with advertisers reinforcing or altering stereotypes about what constitutes an ideal gender; the continued purchase of such goods validates the existence of such stereotypes, perpetuating the system. Of course, it could be argued that people have a choice – most of us will not pay to have cosmetic surgery, for example. And we can always reject the (changing) hegemonic constructs of 'ideal' masculinity and femininity. However, even then, the construction of counter-cultural or minority identities can also be achieved through the purchase of alternative niche products or by references to 'progressive' discourses as shown in the following section.

Commodity feminism and the 'pink pound'

So far, it could be argued that capitalism and hegemonic masculinity/hetero–normativity are mutually-supporting phenomena, with advertisers exploiting hegemonic discourses in order to persuade consumers to purchase products that will allow them to adhere to gender and sexual norms, and so raise their own status or self-image as traditionally masculine or feminine. However, as an economic system, capitalism's goals (inasmuch as we can assign goals to a concept) are growth and profit, achieved by competition and conspicuous consumption (Veblen, 1899). For that reason, those directly involved in capitalist systems (advertisers, corporations, the media, etc.) may often utilise discourses that are hegemonic, because adherence to such discourses is likely to confirm rather than threaten many people's 'common-sense' understandings of the world, making them more likely to purchase the product associated with the discourse. Also, some people involved in the production, marketing and sale of consumer goods are likely to replicate society's hegemonic discourses in any case. Betterton (1987: 10) has argued that advertisements, 'help to define what forms of femininity are acceptable and desirable. In doing so they exclude and deny experiences that contradict or simply do not fit with prevailing values in society'.

However, there is no reason why capitalist structures always have to rely strictly on hegemonic discourses. Within post-modern thinking, there is recognition that a range of possible identities and discourses exist, and while it is still the case that other identities are subordinated or marginalised to hegemonic masculinity, at the same time, advertisers are aware that people possessing these 'othered' identities still have money to spend and choices to make about where to spend it. The relationship between commodification and non-hegemonic identities or discourses is a complex one though. Goldman (1992: 133) notes that, 'A generation after the 'women's movement' scored victories with anti-discrimination suits, advertisers routinely address women and their daughters, in a voice which acknowledges these changes'. Talbot (2000:109) argues that the advertising industry has no stake in subverting conventional forms of femininity, but at the same time advertisers need to show awareness of contemporary issues and have taken feminism onboard (to an extent) since the rise of the Women's Liberation Movement in the 1970s. However, it is liberal feminism which has been co-opted by advertising, rather than more radical conceptualisations of feminism, which are marginalised. For example, Talbot analyses an advertisement for British Telecom which appeared in the *Radio Times* (Britain's biggest selling weekly magazine) in 1994.

1   Men and women communicate differently. Have you noticed?
2   Women like to sit down to make phone calls
3   They know that getting in touch is more important than what you actually say
4   Men adopt another position
5   They stand up.
6   Their body language says this message will be short, sharp and to the point.
7   'Meet you down the pub, all right? See you there.' That's a man's call.
8   Women can't understand why men are so abrupt.
9   Why can't they share the simple joys of talking as other men have?
10 'Conversation is one of the greatest pleasures of life. But it wants leisure'.
    W. Somerset Maugham.
11 Or, as another writer said, 'The conversation of women is like the straw around china.
       Without it everything would be broken'.
12 Even Winston Churchill believed 'Jaw, jaw is better than war, war'.
13 This difference between the sexes becomes rather more academic when the phone bill
       hits the mat.
14 Some men have a way of making women feel guilty about it.
15 Would it help, gentlemen, if you knew the true costs?
16 That a half hour chat at local cheap rate costs less than half a pint, for example?
17 Or that a five minute local call at daytime rate costs about half the price of a small bar of
       chocolate?
18 Not so much when you think about it.
19 Particularly compared with the cost of not talking at all.

From Talbot (2000: 111)

This advertisement could be seen as an example of 'commodity feminism' in that its surface message appears to be something like 'Why can't men be more like women', a different message from the 'women as deficit men' construct of the early twentieth century (see Chapter 2). Women are constructed as *good* communicators, rather than gossips or nags. This preferred use of 'feminine' conversational styles is also discussed in relation to customer service call-centres (see Cameron, 2000). Of course, such discourses also draw on the wider 'gender differences' discourse, which is made explicit from line 1 of the advert. It could be argued that reference to 'gender differences', with its normalising associations of categorising human experience into an over-simplified binary (women are like *this*, men are like *that*), is not always congruent with feminist thinking, particularly postmodern approaches to feminism which see gender as a performance and potentially fluid (see Chapter 3). And we could point to more subtle discourses at work in the advert, which actually reassert sexist thinking.

Talbot points out that women are *spoken for* rather than speaking on their own behalf (particularly in lines 8–9). The three aphorisms of 'common-sense' wisdom used in the advert (lines 10–12) are all attributed to men (Somerset Maugham, Winston Churchill and an unnamed speaker who is intimated to be male – in line 9 there is reference to the 'other men' whose quotes follow on from that). They could be seen as representing the perspective of 'Dead White Men', in other words, a dominant male position.

Talbot notes that these aphorisms contain implicatures which are potentially negative towards women. Consider the Maugham quotation in line 10: 'Conversation is one of the greatest pleasures in life. But it wants leisure'. A possible implicature here is that women are good conversationalists because they have leisure, but men do not have the time to engage in conversation because they have more important things to do. In the second aphorism, the conversation of women is described with a simile – the straw around china. However, this straw/china contrast suggests that women's talk is like packaging material, lacking status in its own right – insubstantial. And the third aphorism, attributed to Churchill, also suggests a less positive stance towards conversation. The sentence at line 12 begins with an adverb, *even*, which indicates that what is to follow is an instance of exception-negating. Churchill is, therefore, constructed as someone who normally preferred action to negotiation. And the term *jaw* is also a somewhat derogatory way to refer to conversation. Finally, in lines 13–19 there is a discourse of economics and domestic budgeting, where women's talk is reduced to a commodity and implied to be cheap, compared to a half of bitter or a small bar of chocolate. Talbot concludes that the text brings together a range of disparate discourses in a way that reads coherently. A feminist discourse is incorporated into marketing material by advertisers, but the presence of other, contradictory discourses within the text shows that feminism is undermined at the same time as it is articulated. As Goldman (1992: 133) argues, 'Advertiser's efforts at bridging the ideological difference between feminism and femininity have spawned new ideological contradictions. Meanings of choice and individual freedom become wed to images of sexuality in which women apparently choose to be seen as sexual objects because it suits their 'liberated' interests'.

Advertising in a 'post'-feminist age is discussed by Lee (1988: 168–69) who writes, 'In the late eighties, bored by feminism and its unglamorous connotations… the media… decided we've done feminism and it's time to move on. We can call ourselves 'girls', wear sexy underwear and short skirts; because feminism taught us that we're equal to men, we don't need to prove it anymore. Is this post-feminism or anti-feminism?' The question is explored further by Levy (2005) who analyses the narratives in the popular American television series *Sex in the City* which centered on the lives of four single women living in Manhattan. Levy observes that, 'the defining pursuit of [the women's] world wasn't sex so much as it was consumption… what it romanticized most of all was accumulation. Buying things became a richly evocative experience' (2005: 172). Sex is also commodified in the series as something that is acquired rather than shared, so Levy argues that when the women do have sex, someone often feels conquered. 'Rather than the egalitarianism and satisfaction that was feminism's initial promise, these sexual marketplaces offer a kind of limitless tally' (Levy, 2005: 174). Lazar (2005: 20) also criticises the impact of 'post-feminism', acknowledging women's visibility and ascendancy in paid work, politics and education in some contexts, but also raising questions about subtle sexism, whether we have moved beyond equality and what the quality of that equality really is.

An example of how capitalist systems are not necessarily wed to heteronormativity but are instead motivated by growth and profit is found within niche marketing schemes aimed at gay men and lesbians. The relationship between homosexuality, heteronormative society and advertising can at times be fraught. For example, in 1994 a planned gay kiss on the American FOX primetime television series *Melrose Place* was not shown due to pressures from mainstream advertisers who were afraid that they would be seen as supportive of homosexuality, possibly alienating conservative and religious viewers. However, gay kisses have appeared in primetime American television since 2000, on programmes like *Desperate Housewives* and *Will & Grace*. And, in particular, within media aimed specifically at gay men and lesbians, advertisers are able to market gay-themed products without fear of backlash. Gay men and, to a lesser extent, lesbians are perceived to have large disposable incomes and few financial responsibilities, leading to the notion of the 'pink pound' in the UK (although Badgett, 2001, disputes the notion that gay men and lesbians are as affluent as we are led to believe).

Two gay marketers, Kahan and Murlyan (1995: 40–42) compare gay and lesbian identities to ethnic identities: 'It's useful to see the gay and lesbian market as similar to an immigrant market. Like immigrants, homosexuals are birds of a feather. They stick together, support each other, and vote for each other… Like immigrants, they are proud of their distinctiveness but fear being branded as different. In addition, gay men and lesbians exhibit all the characteristics of an immigrant tribe. They have distinctive mores and fashions, language, signs, symbols, gathering places, and enclaves'. It could be argued that this is a somewhat reductive view of people who identify as gay and lesbian. There *are* clearly gay men and lesbians who have shared fashions, gathering places, language use etc., but gay and lesbian people also carry many other identities (age, ethnicity, gender, social class, nationality etc), resulting in very large intergroup differences.

But for gay identity to be commodified, it must therefore first be reified – it is in the interests of advertisers to advance the idea of a single gay 'ethnic' community, characterised by a relatively large amount of homogeneity in terms of lifestyle and purchasing choices. Thus adverts aimed at gay men and lesbians are therefore likely to perpetuate the homosexual/heterosexual binary, rather than pointing out that sexuality is potentially more fluid.

For example, gay-targeted advertising makes use of language which specifically constructs and represents homosexuality in a positive way. In the July 2006 issue of *Gay Times*,[1] adverts make use of phrases like 'Come out smiling' (an advert for the Fleet Street Dental Centre), 'We take Pride' (British Airways), 'A Break with Tradition' (holiday in Piemonte) and 'Are you a friend of Dorothy and Toto' (Battersea Dogs and Cats home). Such adverts therefore incorporate gay-specific buzz-words and ideas into their advertising, such as 'coming out', 'pride' or the concept of changing tradition. The phrase 'friend of Dorothy' is an aphorism for homosexuality, referring to the character of Dorothy, played by Judy Garland.[2] The notion of 'gay pride' has been incorporated into gay marketing, for example, through the use of the 'rainbow flag', which Chasin (2000: 120) argues is a symbol of gay nationalism because flags are a standard symbol of nationhood. A flag designated specifically for gay men, lesbians, bisexuals and transgendered people helps to solidify the notion of a united community. Rainbow flags have been applied to a wide range of products such as aprons, beach umbrellas, bath salts, candles, gym shorts, mugs, pillows and jewellery.

On the one hand, it could be argued that the use of the rainbow flag on products is a cynical marketing strategy, drawing on the concept of 'pride' in one's sexual identity in order to sell a product, but, on the other hand, the presence of the rainbow flag could be equated with political power and solidarity – its appearance outside homes, on cars and clothing, suggesting that there are alternatives to heteronormativity. However, Chasin (2000: 131–42) also notes that adverts aimed at gay communities often involve exclusions which reproduce traditional power relations. For example, in an advert for a watch in a brochure aimed at the gay community by the catalogue company, Tzabaco, the text reads, 'Not a limp-wristed watch or one to be hidden in a pocket, this original hangs proudly from your belt loop'. Here, the use of the term *limp-wristed* (pejoratively used to refer to camp or effeminate gay men) suggests a disavowal of such identities in favour of a gay identity which maps more closely onto traditional hegemonic masculinity. Chasin (2000: 126) notes that race is also thematised in advertising, particularly in terms of sex-related products such as commercial pornography aimed at gay men. Looking at the output from Catalina (a company who produce gay pornography), Chasin observes the existence of films with names like *Latin Fever* and *Black Alley*, which are described as, 'The combination of all-male action's best-looking dark-skinned men and Catalina's commitment to quality ensure this black and Latin boner-fest will keep you wet and aroused'. However, there are no films which specifically advertise the 'best looking *white* men'. Non-white men in pornography are therefore reduced to their body parts and ethnic/racial categories, both exoticised and stereotyped, whereas white men are normalised.

The following advert which occurred in *Gay Times*, indicates some ways in which assumptions about ideal gay identities are used in marketing discourse.

Europe's Largest All-Gay Cruise Sails This August

Do you cruise? The most popular all-gay cruises in the world return to Europe this summer with our best itinerary yet. From Barcelona you'll join 2000 gay and lesbian guests as we sail to Cannes, Rome, Ephesus, Santorini and Mykonos for seven nights of unrestrained pleasure and incredible fun. Filled with the stellar entertainment that has made Atlantis world-leader in all-gay cruises.

Atlantis. The way we play (*Gay Times* July 2006, p. 11)

The advert is dominated by a picture of four shirtless young men, smiling and waving from the top of a cruise ship. All are handsome (at least from the point of view of a small survey of friends who I showed the advert to) and have 'six-pack' stomachs and hairless, muscular chests. Below this, three smaller pictures show a Mediterranean building, three clothed men reading a map outside the Roman Forum and finally a picture of the cruise ship sailing across the ocean. Therefore, the written reference to 'lesbian guests' does not appear to be borne out by the accompanying images of holiday-makers who are all male. The tagline 'Do you cruise?' suggests a possible double entendre; the verb *cruise* is also gay vernacular for looking for or engaging in anonymous sex. The references to 'unrestrained pleasure' and 'incredible fun', along with the images of attractive young men and the references to the 'largest all-gay cruise' and '2000… guests', also suggest that a wide choice of sexual partners will be available during the holiday. The final line, 'The way we play', further demonstrates the cruise company's attitude towards sexuality – as something playful, fun and even hedonistic. The advertisement therefore both relies on and promotes a discourse of gay sexuality as fun and potentially promiscuous as well as perpetuating a standard of gay desirability as youthful and muscular (see also Baker's (2005: 191–216) examination of the construction of hedonistic gay tourist identities through safer-sex materials).

As the marginalisation of lesbians in the advert above indicates, it appears that lesbian identities are not marketed as aggressively as gay male ones. Frances

Stevens, the publisher of *Deneuve* magazine (later renamed, *Curve*) aimed at lesbians, is quoted by Johnson (1993) as saying that gay men have set fashion standards for heterosexual men, but, on the other hand, lesbians have not had the same impact on heterosexual women, at least not the 'visible' lesbians, by which she refers to those who match the stereotype of wearing 'a lumber-jack shirt, sandals and no make-up'. This perhaps explains why lesbians are not marketed as rigorously as gay men – they are not seen as arbitrators of fashion, capable of influencing the wider heterosexual market. And lesbians, like all women, tend not to earn as much as men, even when employed in the same capacity. They are not therefore recognised as being the typical holders of the 'pink pound'.

Chasin (2000: 131) notes an assumption on behalf of marketers that lesbians are fundamentally, biologically and stylistically female and feminine, and that they will consume in an accordingly gendered way. A survey of the August 2006 edition of the UK magazine *Diva* (a publication intended for lesbians) reveals adverts for Ladybird Insurance (an insurance company for women), Exclusively Eve (sex toys and lingerie), Strawberry Village (adult store), Juicy Lube (lubricant), Pinksofa.com (a dating service), Tickled Online (gifts and erotic gadgets), The Pink Link (psychic advice telephone line), Pinkmobile (mobile telephone entertainment) and 2getherinpink.com (jewellery). References to the colour pink therefore abound in these adverts, which often employ the colour pink (or related shades from lavender to purple) in the background or as the colour of the typeface. For example, the advert for Tickled Online uses a dark pink font on a light pink background and features pictures of a range of different gifts (all coloured pink). The word *tickled* also strongly collocates in the British National Corpus with *pink*, suggesting that even though the word *pink* does not occur in this advert, there are heavy visual and collocational cues for the concept.

Pastoreau (2004: 82, 223) has argued that colour choices, particularly in terms of clothing, help to establish group identities which are then positioned in relation to society as a whole. Colours can therefore be social codes. Koller's (2006) survey of people's impressions of colours found that over three quarters of her informants associated pink with femininity. Magazines aimed at girls (such as *Girl* magazine discussed in Chapter 4) or heterosexual women (such as *More*) also make strong use of the colour pink. However, the colour pink, 'contains, generates, and tolerates more contradictions than practically any other colour' (von Taschitzki, 2006: 64). Although the respondents in Koller's survey linked pink with femininity and related features such as softness and delicacy, they also associated it with childhood, innocence, fun or vanity, artificiality and lust. Koller argues that pink can be used to signify a post-feminist identity, indexing independence or hedonistic femininity. And pink can also reference homosexuality, possibly due to the fact that gay male prisoners in Nazi concentration camps were made to wear a pink triangle, a symbol which was later reclaimed by gay liberationists. The association with pink and homosexuality is found in the phrase *pink pound* and in gay or queer-themed films such as *Pink Flamingos* (1972), *Ma Vie en Rose* (1997) and *A Touch of Pink* (2004).

Lesbian identity is therefore marketed as feminine, post-feminine, sexual and homosexual through the use of pink and references to sweet tastes (strawberries, juicy). However, the association of pink with femininity, found in social practices such as dressing girls in pink (and boys in blue), is a relatively recent phenomenon. Within western culture, *boys* were dressed in pink until around 1920 (Heller, 1989: 116–18, Pastoreau, 2004: 26–28). Then, pink was used as a lighter version of red, which had masculine associations with blood and fighting. It was not until World War II, that blue became associated with masculinity, through its association with the Navy and other male professions. A number of Koller's older respondents noted how they did not recall the trend for dressing girls in pink in the 1970s. Such research again indicates how practices can have relatively short histories before they become enshrined as 'traditions' as well as indicating how colour is used in an arbitrary and varying way to index sexuality and gender.

An analysis of the relationship between marketing strategies, discourse and gay and lesbian identities therefore reveals contradictions and ambivalence. The fact that pink is associated with femininity makes it possible to argue that advertisers are simply utilising discourses of 'traditional' gender in their marketing campaigns aimed at lesbians. But at the same time, the fact that pink is associated with a range of other traits, such as sexiness, 'post'-feminism or homosexuality, suggests that other readings are possible. Similarly, we can claim that the incorporation of gay pride discourses into advertising may be helpful in fostering positive self-images among gay people. But at the same time, it could be argued that the use of such discourses is cynical and that other aspects of gay advertising simply reinforce hegemonic masculinity in idealising the gay men who appear closest to it, while marginalising or subordinating those who do not. And Chasin (2000: 142–43) argues that when citizenship becomes an effect of market incorporation, only consumer-citizens can be truly enfranchised.

However, identity marketing need not always be connected to commercial institutions with an end goal of financial profit. People can also be engaged in the marketisation (use of practices and discourses associated with marketing) of themselves in a range of ways: in the following section I demonstrate one manner in which this is undertaken with respect to sexual and romantic desire, through the use of personal adverts.

The marketisation of the self: personal adverts

The purchase of products which supposedly improve gender or sexual identities towards a hegemonic (or counter-cultural) ideal is only one aspect of the relationship between marketisation and gender/sexuality. The concept of border crossing (Goodman, 1996), where forms of language associated with a particular situation or context start to occur in other contexts, is particularly relevant here. So promotional discourses, which were initially focused on advertising goods or services and were found in a predictable and limited set of contexts (advertising slots between television programmes, for example), are now crossing into other contexts, where they did not occur in the past. 'It is increasingly difficult not to be involved oneself in promoting, because many people have to be as part of their jobs, but also because self-promotion is becoming part and parcel of self-identity in contemporary societies' (Fairclough, 1995a: 139–40). So researchers have described the ways in which marketisation has occurred in a variety of contexts – from the increasingly scripted, repetitive encounters which telephone operators are required to engage in in order to represent a positive, standardised corporate image (Cameron, 2000) to the presence of promotional discourses in job adverts, university prospectuses and conference materials (Fairclough, 1995a) and the use of informal language in party political broadcasts (Pearce, 2005).

At the same time that we purchase products as one way of constructing gender/sexuality, we can also be engaged in the process of marketing our own identities to others. This occurs for a number of reasons, although particularly in order to develop relationships – not necessarily sexual or romantic relationships, but friendships or working relationships.

In this section I focus on a number of studies where people are involved in 'selling themselves' in a gendered or sexual context through the use of 'personal adverts'. Coupland (1996: 190) argues that, 'commodification can… be thought of as a relationally efficient and a 'natural' response to a particular configuration of societally imposed, modern life circumstances – time-pressured, work-centred, mass mediated'. In the West, the personal advert represents a quest for a romantic partner or perfect mate (Nair, 1992) with partner selection being anticipated through descriptions of the self, the other and the desired relationship (Erfurt, 1985). Personal columns are a kind of 'colony text' (Hoey, 1986) made up of numerous separate entries which may be categorised in different ways (e.g. men seeking women vs. women seeking men) although the meaning of each entry is not affected by the order in which they appear. The personal advert is a minimalist genre (Nair, 1992), often with non-essential items such as function words being omitted (Bruthiaux, 1994). They tend to have an informal, spoken style, often featuring lexical vagueness (Crystal and

Davy, 1975: 111–14), e.g. imprecise references to age or approximations through the suffix –*ish* (*tallish*, *youngish* etc).

Most studies of personal advertisements have tended to focus on the relationship between different identities and people's self-descriptions, and descriptions of their desired other. For example, Shalom (1997) found that heterosexual men were more likely to describe their ideal partner in terms of physical appearance (*attractive, slim, pretty*), whereas heterosexual women desired qualities such as intelligence, education and professionalism. Gay and lesbian advertisers tended to specify that they were looking for someone who was masculine and feminine respectively. Therefore, the majority of Shalom's advertisers, regardless of gender or sexuality, referred to or reinforced hegemonic gendered discourses in different ways. Thorne and Coupland (1998: 240) carried out a study of 100 gay male and 100 lesbian personal advertisements, noting that gay male advertisers prioritised appearance over personality while the reverse was true for lesbian advertisers. They also analysed four types of gay male adverts in some detail, each constructing a different discourse type with specific goals and identities being referenced (e.g. ex-forces bloke, Hollywood iconography, a sexually explicit hard-sell, and older men seeking younger men in exchange for domestic security). My own diachronic analysis of gay men's personal adverts from 1973 to 2000 (Baker, 2005) found evidence to suggest the existence of 'hegemonic homosexuality' (see also Rowe, 2000). Many advertisers focused on an idealised, desirable gay identity (both in terms of their self-presentation and their description of their desired other), consisting of stereotypically masculine qualities, as represented by the following two advertisements.

> Good-looking, 32, 6' tall, slim, straight-acting. Interests: keep fit, weights, badminton, squash, other sports and interests. Non-scene, genuine person, wanting to meet similar, straight-acting with similar interests. 21–34. Photo please. ALA. Box 9333

> Normally straight? Just happened to be looking at these pages? Clean-shaven, non-smoking young-looking guy (21+) wanted by straight-acting totally non-scene male 28. Fun/friendship. London Box 6611

> Baker (2005: 140, 142)

Here, terms like (*totally*) *non-scene* and *straight-acting* indicate a disavowal of the gay subculture or 'scene'. In the first advert, interest in a variety of sports is given as a further indicator of an authentic masculine identity, whereas in the second, the advertiser is seeking someone who 'normally' identifies as straight but 'just happened to be looking at these pages'. Clearly, such men do exist (see the discussion of MSM in Chapter 3). Such men are viewed as desirable because of their association with 'authentic' hegemonic masculinity and because they are not 'tainted' by contact with the gay subculture.

Although many of the adverts I examined articulated stereotypically masculine identities, a very small minority did not:

> Lonely, frustrated student (22), disabled, seeks long-term mate (21–29) for caring, loving, non-casual relationship. Effems welcome. Write with photo, phone number soon. Box 231.19.

> Not quite devastating to look at, occasionally camp, 25, lazy, thin, brown hair, sometimes drunk in Manchester. What butch beauty will sweep me off my feet. Box 37/45.

> Baker (2005: 141, 142)

But to what extent do these non-stereotyped adverts challenge discourses of hegemonic masculinity? In the first, one set of 'less-than-perfect' attributes 'lonely, frustrated, disabled' is offered in exchange for another which could be viewed as having an equally low market-value: 'effems welcome'. While in the second advert, referring to campness is a way of constructing a negative yet 'honest' identity, a strategy also noticed by Thorne and Coupland (1998). Camp occurs within a list of negative qualities: 'not quite devastating to look at', 'lazy', 'sometimes drunk'. By emphasising negative points, the advertiser uses reverse psychology, ensuring that the advert will at least stand out as being different and humorous. And, ultimately, the advertiser is seeking a 'butch' beauty, conforming to the gay fetishisation of masculinity. Therefore, the exceptions to the rule tend to reinforce a discourse of stereotyped masculinity as being the preferred desirable gay identity, constituting a form of 'hegemonic homosexuality'.[3]

However, taking Connell's (1987: 183) point that only heterosexual masculinity is truly hegemonic in contemporary western society, we could refer to such adverts as both creating and extolling a form of 'emphasised homosexuality'. Although heterosexual men do not advertise in gay personal adverts (unless they are 'MSM' or selling sexual services in some capacity), the adverts show that the most highly-valued identity is traditional heterosexual hegemonic masculinity or an approximation to it. The semantic set of words for masculinity: *straight-acting, SA, manly, butch, real man, straight-looking, non-camp, non-effeminate* constituted one of the largest sets of words in my corpus of gay adverts. Emphasised homosexuality therefore defines itself as subordinate to hegemonic masculinity, because it lauds the qualities that society has traditionally associated with heterosexual men. Within the gay subculture, men who look or behave as though they are typically heterosexual are afforded higher status (yet are still positioned as inferior to heterosexual men). The conflation of masculinity and heterosexuality (or gender and sexuality per se) is not just restricted to hegemonic masculine identities, it occurs within subordinate identities also – indeed, one of the tenets of hegemony is that the power hierarchy is enforced or accepted from the bottom up as well as the top down. Just as the girl cliques described by Wiseman and Simmons (see Chapter 5) call each other *sluts* and *bitches*, terms which judge and regulate their sexuality by a male double-standard, gay advertisers also 'buy' into a set of mores that fundamentally stigmatise the widely-held notions of gay identity – that they must be 'straight-acting' in order to be highly valued within the gay marketplace. However, a different, more post-modern 'reading' of such adverts could be that, to an extent, the advertisers are reappropriating aspects of hegemonic masculinity for themselves – refusing to accept mainstream society's stereotyping of gay men as effeminate, or that they are subverting the gender hierarchy by objectifying hegemonic masculinity as a sexual entity, to be consumed or used (see Chapter 8). Such adverts could therefore be read as both complicit *and* empowering.

A number of the texts examined in this and earlier chapters have produced analyses which indicate subtleties or even contradictions. Such texts may utilise a 'gender equality' discourse while also referring to hegemonic masculinity. They may champion the liberation of a minority or oppressed identity, while, at the same time, making stereotyping assumptions, placing expectations or attempting to manipulate holders of that identity in various ways. Such analyses are not limited to advertising texts (although adverts are often exemplars of such contradictions). As noted in earlier chapters, since the 1990s, feminist linguists have moved beyond an approach which classifies language use as being simply sexist or non-sexist, instead, acknowledging that feminism itself has brought about changes in society that have resulted in much more subtle, complex distinctions, open to multiple interpretations – a post-feminist perspective in other words. Two writers who have outlined how such a 'post' form of analysis could be utilised are Mills (1998), who describes post-feminist analysis, and Baxter (2003), who outlines feminist post-structuralist discourse analysis. As Baxter (2003: 9) notes, 'individuals are rarely consistently positioned as powerful across all discourses at work within a given context – they are often located simultaneously as both powerful and powerless'. Such an approach also recognises that women are not a homogenous group. 'Before, it was assumed that there was a universal feminist position of reading and that all women would read in similar ways; since then, it has become clear that women have different access to education, different experience, different affiliations and also different takes on feminism which colour their readings and their reception of individual language items and the overall message as a whole' (Mills, 1998: 239).

To give an example of how post-feminist analysis can be utilised in relation to advertising texts, Mills (1998) examined an advertisement for the dating agency, *Dateline*, which incorporated a questionnaire so that readers could find their 'perfect partner'. She initially notes that the text establishes 'politically correct credentials' by offering a choice of *Mr, Mrs* or *Ms* (and omitting the choice, *Miss*) and referring to *partner* rather than *husband/wife*. However, in other parts of the text, sexist discourses were utilised in more subtle ways. For example, although the text appears to be intended for both men and women, an analysis of the language used and discourses employed, suggests that it is actually only aimed at women. Readers are asked to classify themselves in terms of whether they are *fashionable, somewhat dreamy* or *chatty* – terms which, stereotypically, refer to female identities. Mills (1998: 244–45) argues that the elements in the questionnaire are, 'mostly structured around those things which are stereotypically what males within relationships want. Your age, physical appearance, dress, education and work are seen to be as important as might be expected, but there is a curious expectation on children and whether they are living at home or elsewhere which suggests implicitly that children might be viewed as a problem'. Also, terms like *children* and *homemaking* are listed as options under the heading 'Your interests' rather than under the section on 'Your work', suggesting that bringing up children is not characterised as 'real work'. Therefore, as with the cosmetic surgery brochure or the advert for British Telecom, discussed earlier, the *Dateline* article has a surface appearance of non-sexism or even anti-sexism, but, 'the underlying workings of the text and the meanings which readers negotiate with the text are quite different' (Mills, 1998: 247). Post-feminist analysis therefore acknowledges that multiple readings of a text are possible (see also the discussion of *queer* in Chapter 7), and that sexist discourses are now tempered – although not eradicated – by the presence of equality or feminist discourses.

Resisting commodification?

Leading on from the post-modern conceptualisation of power as non-absolute, some researchers have noted that while commodification plays a significant role in the creation of personal advertisements, advertisers do have the opportunity to 'humanise' their adverts in a range of ways. So, the following example consists of a written and spoken advert, left on the Teletext One-2-One service (Coupland, 1997: 198). Here, advertisers can post written adverts and also leave voice-link adverts where they can be heard on the telephone.

Written advert
YORKS LADY 39 DIVORCED VGSOH GOOD LOOKING, LONG NATURAL BLONDE
HAIR SEEKS FUTURE HUSBAND IN CORNWALL 40–50 BOX 212.

Spoken advert
Hello I'm Jenny and I live in Yorkshire (.) thirty-nine and have been divorced
almost ten years (.) I'm five foot three bluey-grey eyes and have long natural
blonde hair (1.5) I'm considered to be very attractive or (.) well so people say
(laughs) and I have a good sense of humour (.) to get to the point I'm looking
for a future husband in Cornwall (2.0) so leave your number and I'll give you a
call (.) thank-you.

Teletext One-2-One, March 1994

Coupland notes how the advertiser consistently self-presents within existing
sociocultural stereotypes of female desirability, by describing her appearance
in both her written and spoken adverts. However, in the spoken advert she
humanises the commodification by using hedging, 'I'm considered to be very
attractive or (.) well so people say (laughs)'. The use of the discourse marker,
well, her hesitation and laughter allow for modesty and presumably likeability.
Her use of 'get to the point' also serves to make the advert sound more human,
by downplaying the importance of her earlier self-description (again suggesting modesty) in favour of being honest about her goals. Coupland (1997:
202) concludes that, 'the advertisers who have initially subjected themselves
to the formulaicity of the written mode do also command resources to resist
and undermine the process of commodification itself. Some facets of dating
advertising, then, actually show people playing creatively with the strictures
of the media and re-constituting themselves as 'human' *de*-commodified
beings'.
    Other researchers (e.g. Hermes, 1995, Jackson, Stevenson and Brooks, 2001,
Benwell and Stokoe, 2006) have also shown that the relationship between a
product and its (potential) consumer is not necessarily one where the audience
passively accepts its positioning as a consumer or reacts to marketing in a
predictable manner. A commonly-voiced criticism of studies of advertising is
that reception needs to be taken into account and we should not assume that
audiences are homogenous entities comprised of clones who will respond in
the same way. An advert is a 'text', which is open to multiple interpretations.
Some readers may be persuaded to purchase a product and/or internalise the
particular discourses of gender or sexuality that the advert accesses. Others
may consciously reject the advert and its discourses or may react with multiple
or conflicting responses.

For example, Benwell and Stokoe (2006) analysed interactions within focus groups (see Chapter 2) of young male readers of men's magazines. The men's magazine is one way in which new masculinities are 'sold' to audiences (see Mort, 1996, Nixon, 1996, and Edwards, 1997, for more detailed discussion of the commercialisation of masculinity since the 1980s). Benwell and Stokoe (2006: 193) argue that the study of consumers' own talk is useful in that, 'it is able to capture the fine-grained and sometimes contradictory or ambivalent accounts and identity work of the consumers, which is arguably more fruitful for a discursive study of identity than the many studies which view the consumer in abstract economic terms'. In the two examples below, a focus group consisting of 21-year old males discuss the men's magazines' promotions of traditionally 'feminine' grooming products like moisturiser, which construct a sensitive 'new man' identity.

1	Interviewer:	Are there parts of the magazine you always ignore?
2	Mike:	I generally try to skip past the 50 pages worth of adverts
3		(Laughter from them all)
4	Interviewer:	Mike avoids adverts, is that the same for <u>all</u> of you?
5	Greg:	Yeah, I try my best not to look at them
6	Daniel:	There's just so much advertising in them anyway turn a page 'oh no not
7		another advertisement' you're like 'is there anything here worth reading'
8	Jonathan:	I remember doing a Nivea thing that I bought Nivea after reading it years
9		ago like y'know how they have like articles
10	Interviewer:	an article rather than an advert
11	Jonathan:	Yeah it was like a sponsored article-
12	Mike:	(Laughing) Lucky this is anonymous
13		(Laughter from all)

Benwell and Stokoe (2006: 197)

Benwell and Stokoe argue that the members of the focus group shift between a number of different and sometimes conflicting subject positions which relate to their identity choices. In line 2 of the excerpt, above, Mike says that he skips past the fifty pages of adverts, which is confirmed and elaborated on by the group laughter in line 3, and Greg and Daniel's comments in lines 5 and 6. A consensus is therefore constructed: the adverts are annoying and not worthy of attention. Here we could view the subject position as 'cynical consumer'. However, in lines 8 and 11 Jonathan presents a counter-position by revealing that he bought Nivea after reading about it in a sponsored article. Mike's comment in line 12 'Lucky this is anonymous' and the group laughter suggest that Jonathan has occupied a 'troubled subject position' (Wetherell, 1998) whereby he has breached a normative social code. The 'troubled position' is ambiguous: it could be that the group feel that Jonathan has been embarrassed for succumbing to advertising and appearing as a 'passive dupe', or alternatively he could be embarrassed because he has compromised his (hegemonic) masculinity by buying a 'feminine' grooming product (or we could interpret this as a mixture of the two, or something different altogether). Benwell and Stokoe contrast the above excerpt with the following:

1	Daniel:	I think humour is a good way of getting round touchy subjects, like
2		y'know… if you asked a normal kind of lad who'd be like 'oh I'm not
3		going to go and have a facial' or something
4	Interviewer:	Having read it, would any of you be interested in those kinds of products?
5	Mike:	Great! If I had the money I'd have a go at it.

Benwell and Stokoe (2006: 198)

Here, the exchange shows some of the assumptions made about what constitutes a 'normal lad', yet the participants distance themselves from this identity – Daniel uses a third-person distancing strategy 'a normal kind of lad' while Mike (without irony) says that he *would* use the grooming product. This excerpt differs sharply from the earlier one where use of grooming products was marked as being problematic. The focus group participants therefore shift positions both in terms of their relationship to the constructions of masculinity used by the magazines (aligning themselves with the 'normal lad' and the 'new man' identities at different points) and in terms of their relationship to the advertising strategies in the magazines. So subject positions include being a passive dupe: ('doing a Nivea thing'), being a reflexic critic ('If you asked a normal kind of lad…'), being an uncritical consumer (Jonathan's admission to buying Nivea) and being a cynical consumer ('There's just so much advertising'). Benwell and Stokoe (2006: 199–200) conclude that consumers are not a homogenous constituency; their accounts of their practices[4] vary considerably and are demonstrated by the micro demands of the interactional context. The men in their focus group negotiated a line between being detached or disdainful of the magazines and accepting or being deferential to them. Benwell and Stokoe therefore conclude that any attempt to identify a single or 'true' consumer position is a 'red herring'.

Conclusion

In contemporary societies, advertising is an incredibly influential means by which discourses of gender and sexuality are circulated, strengthened or challenged. However, the relationship between advertising and discourse is multifaceted and often contradictory. On the one hand, it is in the interests of capitalism to maximise profit by appealing to a wide range of 'niche' identities, but at the same time the mainstream must not be neglected. Advertising discourse tends to reify identity groups such as women, gay men and lesbians: in targeting and validating such groups by using 'gay pride' or 'feminist' discourses, such adverts may be viewed as empowering. But post-structuralist analysis of such adverts shows that it is also possible to find traces of hegemonic discourse within them, prioritising certain types of identities (even within groups who are subordinated or marginalised) over others. And within capitalist societies, we are all potentially marketers of identity – writers of personal adverts, who are not (usually) motivated by economic profit, can still show adherence to competitive strategies which make use of hegemonic discourses.

Research by Coupland (1996) and Benwell and Stokoe (2006) suggests that consumers are able to recognise such inconsistencies within advertising discourses and can position themselves in relation to them in an equally varied range of ways. As Chasin (2000: 141) notes, 'Most scholars of advertising in the 1980s and 1990s moved beyond the idea that ads provide a transparent window onto values or practices; but clearly ads have something to do with social practice. Serving the plain and singular purpose of selling things, ads attempt to forge associations between specific things for sale and the existing belief systems of their prospective buyers. Of course, ads also manipulate, and thus modify, those belief systems, but ads fundamentally depend on provoking associations to beliefs which are normalized'.

Advertising seems to have resulted in a newer form of equality then, which, rather depressingly, involves *more* people in potentially negative social practices, rather than reducing the impact of such social practices per se. So heterosexual men can be sexually objectified and urged to worry about their appearance in much the same way as women. Similarly, gay men and lesbians can be targeted, too – although it could be asked whether being told what holidays to go on, what to wear, what their bodies should look like and how they should *do* their identities is a form of 'progress'. And this is, potentially, a form of equality which helps to perpetuate yet depoliticise identity categories, reducing them to differences in terms of style rather than politics, with economic clout influencing a person's ability to 'improve' their gender. Yet the analysis of gender and sexual identities in relation to advertising suggests a number of possible 'readings', which position us multiply – sometimes as disempowered 'dupes', but at other times as empowered, active or even resistant consumers. The fact that we, as individuals, can also be involved in marketing our identities to others, suggests an increasing awareness of linguistic strategies used in advertising discourse, which may, ultimately, be empowering.

And at least the enthusiasm with which advertisers have recently begun to target subordinated identity groups suggests that western society is becoming more inclusive in some ways, the extent of which I aim to examine in more detail in the following two chapters.

Notes

1   *Gay Times* is a UK magazine which advertises itself as the 'world's biggest current affairs and lifestyle magazine for the gay and lesbian communities' on its website. http://www.gaytimes.co.uk/gt/. Accessed 17 July 2006.

2   Judy Garland was the lead actress in the 1939 film *The Wizard of Oz* and a favourite of gay fans of cinema. She died of a barbituates overdose on 22 June 1969. During a routine police raid of the Stonewall Inn, a New York gay bar on 27 June 1969, the patrons, many of whom were fans of Garland, were at a low ebb and decided to fight back. The ensuing conflict is believed by some to have kick-started the Gay Liberation movement.

3   My research (Baker, 2005) found that as social attitudes towards homosexuality hardened in the 1980s, due to negative media coverage (mainly regarding AIDS) and resulting in legislation such as Clause 28 which banned the 'promotion' of homosexual lifestyles, gay advertisers responded by categorising themselves and their desired partners even more in terms of words like *masculine, straight-acting, non-scene* and *discreet*. Such words increased by 100 percent between the early 1980s and the early 1990s, returning to their original levels at the turn of the century as the moral panic around gay men faded. References to stereotypically masculine jobs and body hair also increased over the 1980s, whereas references to sexual roles and fetish objects (what Blachford (1981: 192) refers to as *expressive artefacts* and *concrete objects*) popularised within gay communities decreased. The study illustrates the power that mainstream hegemonic culture has over its subordinated and marginalised groups: desire being lexicalised in a way which attempts to erase or deny 'scene-based' gay identity, instead fetishising hetero-sexual hegemonic masculinity even more.

4   Clearly though, accounts of purchasing behaviour are self-presentations and may not be indicative of actual purchasing practices.

7   Queering identity: the new tolerance (and its limits)

Introduction

In previous chapters, we have seen how language use has been one of the major ways by which traditional or hegemonic sexual and gendered identities are constructed, maintained and regulated. In patriarchal society, hegemonic masculinity lies at the peak of an identity hierarchy, having its own boundaries policed, while other identities are subordinated or marginalised. Identities which threaten to blur the illusion of clear distinctions between binary categories can be subject to erasure or marginalisation. For example, they can be 'unspoken' or rejected, as in the case of bisexuality, which has been discursively constructed by both heterosexual and homosexual people as a kind of compromise made by homosexuals who want to retain an amount of 'heterosexual privilege'.

However, in western society, movements such as feminism and gay and lesbian liberation have begun to challenge patriarchal hegemony. Connell (1995: 77) points out that hegemonic masculinity is a "currently accepted' strategy', suggesting that, 'new groups may challenge old solutions and construct a new hegemony'. So, while hegemonic masculinity is still a powerful force, and relatively 'traditional' ways of performing gender and conducting relationships are still highly valued by many people, continuing to be legitimised by political, religious and media institutions, social changes have occurred at an unprecedented rate over the past few decades. As Giddens (1991) notes, contemporary society is 'post-traditional' – people do not necessarily have to rely on old, set ways of doing things. Instead, a range of choices are gradually becoming more available, offering a wider variety of potential lifestyles, relationships and identities that are negotiated and maintained through communication.

In this chapter and the one which follows, I examine the relationship between hegemonic and non-hegemonic identities more closely. Here, the focus is not on powerful identities (as discussed in Chapters 4 and 5), but on identities which are more clearly considered to be subordinate or marginalised.

I have called this chapter The New Tolerance, because, to a large extent, the point I made about increased choice has only come to pass because we (speaking from the point of view of a British resident) generally live in a more tolerant society. However, it should also be acknowledged that there are limitations to that tolerance, hence the codicil (*and its limits*). I also want to use this chapter to focus more closely on the concept of *queer theory*, something which I touched on in Chapters 4 and 5.

Queer theory

As shown in Chapter 4, the concept of *heteronormativity* enables us to understand why sex/gender and gender/sexuality are often conflated, and how this conflation is used to maintain divisions of power within societies. The related concept of *queer theory* also focuses on the ways that 'normal'/'not normal' identities and relationships are 'fixed' and reproduced as binary oppositions in society. In the late nineteenth century, *queer* was used as a pejorative word for sexual deviance (referring to homosexual or effeminate males in particular), derived from its earlier meaning of 'something not quite right', 'strange', 'unusual', etc. However, in the 1990s the term was reclaimed by gay and lesbian communities as a positive concept, with an empowering political agenda attached. While *queer* can be a noun, adjective or verb, the reclaimed usage has emphasised its verb status. Initially derived from idiomatic phrases such as 'to queer the pitch', activists talked of queering identity politics, indicating that this is a more pro-active, involved use of the term, rather than it serving as a derogatory label assigned to others by their detractors. As Sinfield (1994: 205) notes, 'Lately gay has been used continually in the UK gutter press alongside their words ('poof' and so on), and is thereby contaminated with many of their resonances. We can't prevent that happening... we can attempt a new manoeuvre though... the aggression and ambition in the readoption of 'queer' are directly proportionate to the degree to which it proposes to overturn the historic, hostile meaning... 'Queer' says defiantly, that we don't care what they call us'.

Queer theory is also strongly linked to Butler's theory of performativity (see Chapter 3), the idea that gender is a social construct, something that people (continually) do, rather than an essential aspect of their being, and therefore subject to change or disruption. As Butler points out (1991: 24), 'if heterosexuality is compelled to repeat itself in order to establish the illusion of its own uniformity and identity, then this is an identity permanently at risk, for what if it fails to repeat, or if the very exercise of repetition is redeployed for a very different performative purpose? If there is, as it were, always a compulsion to repeat, repetition never fully accomplishes identity... [identity] runs the risk of becoming deinstituted at every interval'. Therefore, a central aspect of queer theory is deconstruction. Instead of concentrating on constructing a 'gay subject' (for example, by asking 'how do gay people use language?') queer theory focuses on deconstructing the underlying logic/rules of a gay subject by examining how the identity itself is constructed through language ('how does language construct gay people?'). One way to achieve this goal is to focus on the (un-)coupling of opposites – the *deconstruction* of the homo/hetero code that structures the social text of daily life (Seidman, 1993: 130). Queer theory is therefore strongly linked to post-structuralism. Poststructuralists propose that the identity of a person or thing is implicated in its opposite (something we considered in Chapter 5), so heterosexuality gains a good deal of its meaning in relation to homosexuality, and these two terms assume a relationship which, due to heteronormativity, is hierarchical. Queer theory therefore promotes a politics of subversion, a belief that polar terms such as *homosexual/heterosexual* are mutually dependent, unstable and subject to reversal. One of the goals of queer theory, then, is to examine and deconstruct the structures and symbolism inherent in the homo/hetero binary.[1]

For example, one strategy of people who incorporate queer theory in their work is to focus on the meanings of the terms *homosexual* and *heterosexual*, by examining their origins and development over time, in order to argue that these identities are socially constructed. As Butler (1990) has argued, heterosexuality could only be established as the normal state of being by the creation of homosexuality as its 'abnormal' alternative. Also, writers like Smith-Rosenberg (1975), Weeks (1977) and Katz (1983) have challenged the assumption that the concept of homosexuality has a single meaning which has remained constant throughout time.

For example, the term *homosexual* was originally coined by Karl Maria Kertbeny in the 1860s as a more positive alternative to an existing term, *pederast*. Kertbeny claimed that many homosexuals were more masculine than other men, being superior to heterosexuals (a well-meaning but still discriminatory stance). However, the word was quickly adopted by doctors, including Richard von Krafft-Ebing, who concluded that homosexuality was a form of inherited medical illness, resulting in effeminacy. Foucault notes that this labelling was an act of reification, so the naming of homosexuality brought it into existence: 'We must not forget that the psychological, psychiatric, medical category of homosexuality was constituted from the moment it was characterised' (1976: 43). Furthermore, Katz (1983: 147–50) notes that the word *homosexual* was created before *heterosexual* – it was only with the creation of 'deviant' homosexuality that the concept of 'normal' heterosexuality could then be conceptualised. Sedgwick (1991: 2) points out that from the point of naming, every person could be assigned a homo- or hetero-sexuality, as well as a gender.

As a result of the reification of homosexuality in the late nineteenth century, popular thinking presupposed that perceptions of sexuality had always existed in this way. Yet historians have shown that this was clearly not the case. For example, Smith-Rosenburg (1975) in her essay 'The female world of love and ritual' pointed out that in the nineteenth century, same-sex intimacies occurred between middle-class women, being maintained at the same time as heterosexual marriages, without incurring public stigma or shame. Halperin (1990: 30–31) describes how in Ancient Greece sexuality was conceptualised in terms of reception and penetration, or active and passive sexual behaviour. This reflected and emphasised the hierarchical social order, rather than constituting an inherent sexual identity. Spencer (1995) observers that in Ancient Greece, acceptance of male-male relationships as part of a 'balanced bisexuality' was viewed as normal (as long as one partner was an adult and the other was aged between 12 and 15), although effeminate adult males tended to incur social opprobrium. While in seventeenth and early eighteenth century Britain a distinction was made between *fops* who were viewed as effeminate but promiscuously heterosexual and *rakes* who took the penetrative role in sex with younger males but were not regarded as effeminate (Trumbach, 1991: 105). By 1710 a new identity, the Molly, had emerged – someone who was effeminate *and* had sex with other men. Such men existed within a subculture based around what were known as Molly Houses, that is, clubs and taverns where working and middle-class men (sometimes dressed as women) would meet, for the purposes of socialisation and to make sexual contacts (Norton, 1992).

Research by Baker and Stanley (2003) and Houlbrook (2005) suggests that in the first half of the twentieth century, male homosexuality in Britain was broadly organised around three distinct social groups: working-class *queens*, who were effeminate and sometimes wore make-up; *trade* who were also working-class but differed from queens in that they were masculine; and 'respectable' middle-class homosexuals who were assimilated into mainstream culture and may have paid for sex. Houlbrook (2005: 137) writes, 'Shaped by broader differences of class, gender, age, ethnicity, and place, men understood and organized their desires and their participation in queer urban culture very differently to each other and to contemporary understandings of 'homo' and 'heterosexuality''. Baker and Stanley (2003) describe how Merchant Navy ships accommodated all three 'classes' of men, with queens taking service roles as stewards or waiters, trade employed in jobs involving manual labour or technical work such as carpentry or engineering, and middle-class men taking command positions as officers. Relationships between queens and trade which resembled heterosexual marriages (and sometimes involved informal ceremonies) were not uncommon, although the trade would often also have a girlfriend or wife waiting back home.

Language use was one way in which the boundaries between the different classes of queer men were defined, with Polari (see Chapter 3) being used as a form of solidarity and identity expression by the queens. Mark, a waiter for eight years in the 1960s, describes how he'd be getting ready for a party, with his *husband* [lover] George and his *sister* [friend], Franny:

> 'I'd say to Franny, 'What are you doing tonight girl?' ... She'd say 'What I'm going to do girl, I'm going to go round and dohbie [wash] the riah [hair], I'm going to do the brows, and then I'm going to put the eek [face] on for the Pig and Whistle [the ship's bar]'. Well, my husband would understand that she's putting on make-up because that's 'putting eek on' you see. But *he* wouldn't use it' (Baker and Stanley, 2003: 83).

In Britain, after the decriminalisation of homosexuality in 1967 and the subsequent gay liberation movement in the 1970s, homosexuality and heterosexuality were conceived as distinct sexual identities and, in some cases, lifestyles. However, even now we can point to people who do not 'fit' these categories, such as men who are labelled MSM. Furthermore, since the 1990s, some people now identify as *queer* rather than gay, as a way of recognising the problematic nature of sexual categorisation. Historical analyses therefore show that society's construction and implementation of categories and roles regarding same-sex desire and behaviour has been subject to change over time.[2] The following two excerpts, both from medical texts about homosexuality written at different times, further illustrate how discourses of homosexual identity have changed from the nineteenth to the twentieth centuries.

From Ellis (1897) *Sexual Inversion in the Male.* Chapter 7, 'The Prevention of Homosexuality' 247–48.

> ...sexual inversion cannot be regarded as essentially an insane or psychopathic state. But it is frequently associated with nervous conditions which may be greatly benefited by hygiene and treatment, without any attempt at all to overcome a homosexual attitude which may be too deeply rooted to be changed...These are conditions which may be ameliorated, and they may be treated in much the same way as if no inversion existed, by physical and mental tonics; or, if necessary, sedatives; by regulated gymnastics and out-of-door exercises; and by occupations which employ, without overexerting, the mind... The inversion is not thus removed. But if the patient is still young, and if the perversion does not appear to be deeply rooted in the organism, it is probable that – provided his own good-will is aiding – general hygienic measures, together with removal to a favorable environment, may gradually lead to the development of the normal sexual impulse.

From Masters and Johnson (1982) *Homosexuality in Perspective* pp. 357, 407–8.

> The therapist must be aware that there are any number of good reasons for the individual to seek change in a homosexual orientation. For example, there may be the real or implied threat of social rejection or a constant concern for job security...
>
> In brief, approximately one in three homosexual men and women treated for sexual satisfaction either failed to convert or revert to heterosexuality during the acute phase of the treatment program or actively or theoretically returned to overt homosexual interaction during the required five-year follow-up period... An important factor that has contributed significantly to failures in treating male homosexual dissatisfaction in the past should prove far less of a barrier to effective therapy in the future. It is anticipated that the degree of cooperation with the therapeutic process by those homosexual men requesting reversion or conversion therapy will improve markedly... The homosexual community will soon realize that there are improved therapeutic procedures available to the dissatisfied as well as the dysfunctional homosexual. This realization should, in turn, increase confidence in and cooperation with the therapeutic process.

Ellis, writing in 1897, characterised homosexuality as a 'sexual inversion'. Although he said it was not an insane or psychopathic state, he points to 'nervous conditions' which are 'frequently' associated with homosexuality. A causal link is not made so it is unclear whether he believes that the nervous conditions cause homosexuality or vice versa, or whether they develop independently of each other. These nervous conditions accompanying homosexuality can be apparently 'treated' with sedatives, tonics, exercise and gymnastics. Homosexuals are, therefore, constructed as 'nervous' and needing to engage in physical exercise – the implication being that homosexuals are effeminate or feminine.

The discourse around homosexuality is couched in terms of change – whether homosexuals *can* be changed or not. Ellis suggests that in some cases, if (unspecified) 'hygienic measures' are employed together with a change of environment (again unspecified), then a 'normal, sexual impulse' may be developed. The use of terms like *perversion* and *inversion* frame homosexuality as a form of mental illness, opposed to heterosexuality which is 'normal'. Ellis does not suggest that all homosexuals can be changed – prognosis seems to be best if the patient is young, suggesting that he viewed homosexuality as a degenerative mental illness, becoming 'deeply rooted' over time.

The Masters and Johnson excerpt is less explicitly negative, only using a single, neutral-sounding term, *homosexual*, rather than *invert* or *pervert*. This is a more research-based, empirical perspective, with references to statistics, follow-up periods and factors, where homosexuals are positioned as experimental subjects. The discourses in the two texts converge, however, by suggesting that homosexual people can be 'converted' or 'reverted', although Masters and Johnson cite therapy or a 'treatment program' as the way of achieving this, and refer to 'homosexual dissatisfaction' – people who are viewed as wanting to become heterosexuals. Therefore, while Ellis implies that homosexuality is a perversion where change is always preferable where possible, Masters and Johnson only advocate change for 'dissatisfied homosexuals'. While Masters and Johnson's more 'neutral' perspective contains an awareness of social reasons why a person might be a dissatisfied homosexual (social rejection, concerns about job security), the 'problem' of homosexuality is constructed as an issue for the individual rather than apportioning responsibility to heterosexism and homophobia within society. So Masters and Johnson do not criticise or question whether it is societal attitudes that require changing, rather than individuals. Also, Masters and Johnson's belief that the homosexual community will recognise improved therapeutic procedures for 'dissatisfied homosexuals' seems overly optimistic. Indeed, the main users of therapies purported to 'convert' homosexuals have tended to be people from religious communities (Yeoman, 1999).

Although the Masters and Johnson excerpt is now only about 25 years old, the concept of providing therapy to change homosexual identity would be seen as unnecessary or unfair (or even regarded as a form of structural violence) by many people today, and this shows how constructions of sexuality are subject to change over time. Both excerpts demonstrate the belief that sexual orientation *can* be altered through some sort of intervention or treatment. While post-modern theory also views sexuality as fluid, it is more focused on viewing *constructions of sexuality* as subject to change over time; where a person's sexual desires or behaviour change it is usually through a more subtle, gradual and natural process, rather than being forced by therapy. In such cases, we could more likely conceive of a model where different aspects of a person's sexuality are (temporarily) backgrounded or foregrounded at any given time, rather than suggesting a dramatic alteration of sexuality (and, of course, it is important to stress that understandings of sexuality could also change in the future).

As well as examining historical change, there are also differences in constructions of sexuality between cultures. For example, Schmitt and Sofer (1992) examined how sexuality is constructed in countries like Morocco, Syria, Iran, Persia, Turkey and Israel, where men who engage in sexual acts with other men do not always consider themselves to be homosexual, especially if they are the active participant: '...the most normal thing is fucking boys. For the man, the buggerer, it is perfectly normal, if he is married and a father... A man should not allow others to bugger him. Otherwise he loses his name, his honor... There is a clear rule: You cannot be fucked. But what this really comes down to is: Saying of somebody that he has been fucked disturbs social relations.... In spite of all of this activity I saw there are no 'homosexuals' and there is no (indigenous) word for 'homosexuality" (Schmitt, 1992: 6-7). As in western cultures, sexuality is also linked to gender, in that there are rules about which sexual acts constitute a masculine gendered performance. However, it is sexual *behaviour* rather than the sex of a partner which determines masculinity – with 'active' penetration (of anyone) associated with masculinity, while passivity is linked to femininity. The concept of homosexuality in terms of being a 'gay identity' as it is recognised in the West is therefore moot.

Herdt (1981) describes a New Guinean tribe called the Sambia, where homosexuality plays an important role in initiation rituals involving men. Among the Sambia, all the men engage in homosexual behaviour at certain points in their lives. Such studies suggest that viewing homosexuality as a minority identity, or even as a stable identity which exists in all cultures, is simply incorrect. Furthermore, research into sexual minorities in other cultures has revealed categories of sexuality which do not map neatly onto the current westernised framework: 'the *hijra* of India, the *yan daudu* of Nigeria, the *kathoey* of Thailand, the Filipino *batut*, Tongan *fakaleiti*, and Brazilian *travesti*, as well as more recently emergent categories such as *gay* in Indonesia and *tong-zhi* in Hong Kong (see e.g. contributions to Campbell-Kibler et al., 2002; Leap, 1995; Leap and Boellstorff, 2003; Livia and Hall, 1997)' (Cameron, 2005b: 494). According to Hall (2003: 101), then, "heterosexual' and 'homosexual' are terms that do not capture the complexity of most human lives when viewed diachronically for past behaviours and always inherent future potentials'. And Seidman (1993: 126) notes that there are 'repressive consequences' of trying to impose current Western thinking on non-Western experiences.

Another tenet of queer theory, however, is the idea that identities are fluid *and* multiple. Therefore, the dominant liberationist opposition between gay/straight or gay/lesbian has passed into multiple divisions such as white/black/Latino gay, middle-class/working-class gay S-M/non S-M gay, etc. (Seidman, 1993: 129). The issues of organising and theorising these multiple differences in light of identity politics has led to the call by queer theorists for the abandonment of identity as a focus of gay politics (see also Cameron and Kulick's (2003: 106–32) discussion of foregrounding desire rather than identity in language and sexuality research.)

The taking, then, of the word *queer* by poststructuralists, is inclusive if not all-encompassing in terms of who it refers to. As Warner (1993: xxvi) notes: 'The preference for 'queer' represents, among other things, an aggressive impulse of generalisation; it rejects a minoritizing logic of toleration or simple political interest-representation in favour of a more thorough resistance to regimes of the normal'. Queer, therefore does not want to be viewed as merely another minority to be 'tolerated' or assimilated. Queer is against the 'normal', not the heterosexual; and because of this, it is able to transcend categories such as 'gay', 'lesbian', 'male' and 'female'. Halperin (1995: 61–2) agrees: 'Queer is by definition *whatever* is at odds with the normal, the legitimate, the dominant. *There is nothing in particular to which it necessarily refers.* It is an identity without essence.

Seidman (1993: 133) links poststructuralist thinking to that of the political activist group *Queer Nation*, noting that both employ disruptive politics of subversion and are opposed to disciplining, normalising social forces. Queer Nation stands for anyone who is outside mainstream society, offering an 'abstract unity of differences without wishing to name and fix' them. Or, in other words, a queer activist can be different from what is considered 'normal' by society's standards in many (or few), deliberately *unspecified*, changing and interacting ways – to specify differences would be to disunify. So both poststructuralists and members of Queer Nation wish to avoid self-identification which would limit and fracture their dynamics.

Barrett (2002: 27) describes this unspecified use of *queer* as a linguistic experiment, where the pejorative term is reclaimed but has no referent – it does not correspond to any real world signified, but instead, 'is intended to index an imagined and undefined set of sexual practices… that fall outside of the heteronormative assumptions of dominant societal discourse'. Barrett warns that in defining a particular group as queer, we aim to 'fill in' the missing signified, but in doing so we will be 'driven by the dominant ideology that demands limitations be placed on acceptable practices and identities'. Therefore, queer linguistics does not study the language of people that mainstream society labels as queer – to do so is to reify identity categories created by a dominant social order. Instead, queer linguistics is a linguistics, 'in which identity categories are not accepted as a priori entities, but are recognised as ideological constructs produced by social discourse… By shifting our focus from how language reflects a priori identity categories to how language constructs identity categories we might be able to develop a more nuanced understanding of the relationship between language and identity that is not based on biased and exclusionary assumptions concerning identity itself' (Barrett, 2002: 28).

However, in being against identity, the poststructuralist refusal to name the subject is potentially problematic in that it can result in confusion about what queer theory actually is and how it can be exploited. As Cameron and Kulick (2003: 148–49) note, 'Scholars working with the term "queer" enjoy pointing out that "queer" denotes that which exceeds definition, that which is undefinable… What is "queer" for you may not be "queer" for someone else: realizing this and trying to understand the ways in which different understandings and uses of "queer" circulate in conversations, political movements or theoretical discussions can lead to a heightened sense of the political work that all seemingly descriptive labels perform'. However, Cameron and Kulick (2003: 148–49) also warn that this can result in a lack of academic clarity. I agree that while this undefinable notion of *queer* is a useful theoretical construct, it has the potential for making analysis of the construct difficult. We may want to examine the ways in which certain types of identities, or forms of sexual desire or behaviour are constructed as queer or not queer – but in order to do that we first have to acknowledge that the identities exist (if only) as social constructs. Obviously this does not mean we should reify or essentialise them, but we do have to refer to them in some way. Clearly, people do self-identify and are labelled by others as male, female, gay, lesbian or heterosexual, etc. These identities 'exist' within discourse, shaping the minds, bodies and lives of many people.

However, queer theory should help us to understand that such identity labels are only 'real' for the here and now – they are not set in stone; instead, there are many other possible configurations. Queer theory can help us to deconstruct the relations between these different identity categories, allowing us to examine the reasons why certain categories are privileged over others. So a queer analysis should allow us to question, challenge or subvert the ways in which societies normalise or problematise different identities at different times.

Livia (2002: 87) writes that some people have conceptualised *queer* more in terms of an umbrella which stands for a range of marginalised sexualities. *Queer* is, therefore, a term which has widened semantically. Rather than referring just to homosexual people, it has instead become a hypernym, used to denote any sexual identity which is seen as 'against the norm', or has been problematised in some way by the values of mainstream society, in which homosexual people are a hyponym of the larger category.

However, Kulick (2002: 67) has questioned whether *queer* actually means anything more than gay and lesbian – and indeed, the majority of chapters within the edited collection *Queerly Phrased* (Livia and Hall, 1997) tend to be concerned with the language of gay and lesbian subjects. The same is true, though to a lesser extent, of *Language and Sexuality* (Campbell-Kibler et al., 2002) where the first half of the book questions the theory of *queer*, whereas the second half mostly contains chapters about gay and lesbian uses of language. Yet, as Cameron and Kulick (2003: 149) observe, 'Queer theory is not exclusively concerned with people designed as 'queer'.. Many heterosexuals are also queer, men and women who never marry, women with lovers or husbands who are much younger than themselves, women who openly reject motherhood as an option, men who purchase sex from women, women who sell sex to men...'[3]

This definition of *queer* is useful in that it enables different sets of people to find common ground, and it also emphasises that a wide range heterosexual identities can be problematised or viewed as deviant. Rather than simply characterising deviance in terms of hetero/homo, it stresses the variety of ways that heterosexuality can be performed (similar to the diversity model of gender which emphasises difference between men or difference between women) and that some ways of 'doing' heterosexuality are considered to be better (or worse) than others.

Therefore one way of understanding *queer*, is by linking it to society's subordination/privileging or legitimisation/marginalisation of different sexualities, rather than by treating it as any specific sexual desire, practice or identity. However, queer theory's focus is on sexuality. As argued at various points in this book, there is a strong link between gender and sexuality – they are often conflated in hierarchies of social relations. Could certain *gender* identities also be seen as queer? For example, could we characterise a heterosexual woman who is masculine or a boy who is interested in a 'traditionally' feminine hobby like ballet (as in the film *Billy Elliot*) as queer? The fact that such people might be (incorrectly) labelled as lesbian or gay suggests that we could helpfully approach such issues form a queer standpoint. It could be argued that *queer* could (or should) be further expanded, to include other categories such as ethnicity, age, (dis)ability or social class, or combinations of such categories with sexuality/gender. This would also mean that groups could both operate as queer and mainstream or 'normal' in different circumstances, being both powerful and powerless (a point which echoes the concept of post-feminist perspectives).[4]

This raises a further issue regarding the definition of 'normal', in much the same way that we can problematise the definition of *queer*. Does normal only refer to the traditional social, religious and legal rules defined by patriarchal mainstream, hegemonic masculinity, or can normal mean 'whoever gets to make the rules' or 'the majority' in any given context? For example, a gay man's identity could be viewed as queer in relation to the rest of society. Yet within a gay community, his identity and desires will be validated and normalised. However, a gay man in a wheelchair or a very effeminate gay man may find himself marginalised, and therefore 'queer', even within a gay community, where here the gay community becomes the hegemonic, controlling force. While it could be argued that the gay community is not hegemonic because it is subordinate to hegemonic masculinity, we could still say that values of hegemonic masculinity (such as the high premium placed on being 'straight-acting' or possessing a muscular ergo masculine body) operate within the gay community to different extents. And if someone chooses to spend most of their time within a particular subcultural context, then is it the subculture which becomes the main factor in defining 'normal' or 'good'?

Seidman (1993: 133) raises a further concern: the refusal within Queer Theory to 'name the subject' or anchor experience in identification could result in 'denying differences by either submerging them in an undifferentiated oppositional mass or by blocking the development of individual and social differences through the disciplining compulsory imperative to remain undifferentiated'. Baxter (2003: 23) notes that post-structuralist theory has been criticised as 'relativist, value-free, nihilistic, cynical, 'a fallacy' and hypocritical in supporting its own 'grand narrative' which specifies sets of insights about the nature of order and meaning'.

It could be argued that identity politics (e.g. gay liberation) and queer theory are therefore opposed to each other – identity politics unwittingly reifies and essentialises the sexual and gender categories constructed by the hegemonic majority, trapping people inside them, making the boundaries between them even more solid and 'real' and downplaying our understanding that such identities are socially constructed and unstable. On the other hand, queer theory disrupts such categories, but leaves us with questions – where do we go from here, and how can we attain improved social and political conditions for people who are currently oppressed because most of society accepts the categories of gay and lesbian as real and discriminates against them accordingly?

However, I do not believe that a queer perspective needs to replace identity politics: it should not be a case of either/or. For example, at some points it may be practically useful for people to align themselves to a 'constructed' identity such as *gay*, and argue from a gay liberation, equality, pride or rights perspective. Organisations such as the Campaign for Homosexual Equality, the Gay Liberation Front and Stonewall have successfully campaigned for improved legal rights and representations of gay and lesbian identities, improving the quality of life for many people.

But under other circumstances, a more useful long-term strategy would be to make it more appropriate to argue from a queer perspective, where we question society's creation, maintenance and representation of categories like *homosexual* and *heterosexual*. Furthermore, campaigns which mobilise a wide range of disenfranchised groups against hegemonic society are likely to be effective in terms of presenting a united front and emphasising the fact that everyone has the potential to become part of a minority. Butler (1991: 19) refers to a concept called 'strategic provisionality', which allows us to preserve sexual identities (such as *lesbian*) as signs, enabling them to function as a site of contest, revision and re-articulation. Gayatri Spivak uses a similar phrase, 'strategic essentialism', referring to the strategy by which groups sometimes find it advantageous to 'essentialise' themselves temporarily and bring forward their group identity in a relatively simplified way in order to achieve certain goals (Landry and MacLean, 1996: 214). Queer should, therefore, be a perspective that is additional to those which already exist. It is important that critical enquiry remains hydra-headed and endlessly adaptable, and is not tied to a single, limiting perspective.

Similarly, Baxter (2003: 12) notes that feminist post-structuralist discourse analysts face a similar problem with terms like woman/man and boy/girl. Yet her analysis is, 'able to recognise… that a term like 'woman' is a necessary category within the feminist critique of power relations, but simultaneously able to problematise that category in its deconstruction of the multiple but nevertheless limited range of subject positions available to individuals'. She cautions against an over-simplistic critique of post-structrualism, saying that it carries with it the potential for transformative projects, although for change to be possible there must be a readiness for forms of enquiry that are less defensive, more multi-faceted and resilient (Baxter, 2003: 29).

The following section demonstrates a couple of ways that the concept of *queer* can be useful in inspiring thought regarding the ways that hegemonic society regulates identity through the use of language and discourse – not simply in terms of heterosexual=good and homosexual=bad, but in the more complex way outlined by Cameron and Kulick (2003), where all forms of sexuality are judged against a 'perfect' heternormative model.

Queer straights

Returning to Bornstein's (1998: 42–45) notion of a gender as a pyramid of power and the post-feminist and post-structuralist analyses described by Mills (1998) and Baxter (2003), it can be understood that while there is a binary aspect of gendered and sexual identities in terms of those which are afforded power and those which are marginalised or subordinated, the situation is in fact more complicated. For example, we could argue that of the heterosexual/homosexual binary, it is heterosexuality which has historically been the powerful, majority, 'normal' identity. However, not all heterosexual identities are equally sanctioned. Thinking of the theory of hegemonic masculinity in Chapter 5, it was noted that the 'nerd' or 'geek' identity was an example of subordinated masculinity. Bucholtz (1999, 2001) has examined girls in American high schools, who are regarded as 'nerds' and use a form of hyper-standard formal English in order to mark their femininity in opposition to their peers (where the use of vernacular English is considered to be mainstream). Cameron (2005b: 492) argues that while heterosexual, nerds could be considered queer in that they, 'reject the heteronormative values of mainstream youth culture: for most high school students engagement in heterosexual activity is a way of displaying 'coolness' and gaining popularity, but nerd femininity is not about being cool, popular or attractive to the opposite sex'.

In order to demonstrate how the concept of queer can usefully conceptualise an alternative system which references (and questions) society's definitions of 'normal'/'not normal', I want to deconstruct critically the language that is used in a text about the sexuality of a heterosexual woman – the American actress, Demi Moore. The text in question is from a newspaper article in a British newspaper, *The Daily Mail*, which described how Moore's male partners were getting progressively younger over time.

1 **How the men in Demi's life are getting younger by the year**
2 Her husband Bruce Willis was eight years her senior. But since they split up, Demi
3 Moore has developed a taste for progressively younger men.
4 The actress, who turned 40 last November, has in the past three years been linked
5 with men of 34, 32, 30, 28, 27 and 26. Now – to the chagrin of Willis, who fears his
6 ex-wife's fondness for toyboys may set their three daughters a bad example – she is
7 dating a 25-year-old.
8 Miss Moore's youngest beau so far is Ashton Kutcher, a little-known actor who was
9 seen canoodling with the star over a late lunch at the Ivy restaurant in Los Angeles
10 at the weekend. In the last month they have been spotted enjoying romantic
11 dinners in New York and at the LA restaurant Dolce, which Kutcher co-owns.
12 Kutcher recently split up with Brittany Murphy, his co-star in the film *Just*
13 *Married*. He has in the past been linked to singer Britney Spears and has partied
14 with President Bush's 21-year-old twin daughters, Jenna and Barbara.
15 Miss Moore has been involved with a number of younger men since the collapse of
16 her 13-year marriage to Willis. The couple – whose daughters Rumer, Scout and
17 Talullah are now 14, 11 and nine – separated in 1998 and finalised their divorce
18 two years later. After the break-up, she moved in with karate coach Oliver
19 Whitcomb, 32, but that relationship ended last year. Since then she has dated actor
20 Owen Wilson, 34, Madonna's business partner Guy Oseary, 30 – for whom she
21 once jumped out of a birthday cake in the skimpiest of bikinis – actor Leonardo
22 DiCaprio, 28, and *Spider-Man* star Tobey Maguire, 27.
23 It was her liaison with 26-year-old actor Colin Farrell, however, that prompted
24 Willis, 48, to speak out in February. A friend of the *Die Hard* star told a U.S.
25 magazine: 'Bruce has been telling Demi to watch it. He says she's old enough to
26 be the mother of some of the guys she's hanging out with.' Miss Moore has
27 worked hard getting in shape in recent months after gaining weight following the
28 break-up.
29 She hired a personal trainer, nutritionist, yoga instructor and kickboxing coach to
30 prepare her for her role in the film *Charlie's Angels 2: Full Throttle* and paid
31 cosmetic surgeons £240,000 for what has been described as a 'head-to-toe
32 makeover'.
Daily Mail, 3 June 2003

Although the main narrative voice of article does not explicitly make a judgement regarding Moore's relationships with younger men, it could be argued that a judgement is present, nonetheless, through the use of a number of linguistic techniques which refer to discourses of gender and sexuality.

The article's first paragraph (lines 2–3) contains two sentences, the first of which implicitly defines an acceptable, somewhat mundane state of existence: 'Her husband… was eight years her senior'. However, the second sentence is placed in contrast to this, using the co-ordinator *but* which signals here that what is to come is a newsworthy fact which justifies the article's existence: 'But since they split up, Demi Moore has developed a taste for progressively younger men'. Such a contrast between the first two sentences is often found in advertising, whereby the first part of an advert represents the 'given' and the second represents the 'new' (Kress and van Leeuwen, 2006).

Lines 4–7 set up a progressive series. The article initially gives Moore's age 'turned 40 last October' (line 4) and then notes that she has 'been linked with men of 34, 32, 30, 28, 27 and 26' (lines 4–5). At the end of this paragraph is the phrase 'Now… she is dating a 25-year old' (lines 5, 7). This list is, therefore, notable in that it focuses on the number of men Moore has had relationships with *and* their decreasing ages. It also reiterates and provides further detail of the proposition found in the first paragraph. The article implies that Moore's relationships with younger men are likely to continue and that she will aim for younger men in the future. Note the article's use of the phrase 'Miss Moore's youngest beau *so far*' (line 8), which sets up an expectation that younger men will follow. Moore is constructed as a sexual recidivist, becoming so jaded that she requires increasingly younger men to satisfy her.

Moore's sexuality is defined as a 'taste for progressively younger men' (line 3) or a 'fondness for toyboys' (line 6). Such phrases diminish the importance of her relationships, the former making use of a metaphor with the word *taste*. As Deignan (1997: 30–32) points out, the metaphor 'Desire is appetite' is largely used in English to focus on desire for sex or for a partner. Moore is therefore constructed as wanting to consume her male partners: it is sexual desire rather than the desire for companionship or security which drives her. Furthermore, the term *fondness* doesn't imply strength of feeling – if we are fond of someone we like them, but not passionately. In the British National Corpus, the phrase *fondness for* occurs 114 times, most of which refer to objects (teddy bears, kites), food and drink (whiskey, alcohol, fruit) or hobbies (sports, reading, wind instruments). It is not a term normally associated with romantic relationships.

It is worthwhile unpacking the meaning of the colloquial term *toyboy*. Based on a rhyming compound, it consists of two morphemes *toy* and *boy*. The term therefore suggests a relationship based on fun and objectification – Kutcher is merely a toy or plaything. Also, the morpheme *boy* exaggerates the youthfulness of the male partner and thus focuses our attention on the age difference of the two people in the relationship (the female equivalents of *toyboy*: *toygirl* and *boytoy*, do not occur often in natural language use, perhaps because younger female partners are expected and normalised, and so are not worthy of note).

The words used to describe Moore's relationships also connote impermanence or casualness: 'The actress... has... *been linked with* men' (lines 4–5), 'Miss Moore *has been involved* with a number of younger men' (line 15), 'her *liaison with* 26-year-old Irish actor' (line 23). The one point at which Moore is described as having a *relationship* is in a sentence which describes its ending: 'After the break-up, she moved in with karate coach Oliver Whitcomb, 32, but that relationship ended last year' (lines 18–19).

Moore's behaviour is further referred to as immature by reference to her actions. She has been 'seen canoodling' (line 9) with Kutcher and 'they have been spotted enjoying romantic dinners' (lines 10–11). A 'discovery' discourse is utilised here: (unnamed) witnesses have noticed public displays of the Moore-Kutcher relationship, which have been reported to the media. In another part of the article, Moore's frivolousness is emphasised when she is described as having 'jumped out of a birthday cake in the skimpiest of bikinis' (line 21) for yet another man, Guy Oseary.

Moore's former husband, Bruce Willis, is mentioned several times in the article. As a film star who played a tough action hero in the *Die Hard* series of films, Willis could be said to be an exemplar of hegemonic masculinity (see Chapter 5) while as a glamorous actress, wife and mother, Demi Moore, on the other hand, constitutes emphasised femininity – at least, before her divorce.

Willis's opinion of his ex-wife's sexual behaviour is referred to in terms of 'chagrin' (line 5). Also, he 'fears his ex-wife's fondness for toyboys may set their three daughters a bad example' (line 6). A friend is reported as saying, 'Bruce has been telling Demi to watch it. He says she's old enough to be the mother of some of the guys she's hanging out with' (lines 25–26). The way that Willis's opinions are characterised is of note: in terms of 'fears' (line 6) and the fact that he has been 'prompted to speak out' (lines 23–24). From this, we are expected to infer that it is wrong for a woman to be old enough to be the mother of her romantic partner. The idea of dating younger men is conceptualised as 'setting a bad example' to children. Moore's relationships are further trivialised by Willis's friend's report, being constructed simply as 'guys she's hanging out with'. While Willis's point of view is privileged, the article does not report Demi's own views of her relationship with Willis or anyone else, nor are we told about Willis's relationships since the split.

Moore's youngest partner, Ashton Kutcher, is described as her 'beau' (line 8). This is an interesting lexical choice. *Beau* is a rather old-fashioned or euphemistic word; it comes from French and means 'boyfriend', although it has a secondary meaning concerned with a man who is overly concerned with his appearance. Its usage in the context of discussing the relationships of Hollywood film stars suggests an enforced delicacy, which is possibly ironic. This is similar to the way that Moore is referred to as *Miss Moore* three times in the article (lines 8, 15 and 26). We may ask why a formal title is used at all (none of the males in the article are referred to as *Mr*), and why *Miss* is used instead of *Ms* (which perhaps applies more often to divorced women). *Miss* has an association with youthfulness or suggests that a woman has never been married. By incongruously referring to Moore as *Miss Moore*, while at the same time describing her involvement in numerous sexual relationships since her divorce and positioning her as an older woman, the article again takes an ironic, mocking stance.

Moore's 'beau', Kutcher, is described as having had relationships with other famous women: Brittany Murphy, Britney Spears and President G. W. Bush's daughters. The lexical choices surrounding these relationships are similar to those used to describe Moore's relationships – he has 'split up with' Murphy (line 12), 'been linked to' Spears (line 13) and 'partied with' Bush's daughters (lines 13–14). Kutcher is therefore constructed as a young Casanova – again suggesting that his relationship with Moore will not last, being based on short-term sexual desire.[5] And, interestingly, he is described as 'a little-known actor' (line 8), which may lead readers to cynically infer that his interest in Moore, who is more well-known, may be motivated by a wish to further his own career.

Towards the end of the article, the sentence, 'Miss Moore has worked hard getting in shape in recent months after gaining weight following the break-up' (line 26–28), presents the reader with a possible explanation for her behaviour. The break-up has affected her to the extent that her physical appearance has deteriorated (by the standards of mainstream society), and it is therefore possible to make a link between her physical decline and her supposed moral deterioration… hence her multiple short-term relationships. Moore might be engaging in sexual relationships with younger men as a way of coping with low self esteem over her appearance and/or the end of her marriage. The final paragraph emphasises Moore's insecurity, pointing out that she has spent £240,000 on a 'head-to-toe' makeover (line 29–32).

So, while this article does not explicitly judge Moore for her relationships with younger men, the fact that her relationships are considered newsworthy at all and that the article is narrated in a way which foregrounds the concerns of her older ex-husband, who claims she should 'watch it' and is 'setting a bad example', accompanied with word-choices which characterise Moore's relationships as trivial or immature, suggest an overall negative or disapproving stance.

I would suggest that the article proposes a number of possible ways in which different heterosexual relations are constructed as 'normal' or problematic in society. First, relationships between people where there is a significant age gap are likely to be problematised or at least seen as worthy of comment. Secondly, this is more likely to be a problem when it is an older woman who is with a younger man. We might want to ask whether men who date younger women receive the same sort of attention and inquiry regarding their relationships, or whether it is reported that they have put on weight after a break-up or paid to have cosmetic surgery. Thirdly, the article also points to other ways in which types of relationships are perceived and regulated, including, for example, divorce and multiple short-term relationships – there are a number of references to Moore's marriage throughout the article: 'since they split up' (line 2), 'since the collapse of her 13-year marriage to Willis' (lines 15–16), 'The couple… separated in 1998 and finalised their divorce two years later' (lines 16–18), and 'the break-up' (line 18). The ending of Moore's long-term marriage to an older man, which produced children, is therefore contrasted with her multiple short-term 'liaisons' with younger men.

This article must be viewed in relation to social context: the changing role of women in society – particularly since the advent of feminism, the marked increase in divorce over the twentieth century, and a reconfiguration of sexuality as a site of pleasure for women and not just a means of procreation. Demi Moore appears to have abandoned the 'traditional' roles assigned to women – being a wife and mother – in favour of roles which position her in ways that are more usually associated with males: the older person in the relationship or a sexual 'player', engaging in multiple relationships. We should also bear in mind that traditionally, such women are regulated with words like *cradle-snatcher*, *slag* or *slut*. So although the article does not make such explicit judgements, there are more subtle regulatory discourses at work, nonetheless.

A post-feminist analysis would note that multiple readings of the article are possible. As Baxter (2003:10) says, 'A feminist post-structuralist perspective on discourse suggests that females always adopt multiple subject positions, and that it is far too reductive to constitute women in general, or indeed any individual woman, simply as victims of male oppression'. So we may view Demi as fortunate or empowered rather than confused or desperate. As a well-known film star, the report of Moore's multiple relationships with younger men could be viewed as validating such relationships for other women. Or her celebrity-status may make her appear somehow 'beyond' normal gender roles – behaviour which is acceptable for celebrities may not be considered appropriate for 'ordinary' people. Along similar lines, Willis's concern could be construed as jealous interference rather than caring concern. Additionally, Ashton Kutcher could be viewed as sexually liberated and progressive in refusing to follow society's age restrictions, rather than a publicity-hungry careerist. So, on a personal level, we could construct the text as being sympathetic towards Moore.

Despite this, it should be acknowledged that there is a *dominant* reading, which is shaped by reference to the context that this text occurs in, along with its methods of reception and production. The fact that the article was written in the *Daily Mail*, one of Britain's most right-wing newspapers, popular among conservative 'Middle England' readers, suggests that the intended message, underlying its 'neutral' reporting stance, is one which views the end of the Moore-Willis marriage as a 'shame' and wishes to present Moore's current situation as troublesome, compared to her previous married state. The article therefore demonstrates 'the new tolerance', characterised by an awareness of alternative discourses which challenge traditional heterosexual hegemony, but at the same time, manages to put its point across in a more subtle way, in much the same way that men's magazines engage in irony in order to distance themselves (but only to an extent) from more objectionably sexist remarks (see Chapter 5). The article, then, reveals how certain forms of heterosexual desire are considered to be preferable to others, and how such categorisations are also gendered. Both a queer analysis, which focuses on sexual identities as normal/abnormal, plus a post-feminist analysis, which foregrounds gender identity, are therefore necessary and appropriate tools to enable us to understand the ways in which sexed and gendered categories interact with each other in the article.

The analysis also demonstrates how sexual identities are unfixed – Moore has gone from the relatively privileged state of wife and mother to now being the subject of gossip and concern: a divorcee with a string of progressively younger toyboys, who is setting her children 'a bad example'. As a celebrity, Moore is held up both as a potential role model to other women, but also as someone who is considered to be a public possession – becoming emblematic of societal concerns about the sexuality of women in general.

Bachelors and husbands

A further conclusion we might want to infer from the Demi Moore article is the relative importance of marriage and the subsequent validation and privilege afforded to married people in society. Therefore, another category of people who we could consider from a queer perspective are adults who do not marry. The English language makes a gender distinction between male *bachelors* and female *spinsters*, although women who do not marry can also be referred to as *bachelorettes*, a term that demonstrates how female terms are derived from male ones (although not usually vice versa). In order to examine how the terms *bachelor* and *spinster* are constructed through discourses, I would like to investigate the ways that they occur in the British National Corpus (in a similar way to the analysis of the term *bisexual* described at the end of Chapter 5). In the

BNC *bachelor* occurs 424 times and *spinster* 140 (a frequency bias towards male terms that we will have come to expect by now).

Interestingly, there are a couple of cases of *bachelor* in the corpus which refer to women, indicating how sometimes male terms (although not female terms) are used in a generic way. However, the frequency bias is partly due to the fact that a proportion of the uses of *bachelor* actually refer to university degrees, rather than unmarried men. The phrases *bachelor of arts* and *bachelor of science* both occur seven times each in the corpus, while *bachelor's degree* appears six times. All in all, references to *bachelor* which refer to university degrees rather than unmarried men account for 62 occurrences. Here the meaning of *bachelor* (a type of degree) is different to the meaning we are concerned with (i.e. a man who has not married). Should these cases be discounted because *bachelor* is a homonym and clearly a bachelor of arts does not imply an unmarried man? It might be best to do this. However, Löbner (2002: 44) states that actual homonyms are a rare and accidental phenomenon. Polysemy, where two words with the same spelling have inter-related meanings are much more common. This is therefore a point at which it is useful to step outside the corpus for a moment and consider other types of historical information.

The term *bachelors degree* can be traced back to the thirteenth century at the University of Paris using a system established under Pope Gregory IX. Historically, the term has also meant a young monk, someone belonging to the lowest stage of knighthood or the younger members of a trade guild. The term has therefore variously referred to young men at the beginning of their careers. Although *bachelor* now means 'unmarried man', it is not difficult to see how this meaning is related to the earlier meaning of a young person (in the past almost certainly male) studying for a preliminary degree. So, while the collocates of *bachelor* which suggest a link to university education no longer have the same association with 'bachelor as unmarried man', the two meanings are likely to be due to historical polysemy rather than being accidental homonyms (see also the different meanings of *gay* discussed in Chapter 5).

Although women can now hold degrees too, the fact that university degrees are still referred to in male terms (the higher *masters* degree also reflecting this), is indicative of the ways that traces of sexist discourses can remain fossilised within language use, surviving long after society has changed.

Putting the degree meaning of *bachelor* and its sexist pedigree aside for the moment, what discourses of *bachelor* can be found in the corpus? The word *eligible* is a strong collocate, always occurring in the phrase *eligible bachelor*, referring to young (heterosexual) men who are either physically attractive or wealthy and therefore eligible for marriage. And there are other references to bachelors, particularly those who are young, whose lives are represented positively.

1. Stefan Edberg, 26, formerly tennis' most eligible **bachelor**, married long time girlfriend Annette Olsen, 27

2. Certainly in his **bachelor** days Johnnie Spencer was the catch of the county.

3. May he enjoy happy **bachelor** days, but not too many, before he realizes the error of his ways

4. Ludo was very popular as a **bachelor**.

5. Gerald Kaufman is a happy-go-lucky **bachelor** who's still waiting for the right girl to come along.

In other cases, bachelors are constructed as having exciting, varied or even scandalous sex-lives (often appearing in the news):

6. I believe he was a real **bachelor** with a ravishing mistress tucked away.

7. Agony Aunt Marje Proops, who confessed to an adulterous 30-year affair with a **bachelor** lawyer, may be in for more agony still.

8. Diana's close friendship with the **bachelor** was revealed in sensational tapes published this summer.

9. Pictures of the Duchess of York on holiday with Texan **bachelor** Steve Wyatt are found.

It is clear, then, that the term *bachelor* does not necessarily refer to men who are unmarriable or will never marry, rather, bachelorhood is treated as a temporary status. In other cases, though, adjectives like *confirmed*, *lifelong* and *steadfast* are used to indicate that bachelorhood can be a more permanent state, while other bachelors are described as living quiet lives, free from sexual scandal:

10. a retired businessman and confirmed **bachelor**, with bald head and circular spectacles

11. He was a steadfast **bachelor** and intended to remain so.

12. 'And ruin your **bachelor** peace with my tattle?'

13. Ackroyd enjoyed a quiet **bachelor** life and lived in a small house by the crossing.

14. He lived the life 'of a spotless **bachelor**'.

15. A **bachelor** who is quiet, modest and with a slight stammer,

Also, other bachelors are seen as being deprived of 'home comforts' in some way, which references a gendered discourse of men as unable to perform the domestic chores required to look after themselves:

16. that vast gloomy kitchen and the clutter of **bachelor** living.

17. The owner, a **bachelor** in his fifties, slept on a camp-bed in the vestibule of the hostel

18. 'the eternal **bachelor**' who could not fry an egg or boil water without burning it.

19. a hapless **bachelor** scrounging free meals.

20. 'Civil enough to supply a few of the home comforts **my bachelor** status denies me, perhaps?'

Bachelors are also described in the corpus as *cynical, difficult, eccentric, madcap, hapless* and *lonely*. Other bachelors are referred to as being misogynist or hating children. There is a mixture of cause and effect here – in some cases, such unattractive qualities are given as the reason for why a man is unmarried. But in others, the unattractive qualities are the result of being unmarried.

21. He had been pathetically shy and awkward, and one particularly painful experience had sent him back to his lonely flat with the firm belief that he would die a **bachelor**

22. The eldest son, who lived out his life as a **bachelor** of somewhat eccentric habits, became deeply estranged from his parents as a young man.

23. An old **bachelor** like him must be lonely.

24. 'Take pity on a lonely **bachelor**.'

25. Frankie, a lifelong **bachelor**, often spoke of his longing to have children of his own.

A number of occurrences of *bachelor* are used euphemistically (or not) to refer to a man who is believed to be homosexual:

26. But Mr Amos, a **bachelor**, denied he had a musical and sensitive sensibility.

27. He was a **bachelor** with (largely) homosexual instincts, melancholy and prone to drinking bouts

And some bachelors are described as being victims, particularly in the news sections of the corpus:

28. A lonely **bachelor** who died in his bath has been found four years later.

29. A lonely **bachelor**, who was the victim of a vicious hate campaign, was found battered to death in his flat.

30. **Bachelor** Brian Claydon, 59, was found beaten to death in a lavatory at Nottingham station with the glue for his toupee in a bag by his side.

Discourses relating to bachelors therefore vary in the corpus, and given that an enormous range of different text genres are represented within it, this is perhaps to be expected. However, a number of themes emerge. First, a bachelor is not necessarily a problematic identity for society. Bachelors are required for society so that women will have someone to marry. And young, attractive, heterosexual bachelors in particular are viewed as eligible and characterised as having happy lives. However, not all bachelors are viewed in this way, particularly those who remain unmarried for a long time. The phrase 'may he enjoy happy bachelor days but not too many' (example 3) summarises a belief that a bachelor identity ought to be temporary rather than permanent.

An aspect of the 'queering' of bachelors is in the large number of explanations that society requires of them: we need to understand *why* they are not married. So reasons such as not liking women or children, being shy, eccentric, etc., are often presented in texts about bachelors. Reference to characteristics such as a 'bald head', 'a slight stammer' or even objects, 'the glue for the toupee in a bag by his side', appear as cues for the reader, helping to explain why such a person may be a bachelor. Other reasons are suggested: the man is or might be homosexual.

A set of long-term consequences of not marrying is also given and this helps to contribute to the negative characterisation of bachelors: they are lonely, victims of crime or unable to look after themselves – the latter consequence refers to the 'gender differences' discourse I discussed earlier, in which men and women are viewed in terms of the different qualities they possess. The implicature is, then, that a man needs a woman to look after him and take responsibility for the domestic chores of daily living – a 'different yet complementary' discourse of gender. Furthermore, the description of bachelors as being involved in scandals with married women also suggests that they can be problematic for society – the implication being that if they had their own wives, they wouldn't have to pursue women who were already 'taken'. Perhaps the most telling construction of the bachelor identity is in the following sentence from the corpus:

31. Falconer was a **bachelor** but a man in love with life.

The use of the co-ordinating conjunction *but* is interesting here. It implies that the two propositions, to be a bachelor and to be in love with life, are usually mutually exclusive. The use of *but* tells us that what is to follow is unexpected.

Although Falconer himself is not presented negatively, by presenting him as against the norm, through use of *but*, the writer implies that the norm is for bachelors to *not* be in love with life.

At this stage, in addition to examining bachelors, a queer analysis would suggest that we see how the opposite side of the binary is constructed. However, we should not assume that identities have only one binary. For example, we could position bachelors in relation to spinsters (a gender distinction), or we could think about them in relation to men who *are* married. It is this latter distinction that I want to focus on here, in order to 'queer' the concept of marriage.[6] The word *husband* occurs 10,725 times in the British National Corpus – it is therefore much more frequent than *bachelor* (about 25 times more frequent). The large number of examples means that it is more difficult to summarise patterns, and a reliance on collocates, along with a closer look at a random or a more focused sample of data is, therefore, required. High frequency does not always equate with a dominant or majority identity; for example, as shown in Table 4.2 *homosexual* occurs more often *heterosexual* (821 vs. 377 cases) in the BNC, and an examination of these terms indicates that heterosexuality tends to be more often taken as an unspoken norm. However, we would perhaps expect *husband* to be frequent because it is a high-status male term – words like *man* are also very frequent in language usage.

One point that is of immediate interest about the strongest collocates of *husband*, is that they are very frequently talked or written about in relation to their wives. The two strongest collocates using the log-log algorithm (Kilgarriff and Tugwell, 2001) of *husband* are *wife* and *her*, with *my*, *woman*, *mrs*, *she* and a number of female names also being strong collocates. Another set of collocates concern financial and legal matters (*conveyance, debts, creditor, settlor, mortgage, pension, solicitors*), suggesting a discourse of marriage in terms of a partnership sanctioned by law. However, an interesting aspect of many of the collocates is that they relate to instances where a marriage is potentially threatened, either through the death of one partner (*widow, killed, murder, murdered, dead, dies, funeral, late*), separation (*estranged, divorced, divorce, deserted, ex-wife*) or through infidelity (*jealous, unfaithful, cuckolded, affair, lover, infidelity, deceiving*). These collocations suggest one reason why *husband* is so frequent in naturally-occurring language data: like *bachelor, husband* also has the potential to be a temporary identity (which can be brought to an end through death or divorce), but unlike *bachelor*, the cessation of a husband identity is problematic for society rather than a cause of celebration. It therefore requires comment, explanation and analysis as the following examples from the corpus demonstrate.

1. She said she was a widow, her **husband**, Malcolm, had died at the beginning of her pregnancy.

2. She lost the baby and she and her **husband** divorced three years later.

3. Dawn and her first **husband**, Brian, divorced as a result of the affair.

4. She divorced her alcoholic **husband** four years ago when he started beating her up

5. A jealous **husband** stabbed his wife and her toyboy lover to death

6. A married woman in her forties has her **husband** killed in an accident.

7. When Vera Czermak found that her **husband** had been unfaithful, her first thought was to throw herself out of the window of their third-floor flat in Prague and put an end to her misery.

8. She may even one day be able to form a real friendship with her estranged **husband**.

Some of the examples here suggest reasons why marriages have ended: losing a baby in line 2, an affair (3, 5), a husband who is alcoholic and violent (4), an 'accident' (6). In the same way that the long-term bachelor identity requires explanation, so the end of a relationship also needs a similar level of justification. Thus, a significant proportion of the discussion of husbands is marked as against the norm because a marriage is under threat or has ended. In (7) an unfaithful husband causes a woman to want to commit suicide. It is clear, then, that the husband identity is not always characterised as a perfect, permanent state, but as having the potential to 'go wrong'.

We can examine discourses of husbands by considering the ways in which 'ideal' husbands are represented. A possible way of doing this is to analyse sentences which involve strong modality: verbs like *should*, *ought* and *must*. Such sentences are likely to reveal expectations concerning the husband identity:

9. The **husband should** fulfil his marital duty to his wife

10. If couples are not receiving any extra but believe they should be, the **husband should** write to their local tax office stating their ages.

11. 'I know I haven't always been what a **husband should** be to you – but that doesn't mean I don't appreciate and admire your beauty.'

12. A **husband should** never get involved in these intense little debates a woman has with herself.

13. When I gave birth to Reuben, I believed that my **husband must** love me for giving him a son.

14. 'No, but a **husband should** not have to look up to his bride.'

15. The **husband must** give the wife what is due to her, and the wife equally must give the husband his due.

16. a **husband** paying CGT **should** give some of his assets to his wife.

17. Agreement was reached and a consent order subsequently made to the effect that the house should be sold and that the **husband should** pay the wife a lump sum of £9,000 from his share of the proceeds of sale.

The sample above is only small, but it outlines a number of expectations about the role of husbands – particularly in relation to women: their love can be dependent on their wife's ability to produce children, they should fulfil a 'duty' to their wives and give her what 'is due' to her (although it is not always clear what these sentences actually refer to – in some cases they reference financial obligation), they should admire a woman's beauty but at times keep their distance from her. Other cases of modality suggest that the relationship between husbands and wives is not one of equals; for example, 'a husband should not have to look up to his bride' and in example 10 (from a guide to retirement) it is the husband who is specifically told to write to the tax office, not the wife or the couple jointly.[7]

Examining modality has showed some of the ways in which people have characterised husbands, most of which relate them to their wives. Another way of looking at an identity group is to consider the ways that good and bad members of that group are explicitly referred to:

18. he is brave, heroic, loyal, a **good husband** and father, a redoubtable foe and a man of honour.

19. He became a **good husband**, quiet and kind

20. A girl should think about making herself look attractive so she can get a **good husband** later on.

21. Fred was a **good husband** to her and the difference in their ages did not matter to Carrie.

22. Peter was a pianist, had a job as a pianist, and always seemed to have money, which made Cecilia see him as a potentially **good husband**.

23. No doubt a conscientious worker; no doubt a **good husband** and father; but totally unremarkable.

24. for the girls it was the problem of finding a **good husband** and the inevitable hardship of raising a family.

25. 'I'll have no trouble finding you a **good husband**.'

26. Besides, she's got a **good husband** and I hope she'll be very happy with him.

A good husband is clearly something of value to (presumably heterosexual) women – the examples above refer to 'finding a good husband' (24, 25), the consideration of someone as 'potentially a good husband' (22) and a reference to someone being 'very happy' with their good husband (26). However, finding a good husband is viewed as a potential 'problem' for 'the girls' (24) who are instructed to make themselves attractive in order to get one (20). Good husbands themselves are described with adjectives like *brave, heroic, loyal, honourable* (18), *quiet, kind* (19), they are conscientious workers (23) and also wealthy (22). Line 23, however, predicts that someone who will be a good husband is also unremarkable. In this sense, being a good husband is constructed as uninteresting and ordinary: it is the norm. Other adjectives that depict husbands as good in the corpus mainly refer to their faithfulness (*devoted, loving, faithful, loyal*) but also reference other qualities, including *kind, handsome, clever, smiling, proud, innocent, rich, wonderful* and *happy*.

What about bad husbands? There are only two references which explicitly use the phrase 'bad husband' in the BNC. However, both reveal interesting discourses of marriage and gender:

27. I think what had happened to my father was this. He had been married to my mother for fifteen years and had been called a **bad husband**, whereas she had been what is known as a good wife. That is, she had been faithful, and domineering, and had demanded proper behaviour of him. Under her crumpled linen skirts had been concealed the pants. Since she had begun by taking charge he had let her continue doing so, and had responded by being more feckless, lazier and more contrary than he was by nature. A marriage only needs, can only support, one strong partner, and my mother had claimed that role for herself.

28. Margaret Wynne Nevinson, an active suffragist, rebelled against the way 'marriage was dinned into me from morning till night … from a business and commercial standpoint'. As a result she developed a 'repulsion' to men and to her mother's creed that 'a **bad husband** is better than none'.

In order to understand the uses of 'bad husband' in examples 27 and 28, I have quoted text beyond the immediate sentences. In (27) the writer explains why the husband is labelled as bad. The reason that the writer gives, involves blaming the man's wife, who is described as domineering, which resulted in the man becoming more lazy and feckless. This writer claims that a 'marriage can only support one partner' and seems to imply that the wife, who had 'claimed that role for herself', is therefore responsible for her husband being bad. The implication here is that it is the man who should be dominant in a relationship, not the woman. The second example cites a piece of folklore, 'a bad husband is better than none', which again emphasises the importance of marriage to society – although in this text, which is about women in history, it is stated that the woman being written about has rejected this belief. The woman is a suffragist, so her rejection of the folklore advice is therefore positioned as sensible. Adjectives used to describe bad husbands in the corpus include references to violence and rage (*brutal, violent, furious, cruel, mad, terrible, outraged*), being uninteresting (*boring, dull*) and unfaithfulness (*guilty, jealous*).

Finally, as with the case above of the man who is a bachelor 'but in love with life', I examined uses of *but* in connection with *husband*, as such cases suggest exceptional cases or situations that are unexpected.

29. Nina adores her saintly **husband but** lusts after the sordid Howard.

30. She did not love her **husband but** instead her husband's brother.

31. Signora Neroni is very unusual – she has a **husband but** is not at his side which seems to suggest independence

32. Mrs. Proudie supports her **husband but** is not quiet

33. Mada Joyce had, it seemed, no **husband but** seven children from three different fathers

34. Patricia Martin, 38, had hoped to keep an affair secret from her **husband but** she fell pregnant

35. Not many wives would be happy to watch two other women fighting over her **husband but** Chris Broughton, receptionist at Torness, found it hilarious.

The sentences here actually refer to the attitudes and behaviours of wives rather than husbands. However, the range of expectations regarding husbands is still interesting – it is noteworthy for married women to find other men attractive, love them or have their children (29, 30, 34). It is noteworthy for women who are not married to have children (33). And it is noteworthy that a wife is not by her husband's side (31) or to support him but not be quiet (32). The final example (35), suggests that it is noteworthy that the receptionist is happy or amused by two other women fighting over her husband, implying that another, more negative, emotion is more appropriate – such as jealousy.

Clearly, with over 10,000 cases of *husband* to examine in the corpus, this is only a small sample of the range of ways that such men are represented in society. However, what the analysis so far has uncovered is a discourse of husbands as a powerful identity: women are expected to want to find a 'good husband' and a great deal of time is given over to writing about husbands in the context of marriages that are threatened. Lack of faithfulness is given as one of the main qualities of a threatened marriage, whereas good husbands are regularly described as loyal, devoted and faithful. Bad husbands, on the other hand, are referred to in terms of their propensity to violence, although violence is also often linked to descriptions of the end of a marriage, due to infidelity.

How does the construction of *husband* compare to that of *bachelor*? It is not a simple case of husband=good, bachelor=bad. However, a theme that arose from the analysis of both words was a normalisation of marriage, whereas an explanation is often required when referring to someone who does not marry, or someone who has been married in the past but is not married at present. Non-marriage, in a range of forms, is therefore marked in natural language use as needing to be explained. A bachelor identity is only sanctioned as short-term, whereas long-term bachelors are characterised in a number of negative ways (eccentric, unable to look after themselves, victims, lonely, seducers of married women). On the other hand, husband identities are problematised mainly when they occur in the context of male violence and/or unfaithfulness (there is a strong link between the two: men are regularly described as violent after their wives have been unfaithful, see below). There is a very strong discourse of monogamy and faithfulness suggested by the corpus data for *husband*, which cuts across gender divisions. Although it is not possible to expand the analysis further due to space limitations, it would be fruitful to examine other words and phrases like *wife, divorce, divorced, married man, marriage*, etc., in the corpus.

Gendered discourses suggest subtle ways in which certain types of identities and the expected roles and restrictions within them are maintained. Western society does not force marriage onto people, but our need to explain bachlorhood/separation, alongside the negative characterisations of long-term bachelors and descriptions of the violent consequences of unfaithfulness serve as warnings: we do not want to become like these people. It could be argued that the discourses of marriage and non-marriage discussed here go one step further than acting as warnings – they are instructional discourses, helping to create, reinforce and normalise identity categories and behaviours based around them. A man who does not marry may therefore expect to feel lonely or unattractive – that there is something wrong with him. A man whose wife is unfaithful may feel that in order to perform hegemonic masculinity correctly, he should replicate the outraged or even violent responses of so many other men (both real and fictional) that he has read about and heard of in the course of conversations, reading newspapers, viewing television programmes and films during his lifetime:

36. Jealous former **husband** 'arranged acid attack'

37. A jealous **husband** using an axe on his wife.

38. Julia Roberts' latest film is Joseph Reuben's Sleeping With The Enemy, in which she is terrorised by a jealous, violent **husband** (Patrick Bergen).

39. When Anna May Reese took a new lover her estranged **husband** was seized with murderous jealousy.

40. Their friendship stands the test when Ruth's brutish estranged **husband** tries to kidnap her baby.

41. A primary school teacher was shot dead in front of a class by her estranged **husband** yesterday.

42. Family were terrified when the estranged **husband** of their neighbour burst into their home wielding a knife.

43. It is the cuckolded **husband** who kills who gets the sympathy.

That is not to say that discourses are all-powerful – most men do not arrange an 'acid attack' if they discover their wife is having an affair. And constructions of jealous and violent husbands in contexts like soap operas or other forms of fiction are not necessarily accurate reflections of actual domestic violence. Furthermore, constructions of jealous/violent husbands are not usually explicitly sanctioned in public discourse; instead, text producers often draw attention to the inappropriateness of such responses, which are framed as crimes.

But with that said, rates of domestic violence are high,[8] and certain types of depictions of male violence towards women may be a contributing factor in normalising such violence – at least for some people. Cumulatively, such articles contribute to one aspect of the gender differences discourse, positioning men as 'losing control' in certain situations, similar to the 'male sexual drive' discourse, which can also result in violence against women, described in Chapter 5.

Also, such discourses act as a form of social control on women, serving as a warning of what *could* happen if they ever feel tempted to have an extra-marital sexual relationship or be a 'bad wife' in other ways. The news media tends to focus on extreme responses, which can have the effect of altering or confirming discourses. Similarly, fictional stories, soap operas, reality television, etc., tend to centre on eye-catching stories that involve conflict, betrayal and revenge; we could argue that this is inevitable if news and entertainment are consumed as products within a capitalist system where ratings, advertising and sales figures are crucial. The maintenance of discourse is, then, cyclical: a phenomenon is characterised in a certain way through discourse; the media latch onto it and refer to it frequently; this results in its consumption and uptake in real life, which the media then reports on; and, realising that the phenomenon attracts audiences, this, in turn, translates to capital.

A corpus-based analysis of the contexts that identity categories occur in is by no means the only way in which queer categories can be deconstructed. If anything, applying this sort of analysis to queer theory is unusual. My aim in choosing this methodology was to contrast it with the more detailed qualitative analysis of the newspaper article I carried out earlier in this chapter in order to show that both small- and large-scale analyses offer different methodological pros and con. It may be difficult to generalise from a single newspaper article, but a corpus approach may result in there being too much data to summarise adequately. Just as queer theory aims to deconstruct a range of different identity constructions and the discourses surrounding them, so, too, are the range of possible sources of data and analytical methods available to queer theorists.

Conclusion

I do not wish to end this chapter by suggesting that a queer analysis of the identity categories surrounding marriage ought to conclude that the institution of marriage should be dismantled. Rather, I would suggest that, as a society, we examine more closely the ways that certain categories or social practices surrounding marriage (or non-marriage) are problematised, backgrounded or stereotyped while others are validated, foregrounded and privileged, and that we consider the consequences that this is likely to have on a range of different types of people – particularly those who do not seem to be benefitting from the system as it stands. Returning to some of the concepts discussed in earlier chapters of this book, marriage and its associated discourses can play an important role in the maintenance of heteronormativity and hegemonic masculinity. Discourses of marriage which present it as a normal, expected state, effectively legitimise those who follow the prescribed route, while subordinating or maginalising those who, for various reasons, do not (homosexuals, long-term bachelors and spinsters, divorced people, older women/younger men pairings, etc.).

This chapter has aimed to show how queer theory can be used in order to query the ways in which different types of *heterosexual* identities or sexual practices are subject to regulation. A key goal of queer theory is to move the debate on sexuality beyond the focus of gay and lesbian identities by taking into account the ways in which *all* forms of desire and all social practices connected to sexuality and gender are influenced by powerful, normalising discourses which are mostly accepted as unremarkable. In the following chapter, I maintain an emphasis on the power of a 'queer' analysis to deconstruct categories, but this time I wish to go beyond the margins of identities that are regarded as 'normal' or tolerated as 'different' or 'a bit strange' by most of us. In what ways does queer theory relate to these more tabooed categories of identity? What can be gained from a queer perspective on sexual identities and practices that we may find problematic and does this suggest that even the concept of queer has its limits?

Notes

1   Queer Theory could be treated as comparable with post-feminist forms of analysis suggested by Mills (1998) and Baxter (2000) which were discussed in Chapter 6. The two approaches differ in that a post-feminist analysis takes gender as its focus and, in particular, examines the ways in which discourses impact in multiple ways on (different sorts of) women. The queer perspective is instead organised around sexuality and has tended to focus either on homosexuality (although it retains the potential to query any form of oppressed sexual identity) or refuse to explicitly 'name the subject' of its enquiry.

2   We should not assume, however, that different ways of categorising sexual identi-ties altered overnight, rather, this was a fluid process taking decades, and some people would have always identified with older categories. For example, after the Gay Liberation period of the 1970s, there were still men who were more easily classified according to the trade/queen/respectable middle-class distinction rather than identifying with the new category of *gay*.

3   This list of heterosexual 'queers' raises a potential question: would everyone be happy with conceiving of men who purchase sex from women as queer? A feminist stance could argue that the commodification of women's bodies for male gratification is a prime example of reifying patriarchy. On the other hand, such men are stigmatised (to an extent) in society. The problems of identifying who can claim 'queer' and who can not are further discussed in Chapter 7.

4   A further issue could concern what we consider to be the 'dominant society' in different contexts. For example, within certain communities (e.g. religious communities), homosexuality or effeminacy (for men) may still be viewed as shameful or wrong – a position which is increasingly at odds with the more liberal acceptance of homosexuality in other contexts. Could we also consider 'society' in terms of a person's immediate family or community? For example, the central characters in Shakespeare's play *Romeo and Juliet*, although heterosexual, found that their respective families disapproved of their relationship due to a long-standing feud. Would a 'queer' reading of this text be applicable or would it

serve to trivialise or 'dilute' the notion of queer as 'any form of sexuality which people/society disapproves of'?

5   Moore and Kutcher married in September 2005.

6   That is not to say that an analysis of spinsters is not worthwhile. Unsurprisingly, spinsters are also constructed as a problematic identity, although rather than being viewed as eccentric or shy, they are regularly described as unattractive, plain, sex-starved or sexually frustrated. Compared with bachelors, there is no 'happy young spinster' identity, so the sexual freedom afforded to unattached young males is not similarly given to women. Yet the more distinctly negative discourse of spinsters is so marked that it has prompted a counter-discourse, where writers note how spinsters are often characterised by cruel stereotypes, negative language and stark portrayals. Such a discourse has a strong grounding in feminist writing and is most often found in the social sciences genre of the British National Corpus (see Baker, 2006, for a more detailed analysis.)

7   This text was published in 1993.

8   For example, the *British Crime Survey* for the year 2001–2 (Walby and Allen, 2004) reported that there were an estimated 12.9 million incidents of domestic violence acts (non-sexual threats or force) against women (84 percent) and 2.5 million against men (16 percent) in England and Wales in the year prior to interview. Four percent of women and two percent of men were subjected to domestic violence (non-sexual domestic threats or force) during the last year. In 2001, according to the United States Census Bureau there were 691,710 non-fatal domestic violence acts committed and 1,247 fatal incidents. The Bureau estimates that 6–12 percent of women are abused in a given year.

8 Exploring taboo: on and beyond the margins

Introduction

As indicated in the previous chapter, there are a number of potential problems with the theoretical notion of *queer*. On the one hand, the fact that it has no real-world signified may lead us to argue that its status as a linguistic experiment is likely to fail (Barrett, 2002: 27). It is simply too difficult to sustain a purely indexical sign. On the other hand, if we take *queer* as an inclusive 'umbrella' category, then this could result in *too many* signifieds, and little agreement regarding where category boundaries lie (see below). Seidman (1993: 135) points out that the disruptive nature of Queer Theory may mean that it forfeits an integrative, transformative politic, lacking coherence and is to an extent 'abstracted from institutional contexts'. A related criticism of movements that take post-structuralism as their motivation, is that the focus on the metaphorical and symbolic can result in an inaccessible and confusing theory. As Baxter (2003: 3) notes of post-structuralism, 'Colleagues and students have admitted to me that they "just don't get it". This is especially ironic in the light of the post-structuralist quest (Derrida, 1987) to demystify the ways in which both discourse and language "do power"'. Post-structuralists risk becoming the new elite, simply replacing one form of hegemony with another hierarchical binary (those who engage with queer theory vs. those who do not). We could also conceive of a new 'queerer than thou' hierarchy, whereby people who possess multiple identities that are subordinated or marginalised in some way by society, are now validated or prioritised within queer communities over those whose identities are closer to the 'norm'. Is Demi Moore, a woman who has sex with younger men (see Chapter 7), less queer than a transgendered sex-worker? If gender/sexuality is seen as a hierarchy, then all identities exist in relation to the 'top' of the hierarchy. Also, there may not always be consensus regarding how the hierarchy is organised, particularly as it has the potential to change.

219

Watney (1997) complains that, 'there is an air of unpleasant snobbishness in some academic pronouncements concerning 'ordinary' (e.g. non-academic) lesbian and gay lives'. Gamson (1998: 592) also notes that younger people can only 'reclaim' the word *queer* because they have not felt as strongly 'the sting, ostracism, police batons and baseball bats that accompanied it one generation earlier'. Older people may never be able to reclaim *queer*, because of its associations with oppression. However, Hall (2003: 80) reminds us that queer was a concept which 'came from the activists and was appropriated by the academics, not the other way round'.

Even if we accept a modified 'umbrella' definition of *queer*, it may be over optimistic to hope that a wide range of diverse identity groups will be able to find enough common ground to cause political change or even to reconceptualise the way we orientate to the concept of identity. Indeed, certain queer groups may want to *distance* themselves from others or possess antagonistic viewpoints. Others may want to set boundaries, depending on moral, spiritual or legal considerations. For example, should people who have consensual sado-masochistic sex be viewed as part of a queer community? What about gay men who engage in 'bare-backing' (anal sex without a condom, where the risk of HIV infection is high)? Weeks (1985: 214) notes that, 'There is little solidarity among the sexually oppressed. Lesbians disassociate themselves from the "public sex" of gay men. Gay leaders dissociate themselves from paedophiles. Paedophiles can see little relevance in feminism. And the ranks of feminism are split asunder on topics such as pornography, sado-masochism and sex itself'. Such topics are difficult to address, because they tend to polarise opinion. As English et al. (1981: 51) say of pornography, '[it] pushes people's buttons. [People] polarise and go into their corners very fast'. Because of this, such 'controversial' topics can be avoided by researchers of language, sexuality and gender, resulting in a form of academic erasure. A motivation in writing this chapter, therefore, is to address a few of these more tabooed areas, with the aim of giving focus to subjects that are sometimes too politically controversial or sensitive to mention in 'polite company', academic or otherwise. What can be gained from considering tabooed sexual groups in terms of queer theory and related theories regarding hegemony and discourses of gender or sexuality?

Vile perverts

So if *queer* is not 'owned' by any group, but open to appropriation by anyone who is 'against the norm' then would it be possible, say, for an organisation such as NAMBLA (North American Man/Boy Love Association) which opposes age of consent laws, or a rapist, to characterise their sexuality as queer? Hall (2003: 166) notes that, '"age of consent" and questions of children's/adolescent's sexual "rights" are particularly nervously avoided among queer theorists... Even with the prospect of "tenure" and the shield of "academic freedom", queer theorists are usually employed by institutions... that put many forms of overt and covert pressure on them to avoid discussing topics that might engender hysterical (often media-driven) public reactions'. It could be argued that casting *queer* as 'the range of problematised sexual relationships, identities, desires or acts that involve *adults who are able to give informed consent*' would be sensible. But how is a term like 'adult' defined? We could take the legal age of consent into account, but just as categories like 'homosexual' are socially constructed and subject to change across time and between societies, so is 'adult'. The age of sexual consent (the age at which people are considered 'adult' enough to have sex legally) has not remained historically or geographically stable, and the onset of sexual activity, regardless of laws, can also fluctuate. Wellings (2005) reports that for British men and women reaching sexual maturity in the 1950s, their average ages at first intercourse were 20 and 21 respectively; by the mid-1990s, this figure was 16 for both sexes. And by the year 2000, 25 percent of young women were having sex below the age of consent, compared with one percent in the 1950s. Weeks (1985: 230) suggests that young people should be given full access to both sexual knowledge and protection as it becomes appropriate, although each young person will have their own timescale, making it difficult to impose social policy in a one-size-fits-all fashion.

I would argue that restricting *queer* to an 'adults only' category (however we define the term *adult*) would betray many children who are under the age of consent. People (including children) need not necessarily be sexually active in order to be labelled as 'abnormal' in terms of their gender or sexuality. Indeed, adults who are celibate could be considered from a queer perspective. And we ought to acknowledge that some children *are* sexually active. It could, therefore, be possible to view a consenting relationship between, say, two 15-year olds as 'queer' (in the UK, the age of consent is 16), yet, if one of the teenagers was younger, or if one of them were above the age of consent, then we may become increasingly uncomfortable about the appropriateness of arguing that the relationship was queer. I would argue that each case needs to be considered carefully and individually.

And to what extent would we want to label as queer any sexual behaviour which resulted in (consensual) injury or even someone's death? In 2001, a 42-year-old man called Armin Meiwes posted an advert on the Internet seeking a young man for 'slaughter and consumption'. A man called Bernd Jürgen Armando Brandes responded and after the men had engaged in sado-masochistic sex, Meiwes killed and ate Brandes. Psychologists said that Meiwes was mentally fit to stand trial, and he was given a life sentence. Here the two participants were over the age of consent, yet their sexual desires led to the death of one.[1] Again, I am unsure about the appropriateness of considering this relationship under the queer umbrella. It could be argued that the distinction between *queer* and *normal* is itself not a simple binary, but instead consists of subtle gradients, where everyone is engaged at some level in defining a personal hierarchy which is likely to be governed, at least to an extent, by the norms of the society of which we are a part. *Queer* and *normal* are therefore shifting categories, as society taboos or accepts certain gendered or sexed identities and their corresponding relationships.

Importantly, a (queer or otherwise) analysis of the construction of a sexual identity should not a priori assume the emancipatory goals of legitimisation or legalisation. The deconstruction of an identity category, type of relationship or sexual desire need not lead us to an argument for its automatic validation. Indeed, a central tenet of queer theory is that identity categories are socially constructed, which is a very different goal from seeking acceptance. However, there is a great deal of value in carrying out analysis of the ways in which such tabooed or 'problematic' sexual categories are discursively constructed, which can only enable a greater understanding of sexuality, 'normality' and taboo in our own society. For example, Becker (1963: 9) observes that, '…social groups create deviance by making the rules whose infractions constitute deviance and by applying those rules to particular persons and labelling them as outsiders'. In particular, the media have an important role to play in defining taboos, as Erikson (1966: 12) notes, 'a considerable portion of what we call 'news' is devoted to reports about deviant behaviour and its consequences'. An analysis of the linguistic strategies adopted in media reports on such behaviours is therefore likely to be illuminating in terms of revealing how discourses of sexual taboo are constructed and maintained. We may agree with or condone a societal taboo, but even here there are a range of possible ways that such a taboo is represented; some of these may be damaging or may have wider implications that impact in negative ways beyond the tabooed group.

For example, Hechler (1988) writes about a 'backlash' which was characterised by the media's 'discovery' of the existence of child sex abuse, which led to a large increase in the number of cases covered. Finkelhor (1994: 2) argues that child sexual abuse has 'clearly arrived on the public agenda' and has been 'occupying centre stage' for far longer than most social problems do. Myers (1994: 86) writes that the 'coverage of child sex abuse is particularly vitriolic', with child protection seen as a witch-hunt, the child protection system viewed as out of control and welfare professionals portrayed as unstable and contributing to hysteria. The concept of the 'moral panic' is perhaps useful to note here. First outlined by Cohen (1972) and later defined by Thompson (1998: 98), a moral panic is described as the efforts of a particular group to exert collective moral control over another group or person. Moral panics involve the identification of a 'problem' which is perceived as a threat to a community or section of a community's values or interests. There is a rapid build-up of public concern focused on the problem, and numerous solutions are proposed until the panic either recedes or results in social change. Hall et al. (1978) and Goode and Ben-Yehuda (1994) claim that moral panics can be 'elite-engineered' instruments of state control or can occur as a result of a bottom-up 'grassroots' manifestation of genuine public concern. Spargo (1999: 5) argues that, 'Scenes of mob hysteria about convicted or even suspected paedophiles reveal the frightening side of people power. Freud may have uncovered infantile sexuality, but it's not something late 20th-century society can discuss rationally'.

With these points in mind, I would like to examine the use of language in a newspaper article which is about paedophiles and child sex abuse. I am interested in the ways that acts and actors are represented in the article, as well as the range of discourses that the article accesses – particularly because the article contains multiple 'voices', which reflect different discursive positions.

1   SEX BEAST CAUGHT BY PHONE
2   A PAEDOPHILE was tracked down and arrested by police after they found a
3   photograph on a mobile phone of him abusing a nine-year-old schoolgirl. Trevor
4   Haddock, 55, from Warndon, Worcester, has pleaded guilty to 14 child sex offences
5   including rape and conspiracy to rape, and could now face life behind bars. The
6   vile pervert was head of a sick nationwide paedophile ring which was smashed by
7   cops after a tip-off from an undercover reporter.

8   Ruth Lumley had spotted sick graffiti on a train from London to Brighton which
9   read: "Girls 8–13 wanted for sex. Text XXX." Posing as an 11 year-old girl,
10 she replied - and was sent sexually explicit messages in response. Police were
11 alerted and a 10-month investigation eventually discovered a paedophile
12 network that had abused eight young girls over a number of years.

13 Haddock was tracked down after cops arrested Ian Jones, 43, from Worthing, and
14 discovered mobile phone pictures of the Midlander abusing a young girl, together
15 with another pervert. The victim was just nine years old.

16 More than 800 exhibits, some of them videos, were taken from Jones' flat and text
17 messages linked him to two men, including Haddock.

18 West Mercia Police arrested him on March 27, along with Derek Moody, 43 from
19 Newcastle and John Farmer, 67, from Pevensey in East Sussex. The four men
20 pleaded guilty at Hove Crown Court last week to a series of sexual offences and
21 are now awaiting sentencing. Haddock, who admitted charges including rape,

22 attempted rape of a child and conspiracy to commit rape on a child under 13, could
23 face a life sentence.

24 Senior investigating officer Jeff Liste of Sussex Police said: 'This has been a
25 complex investigation into horrific offences against young children. These young
26 victims have had their childhoods taken away from them. Haddock was actively
27 seeking and conspiring with other men across the country to further abuse these
28 children. I am relieved that the defendants at the last minute pleaded guilty, so
29 that these young children were spared the pain of reliving their abuse by giving
30 evidence. The investigation has involved officers from Sussex Police, West
31 Mercia Constabulary, British Transport Police and Northumbria Police. It has
32 demonstrated how well police forces can work together when faced with such
33 serious crimes.'

Sunday Mercury, 7 May 2006

It is difficult to read this article without having an emotional reaction to it: not only does it refer to child abuse, but, like many news stories about paedophiles, the language of the narrative voice is couched in an extremely evocative way. For example, the paedophiles are dehumanised with the phrase *sex beast* (line 1), while another strategy references illness: the graffiti is described as *sick* (a word which occurs twice in the narrative), while one paedophile is referred to as a *vile pervert* (line 6). Some of the colloquial language use in the article appears similar to those found in (American) detective fiction (*cops, tip-off*), although it should be noted that informal language is common to tabloid newspapers. In this case, such terms help to dramatise the events being described. Perhaps this is unsurprising: popular television drama series like *CSI* and films like *Silence of the Lambs* show sex crimes and autopsies in explicit detail, while many bookshops have a 'true crime' section, reflecting the fascination that mainstream society has with sexual crime and deviance.

Another aspect of the article is its emphasis on paedophiles as being well-connected and widespread. There are references to a *sick nationwide paedophile ring* (line 6) and a *paedophile network* (line 11). Words like *ring* and *network* are often used to refer to secret and/or criminalised or tabooed behaviour: Baker (2005: 84) describes how homophobic news discourses have used the phrase 'homosexual ring', while in the British National Corpus the word *ring* collocates with *spy, espionage*, and *smuggling* and *network* collocates with *informers* and *spy* (again referencing the 'detective' discourse of the article). The phrasing here could be indicative of moral panic, whereby a threat is characterised as widespread and difficult to police. The terms *nationwide* and *network* in particular, imply that the threat is everywhere – which is hyperbolic given that only four people were involved.

The police operation is described as *complex*, involving police from four different authorities, and lengthy (a ten-month investigation). This emphasises both the complexity of the operation but also the dedication of the police and the seriousness of the crime. However, let us compare the use of language of the narrative voice of the article to the direct quote from the police officer. The officer refers to the illegal acts with a combination of intensifying adjective plus criminal word: *horrific offences* (line 25) and *serious crimes* (line 33), but he does not use the words *paedophile* or *pervert*, instead referring more neutrally to *men* (line 27) and *defendants* (line 28). The police officer uses the word *young* on three occasions: *young children* (line 25 and again at line 29) and *young victims* (lines 25–26). However, this differs from the narrative voice of the article, where the exact age of the child is given twice: *a nine-year old schoolgirl* (line 3) and *The victim was just nine years old* (line 15). Here the age of the child is stressed: note the emphasising choice of the word *schoolgirl*, rather than say, *girl*, and the use of the intensifier *just* in the second example. The more muted use of professional police discourse in the context of an official statement to the media strongly contrasts with the sense of outrage and fear which is communicated in the first half of the article.

It would be interesting to examine articles from other newspapers on the same story – many newspapers take press releases as the basis for their stories and then build on them, colouring them with their own commentary; this may be true here. It is notable that the second half of the article, from 'More than 800 exhibits…', is more descriptive and does not use terms like *pervert* or *beast*. Finally, the use of names is worth noting: the paedophiles are identified by their full names, which are given alongside the towns where they live. Also, within the article (not shown here) are photographs of the four convicted men.

A queer analysis of a text like the one above could focus on the way that a deviant group is constructed (in relation to an unspoken norm of non-paedophile), e.g. via the casting of paedophiles as beasts. It is important to note that an analysis like this need not (I would argue *should* not) question the morality of criminalising child sex offenders. However, what is more at issue here is an acknowledgement of the range of possible ways in which child sex offenders, or other sexual offenders are (or could be) represented linguistically and the effects that such representations may have on the populace, for example, by instilling fear and paranoia, or inciting people to 'take the law into their own hands' by engaging in violent mob behaviour against paedophiles or suspected paedophiles. For example, in 2000 and 2002 the British tabloid newspaper *The News of the World* published lists of names and addresses of sexual offenders, urging readers to sign a petition to expose the '110,000 perverts still on the loose in Britain'. The campaigns resulted in some paedophiles and non-paedophiles being attacked and having their homes vandalised.

It could also be argued that the extreme dehumanisation of a tabooed group may drive members of the group further underground, rather than encouraging them to seek help so that they do not re-offend. Studies have shown that the majority of child sex abuse tends to occur where the victim either already knows or is related to his or her attacker (e.g. Lieb, Quinsey and Berliner, 1998). If the media continually constructs paedophilia as only or mainly relating to a small number of high-profile 'snatchers' or 'organised rings', then it could draw attention away from family-situated sexual abuse, or may impact on children's and adult's understandings of what such abuse actually means – even resulting in children falling into danger. The potential erasure of child abuse which occurs within 'normal' family settings suggests another way in which a binary distinction between 'beasts' and everyone else is solidified, over-simplifying and under-playing the true extent of child abuse.

Clearly, we would need to consider a much wider range of news texts about paedophiles in order to ascertain whether the constructions within it are typical or not – the *Sunday Mercury* article is only one example of such a text (although other studies of media discourse, e.g. Hechler (1988), Myers (1994), suggest that this article *is* fairly typical). Also, a queer analysis may want to ask why paedophiles are constructed in such a way, whether this has always been the case (it appears not), and, if so, why are they *now* constructed in this way? It is worth noting that homosexuals were demonised by the media forty to fifty years ago; for instance, in a 1963 *Sunday Mirror* article (quoted in Baker, 2005: 60) they were described as perverts. The *Sunday Mirror* article claimed, 'They are everywhere and they can be anybody', a warning which echoes the descriptions of the 'nationwide paedophile ring' above. Other societies at different points in history, on the other hand, have not always demonised behaviour that we would deem to be paedophile (see Herdt, 1981, and Schmitt, 1992, described in the previous chapter). A report by UNICEF (2001) claims that marriage of young teenage girls is relatively common in many parts of the world, including Africa, India, Bangladesh and Albania. For example, 44 percent of 20 to 24-year old women in Niger were married under the age of 15. We might also consider whether such cases of 'child marriage' are considered as newsworthy by western media or written about in similar ways.

Also, we might want to consider how children's sexuality is constructed in a range of other texts. For example, consider the magazine aimed at girls, discussed in Chapter 4, where readers are presented with a photograph of a shirtless man and told 'we can't argue with the results, can we?!' This article references a discourse of children's sexuality which appears to construct girls as capable of finding adult males desirable. Clearly, the capacity for experiencing desire is different from sexual abuse, but the *Girl* text seems to present child sexuality in a different way to the *Sunday Mercury* article.

Not all research on newspaper articles about paedophilia has taken a moral panic perspective. Goddard and Saunders (2000) examined the coverage of child abuse cases in Australian and UK newspapers. They showed how in some cases abused children lost their gender as the story unfolded in an article, being substituted with the word *it*; they were at first described as a boy or girl, but then became an object – a phenomenon that Goddard and Saunders refer to as 'gender slippage' (2000: 42), which may be an emotional or even unconscious response to unpleasant situations. In one article they examined (from the British broadsheet newspaper *The Guardian*) concerning a man who was jailed for having sex with a ten-year-old girl, Goddard and Saunders noted that the story was reported in a way which reduced the impact of the crime. For example, the assault was referred to as an *affair*, the perpetrator and victim were referred to as *the couple* and they were described as being in a *relationship*. The research by Goddard and Saunders thus stresses the importance of maintaining balance between a position which incites hysteria or encourages violent vigilante reaction, and one which inadvertently validates a sexual desire or behaviour which puts innocent or vulnerable people in danger. Understanding that current responses to paedophiles are transitory, as well as localised, and attempting to place such constructions within a wider transhistoric context, will allow us a greater understanding of our own society's response to tabooed sexualities.

Doggers, feeders and swingers

As shown in the analysis of *bachelor* and *husband* in the previous chapter, mainstream society presents married (monogamous) relationships as normal and consequently problematises adults who are not in such relationships – for example, by having to 'account for' bachelorhood, or referring to husbands in contexts where married relationships are under threat or have ended due to death or unfaithfulness. Pressures on people to form long-term relationships which are sanctioned by the institutions of religion, law, the media and the family are relatively high (although, we could argue, not as high as they used to be). But as Welling's (2005) study of British attitudes suggests, what is referred to as 'unfaithfulness' (itself an interesting term), continues to be tabooed:

> There has undoubtedly been a relaxation in social attitudes towards sexual behaviour, particularly towards the sexual behaviour of the young. Attitudes towards homosexual behaviour, non-exclusive sexual relationships and sex outside of marriage have all softened over recent decades. The exception is monogamy. Whatever our practices and for all our interest in the peccadilloes of celebrities, in principle, the UK public are firmly in favour of sexual exclusivity. One of the most striking findings

of Natsal [The National Survey of Sexual Attitudes and Lifestyles] 1990 and 2000 was the near universal condemnation of sexual relationships outside of regular ones, which the vast majority of both men and women believe to be wrong. The degree of disapproval varies only slightly with the degree to which the relationship is institutionalised and there are no major differences between the sexes. The majority of people of both sexes – four out of five – are strongly disapproving of sexual infidelity, either in relation to regular, live-in or marital relationships, and there are no major differences between the sexes. (Wellings, 2005: 18)

Given that attitudes to monogamy are reasonably balanced across the sexes, it might be best referred to as a discourse of sexuality rather than a gendered discourse (although it could be argued that men are still afforded more sexual freedom under the present system of gender relations). The media have also reflected, and possibly strengthened, the dominant 'monogamy' discourse. For example, on British and American television (and on television in many other parts of the world), daily talk-show programmes like *Trisha*, *Rikki Lake*, *Jerry Springer*, etc., feature family members who confront one another over real or suspected infidelities. Story lines involving 'unfaithfulness' are staples of soap operas, telenovellas and other dramatised television programming. Furthermore, newspapers regularly report scandals involving famous people who are 'caught' having extra-marital affairs. More recently, a number of scandals have occurred in Britain involving 'dogging' – the practice of engaging in or viewing sexual activity which involves strangers in secluded public places such as parks.[2] Dogging is, chiefly, a heterosexual activity, usually involving couples or single heterosexual men. It has been constructed as problematic through the media because it breaks a number of sexual taboos simultaneously: it involves public or semi-public sex, anonymous sex and (sometimes) group sex or extra-marital sex. An example of the taboo placed on dogging can easily be found in the following short excerpt from a newspaper story about Stan Collymore, a British footballer who was reported to have engaged in the practice.

COLLYMORE'S CAR PARK SEX SHAME
Sun exposes ace's lust for thrills with strangers
THE Sun today exposes soccer star Stan Collymore as a sleazeball who trawls car parks for sex with strangers.
The married ex-England ace, 33, indulges in sordid 'dogging' near his home in Cannock, Staffs.
He told undercover Sun reporters: 'It'd be great to hook up with you.'
The Sun 3 March 2004

The lexis used in the article constructs dogging as a shameful activity: Collymore's marital status is noted and he is described as a *sleazeball*, while dogging is labelled as *sordid*. The term *dogging* occurs within quotes, marking it as a subcultural lexis from which the newspaper wishes to distance itself. The telegraphic headline, *Collymore's car park sex shame*, is ambiguous in that we are unsure as to who has attributed shame to Collymore – is it something he personally feels, or does the newspaper imply that he ought to feel ashamed? Verbs such as *trawls* and *indulges* are indicative of the moral stance that *The Sun* appears to take on the practice. *Trawl* is a fishing term, referring to a way of catching fish at great depths; the verb thus references Collymore's sexual activity in terms of being 'low' and 'submerged'. In the British National Corpus, *indulge* and its related grammatical forms collocate with *whims*, *idle* and *luxury*, suggesting a semantic preference for unnecessary pleasure. The application of abstract nouns like *lust* and *thrills* also suggest a moral discourse which disapproves of sex as pleasurable. The word *lust* has a particular saliency in language use as it is characterised as one of the religious 'seven deadly sins', while a strong collocate of *thrills* (as a plural noun) is *cheap*: when we read the word *thrills*, we may be primed to make a negative judgement, even when the word *cheap* is not present, because of all our previous encounters of the word in a range of negative contexts (see Louw, 1993, and Stubbs, 2001, for further discussion of these sorts of semantic/discourse prosodies).

The article's focus on the phrase *with strangers* (which occurs twice in the short article) also suggests a moral disapproval of sex outside marriage. We are not told whether Collymore's wife was aware of his sexual activities or if she sanctioned or disapproved of them (some people might regard lying to a husband or wife more morally reprehensible, although the article focuses more on the 'exotic' sexual practice itself, rather than this aspect of the story). Collymore's dogging is thus 'exposed' by *The Sun*, necessitating the use of 'undercover reporters'. The article's 'hunt' discourse therefore bears a similarity to the article on paedophiles discussed earlier in this chapter.

Detailed news stories in British newspapers involving scandalous sexual activities of footballers are increasingly common. Yet, paradoxically, *The Sun* is well-known for its 'Page 3 girls' – topless female models who appear on page 3 (see also Maybin, 2002), and tabloid newspapers also regularly include adverts for sex phone lines and pornographic films. Considering the more sexual context of the article, then, it would appear that the exposé on Collymore serves multiple purposes. It appears to reinforce conservative sex mores by engaging in moral outrage, but at the same time, it titillates the reader with details of the sex-life of a celebrity footballer, and it also informs the audience of a sexual practice they may not know about, in effect, giving publicity to dogging.

Ironically, such articles, which place hitherto-unknown sexual activities in the public consciousness, may result in an increase of those behaviours.

The article on Collymore therefore simultaneously accesses:

- a moral discourse, through evaluative terms like *shame, sleazeball* and *sordid*;

- an instructional discourse, by introducing the term *dogging*, which can be inferred to mean *sex with strangers*, associating the practice with a celebrity and detailing where it took place: car-parks, Cannock, Staffordshire; and,

- a prurient discourse, in allowing the reader to identify with the position of a (presumably female) undercover reporter, whom Stan contacts as a potential sexual partner. The article also evokes a (possibly erotic) visualisation of Collymore engaging in sexual acts. Although Stan is constructed negatively in parts of the article, he is also referred to in more positive terms, as an *ace* (twice) and a *star*.[3]

A range of responses are possible on reading the article. People could feel angry or disgusted about dogging. They could feel sorry for Collymore or his wife, or be curious about the practice of dogging, or even aroused. They might be angered by the newspaper's decision to report the story, or find it funny, or they might not care.

Mixed messages regarding sexuality and sexual practices are not uncommon. For example, the link between sexual health and erotica stretches back to at least the 1930s. Marketers of films such as *Forbidden Desire* (1936), *Know For Sure* (1939), *Sex Hygiene* (1942) and *VD-Damaged Goods* (1962) emphasised their 'health' aspect, thus justifying the sensationalistic content. Similarly, early American gay 'beefcake' magazines from the 1950s and 1960s placed importance on physical grooming, cleanliness and regular exercise. Audiences who want to consume erotic material can be assured that there are socially-sanctioned reasons for doing so. Tabloid newspapers can therefore justify articles about sex by appearing to take a moralistic position, ensuring that their newspapers sell, but at the same time, countering criticism from religious, moral and political leaders. Such articles therefore reveal a great deal about society's attitudes towards sexuality, suggesting that the distinction between 'normal' members of society and 'perverts' is not clear-cut.

While the media play a significant role in circulating or influencing discourses of sexuality, it is by no means the only way in which people's beliefs and attitudes are shaped. Particularly with the popularity of the Internet, information about sexuality, from a range of sources, is increasingly available to a wide audience. The fact that ordinary people can create specialised websites or use chat-rooms, bulletin boards and other interactive forums has resulted in the creation of online communities based around specific sexual practices (see also the description of Second Life in Chapter 3). As Gates (2000: 6) writes in her description of a range of 'deviant sexualities' such as *looners* (people who have sex with balloons), *ponyplay* (people who dress up as ponies), *crush freaks* (people who derive sexual pleasure from being walked on or squashed) and *fat admirers* (people who are attracted to overweight people), 'The internet has transformed these deviants' lives, enabling them to come out of the closet and to band together in small groups with shared erotic aesthetics'. The creation and use of a shared language, which describes sexual activities, participants and relationships, is one way in which such communities of practice initiate and maintain their group identities. For example, Gates (2000: 181) lists a number of terms used by the Fat Admirer Community.

> FA: Fat admirer. A person – typically small-to-average-sized – who prefers a fat sexual partner. Generally an FA is a man who seeks a fat woman.
>
> BBW: Big, Beautiful Woman. The object of an FA's desire.
>
> SSBBW: Super-sized BBW. A woman who's dress size exceeds 28.
>
> FFA: Female fat admirer. A woman who prefers fat men.
>
> BHM: Big, Handsome Man. The object of an FFA's desire.
>
> Chaser: A man who prefers fat men.
>
> Chubby: The object of a chaser's desire.
>
> Feeder: One of a small subset of male FAs who enjoy the fantasy or reality of their fat girlfriend getting fatter.
>
> Feedee: A woman who experiences sexual pleasure at the thought or reality of gaining weight. Also known as a BBGP or Big, Beautiful, Growing Person.
>
> Encourager: The gay male version of a feeder.
>
> Gainer: A gay male feedee.
>
> From *Deviant Desires*, Gates (2000: 181)

This lexicon is interesting in a number of ways. First, it echoes the gay subcultural lexica discussed in Chapter 2, listing different types of people who are found within a particular community. However, in the case of Fat Admirers, sexual desire is organised not so much around homo- or heterosexuality, but around the fetishisation of fat. The Fat Admirer Community is therefore open to any sexuality, although different terms are used to refer to heterosexual and gay people, to describe essentially the same kind of desire.[4]

Also, the use of lexis could be said to operate at the level of anti-language (Halliday, 1978). For Halliday, *anti-language* is to anti-society what language is to society. An anti-society is a society within a society – a conscious alternative to society, existing by resisting either passively or by more hostile, destructive means. Anti-languages are created by anti-societies and in their simplest forms they are a partially relexicalised language, consisting of the same grammar but a different vocabulary (Halliday, 1978: 165) in areas central to the activities of the subculture. Many sexual subcultures exist as anti-societies and language becomes a central way in which such anti-societies define themselves and their reality. According to Halliday (1978: 170), 'An individual's subjective reality is created and maintained through interaction with others, who are 'significant other' precisely because they fill this role: and such interaction is, critically, verbal – it takes the form of conversation'. Anti-languages therefore allow members of an anti-society to give names for things that do not exist in mainstream society but also afford them a new way of understanding the world. Crucially, 'Anti-language arises when the alternative reality is a *counter-reality*, set up *in opposition to* some established norm' (Halliday, 1978: 171). So by using terms like *Big Beautiful Woman*, *Big Handsome Man* and *Big Beautiful Growing Person*, the FA Community reject society's negative representations of fat people, reframing such representations with positive-sounding labels. We could refer to this aspect of anti-language in terms of it accessing an alternative, subversive or liberating discourse (Sunderland, 2003: 47, 102, 162).

Along similar lines, Gates (2000: 182) refers to social constructionist arguments, pointing out that in societies such as Africa, Arabia and the Far East, fat men are viewed as powerful and potent whereas in certain African tribes, young women are sent to 'fat farms' to be grown to marriageable size. In earlier centuries, larger women were lauded as beautiful in Western Europe, depicted by artists like Peter Paul Rubens, Rembrandt van Rijn and Pierre Auguste Renoir. Western society's current pre-occupation with diet, gyms and weight loss is therefore a recent development which Gates suggests is a way of controlling women's femininity (the growing numbers of people (particularly women) with eating disorders, such as bulimia and anorexia indicate a worrying societal obsession with thinness). The focus on thinness is certainly also related to a capitalist economic system, with marketisation being used to encourage spending on magazines, dietary products, exercise equipment and gym membership, while ultra-thin female models and actresses are staples of the fashion and film industries (see also Wolf, 1991, Orbach, 1998).

The recasting of fat as beautiful through the invention of new terms, the critique of 'thin' as a means of gender control and the focus on changing standards of beauty suggests a celebratory or queer reading of fat identities, by Gates at least. On the other hand, Gates later discusses the potential negative aspects of the FA identity, such as health risks, cases where women feel obliged to gain more weight to retain their partner's sexual interest and the possibility that Big Beautiful Women and Big Handsome Men may end up in wheelchairs needing full-time care. The issue of 'feeding' is particularly controversial within the FA Community (Gates, 2000: 194–95), with Internet sites which compare feeders to paedophiles, while feedees are constructed as victims. What the FA Community does reveal, however, is that current western mainstream conceptualisations of physical desirability are unstable, being subject to subversion and change. As Gates (2000: 11) writes, 'The sexual conversation is changing, and it's changing rapidly… New erotic communities are forming every day… Our old monolithic view of human sexuality, as a bunch of normals (us) vs. abnormals (them), is being replaced by a far richer picture of the human sexual imagination as a vast, complex web of images and cultural narratives that we can disassemble and reassemble in thrilling new forms'.

So rather than having to locate and then subscribe to specialist magazines, which, in the past, may have only been available from sex shops, a range of 'deviant' sexual communities are now a mouse click away. The way that such communities describe themselves and their sexual practices may be in conflict with the moral or prurient discourses found in the mainstream media. I would like to examine one such online community, closely related to that of dogging, which is based on the sexual practice of *swinging* – or recreational sex between adults. The most popular swingers' website in the UK is www.swingingheaven.co.uk.

The website is divided into public and members only sections. Members who sign up for an account are given access to other parts of the site which contain photographs and advertisements. The text that I wish to analyse is called 'Advice on Swingers' Clubs'. It is available on the public part of the website http://www.swingingheaven.co.uk/advice/swingers-clubs.html.

1   Advice on Swingers' Clubs
2   My first experience at a swingers' club was with a man I met on an Internet site
3   when I was advertising for sex as a single female. He was a relatively experienced
4   swinger, and although I had done group sex before in private I had never even
5   contemplated going to a club before this man suggested that we pay one a visit
6   together. My first reaction was, 'Oh no, I can't do that!' However, once I'd given
7   the idea some consideration, I thought, 'Hey, hey, this could be fun!', and decided
8   that I would give it a go, 'just for the experience'!
9   Swingers' clubs are portrayed in the media as wall-to-wall, non-stop sex dens, and
10 to be honest, I was expecting to be greeted by hoards of rampant people who
11 wouldn't understand that I was a swinging club 'virgin'. I was very nervous about
12 the whole thing, and for a few days before the 'big night' I e-mailed a whole host
13 of questions about the club to my Internet friend. Part of me thought I was being

14 silly for asking questions like, 'Will men take no for an answer?', but it was really
15 playing on my mind that I would be expected to 'perform' before I'd barely had
16 chance to take my coat off. My friend was totally reassuring, and I believe now
17 that without his patience and willingness to answer even the silliest of my
18 questions I would have bottled out, and would not be here to tell the tale now.
19 Almost from the minute I walked into a club for the first time, I felt relaxed and
20 welcome, and under no pressure whatsoever to 'perform'. Clubs have a very clear
21 policy regarding sexual behaviour: basically 'no means no' at all times. The
22 majority of people are very careful not to over-step this mark. Sometimes this can
23 result in a group of people sitting around, all secretly wishing something sexy
24 would happen, but no one wanting to make the first move at risk of appearing
25 pushy or offensive. If you've been to a club before and experienced this kind of
26 situation you will know exactly how frustrating it can be! Sometimes, even if
27 you're quite experienced, it is difficult to work out what people are doing there,
28 who wants to play and who just wants to watch. So much for the stories of sex-
29 crazed hedonism told by the tabloid media; it really isn't that easy, believe me!
30 At some clubs (excepting couples only nights) single men are in the majority.
31 Some of these men just go to watch, but the ones that go in hope of sex have to
32 'compete' for the attentions of the women. Single women at clubs are quite rare,
33 although some women do go alone, and seem to have a great time! Most women
34 however, attend with their partners. Some couples go to meet and swap with other
35 couples. Others go for 'same room fun' only. This means playing with each other
36 in the presence of others but not actually swapping partners. Still more couples go
37 to 'choose' one or more single men, who they might take into a private area (if
38 available) for sex. In addition, there are some women who go to play with large
39 groups of men, and who are happy to perform in public areas in front of a crowd.
40 Whether you are male or female, if you are going clubbing to do anything other
41 than watch, your first job is to suss out who is up for what you want and who isn't.
42 Getting it wrong happens, even if you are very experienced. I've been in a few
43 situations where I have misunderstood peoples' intentions and ended up feeling
44 slightly embarrassed! Of course, the most direct way of finding out what
45 someone's intentions are is to ask them. As in all situations where the negotiation
46 of sexual favours is the issue, being friendly and polite is a must! You might think
47 that because you are in a sex club, being blunt and to the point is a good way to go,
48 but a brutal 'Fancy a shag, darlin'?' might well come across as being a little too
49 rude, even for the most hardened of swingers!
50 Having said that, there are situations where it is not appropriate to engage in a
51 conversation to establish intentions. Perhaps, for example, you are in a situation
52 where a couple is playing quite happily with one or two single guys in a private
53 room. They have left the door open, which is normally a sign that they are happy
54 for people to watch, and even join in. You would like to join them, so what do you
55 do? Going over to them, tapping one of them on the shoulder and trying to start up
56 a friendly conversation might well dampen the mood a little! In situations like this,
57 going over and sitting close to them, and appearing obviously interested might well

58 get you an invite to join in. If not, some people try the 'light touch' technique,
59 such as stroking one of the 'players' on the arm or leg, just to test the water. If this
60 is not welcome they will stop you, normally by moving your hand away or politely
61 saying no. Yes, this can be slightly embarrassing, but nothing ventured, nothing
62 gained. This type of 'testing the water' is not generally considered too pushy
63 unless you do not get the message straight away. If you are rebuffed, take the hint
64 and keep your distance. If you don't stop touching, or then start again thirty
65 seconds later hoping that they might have changed their minds, [it] will not make
66 you popular and in extreme cases is more likely to get you banned from the
67 club than some sex!
68 Before my first ever trip to a club I only had a vague idea of what I might want to
69 get up to in there. I sort of liked the idea of playing with lots of men (and maybe
70 some women), but could not quite imagine how it would work in reality. Since
71 then, I have explored my sexuality, my limits, and now have a very definite idea of
72 what I want to happen on a particular night. If you think that swingers' clubs sound
73 like fun I think it is important to have at least an idea of what you hope to get out
74 of the experience before your first visit. That way you can choose a club that has
75 the right facilities and the right type of night for you. You also need to be realistic
76 in your expectations. Expecting clubs to be like they are portrayed in the media
77 will only leave you disappointed. You must remember that swingers are just
78 normal people, not sex-crazed demons willing to do anything you desire, and very
79 few of us have super-model looks!
80 Clubs differ widely on what facilities they have available. Of the three clubs that I
81 have been to over the last three years, all have at least one 'couples room', which,
82 as the name implies, is for couples only. Single men get booted out – fast!
83 However, these rooms have windows that allow people to watch the action from
84 outside the room. These rooms are great for both voyeurs and exhibitionists! Some
85 clubs also have rooms that are totally private, there are no windows and the door
86 can be locked, and people just have to imagine, or listen to what is going on inside!
87 In addition, for the people who like to play with big groups, and be watched
88 performing (probably by the entire club!), clubs have open 'romping' areas or
89 'orgy rooms' where basically anything (consenting) goes! You might also find
90 dark rooms, bondage equipment (ties, harnesses etc.), saunas, Jacuzzis, and a
91 whole host of other 'goodies'! Check out the web sites of the clubs in your area to
92 see what facilities are available, and what whets your appetite, and then go for it!
93 Before you get your sexy undies on and tootle off to a club that tickles your fancy,
94 you might consider which night you plan to go. Some nights are busier than others:
95 Fridays and Saturdays tend to be the busiest nights, although it does vary both
96 between and within clubs. If you want to throw yourself in at the deep end, I would
97 say try one of these nights! If you want to paddle in the shallow end first, try a
98 Sunday or a night in the week when it is likely to be less busy. Not all clubs open
99 every night; so check the opening times before you go – there's nothing worse than
100 being all dressed up with no place to go!

www.swingingheaven.co.uk/advice/swingers-clubs.html

The article serves as an introduction to the swinger's 'community of practice', in that it is placed in the non-members section of the website and written in an accessible, conversational style. There are many references to the reader as *you*, which could imply a one-to-one relationship between author and reader, but could also stand as an informal way of denoting 'people in general'. There is also frequent use of colloquial English (*suss out, booted out, bottled out*) which contributes to the informal, conversational, personalised tone of the article. In the introduction to the article (not shown here) we are informed that the person who wrote it is called Marie – the use of a first name, rather than a surname, therefore frames the author as more approachable.

There are a combination of discourse styles in the article. The first part is written as a 'my first time' narrative, where Marie describes her reasons for wanting to visit a club, what she expected, how she felt and what she eventually found. By the third paragraph, the article moves away from outlining Marie's 'first time' and is more concerned with detailing the social conventions of swingers' clubs, illustrated with reference to different situations. A notable aspect of the article is its intertextual orientation to existing discourses of swingers, which the author acknowledges as being perpetuated in wider society, through the media.

- 'Swingers' clubs are portrayed in the media as wall-to-wall, non-stop sex dens' (line 9);

- 'So much for the stories of sex-crazed hedonism told by the tabloid media; it really isn't that easy, believe me!' (lines 28–29); and,

- 'Expecting clubs to be like they are portrayed in the media will only leave you disappointed' (lines 76–77).

As well as countering media discourses, the writer explicitly states, 'You must remember that swingers are just normal people, not sex-crazed demons willing to do anything you desire, and very few of us have super-model looks!' (lines 77–79). Media discourses are therefore dismissed by the author as *stories* or *portrayals*, implied to be inaccurate or exaggerated. We are encouraged to trust Marie's 'insider' perspective as someone who is in a position to give a real account of swingers' clubs. She refers to the amount of experience she has had: 'Of the three clubs that I have been to over the last three years...' (lines 80–81).

I would argue that the article helps to normalise the experience of going to swingers' clubs in a number of key ways. The 'my first time' part of the article (the first three paragraphs), constructs a series of dependent events: Marie is interested in going to a swinging club, but nervous. However, she is helped to overcome her fears through her friend's 'patience and willingness' and is able to attend a club. Her first time is therefore characterised as a feat which required positive qualities to overcome – her friend's patience and a certain amount of bravery on her part – she writes, 'I would have bottled out, and would not be here to tell the tale now' (line 18). This first visit is defined as a character-building experience, worthy of the telling of a tale. In addition, Marie twice labels her own nervous expectations as 'silly' and points out that when she arrived at the club, she felt 'relaxed and welcome' and 'under no pressure to perform'. Marie therefore positions the reader as possibly similar to herself, someone who might be interested in going to a club, but is unsure, being familiar with media stories. However, the narrative works to reassure the reader that although their fears are normal (she has had them too), they are unfounded. The writer refers to the importance of consent at several times throughout the article, 'If you don't stop touching…is more likely to get you banned from the club than some sex!' (lines 64–67), 'no' means 'no' at all times' (line 21), 'anything (consenting) goes' (line 89), which emphasises the moral framework under which the clubs operate. At other points in the text, the writer explicitly notes how members of the club orientate to politeness conventions that exist in wider society:

- 'Sometimes this can result in a group of people sitting around, all secretly wishing something sexy would happen, but no one wanting to make the first move at risk of appearing pushy or offensive' (lines 22–25);

- 'I've been in a few situations where I have misunderstood peoples' intentions and ended up feeling slightly embarrassed!' (lines 42–44); and,

- 'As in all situations where the negotiation of sexual favours is the issue, being friendly and polite is a must!' (lines 45–46).

Choice of lexis is interesting. The writer does not use any unfamiliar terms for exotic sexual practices which are sometimes found within the lexicons of sexual subcultures (see Gates, 2000, or Baker, 2002). Instead, the words which are used to refer to sexual experience are all reasonably well-known. Sexual activity and desire is often referred to euphemistically or metaphorically: *action, perform, play, swapping partners, romping, anything (consenting) goes, tickles your fancy, throw yourself in at the deep end, paddle in the shallow end*. Such metaphors serve to desexualise the text, preventing it from being read as an erotic text in itself, but instead centring its discourse on the social practices of swinging – the rules, advice and expectations. Also, the use of familiar euphemisms helps to normalise rather than exoticise the swinging community. For example, the use of a colloquial verb like *tootle* serves to defuse the earlier reference to sexy undies: 'Before you get your sexy undies on and tootle off to a club that tickles your fancy…' *Tootle* means to walk in a leisurely manner. It only appears rarely in general corpus data, but analysis of its usage on the Internet suggests that it is not normally associated with erotic discourse.

Sexual activity is therefore characterised in terms of performance, play or sport (note the swimming/bathing metaphors such as *throw yourself in at the deep end*). This enforces the concept of swinging as a practice-based community, with sex as a pleasurable hobby. The words *fun*, *great time*, *great* and *goodies* also construct swinging in a positive way, yet are unspecific so they can be interpreted by different readers in a way which allows individuals to relate to their *own* ideas of fun.

The writer frequently uses quotes around various words and phrases: 'virgin', 'big night', 'perform', 'compete', 'same room fun', 'choose', 'no means no', 'light touch', 'players', 'testing the water', 'couples room', 'romping', 'orgy rooms', 'goodies'. Some quotes directly reference speech, e.g. 'no means no'. And sometimes quotes can be distancing in that they suggest that the writer wants to show implicit disapproval of someone else's use of a word, as in the media's use of 'dogging' in the Stan Collymore article discussed above.[5] However, here I would suggest that in most cases the writer is instead euphemistically re-contextualising these often familiar words within the context of swinging. So for example, consider the phrase, 'but it was really playing on my mind that I would be expected to 'perform''. There are many possible meanings to the word 'perform', perhaps the most common or prototypical usage is to do with performance onstage, in a theatre production. This word clearly has a different yet related meaning within the context of the swinging club, so the use of quotes signifies this.

There is also a subtly persuasive discourse at work in the text, particularly towards the end. Consider the following:

- 'Check out the web sites of the clubs in your area to see what facilities are available, and what whets your appetite, and then go for it!' (lines 91–92);

and,

- 'Before you get your sexy undies on and tootle off to a club that tickles your fancy, you might consider which night you plan to go' (lines 93–94).

These sentences could be understood in terms of what Omoniyi (1998: 6) refers to as *invitational imperatives*, where the reader is invited to participate in an activity but is under no obligation to do so. Also, the phrase 'Check out the web sites of the clubs in your area' contains an implicature that there *are* clubs in your area, where the writer implies that swinging is not a minority practice, but one which occurs throughout the country. In a similar way, in the sixth paragraph, the writer places the reader in a hypothetical situation: 'you are in a situation where a couple is playing quite happily with one or two single guys in a private room... You would like to join them, so what do you do?' (lines 51–55). By personalising the situation with the second person pronoun *you*, rather than say, giving a third-person description, e.g. 'A woman is in a situation where…', the reader is positioned as someone who could find themselves in this situation, experiencing the reaction of wanting to join in. Both the hypothetical situation and the reader's assumed response are therefore constructed as normal or expected. What is *not* taken for granted is how the reader is expected to negotiate the sexual activity. The text therefore employs an 'instructional' discourse as well as a 'first-time narrative' discourse.

An interesting aspect of the text is its reference to gender. For example, the author points out that males are often in the majority at clubs and that 'single women at clubs are quite rare'. There are other references to the abundance of men and scarcity of women: 'more couples go to 'choose' one or more single men' (lines 36–37) and 'some women who go to play with large groups of men' (lines 38–39). The article does not explain or problematise why there are more single men than women, but it does imply that single women are present: 'although some women do go alone and have a great time' (line 33). The article also positions men as competitors: 'the ones that go in hope of sex have to 'compete' for the attentions of the women' (lines 31–32), again suggesting a traditional gender-differences stance, although here women are constructed as potentially powerful because their scarcity allows them to select or reject men. But men are also defined as possible trouble-makers who may over-step the club's rules: 'Single men get booted out – fast!' (line 82). Women, on the other hand, are not explicitly referred to as rule-breakers.

The article therefore serves to normalise rather than exoticise swingers' clubs, re-framing the 'reality' as different from media portrayals, populated with normal people who are likely to live locally, who abide by society's politeness norms and operate by a strict system of rules designed to protect its members (especially women) from unwanted attention. Sexual activity is constructed in terms of a pleasurable hobby or sport through subtle euphemisms rather than the use of explicitly arousing or subculturally-exclusive language use.

What I find most interesting about the text are the ways in which it is orien-tated to wider discourses of gender and normal/abnormal sexuality within society – choosing to reject the more negative ones, but accepting others. As a sexual practice which rejects society's conceptualisation of sexual monogamy, swinging seems to be increasingly popular, indeed, www.swingingheaven.co.uk/ claimed over half a million members in 2006. New technologies like the Internet and mobile phones appear to be accelerating the development of new sexual commu-nities and, crucially, unlike older forms of media, such as print newspapers, they are democratising in that they allow for more interaction between participants. In addition, they tend to be less concerned with profit margins and they are not required to pay lip service to the more sexually-conservative institutions based on religion, politics and the law. It will be interesting to see the extent to which internet discourse influences discourses of sexuality in other forms of media.

The inclusion of the swingers' article also demonstrates that the analysis of texts does not necessarily have to focus on negative (hidden) agendas or the creation and maintenance of unfair power structures. As Martin (2004) points out, it is possible to carry out 'positive discourse analysis' or constructive CDA, which examines how people get together and make room for themselves in the world. While not everyone is likely to agree with swingers' clubs, the frank, normalising, sex-positive and ethical discourses that are presented in the 'Advice on Swingers Clubs' article, at least suggests a more positive conceptualisation of sexuality, particularly in comparison to the more salacious and demonising tabloid representations of similar sexual practices.

Straight to hell

For the final part of this chapter, I wish to turn to a form of language that is more straightforwardly designed to articulate desire and inspire arousal in its readers, but is also considered to be taboo by many people. Defining this genre is difficult, due to the fact that the two most commonly-used terms surrounding it, *erotica* and *pornography*, are both politically loaded. Bright (2001: 42) points out that there is rarely agreement over what the two terms mean: 'It's simply impossible to find two people who agree straight down the line as to what is in the E section and what belongs under P'. For some, the difference between the two is a matter of taste or personal preference. The Meese Commission of 1986 defined pornography as, 'any depiction of sex to which the person using the word objects'. Erotica was viewed as sexually explicit material but the committee found that the term was used to refer to material 'of which the user approves'. The distinction between pornography and erotica is further complicated by conflicting feminist critiques, and played a part in what was known as the 'sex wars', also called the 'lesbian sex wars', the 'feminist sex wars' and the 'porn wars'. These 'wars' centred around debates between anti-pornography feminists and sex-positive feminists over issues like pornography, sex-work, sado-masochism and other sex-related issues. They took place in the late 1970s and early 1980s and, being largely unresolved, are to some extent ongoing (for further details see Leidholdt and Raymond, 1990, Duggan and Hunter, 1995, and Healey, 1996).

Some feminist perspectives of pornography have cast it in terms of unequal gender relationships. Brownmiller characterises it as, 'the undiluted essence of anti-female propaganda' (1975: 394), whereas Longino (1980: 42) defines it as, 'the degrading and demeaning portrayal of the role and status of the human female'. On the other hand, Steinem (1978: 37) describes erotica as, 'a mutually possible, sexual expression between two people who have enough power to be there by positive choice... It doesn't require us to identify with a conqueror or a victim'. Bright (2001: 44) notes that porn has come to be defined as pictorial rather than textual, whereas Dworkin (1981: 9) suggests that the only difference between erotica and pornography is in terms of production values: 'Erotica is simply high-class pornography; better produced, better conceived, better executed, better packaged, designed for a better class of consumer'. I am not sure, therefore, that making a distinction between erotica and pornography is helpful, except in revealing a person's political stance in relation to certain aspects of sexual representation. In this chapter I mainly use the term *pornography*, but choose to define the word widely, where it refers to explicit (an admittedly objective criteria) depictions (visual, spoken or written) of situations in which sex takes place. I use the word *pornography* rather than the more euphemistic *erotica*, because I think it is useful to acknowledge that some people find the term and subject-matter problematic. In cases where another researcher has chosen to write about *erotica* instead, I use their term.

The small amount of previous work on the *language* of erotica/pornography has tended to focus on professionally-published literature. Hoey (1997) examined patterns of narrative organisation in first-person erotic stories written by heterosexual men and women. He found that males tended to employ a narrative structure of Opportunity-Taking most often, whereas female narratives tended to follow a pattern characterised as Desire-Arousal-Fulfilment. In other words, women tell stories that begin with them having a positive reaction to another person, whereas men are more likely to tell a story that begins with them discovering an opportunity to have sex, which they consequently take; the other person is not particularly relevant to their story. As Hoey notes, 'many men think of [women] as sex objects' (1997: 104). Patthey-Chavez and Youmans (1992) also found differences between erotica aimed at men and women, pointing out that in women's texts, the principal characters are well-developed, context is explored in more detail and genitalia are romanticised by the use of metaphor. The men's texts, however, only develop the character of the narrator, are concerned with sexual variety and explicitness, and draw on a smaller lexicon, which is used creatively. Erotic narratives consequently appear to be sites where the 'gender differences' discourse functions at full throttle.

Bolton (1995) carried out a quantitative study of ten books containing gay male erotica published between 1981 and 1992, looking at the frequencies of body parts and the descriptors applied to them. He concluded that such narratives were important in that they, 'instruct us in knowledge which can help us promote a sexuality that is rich and satisfying' (Bolton, 1995: 205). One consequence of this could be in the design of health promotional materials. Indeed, Wilton (1997) and Baker (2005) have shown how erotic imagery is used in safer sex materials for gay men by the Terrence Higgins Trust charity, although Wilton warns that such materials may also exclude some gay men.

Harris (1997: 158) tracks the evolution of commercial gay pornography throughout the twentieth century, noting that it has resulted in the, 'active suppression of the gay sensibility, a process in which manufacturers divest us of our subcultural identity'. However, a similar finding was noted by Baker (2005) who compared a two million word corpus of *non-commercially* written gay and lesbian erotic narratives.[6] Both sets of narratives frequently utilised hyper-gendered discourses – the male characters in the gay narratives were constructed as possessing stereotypical hegemonic masculinity, described as big, tough and confident. They often participated in contact sports, drank beer, used non-standard or impolite language and experienced desire as an almost animalistic urge to penetrate and ejaculate. In these narratives, male bodies were described as machine-like, sex was viewed in terms of hard manual work, rough to the point of almost being violent, and sometimes a painful experience that needed to be endured. Sexual arousal was demonstrated through physical action rather than by references to feelings. Gay erotic narratives tended to be egocentric, focusing more on the narrator, and experienced through first person narration.[7]

On the other hand, the lesbians in the narratives matched Connell's (1987: 183) description of 'emphasised femininity', being represented as smaller, softer and less confident. They drank tea or wine rather than beer and they liked to listen to music. Atmosphere and emotions were important features of the narratives, as was conversation, before and during sex. The language used by lesbian characters was more formal and there were more references to the passage of time, depth of feelings, subtleties of mood and descriptions of surroundings. Lesbian erotic narratives tended to place more distance between the reader and the characters because the story was narrated in the third person. Also, characters within lesbian narratives communicated with each other more than gay men, as well as blushing and giggling more often. Love and relationships were also viewed as important, and, on the whole, physical contact was more tender than in the gay male narratives. Baker's comparison of gay/lesbian erotic narratives is therefore similar to Patthey-Chavez and Youmans' (1992) male/female study. This suggests that erotic discourses are first and foremost organised around gender differences, with mainstream gendered discourses providing the strongest template for the way that sexuality and desire are articulated. Even when the characters are gay or lesbian, they still adhered to hegemonic discourses.[8]

Rather unsurprisingly then, both Harris (1997) and Baker (2005) found that characters who claimed a gay identity were rarely present in so-called gay narratives, instead, the stories dealt with MSM (men who have sex with men) identities, men who were stereotypically masculine and ostensibly heterosexual, who just happened to be having sex with other men. Harris (1997: 158), rather pessimistically observes that, '…literary pornography is often based on acts of disavowal, as in the case of the nongay homosexual'. This point was also observed by Heywood (1997), who analysed 'gay' true-life narratives taken from a magazine called *Straight to Hell*, which was published in America in the 1970s and 1980s. The magazine's title is derived from a curse but also operates as a pun – again, most of the participants in the sexual narratives are heterosexual men. *Straight to Hell* has little alliance to the Gay Liberation movement, often attacking the gay cultural establishment by associating it with middle-class or mainstream values. For example, in a piece entitled 'Wax Fruit', the editor writes of gay liberationists, 'They are the sorts of 'gays' their mothers always wanted, but no one else does; they are the true undesirables' (*Straight to Hell*, issue 48).

Heywood (1997: 195) notes that, 'The discourse frame sets the presumption of 'straightness' so firmly that the majority of the narratives make no explicit reference to the sexual identities of either the writers or the objects of their desire'. Instead, the writers are preoccupied with whether the object of their desire is authentically masculine. Terms such as *butch*, *trade*, *hunk* and *macho* are used frequently, and there is a focus on the size of the muscles and length of the penis. Ethnicity is also used to index masculinity, with non-white participants afforded a masculine identity simply because they are Mexican, Italian or black (see also the discussion of gay-targeted advertising in Chapter 6). Furthermore, roles such as sailor, police officer, father and solider frequently occur, again referencing hegemonic (heterosexual) masculinity.

Heywood points out that although the narratives sometimes read like accounts of rape (titles include, 'I was scared of choking to death', 'Gets sore, but it was worth it', '4 boys raped me – thank God'), the writers exhibit a 'kind of pride' in their accounts of enduring rough treatment and sexual 'violence': 'You've heard of too little too late. Well this was too much, too big, too fast. The moans and screams I heard were coming from me. But I never tried to get him off me. I guess the truth is that I wouldn't have missed it for anything' (*The Guide*, November 1993: 115). Eighty percent of the stories that Heywood examined were written from the point of view of the narrators taking 'passive' or receptive roles, being 'topped' by a 'masculine stud'. However, in sexual narratives terms like 'passive' and 'receptive' often misconceptualise agency. Most of the narratives involved descriptions of oral sex rather than anal sex, and the man being penetrated was therefore often a more active participant, having control of the sexual encounter.

Paradoxically, the narratives must dissolve or at least subvert the category of *heterosexual*, because these men are, after all, engaged in sex with other men. The editors of *Straight to Hell* write, 'Pure heterosexuality as a sexual category does not exist, while pure homosexuality does, according to a lay analyst… Heterosexuality is not primarily sexual at all, but mainly social, and therefore unnatural' (McDonald and Leyland, 1982: 111). So the narratives invert traditional understandings of sexuality – it is heterosexuality which is a deviation from a normal state, something which is the result of proselytisation, requiring defences so that it can be maintained against the face of the 'natural', instinctive force of homosexuality. A number of the narrative's titles also refer to the ambiguous sexuality of the participants: "Straight' queer', 'hubby's night out with the boys', 'Sailor: 'here it comes faggot''. The following short story, taken from *Meat* (1981), an anthology of stories that were originally published in *Straight to Hell*, demonstrates some of the paradoxes inherent in these 'straight man' narratives.

Sailor in Heat

At the baths in Philadelphia, this one guy stood up against the wall for one fuck, two, three. I was number 4. My cock slid in part way and I felt a hand on my balls from back behind. I turned around and there was a guy lying on a cot, naked, sporting a 9-inch hard on, and wearing a sailor cap.

'You guys don't know how to fuck,' the sailor said: 'You're supposed to *ram* your cock in like a man'. He kept talking about what a big man he was and how he only fucked ass because his girl was in Dayton for a week.

I had me a really good fuck and then watched the sailor fuck the guy. 'You fucking queer' he'd say, 'you take all the cock you can get don't you? Want a real man to fuck you? Fuck you, bitch, I'll bet you drink piss for breakfast too.' He kept yelling about cocksuckers on the streets.

Now the next thing really happened, no shit. After the sailor shot his wad he kissed the guy on the neck and back. You could see the cum dripping out of his asshole from all the guys who'd fucked him. Sailor boy started licking the cum off the guy's legs and before I knew it he was right in there eating the guy's asshole – rimming, sucking, licking, swallowing and moaning. He really dug sucking assholes. He sucked that ass longer than he had fucked and had nothing to say now about queers and cocksuckers. At least 5 guys stood around watching and jacking off. I was one of them. I even got my finger up the sailor's asshole a little and he never noticed (or cared).

The big 'straight' tough sailor finished getting all the cum he could and then turned the guy around and kissed him – gently. Really kissed him like a buddy and stroked his balls and stiff cock.

I'd seen enough and wanted more action so I left. This is true.

Meat, 1981: 18

The narrative takes place 'at the baths' – a subcultural term for 'bath-houses', commercial buildings which contain saunas or steam-rooms, where sex between men can take place. Although there are potentially ten participants in this narrative, the focus is on the sailor, whose physical description is limited to just two aspects, both of which emphasise his masculinity: his penis size and his sailor cap.[9]

This narrative has two distinct parts to it. In the first, the sailor is constructed as critical of the other patrons of the bath-house, due to their inadequate sexual technique. He positions himself as knowing how men fuck: 'you're supposed to *ram* your cock in like a man' (the implication being that the other patrons are unmanly). Note the use of the high impact verb *ram*, written in italics to stress the emphasis that the speaker placed on it. The merging of heterosexuality and masculinity is further demonstrated by the sailor's assertion that he has a girlfriend and is only at the baths because she is away – so a form of 'situational homosexuality' is used as a justification for his sexual behaviour. The sailor's abuse of his sexual partner, using *queer* (in its older, non-reclaimed, homophobic sense) as well as the feminising *bitch*, serve to subordinate the other men to him. His use of taboo language, 'fucking queer', 'fuck you', emphasises a form of 'authentic' working-class masculinity and also demonstrates his contempt for the homosexual patrons of the bath-house. At the same time he refers to himself as a 'real man' and extends his homophobia to gay men in general: 'he kept yelling about cocksuckers on the streets'. The sailor therefore constructs himself as different from and superior to the other (faceless) participants; gay characters are marginalised in this narrative, in favour of the one character whose behaviour is more closely associated with traditional heterosexual masculinity.

The second part of the narrative, however, questions the sailor's heterosexual identity by describing his engagement in a wider range of sexual activities: kissing, rimming, sucking, licking and stroking. Previously, the sailor's heterosexual or MSM identity had been accepted because he had been abusive to gay people (even while having sex with them) and only engaged in an active, inserter role. However, when he shows affection towards his partner and engages in sexual activity which is less involved in penetration but more about transgression of his MSM identity, 'he really dug sucking assholes', or being penetrated, 'I even got my finger up the sailor's asshole', his sexual identity is destabilised. Note the use of adverbials *really* and *even* in the second part of the narrative, which serve to emphasise the surprising 'turn' of events. In addition, the second part of the story is both prefaced and post-scripted with an assertion of its veracity: 'Now the next thing really happened, no shit', 'This is true'. Therefore, we could infer that, from the narrator's viewpoint, the first part of the story, a masculine, heterosexual sailor having situational gay sex while abusing his partners, is common-place. Yet the second part, in which the same sailor is affectionate and derives pleasure from being penetrated and servicing other men, is fantastic and unusual. The description of the sailor at the end of the story is re-evaluated: 'The big 'straight' tough sailor'. While he is still constructed with three masculinising adjectives and a reference to his profession (which further denotes masculinity), the adjective *straight* now occurs in ironic, distancing quotation marks.

A number of different 'readings' of this narrative are possible. The construction of a masculine MSM sailor as becoming open to 'gay' sex serves to destabilise the assumption that masculine and heterosexual identities are fixed, suggesting that they can be subverted. Or it could be that the sailor was 'gay' from the outset, but was simply performing a masculine or MSM identity in the first half of the narrative for erotic effect. Or it could be that the sailor was ostensibly MSM but became overwhelmed with desire, abandoning himself to sexual acts, the gender of his partners becoming less important than the acts themselves. It is difficult to assign definitive labels to classify the sexuality of the sailor by the end of the story. Is he heterosexual, 'heterosexual', bisexual, MSM, gay or polymorphously perverse? *Straight to Hell* narratives are subversive in that they continually blur categories of sexual identity, presenting desire as fluid.

Despite the fetishisation and admiration of hyper-masculine 'heterosexual' men like the sailor in the *Straight to Hell* narratives, at other times they are not afforded much respect. In another STH anthology, the editors write: "Straight males' can be used for fun in bed but they are not worth talking to, their writing is not worth reading, their films are not worth seeing, their attempts to give leadership in religion or psychiatry or any field are not to be followed, and they should not be allowed power in business or government... Inadequate use of their pricks has turned America into a nation of pricks' (McDonald and Leyland, 1982: 5). As Shively (1981: 6) points out in the introduction to *Meat*, 'STH does not address itself to the needs and sensibilities of straight people: they can go to hell, straight to hell'.

There is, therefore, an ambivalence running through these narratives. On the one hand, gay liberationists are labelled as undesirable while 'straight' men are worshipped as objects of desire, their violent sexual acts and rough treatment – which in other circumstances, would be viewed as a form of abuse – are enjoyed at the same time as they are endured. But on the other hand, such men are derided as a 'nation of pricks'. As Heywood (1995: 202) observes, 'the object of desire is also the object of contempt'.

The paradoxes of such narratives present potential problems for language and sexuality researchers; the aspect of subverting the so-called stable categories of 'heterosexual' and 'homosexual' is attractive from a queer theory standpoint.

But at the same time, the fetishisation of masculine hegemonic power and violence, along with the subordination of liberationist or community-based gay identity, suggests an acceptance of more traditional discourses of gender. As in Chapter 5 in the narrative *A Real McCoy*, which involved a heterosexual couple, the masculine male's dominance is established by his taking control of the sexual encounter. Hegemonic masculinity is therefore constructed as sexually desirable, while the oppression of gay men and women is legitimised. Stories like 'Sailor in Heat' code the participants as desirable by referencing their masculinity/heterosexuality, a large part of which requires them to subordinate openly gay identities, treating their partners with contempt. The second part of the narrative about the sailor, discussed above, suggests that such abuse could be unnecessary – it is simply a 'front'. Yet at the same time, homophobic abuse and rough treatment is fetishised and enjoyed as part of the sex *because* it is linked to masculinity.

But as Baker (2005:190) writes, 'an ideal sexual partner is not necessarily someone who would be an ideal romantic partner, work colleague or friend. Therefore an analysis of erotica only tells us so much about 'perfectly gendered'... *sexual* stereotypes. Outside of the bedroom (or sauna or hayloft etc), such ideals may be viewed more cynically or with contempt. For example, the stud who services an entire rugby team may not be viewed as long-term partner material'. A post-structuralist account of pornography, then, needs to take context into account – sexuality and desire being both *multiple* and *aspects* of a person's identity that is not necessarily consistent over different contexts.

Furthermore, we should not assume that pornographic narratives always feature masculine 'heterosexual' men dominating others. A wide range of pornography exists: some is concerned with dominant/submissive encounters; some involves relationships which occur on a more equal basis. In narratives where power plays a central part, it is not always the case that one person maintains all the power: roles can shift as the narrative progresses. And pornographic narratives exist where women dominate men (or other women), thus reversing or ignoring the traditional hegemonic social structure. What we can perhaps glean from this is that power is sometimes, but not always, a key aspect of sexuality and an important site of desire. I would argue that an examination of the ways that power functions in relation to desire, along with all its inherent inconsistencies and paradoxes, is paramount in affording us an understanding of gendered relations in wider society.

Weeks (1985: 239–40) argues that sado-masochism is, 'the most radical attempt in the field of sexual politics to promote the fundamental purpose of sex as being simply pleasure... pleasure becomes its own justification and reward. It is this, rather than the mystical or therapeutic value of S/M, that is the real scandal of sado-masochism.[10] Desire is, therefore, paradoxical – and the language of desire reflects this. Sexual practices like producing or consuming pornography and S/M can simultaneously oppress and liberate participants. In some gay pornographic narratives, hegemonic masculinity or other forms of power are both worshipped and derided while the object of desire is constructed as simultaneously heterosexual *and* gay. The nature of such paradoxes indicates that when issues of sexuality and desire are considered in relation to gendered social relations, some debates simply become irresolvable. However, post-modernism allows for multiple interpretations, rather than forcing people into binary positions. A both/and response is therefore useful in allowing a realisation of the ambivalent nature of desire: different aspects of identity can be represented as both heterosexual and homosexual; sexual desire is both socially constructed and inherent, political and apolitical; pornography can be both oppressive and liberating; dominance can be both sexy and offensive.

Conclusion

I have examined a range of texts in this chapter that, in certain respects, appear to have little in common with each other – except that they concern sexual practices that are, to various extents, 'taboo' in western society (paedophilia, swinging, dogging, fetishisation of fat people), as well as analysing a pornographic text which explicitly described anonymous, multiple male-male sexual encounters. What patterns or themes emerge if we consider the analysis of such texts collectively? And what, if anything, is gained from a linguistic focus on such texts, other than providing a kind of 'Cook's Tour' of the linguistics of sexual 'deviance'?

On one level, the analysis of texts about sexual taboo is helpful in terms of making analysts reflect on and address their own positions regarding issues of sexuality. This has the potential to make us consider the internalised discourses of sexuality that we tend to access ourselves, where they came from and how we articulate them. Taking a queer or post-structuralist perspective, analysis ought to address the ways that social categories of identity are constructed and reified, particularly in terms of power relations (who benefits?), but this should not necessarily lead to a liberationist/acceptance position regarding tabooed sexual identities.

Texts about tabooed sexual identities are good epistemological sites for exploring discourses of sexuality, because they often police sexual boundaries, orientating to distinctions like normal/abnormal, right/wrong and good/bad. They also reveal contradictory discourses that tell us a lot about society's complex relationship (repulsion/fascination) with sexual taboo, and they show us how difficult it can be to define and fix identity boundaries such as 'gay' or 'child'.

Such texts also reveal the range of sexual diversity in existence, making us question the idea of certain types of sexual expression as normal/right while others are deviant/wrong. And they reveal changing conceptualisations of sexuality – particularly in terms of competing discourses and the emergence of communities based around new forms of media. Finally, in focusing on desire, they offer new ways of considering the relationship between sexuality and gender.

It is with these points in mind that I turn now to the concluding chapter of the book, where I summarise some of the key findings and offer several suggestions about directions that future research in the fields of language, sexuality and gender could take.

Notes

1 Meiwes is not the only case of Internet-mediated killing. In October 1996, an American called Sharon Lopatka was tortured and strangled to death by Robert Glass, a man whom she had contacted over the Internet with the intention of finding someone to murder her. Glass was convicted of voluntary manslaughter.

2 The etymology of the term is vague, although it possibly originates as a result of participants using the excuse of taking their dogs for a walk in woodlands or parks, where the sexual activity may occur, or it may come from the fact that men who spied on couples having sex would 'dog' their every move in an effort to watch them.

3 Traces of multiple discourses can be embedded within the same word, phrase or sentence. For example, the phrase 'lust for thrills with strangers' could simultaneously access a moral discourse or a prurient discourse.

4 It is not necessarily the case that a desire for fat people will 'over-ride' a person's sexual orientation. However, in some sexual communities, e.g. BDSM communities, the gendered object of desire is not always foregrounded, rather, the sexual aim (dramatising power differences) takes precedence.

5 Similar news stories to the one about Stan Collymore have also been written about high-profile figures and swingers' clubs. For example, in 2006, the co-chair of the Scottish Socialist Party, Tommy Sheridan, resigned, just before the *News of the World* alleged that he had engaged in an extra-marital affair and attended a 'grubby swingers' club' in Manchester (8 October 2006).

6 It could be that decades of commercially-produced pornography have influenced recent non-commercial representations, and/or the presence of stereotypically 'masculine' and ostensibly heterosexual men in gay non-commercial pornography could be due to such men being represented as either normal or powerful and desirable in society, while gay men are stigmatised as effeminate and deviant.

7   These men were therefore constructed as possessing working-class 'blue collar' masculinity rather than middle-class 'white collar' masculinity, associated with managers or businessmen. Although on the one hand, managers could be said to possess greater power, traditional working-class constructions of masculinity offer a gendered performance based on the ways that they are physically stronger than women and other men. In gay pornography, the ways that such men's bodies look, and the ways that they conduct and express themselves, are therefore more obviously expressive of an exaggerated 'tough' masculinity than the more refined manners of a middle-class manager at a desk job, where power is institutional rather than physical.

8   One question Baker raises in his analysis concerns the author and intended recipients of the erotic narratives, which were stored at a large Internet repository called nifty.org. It was not possible to identify the gender/sexuality of either, although it might be possible to make educated guesses. If the lesbian texts had been written by and for heterosexual men, we may be able to explain why the 'lesbians' in these texts were constructed as hyper-feminine. Erotic texts written by and for lesbians may represent women in more varied ways. It would also be worth examining gendered constructions in 'slash' fiction, which is often written by women.

9   It is not possible from the story to ascertain whether the sailor was a 'real' sailor or not. However, his wearing of a sailor cap in a gay space, suggests a self-conscious recognition that such an item of apparel would function as erotic in this context, indicating the performative aspect of the presentation of his sexual identity, whether he is a sailor or not.

10   Although power and different roles (e.g. dominant/submissive, penetrator/penetrated) are eroticised in the *Straight to Hell* narratives, the texts seem different from the foregrounding of dominance and submission in ritualised discourse that characterise S&M. However, on the other hand, *Straight to Hell* references masochistic pleasure in suffering, suggesting the existence of an S&M continuum.

9   Conclusion

When I started writing this book, I approached the subject of gender and sexuality relations within society from a fairly optimistic position. In Chapter 1, I pointed out, for example, that movements such as feminism and gay liberation in the second half of the twentieth century had resulted in an improved, more tolerant society – in Westernised countries at least. The last few decades *have* seen social advances, resulting in the removal of some of the stigma associated with being gay or lesbian, while to an extent, women appear to be edging towards equality with men.

However, in the process of writing this book, it has perhaps become apparent that such optimism requires qualification, along with an acknowledgement that there is still a long way to go before movements for equality can confidently claim success. The 'diversity' model of language and gender (discussed at the beginning of Chapter 3) has focused on differences between individual men or between individual women, while de-emphasising an over-simplistic difference model based on men vs women. However, Philips (2003: 260) expresses concern that the diversity model may obscure the broader picture: 'While a great deal was gained by the new feminist conceptualizing of women as intersections of various aspects of social identity, a great deal was lost too. The rhetorical force of the focus on the universal key problem of a very broad male power over women, rather than the particularities of problems such as domestic violence and rape, was obscured, and has not regained centre stage in feminist writing since'. Cameron (2005a: 4) agrees, '…we may do women a disservice if in our eagerness not to (over) generalize or stereotype we deny that it is an issue'.

A recurring theme throughout this book is that over the last few decades, hegemonic masculinity has been challenged on a variety of fronts. Yet hegemonic masculinity has responded to such challenges in a number of (often subtle) ways that seem likely to prolong its existence into the near future at least. One strategy involves the adoption of an ironic, 'post-modern' stance towards sexism, as noted by Benwell (2002) and Levy (2005). Male writers are able to 'double-voice' sexism, making the issue appear like a joke that they don't actually agree with. Such a strategy provides an advance defence against criticism – the writer was 'only joking' and anybody who doesn't 'get the joke' is over-reacting or has no sense of humour. However, in double-voicing there is still ambiguity. As Bakhtin (1984: 199) notes, at times the boundary between a speaker and the 'voice' that they are adopting can diminish so that there is a 'fusion of voices': the discourse ceases to be double-voiced, and instead becomes 'direct unmediated discourse'.

Another example of how hegemonic masculinity persists is in the fact that professional success must still be negotiated in relation to it. Women who want to get on at work, for example, are advised (by other women such as Evans, 2000, and Frankel, 2004, to adopt stereotypically masculine ways of speaking and behaving. As Levy (2005: 117) says, 'It can be fun to be exceptional... to be the loophole woman, to have a whole power thing, to be an honorary man. But if you are the exception that proves the rule, and the rule is that woman are inferior, you haven't made any progress'. The problem stems from the fact that certain types of behaviour are tied to gender and sex norms (which are in turn tied to one another). So giving direct commands, being tough, etc., is viewed as masculine and (therefore only) appropriate for males, while a more sensitive or caring style of interaction is seen as feminine behaviour and appropriate for women. While these sorts of behaviours are accordingly gendered and assigned to different sexes, women managers will always be in a double-bind because the set of behaviours they are 'expected' to engage in will not always engender success in the workplace, while if they change their behaviours they are negatively viewed as either acting like men or being complicit with male norms. The system also restricts male behaviour, however, equally placing expectations on male managers to behave in gender-appropriate ways.

So the assertion that we live in a 'post'-feminist age is perhaps premature. Budgeon (1994: 68) notes that, 'the images of 'liberated' women in advertising who are shown enjoying their freedom and success within the context of commodity consumption obscure issues that feminists argue are important... the widening wage gap between men and women, the concentration of women in lowest-paying and lowest-status jobs, violence against women, and the feminisation of poverty'. It is too soon to reject Connell's notion of hegemonic masculinity which remains a driving force in determining societal norms along with access to resources and advancement. Connell (1995: 82–83) reminds us that, 'in rich capitalist countries, men's average incomes are approximately double women's average incomes... Men are much more likely to hold state power... It is overwhelmingly the dominant gender who hold and use the means of violence... Domestic violence cases often find abused women, physically able to look after themselves, who have accepted the abusers' definitions of themselves as incompetent and helpless'. He concludes (1995: 82) that, 'Social struggle must result from inequalities on such a scale'.

The way that conservative commentators have responded to the issue of non-discriminatory language also shows another way in which hegemonic masculinity continues to flourish. By characterising 'political correctness' as a series of extreme, inconsistent and ridiculous policies ('PC gone mad!') that are imposed on society by left-wing councils and idealistic academics, the goal of removing gender and other inequalities that are inherent in language has been compromised (although 'political correctness' could still be argued to have made a significant impact). The creation of parodic, hypothetical PC terms, designed to tarnish the more sensible suggestions, along with media circulation of myths regarding outrageous 'bans' has resulted in a movement which hardly anyone dares to associate with. This is unsurprising; PC was never an official movement from the outset, but its reification was necessary so those who wanted to keep the status quo would have something concrete to vilify.

The linking of the 'gender differences' discourse to advertising and the marketisation of identity suggests another way in which hegemonic masculinity is likely to thrive. The goals of capitalism are ultimately materialistic and, one could say, stereotypically 'masculine' in their celebration of a survival-of-the-fittest competition. Gender is assigned an economic value in that products which supposedly 'improve' our gender are given a price-tag and exulted in advertising discourse. The advertiser's promise of increased confidence, desirability and power is linked to the notion of conforming to a small set of gender stereotypes, yet, at the same time, the exchange of capital must perpetuate for capitalism to succeed – no product or set of products can ever be allowed to fulfil our needs to the point where we attain a state of perfect being... and stop purchasing. So the boundaries must be shifted continually. The package of products guaranteed to make you 'feel and look more feminine' ten years ago are unlikely to be up to the job today. And as McCracken (1993: 79) notes, 'advertising falsely links people's internal feelings to an external object through what comes to be seen as a logical connection; the unattainable is associated with what can be attained – the purchased product'. Just as our gender must continually be performed in order for it to appear inherently stable, consumption must also be a continuous process, never finalised.

And just as discourses of hegemonic masculinity have relied on irony and humour in order to counter feminist critiques, so has advertising responded by adopting self-aware techniques which (only) *appear* to award control back to the consumer: 'the quest for endless renewal may sometimes involve the strategic recuperation of what seem initially to be acts of resistance to consumer culture' (Benwell and Stokoe, 2006: 192). So again, by using humour, by being self-reflexive regarding the value of advertising and by co-opting feminist discourse, advertisers may appear to offer an alternative 'ethical' choice. Yet it could be cynically argued that these appeals to our sense of humour or our morals are simply new ways to get us to engage in the market. As Goldman (1992: 153) writes, 'commodity feminism declares that control and ownership over one's body/face/self, accomplished through the *right* acquisitions, can maximise one's value at both work and home'. Commodity feminism is therefore restructured around purchasing choices rather than political ones.

But another view of marketisation, outlined by Coupland (1996) and explored in focus group data by Benwell and Stokoe (2006) suggests, more hopefully, that consumers are not mindless dupes. Benwell and Stokoe (2006: 201) say they might be encouraged to, 'reappraise the customer as more discerning, resistant and fickle than traditional accounts have suggested'. However, it could be argued that customers are only fickle because they have been distracted by a better form of advertising. And advertising discourse is often incredibly clever – demonstrated by the fact that it requires a close linguistic analysis in order to unpack the myriad ways in which it persuades. The vast majority of people rarely engage consciously with advertising texts in this way, suggesting that we all have the potential to continue to be 'duped'. In an age of information-overload, the process of engaging with texts becomes ever more arduous. The power of the media in particular, including its newer electronic forms, will continue to be a major battle-ground for gender and sexual relations. Competing discourses of gender and sexuality are emerging, potentially offering the creation of new communities, which can develop with less interference from the influences of commercialisation and mainstream moral approbation. Focusing on the wider range of ways that discourses enable gendered/sexed power structures not only acknowledges that women and gay men are not always victims (a politically disabling concept) but also allows us to shift focus away from an over-simplified 'heterosexual men vs. everyone else' position.

And, more positively, it could be argued that the fact that hegemonic masculinity has needed to adapt, suggests that at least *some* progress has been made. Regarding gay and lesbian rights in the UK, for example, there have been significant political changes over the past decade: civil partnerships for same-sex couples, equalisation of the age of consent, removal of the ban on gay people in the military, longer prison sentences for those who commit homophobic crimes. Most cities now have their own 'gay village' containing bars, clubs, shops, cafes, etc. Yet with the acceptance of gay and lesbian identities has also come their commercialisation. As Harris (1997: 78) writes of American gay culture, 'Having failed to win acceptance through the customary routes of political reform, we are experimenting with another technique of effecting change, one that involves strategic acts of shopping, of flexing our economic muscle'. The commodification of gay identity has also helped to cement its own hierarchical structure, based, among other things, on hegemonic ideals of gender. The notion of a perfect masculine gender is used to sell products – images of semi-clothed, muscular young men are used to advertise everything from mortgage advice to porn. Adverts aimed at lesbians make use of the colour pink, suggesting a link between stereotypical femininity and lesbian identity. Such images help to validate 'straight-acting' gay and lesbian identities, thus acknowledging hegemonic masculinity (and emphasised femininity) as desirable, and also setting the standards which gay men and lesbians *should* consider to be desirable. While we should acknowledge that power relations are borne out where hegemonic masculinity is rather more backgrounded – gay people can oppress other gay people, women can oppress other women – we should also be aware that, ultimately, everyone orientates to hegemonic masculinity in one way or another.

The reification and tabooing of homosexuality in the nineteenth century had an unexpected consequence: people then could not know that the creation of a stigmatised identity would eventually result in people uniting around it and demanding liberation. As Foucault (1976) points out, where there is power there is also resistance. The discourses that created the homosexual as a 'deviant' sexual category also provided a lexicon for articulating resistance: 'homosexuality began to speak in its own behalf, to demand that its legitimacy or 'naturality' be acknowledged often using the same categories by which it was medically disqualified' (Foucault, 1976: 101). Therefore, the politics of liberation also contributed towards the reification of identity categories, coinciding with the creation of a gay 'scene', a gay 'lifestyle' and a gay 'village'. While liberation has undoubtedly improved the lives of many people who do identify themselves as gay, I am not sure about its effects on people who do not feel able to position themselves neatly at either end of the heterosexual/homosexual binary. The continuing erasure of the potential for a bisexual identity (on both sides of the binary), combined with the privilege afforded to those who identify as heterosexual, suggests that our categorisation system continues to afford power to some at the expense of others, rather than reflecting people's sexual potential as being less 'fixed'.

Queer theorists and social constructionists point to the fact that our categories of *gay*, *lesbian* and *heterosexual* are constructs: the examination of other cultures, separated from ours in terms of their geographic location and time, provides evidence that our categories of gender and sexuality and the ways we organise ourselves into relationships based on desire are localised and hence transient, subject to change and subversion. As Freud (1905) has argued, humans are born polymorphously perverse, meaning that any number of objects could act as a source of sexual pleasure. Research by Kinsey (1948, 1953) suggests that although most people identify and live as heterosexuals, a large proportion of them have the *potential* to be bisexual, allowing societal norms to background aspects of their sexuality. Just as language itself is shaped by contact with society, so do specific societies shape our gender, our sexuality and the way we experience desire. Kinsey suggested a 'third way' of viewing sexuality – not as purely for procreation or for recreation, but as, 'a normal biological function, acceptable in whatever form it is manifested' (1948: 263). Similarly, Cixous (1975: 84–5) seeks, 'a reconsideration of bisexuality... evident and insistent in different ways according to the individual, the nonexclusion of difference or of a sex, and starting with this 'permission' one gives oneself, the multiplication of the effects of desire's inscription on every part of the body and the other body'.

In a similar way, western society continues to privilege monogamous relationships over other types. The institution of marriage (ideally between heterosexual people of a relatively similar age, ethnicity and social background) proscribes extra-marital sexual conduct. However, the high rate of divorce in western societies perhaps indicates that monogamy is a difficult goal for many people.[1] And the circulation of 'revenge for cheating' discourses in the media further suggests that the current system is not working for everyone. Perhaps a reconsideration of people's sexual capabilities is required. We could raise a question here about what a more 'accurate' gender/sexuality system would be – and whether such a thing even exists. I am not sure that a concrete, definitive answer can be found. Perhaps a more productive consideration is how a 'fairer' system would look: one where particular gender and sexed identities are *not* unthinkingly accepted as better than others and where the concepts of identity and sexual desire are more widely acknowledged as fluid would be a start. Hall (2003: 101) offers a slightly more qualified version of sexuality: '....desires do not necessarily *remain* true. That is not to say that we are 'all' really bisexual. The point of queer theories generally is that we are not all 'really' any one thing'.

However, I do not think that discourse alone can account for all expressions or configurations of gender and sexuality. Although it is, currently, an unpopular stance to take, I would advocate some role for genes and biology. Discourse might help to explain why many of us appear to express gender and sexual identities in terms of fixed categories but I am unsure that we are all born with identical 'factory settings' which specify that everyone's gender and sexuality has exactly the same potential for fluidity. Discourse does not explain so easily why some people *do* engage in same-sex relationships in societies where such relationships are erased, heavily tabooed or criminalised. And it does not explain why many gay and lesbian children feel 'different' from other children from an extremely early age – even before they are consciously aware of sexuality. Similarly, I am not sure how performativity theory can explain why some children enact 'inappropriate' gender performances from an early age. Perhaps they are 'modelling' opposite sex role models, but why would they (unconsciously) choose such role models in the first place, particularly once they begin to encounter gendered discourses which serve to restrict the potential range of ways we are each expected to perform gender? Such phenomena point to something 'extra' to discourse: the possibility that our sexuality and/or gender are not completely 'blank slates', but that individuals may be born with a range of potentials (which might differ from person to person), and which would then be realised within the limits of the discourses that a society provides. Furthermore, we should not under-estimate the role of agency or choice. People are often influenced by discourses or ideologies, but as this book has shown, they also have the ability to challenge and change discourses, imagining new configurations or refusing to go along with 'the way things are'. Understanding the expression of sexual and gender identities as dependent on a series of multi-faceted, interacting components, perhaps helps to account for their complexity and dynamism.

The issue of whether queer or feminist theory has the power to transform wider society outside academia is discussed by a number of researchers (see Gilbert, 2001). Also, Hall (2003: 90) rather pessimistically compares aspects of queer research to marketing strategy: 'Just as with marketing ploys in which corporations offer to donate a tiny percentage of profits to a charitable organisation as a way of attracting consumers (who are encouraged to think of themselves as significantly helping the poor, ill or oppressed by purchasing a greasy hamburger or buying fashionable new clothes), so too it is seductive and somewhat grotesque to think that we are performing important 'queer' political work by piercing our noses, purchasing a bumper sticker or t-shirt or, frankly, by writing a piece of abstrusely worded literary criticism for publication in a scholarly journal'. Wider participation in higher education may help to introduce greater numbers of students to the transformative power of feminism, gay liberation and queer theory, although as Schwarz (2006) noted in her research on interpretative repertories surrounding non-sexist language, it tended to be life experience rather than academic training which had the most impact on the value that women placed on non-sexist terms like *he/she* or *Ms*. Finding ways to make academic theory relevant to real-life concerns is an urgent goal – whether by dedicating research to exploration of sexism in the workplace, law reform, issues such as 'gay marriage' or the media representation of sexual practices and gendered identities. The potential within everyone to be queer, including many heterosexuals, is also worthy of consideration, as are the ways that the bastions of normality – marriage and monogamy – continue to be upheld as ideals.

Queer Theory has the potential to unite all identities which are something other than 'normal', although in purposefully refusing to specifically name the subject of its enquiry, it could also result in a diluted movement with little focus. It should be remembered that identity-based political movements such as feminism and gay liberation *have* resulted in real-world improvements for people and we should not abandon identity so quickly. As always, context is important: at times it is useful to 'claim' an identity, while on other occasions acknowledging that identity is fluid, socially-constructed and contradictory, and that there is value in its deconstruction. Such a multi-pronged strategy stands well with the *both/and* philosophy of post-modernism, enabling 'minority' movements to adapt to changing circumstances.

However, a potential problem with queer theory is its relation to 'morality'. While it can be argued that the subordination and marginalisation of women, gay men, lesbians, bisexuals, transsexuals, etc., is morally wrong, for most people there is a point where a boundary is set. For many this boundary is set in relation to informed consent. So, sexual practices such as rape and paedophilia will always be on the other side of boundary. There may be questions which complicate these decisions such as 'how do we define the concept of a child?' But, on the whole, informed consent provides a reasonably robust model in boundary setting. The issue of harm is another issue – where do we draw line there? Is mild consensual S/M acceptable, but a man who kills and eats another man for sexual pleasure (where both consent to this) not? As Weeks (1985) notes, 'categories such as 'exploitation', 'corruption' and 'harm', which must be controlled, and the 'vulnerable' or the 'young', who must be protected, are obviously flexible and changing ones'.

And while we may decide that certain expressions of sexuality are simply 'wrong', the *ways* that we decide to represent them may have the effect of making them more fascinating. The hysterical, demonising media discourses surrounding paedophilia could encourage vigilante behaviour, force paedophiles underground rather than encouraging them to seek help so that they do not act on their desires, or commit murder in the hope of silencing their victims forever. Such discourses also effectively instil fear into the majority of the population, and potentially 'imprison' children in their own homes –where ironically, they are more likely to be under threat from abusers whom they already know.

And what about sexual desires and practices which appear to be consenting, yet affirm discourses that could be construed as damaging? Ardil and Neumark (1981: 11), two lesbian S/M practitioners, write, 'The main problem for us is when fantasies and the play involve scenes with highly reactionary political meanings – e.g. Nazi uniforms or slave scenes. We wonder if there is a limit to how far the individual context of sexual sex can transform their social meanings'. Furthermore, Heywood (1997) outlines how in gay pornographic 'real-life' narratives, gay men take erotic pleasure in relinquishing power and being abused by ostensibly heterosexual men. While he notes that there is ambivalence in these texts, with heterosexual men simultaneously worshipped sexually but also vilified as 'a nation of pricks', such narratives can still be interpreted as fetishising hegemonic masculinity. It is hardly surprising that the study of pornography or erotica has resulted in some of the most divided debates in academia. Representations of sexual desire can often be 'politically incorrect'. We desire that which is forbidden or tabooed, yet our desires can reflect the social structures in our society, with a focus on dominance and hierarchies.

The post-modern 'take' on power is described by Hall (2003:66) who notes, 'In his notion of the 'tactical polyvalence of discourse' Foucault opened up the conceptualisation of power from a simple model of oppressor and oppressed to a multidimensional investigation of oppression, reaction, metamorphosis and group empowerment over time...' Just as anyone can be queer, in different contexts, we all hold power and/or are powerless. Foucault (1984: 61) himself warns that power should not always be viewed as negative, but instead constituting and giving energy to all discursive and social relations: 'If power were never anything but repressive, if it never did anything but say no, do you really think one would be brought to obey it? What makes power hold good, what makes it accepted, is simply the fact that it doesn't only weigh on us a force that says no, but it traverses and produces things, it induces pleasure, forms knowledge, produces discourse. It needs to be considered as a productive network which runs through the whole social body much more than a negative instance whose function is repression'. Connell and Messerchmidt (2005) have more recently suggested that Connell's original concept of hegemonic masculinity is reformulated to take into account a more complex model of gender hierarchy. They argue that the agency of women needs to be emphasised, together with a recognition of the geography of masculinities – the interplay of local, regional and global levels. They also suggest that more focus is given to understanding the internal contradictions inherent within hegemonic masculinity and the possibilities of movement towards gender democracy.

This direction, along with the kind of post-feminist text analysis suggested by Mills (1998) or Baxter's (2003) feminist post-structuralist discourse analysis, indicates that the movements begun by feminists and gay liberationists in the second half of the twentieth century continue to present a challenge to hegemonic masculinity's grip. The post-feminist account of gender relations, rather than simply stating 'equality achieved: feminism unnecessary' instead acknowledges that since the advent of feminism, gender relations are now a more subtle and complex affair than ever before. As Mills (1998: 247–8) argues, 'If texts are overtly sexist, they are easier to deal with, since overt sexism is now very easy to identify... It is clear that feminist pressure around the issue of sexism has had a major effect on the production and reception of texts. Sexism has not been eradicated but its nature has been transformed into this more indirect form of sexism. What is necessary now is a form of feminist analysis which can analyse the complexity of sexism... now that feminism has made sexism more problematic'. Post-feminist research therefore favours the critical analysis of less obviously sexist texts, instead showing how authors use language to negotiate and orient to a wide range of traditional and progressive discourses – how they attempt to resolve such apparent contradictions and the impact that such ambivalent texts have on a range of audiences.[2] It also acknowledges that power is rarely absolute, but continually up for grabs. As Lazar (2005: 17) argues, 'The discourse of post-feminism is in urgent need of critique for it lulls one into thinking that struggles over the social transformation of the gender order have become defunct in the present time'.

Although post-structuralist forms of analysis have been critiqued as nihilistic, unconcerned with liberation politics or lacking a grand narrative, Baxter (2003: 37) claims that they *can* be successfully utilised in order to promote the free play of multiple voices. An important facet of post-structuralism is its emphasis on understanding the ways in which a range of different discourses position people and interact with each other. She argues, then, that post-structuralist forms of analysis are perfectly placed to give voices to minority or oppressed groups, allowing them to be heard clearly alongside the more dominant minority groups, which will potentially undercut or overturn the status quo. Dominant discourses are interested in silencing, inhibiting and fore-closing all other positions except their own, and, therefore, post-structuralism enables such relatively silenced groups to be heard.[3] Additionally, Martin (2004) reminds us that critical forms of analysis need not always be concerned with exposing hidden *negative* agendas (even though the analysis of some forms of media such as tabloid news, romantic fiction or advertising are likely to orient to power relations in ways which maintain the status quo or unequal relationships to different extents). Martin's 'Positive discourse analysis' suggests that positive readings of texts are possible and that not all discourses are simply damaging or negative. A recurrent theme of this book has been that some texts may appear to be sensitive to feminist or gay concerns 'on the surface', but they contain underlying aspects of language use that are more hegemonic or sexist. However, we also need to assign credit where it is due, lest we paint an overly depressing (and inaccurate) picture which does not acknowledge *any* existence of change or improvement. For example, the *Guidelines for Social Diversity and Inclusive Language* in Chapter 4, the interview with Ben in Chapter 5 and the 'My first time' narrative from Chapter 8 all contain uses of language which orient to more positive, inclusive discourses. We could argue that some aspects of these texts are potentially problematic: for example, Ben's lengthy negotiation of his sexual identity reveals the awkwardness that some heterosexual men feel when approaching such subjects, but the fact that Ben words his response in a way that is intended to be sensitive rather than offensive, is equally worthy of note.

While there is value in making gender or sexuality the main object of enquiry in a particular form of analysis, researchers working in both areas would benefit from acknowledging that these two components of identity are linked at their core – and that both post-feminist analysis and queer theory hold much in common. Both are concerned with showing how identity categories are reified and organised around power, yet at the same time both stress the multiplicity and complexity of power relations, a view of power as a web or network, rather than as, say, a ladder. Theoretical concepts like the discourse of 'gender differences', heteronormativity and hegemonic masculinity all require us to take the close relationship between gender and sexuality into account. As Cameron (2005b: 494) argues, 'Sexual identities, like gender identities are... culturally and locally variable. Yet, in fact, these are intersecting rather than parallel developments, because sexual and gender identities do not only inflect one another, they are to a considerable extent mutually constitutive'. That is not to say that approaches to gender and sexuality ought to be merged into one over-arching framework, but at the same time each could usefully draw on and learn from the other.

The research in this book is limited in that it has mainly taken a westernised perspective of sexuality and gender. Many of the texts which I examined were chosen because they were reasonably close to hand: I was able to encounter or gain access to them easily while going about my everyday life. While this was a decision taken on grounds of practicality, I also felt that it conferred an amount of authenticity to the texts that were chosen: their accessibility indicates that they possess real-world saliency, in my life at least. References to other cultures or other time periods have generally either been made as part of the historical literature review that formed part of Chapter 2, or as examples of social constructionist arguments, in order to show that the gender/sexual relations of the present-day were not always that way and are likely to differ considerably if one takes an aeroplane to a different part of the world. As a result, any findings or conclusions must be issued with the caveat that they can only relate to my 'here and now' – in this case, early twenty-first century, western (mainly British) society. To take into account a wider range of texts is unfortunately beyond the space limitations of this book. There is enormous value, however, in extending the remit of this book to consider sexual and gendered relations within other cultures; many researchers are already engaging in this type of work. Not only will such research confirm social constructionist arguments, thus further destabilising discourses which validate and perpetuate inequalities and appear to be written in stone, but they also give a deserving focus on non-western societies, reminding the West that its preoccupation with itself is just that: a preoccupation.

The spread of western discourses to other cultures is also worth addressing. When we speak of globalisation (McLuhan, 1964), what we most often mean is Americanisation. Crystal (1997) outlines the massive impact of global English across the world, while researchers like Graddol (1997) and Ross (1995) have

demonstrated the impact of American media, modernisation and global econo-
mies on non-western cultures. The proliferation of western or American media,
in the form of films, news, soap operas, game-shows, sports, advertising, etc., are
all likely to ensure that the discourses of gender and sexuality which originate
in the West will continue to make a strong impression on the rest of the world.
An analysis of the ways that westernised discourses are negotiated in a range
of cultures would therefore provide an interesting picture of gender and sexual
relations across the world. For example, Ellece (2005) has examined gendered
discourses surrounding marriage in Botswana. Her analysis of Botswana media,
along with interviews with members of the public, has found that while aspects
of marriage are considered to result in great inequalities between men and
women, at the same time, it is argued that the status quo should be preserved
through references to a nationalistic discourse of Botswanan identity. Marriage
reform is seen by critics to be unnecessary because it emulates a Western model
of marriage, constituting an unwanted form of imperialism. It will be interesting to see how the West's model of advanced capitalism will impact on other
cultures, in terms of the marketisation of gender and sexual identities. Cameron
(2005b: 499) points to 'transidiomatic practices', whereby service-based work
(such as telephone call-centre operators handling customer accounts) are
internationally out-sourced, resulting in large numbers of people conducting
workplace interactions in second languages. Such interactions require workers
not only to use English, but to adopt westernised patterns of interaction (where
a high premium is placed on scripted 'feminised' styles of speaking which appear
warm and caring). Will westernised notions of stereotyped masculinity and
femininity become globally recognisable commodities? And will the Pink Pound
translate into other currencies, influencing eventual reification and acceptance
of gay and lesbian identities around the world, yet at the same time, presenting
such communities with problems relating to stereotyping and the creation of
competitive sexual hierarchies?

At the beginning of this book I gave a short anecdote about the 'gendering'
of muffins in a coffee shop. Although the example appeared trivial and relatively
mundane, I hope that this book has shown how language is used to influence
discourses in ways which are both banal and wide-reaching – and that the
cumulative effect of many 'small' everyday encounters we have with discourse,
can be as important as something like the use of language in a Parliamentary
Act. Also, such banal examples of discourse both reflect and influence the more
'important' arenas of law, politics, religion, education and the workplace.

Cumulatively, the research discussed in this book suggests that, as a society,
we are at a stage where older, traditional configurations of gender and sexuality
are on the verge of being dismantled, resulting in a potentially more liberated
system. This is evidenced both by the great variety of discourses, circulating,

co-existing and clashing, even within the same texts, and of more sophisticated strategies which either perpetuate or challenge older discourses. It is not a foregone conclusion that hegemonic masculinity and heteronormativity will at some time in the future be replaced by gender equality, liberation for sexual 'minorities' or a wider acknowledgement that people's sexual or gender potential is more fluid. Indeed, in some enclaves of western society, traditional configurations continue to be retained.

As a society and as individuals, we therefore need to develop a critical consciousness of the power of everyday language in all its forms to shape discourses of gender and sexuality, the ways that the dozens of different types of 'texts' that we encounter on a daily basis inform, persuade, normalise and taboo. We require a wider appreciation of the way that linguistic phenomena, e.g. lexis, collocation, metaphor, agency, passivisation, nominalisation, implicature, problem-solution patterns, irony, sentence structure, etc., can be used to validate or manipulate discourses along with learning strategies for challenging those discourses which are ever-more subtle yet still potentially harmful in terms of retaining oppressive or unfair power structures.

Post-structuralist theories emphasise that we all have the potential to be powerful or powerless. But we also have the potential to recognise this, and to do something about it – to make our own difference both in the language and discourses we use ourselves and the ways we orientate ourselves to the language and discourses of others. As this book has shown, language enables us to make sense of the world, ourselves and others. While a greater awareness of the role that language plays in positioning us in relation to the world will not automatically result in beneficial changes to society, it will enable us to articulate the complex ways that gender and sexuality inequalities are enshrined and maintained by societies – an essential first step if we are ever to present a challenge to the status quo.

Notes

1   A study by management consultants Grant Thornton in 2004 found that extra-marital affairs were given as the main reason for divorce that year, cited in 27 percent of cases. See http://www.grant-thornton.co.uk

2   That is not to say that we ought to assume that no 'obviously' sexist (or homophobic) texts are now being produced, or that if they do, there is no point in subjecting them to critical enquiry. While there may be increased awareness of newer discourses in public or official capacities, in other instances – private conversation or internet-based discussion for example, discourses may continue to be straight-forwardly overt and 'damaging'. Addressing such texts, their discourses and strategies of legitimation in relation to their social, political and historical context is worthwhile, if at least to demonstrate how far there is yet to go.

3   Although others have argued that such an inclusive view of discourse analysis could therefore give a voice to extremist (violent, fascist) groups who would also be considered to be a 'minority' in democratic society the difference between those groups and other minorities, is that they are rarely interested in having their voices heard alongside others – instead they aim to become the dominant discourse. Baxter (2003: 37) equivocally points out then, that all marginalised groups could be allowed the space to make their case alongside and in opposition to other voices, but this does not mean that each perspective is equally valid; rather, each should be interrogated from a stance which accepts that no perspective is unbiased.

References

Adler, S. (1992) 'Aprons and attitudes: feminism and children's books', in Claire, H., Maybin, J. and Swann, J. (eds) *Equality Matters*. Clevedon: Multilingual Matters, pp. 111–23.

Allen, L. S. and Gorski, R. A. (1992) 'Sexual orientation and the size of the anterior commissure in the human brain', *Proceedings of the National Academy of Sciences of the U.S.A.* 89: 7199–7202.

Anderson, B. (1983) *Imagined Communities: Reflections on the Origins and Spread of Nationalism*. London: Verso.

Angelides, S. (2001) *A History of Bisexuality*. Chicago IL and London: University of Chicago Press.

Ardill, S. and Neumark, N. (1981) 'Putting sex back into lesbianism: Is the way to a woman's heart through her sado-masochism?' *Gay Information* 11 (spring): 11.

Aries, E. and Johnson, F. (1983) 'Close friendship in adulthood: conversational content between same-sex friends', *A Journal of Research* 9 (12): 1183–96.

Armistead, N. (1974) *Reconstructing Social Psychology*. Harmondsworth: Penguin.

Austin, J. L. (1962) *How To Do Things With Words: The William James Lectures Delivered at Harvard University in 1955*. Oxford: Clarendon.

Babcock, B. (1978) *The Reversible World: Symbolic Inversion in Art and Society*. Ithaca, New York: Cornell University Press.

Badgett, M. L. V. (2001) *Money, Myths and Change – The Economic Lives of Lesbians and Gay Men*. Chicago: University of Chicago Press.

Baker, P. (2002) *Polari: The Lost Language of Gay Men*. London: Routledge.

Baker, P. (2005) *Public Discourses of Gay Men*. London: Routledge.

Baker, P. (2006) *Using Corpora for Discourse Analysis*. London: Continuum.

Baker, P. and Stanley, J. (2003) *Hello Sailor. The Hidden History of Gay Life at Sea*. London: Pearson.

Bakhtin, M. (1984) *Problems in Dostoevsky's Poetics*. Minneapolis: University of Minnesota Press.

Barker, C. and Galasinski, D. (2001) *Cultural Studies and Discourse Analysis. A Dialogue on Language and Identity*. London: Sage.

Barthes, R. (1977 [1968]) *Image, Music, Text*. New York: Noonday Press, Ed. and trans. S. Heath.

Barret, R. (1995) 'Supermodels of the world, unite! Political economy and the language of performance among African American drag queens', in

Leap, W. (ed.) *Beyond the Lavender Lexicon: Authenticity, Imagination and Appropriation in Lesbian and Gay Languages*. New York: Gordon and Breach Press, pp. 207–26.

Barrett, R. (1997) 'The 'Homo-genius' Speech Community', in Livia, A. and Hall, K. (eds) *Queerly Phrased*. Oxford: Oxford Studies in Sociolinguistics, pp. 181–201.

Barrett, R. (2002) 'Is queer theory important for sociolinguistic theory?' in Campbell-Kibler, K., Podesva, R. J., Roberts, S. J. and Wong, A. (eds) *Language and Sexuality: Contesting Meaning in Theory and Practice*. Stanford, California: CSLI Publications, pp. 25–43.

Baxter, J. (2003) *Positioning Gender in Discourse: A Feminist Methodology*. Basingstoke: Palgrave Macmillan.

Beck, A. T. (1988) *Love is Never Enough*. New York: Harper and Row.

Becker, H. (1963) *Outsiders: Studies in the Sociology of Deviance*. New York: Free Press.

Behrendt, G. and Tuccillo, L. (2004) *He's Just Not That Into You: The No-excuses Truth to Understanding Guys*. New York: Simon and Schuster Inc.

Bell, S. (1993) 'Kate Bornstein: a transsexual, transgender, postmodern Tiresias', in Kroker, A. and Kroker, M. (eds) *The Last Sex: Feminism and Outlaw Bodies*. New York: St Martin's Press, pp. 104–20.

Benjamin, W. (1936) *Das Kunstwerk im Zeitalter seiner technischen Reproduzierbarkeit*. English translation: Zohn, H. (1968) *The Work of Art in the Age of Mechanical Reproduction*. New York: Schocken Books

Benwell, B. (2002) 'Is there anything 'new' about these lads?: the textual and visual construction of masculinity in men's magazines', in Litosseliti, L. and Sunderland, J. (eds) *Gender Identity and Discourse Analysis*. Amsterdam: John Benjamins, pp. 149–74.

Benwell, B. and Stokoe, E. (2006) *Discourse and Identity*. Edinburgh: Edinburgh University Press.

Benyon, J. (2002) *Masculinities and Culture*. Buckingham: Open University Press.

Berger, J. (1972) *Ways of Seeing*. London: BBC.

Bernstein, B. (1990) *The Structuring of Pedagogic Discourse: Class, Codes and Control. Volume IV*. London: Routledge.

Betterton, R. (ed.) (1987) *Looking On*. New York: Pandora.

Biber, D., Johansson, S., Leech, G., Conrad, S. and Finegan, E. (1999) *Longman Grammar of Spoken and Written English*. London: Longman.

Billig, M. (1995) *Banal Nationalism*. London: Sage.

Blachford, G. (1981) 'Male dominance and the gay world', in Plummer, K. (ed.) *The Making of the Modern Homosexual*. London: Hutchinson, pp. 184–210.

Blommaert, J. (2005) *Discourse*. Cambridge: Cambridge University Press.

Blumstein, P. and Schwartz, P. (1984) *American Couples: Money, Work, Sex*. New York: William Morrow.

Bolton, R. (1995) 'Sex talk: bodies and behaviours in gay erotica', in Leap, W. (ed.) *Beyond the Lavender Lexicon*. Amsterdam: Gordon and Breach, pp. 173–206.

Bordieu, P. and Boltanski, L. (1975) 'Le fétichisme de la langue', *Actes de la recherché en sciences socials* 4: 2–32.

Bordo, S. (1993) *Unbearable Weight: Feminism, Western Culture, and the Body*. Berkeley: University of California Press.

Bornstein, K. (1995). *Gender Outlaw: On Men, Women, and the Rest of Us*. New York: Vintage Books.

Bornstein, K. (1998). *My Gender Workbook*. New York: Routledge.

Bowker, L. (2001) 'Terminology and gender sensitivity: a corpus-based study of the LSP of infertility', *Language in Society* 30: 589–610.

Bright, S. (2001) *How to Write a Dirty Story: Reading and Publishing Erotica*. New York: Fireside.

Brooks, A. (1997) *Postfeminisms: Feminism, Cultural Theory and Cultural Forms*. London: Routledge.

Brown, P. (1973) *Radical Psychology*. London: Tavistock.

Brown, P. and Levinson, S. (1978) 'Universals in language use: politeness phenomena', in Goody, E. (ed.) *Questions and Politeness*. Cambridge, Cambridge University Press, pp. 55–289.

Brown, G. and Yule, G. (1983) *Discourse Analysis*. Cambridge: Cambridge University Press.

Brownmiller, S. (1975) *Against Our Will: Men, Women and Rape*. London: Secker and Warburg.

Bruthiaux, P. (1994) 'Functional variation in the language of classified ads', *Perspectives: Working Papers of the Department of English*, City Polytechnic of Hong Kong 6(2): 21–40.

Bucholtz, M. (1999) "Why be normal?' Language and identity practices in a community of nerd girls', *Language and Society* 28: 203–33.

Bucholtz, N. (2001) 'The whiteness of nerds: superstandard English and racial markedness', *Journal of Linguistic Anthropology* 11: 84–100.

Budgeon, S. '(1994) Fashion magazine advertising: constructing femininity in the 'postfeminist' era', in Manca, L. and Manca, A. (eds) *Gender and Utopia in Advertising: A Critical Reader*. Lisle IL: Procopian Press, pp. 55–70.

Burgess, E. W. (1949) 'The sociological theory of psychosexual behaviour.' In P.H. Hoch and J. Zubin (eds) *Psychosexual Development in Health and Disease*. New York: Grune, Statton, pp. 227–43.

Burr, V. (1995) *An Introduction to Social Constructionism*. London: Routledge.

Burroughs, A. (2004) *Magical Thinking*. New York: St Martins.

Burt, R. (1998) *Unspeakable Shaxxxspeares: Queer Theory and American Kiddie Culture*. London: Macmillan.

Butler, J. (1990) *Gender Trouble: Feminism and the Subversion of Identity*. New York: Routledge.

Butler, J. (1991) 'Imitation and gender insubordination', in Fuss, D. (ed.) *Inside/ Out. Lesbian Theories, Gay Theories*. New York: Routledge, pp. 13–31.

Butler, J. (1993) *Bodies that Matter*. New York: Routledge.

Caldas-Coulthard, C. R. and van Leeuwen, T. (2002) 'Stunning, shimmering, iridescent: toys as the representation of gendered social actors', in Litosseliti, L. and Sunderland, J. (eds) *Gender Identity and Discourse Analysis*. Amsterdam: John Benjamins, pp. 91–108.

Cameron, D. (1994) 'Words, words, words: the power of language', in Dunant, S. (ed.) *The War of the Words: The Political Correctness Debate*. London: Virago, pp. 15–34.

Cameron, D. (1995a) 'Rethinking language and gender studies. Some issues for the 1990s', in Mills, S. (ed.) *Language and Gender: Interdisciplinary Perspectives*. London: Longman, pp. 31–44.

Cameron, D. (1995b) *Verbal Hygiene*. London: Routledge.

Cameron, D. (1997) 'Performing gender identity: young men's talk and the construction of heterosexual masculinity', in Johnson, S. and Meinhof, U. (eds) *Language and Masculinity*. London: Blackwell, pp. 47–64.

Cameron, D. (2000) *Good to Talk?* London: Sage.

Cameron, D. (2001) *Working with Spoken Discourse*. London: Sage.

Cameron, D. (2003) 'Gender and language ideologies', in Holmes, J. and Meyerhoff, M. (eds) *The Handbook of Language and Gender*. Oxford: Blackwell, pp. 447–67.

Cameron, D. (2005a) 'Theorising the female voice in public contexts', in Baxter, J. (ed.) *Speaking Out: The Female Voice in Public Contexts*. Basingstoke: Palgrave Macmillan.

Cameron, D. (2005b) 'Language, gender and sexuality: current issues and new directions', *Applied Linguistics* 26 (4): 482–502.

Cameron, D. and Kulick, D. (2003) *Language and Sexuality*. Cambridge: Cambridge University Press.

Cameron, D. and Kulick, D. (2006) *The Language and Sexuality Reader*. London: Routledge.

Campbell-Kibler, K., Podesva, R. J., Roberts, S. J. and Wong, A. (2002) *Language and Sexuality: Contesting Meaning in Theory and Practice*. Leland Stanford Junior University: CSLI Publications.

Canary, D. J. and Hause, K. S. (1993) 'Is there any reason to research sex differences in communication?' *Communication Quarterly* 41: 129–44.

Chambers, S. A. (2003) 'Telepistemology of the closet; or, the queer politics of *Six Feet Under*', *Journal of American Culture* 26 (1): 24–41.

Chasin, A. (2000) *Selling Out: the Gay and Lesbian Movement Goes to Market*. New York and Basingstoke: Palgrave.

Chesebro, J. W. (ed.) (1981) *GaySpeak: Gay Male and Lesbian Communication*. New York: Pilgrim Press.

Cheshire, J. (1982) 'Linguistic variation and social function', in Romaine, S. (ed.) *Sociolinguistic Variation in Speech Communities* London: Edward Arnold, pp. 153–66.

Chilton, P. (2004) *Analysing Political Discourse: Theory and Practice*. London: Routledge.

Choi, P. Y. L. (2000) *Femininity and the Physically Active Woman*. London: Routledge.

Cicourel, A. V. (1964) *Method and Measurement in Sociology*. New York: Free Press.

Cixous, H. (1975) 'Sorties', in *La Jeune Née, Paris Union Générale D'Editions*, 10/12; English translation in Marks, E. and de Courtivron, I. (eds) (1980) *New French Feminisms: An Anthology*. Amherst MA: The University of Massachusetts Press.

Coates, J. (1993) *Women, Men and Language: a Sociolinguistic Account of Gender Differences in Language* (second ed.) London: Longman.

Coates, J. (1996) *Women Talk*. Oxford: Blackwell.

Coates, J. (2002) *Men Talk*. Oxford: Blackwell.

Coates, J. and Cameron, D. (eds) (1988) *Women in their Speech Communities*. London: Longman.

Cohen, S. (1972) *Folk Devils and Moral Panics: The Creation of the Mods and Rockers*. London: MacGibbon and Kee.

Connell, R. W. (1987) *Gender and Power*. Stanford, CA: Stanford University Press.

Connell, R. W. (1995) *Masculinities*. Oxford: Polity Press.

Connell, R. W., Davis, M. and Dowsett, G. W. (1993) 'A bastard of a life: homosexual desire and practice among men in working-class milieux', *Australian and New Zealand Journal of Sociology* 29: 112–35.

Connell, R. W. and Messerschmidt, J. W. (2005) 'Hegemonic masculinity: rethinking the concept', *Gender and Society* 19 (6): 829–59.

Cory, D. W. (1965) 'The language of the homosexual', *Sexology* 32 (3): 163–65.

Corrigan, P. (1997) *The Sociology of Consumption. An Introduction*. London: Sage.

Coupland, J. (1996) 'Dating advertisements: discourses of the commodified self', *Discourse and Society* 7 (2): 187–207.

Crist, S. (1997) 'Duration of onset consonants in gay male stereotyped speech', *University of Pennsylvania Working Papers in Linguistics* 4 (3): 53–70.

Cromwell, J. (1999) *Transmen and FTMs. Identities, Bodies, Genders and Sexualities*. Urbana: University of Illinois Press.

Crosby, F. and Nyquist, L. (1977) 'The female register: an empirical study of Lakoff's hypothesis', *Language in Society* 6: 313–22.

Crystal, D. (1997) *English as a Global Language*. Cambridge: Cambridge University Press.

Crystal, D. and Davy, D. (1975) *Advanced Conversational English*. London: Longman.

Darsey, J. (1981) "'Gayspeak': A response', in Chesebro, J. (ed.) *Gayspeak: Gay Male and Lesbian Communication*. New York: Pilgrim Press, pp. 58–67.

Davies P. (1990) *Longitudinal Study of the Sexual Behaviour of Homosexual Males under the Impact of AIDS: A Final Report to the Department of Health* (Project SIGMA Working Papers). London: Department of Health.

Deignan, A. (1997) 'Metaphors of desire', in Harvey, K. and Shalom, C. (eds) *Language and Desire*. London: Routledge, pp. 21–42.

Derrida, J. (1974) *Of Grammatology*. Baltimore, MD: Johns Hopkins University Press.

Derrida, J. (1978) *Writing and Difference*. Chicago: University of Chicago University Press.

Derrida, J. (1981a) *Dissemination*. Chicago: University of Chicago University Press.

Derrida, J. (1981b) *Positions*. Chicago: University of Chicago University Press.

Derrida, J. (1987) *A Derrida Reader: Between the Blinds*. Brighton: Harvester Wheatsheaf.

Dindia, K. and Allen, M. (1992) 'Sex differences in self-disclosure: a meta-analysis', *Psychological Bulletin* 112 (1): 106–24.

Douglas, M. (1966) *Purity and Danger*. London: Routledge and Kegan Paul.

Duggan, L, and Hunter, N. D. (1995) *Sex Wars: Sexual Dissent and Political Culture*. New York: Routledge.

Dull, D. and West, C. (1991) 'Accounting for cosmetic surgery: the accomplishment of gender', *Social Problems* 38: 54–70.

Dunant, S. (ed.) (1994) *The War of the Words: The Political Correctness Debate*. London: Virago.

Dworkin, A. (1981) *Pornography: Men Possessing Women*. New York: G. P. Putman's Sons.

Dyer, R. (ed.) (1977) *Gays and Film*. London: British Film Institute.

Eakins, B. and Eakins, R. (1978) *Sex Differences in Human Communication*. Boston: Houghton Mifflin.

Easlea, B. (1981) *Science and Sexual Oppression: Patriarchy's Confrontation with Woman and Nature*. London: Weidenfeld and Nicolson.

Easton, D. and Lizst, C. A. (1997) *The Ethical Slut*. San Francisco: Greenery Press.

Eckert, P. (1998) 'Gender and sociolinguistic variation', in Coates, J. (ed.) *Language and Gender: A Reader*. Oxford: Blackwell, pp. 64–75.

Eckert, P. and McConnell-Ginet, S. (1998) 'Communities of practice: where language, gender and power all live', in Coates, J. (ed.) *Language and Gender: A Reader*. Oxford: Blackwell, pp. 484–94.

Eckert, P. and McConnell-Ginet, S. (2003) *Language and Gender*. Cambridge: Cambridge University Press.

Edley, N. (2001) 'Analysing masculinity: interpretative repertoires, ideological dilemmas and subject position', in Wetherell, M., Taylor, M. and Yates, S. J. (eds) *Discourse as Data: A Guide for Analysis*. London: Sage, pp. 189–228.

Edley, N. and Wetherell, M. (1997) 'Jockeying for position: the construction of masculine identities', *Discourse and Society* 8 (2): 203–17.

Edwards, T. (1997) *Men in the Mirror: Men's Fashions, Masculinity and Consumer Society*. London: Cassell.

Ehrenreich, B. (1992) 'The challenge for the left', in Berman, P. (ed.) *Debating PC: The Controversy over Political Correctness of College Campuses*. USA: Laurel, pp. 333–38.

Ellece, S. (2005) 'Cultural identity and gender in a TV talk show in Botswana: a CDA approach', paper presented at *Theoretical and Methodological Approaches to Gender and Langauge Study. BAAL/Cambridge University Press Seminar*. 18–19 November. Birmingham University, UK.

Ellis, H. (1897) *Sexual Inversion in the Male*. London: Wilson.

English, D., Hollibaugh, G. and Rubin, G. (1981) 'Talking sex: a conversation on sexuality and feminism', *Socialist Review* 4: 43–62

Epstein, D., Elwood, J., Hey, V. and Maw, J. (1998) (eds) *Failing Boys: Issues in Gender and Achievement*. Buckingham: Open University Press.

Epstein, S. (1998). 'Gay politics, ethnic identity: the limits of social constructionism', in Nardi, P. M. and Schneider, B. E. (eds) *Social Perspectives in Lesbian and Gay Studies*. London: Routledge, pp. 134–59. Reprinted from *Socialist Review 93/94* (May–August 1987) pp. 9–54.

Erfurt, J. (1985) 'Partnerwunsch und textproduktion: zur strujtur der intentionalitat in heiratsanzeigen', *Zeit für Phonetik, Sprachwiss und Kommunikforsch* 38 (3): 309–20.

Erikson, E. (1956) 'The problem of ego identity', *Journal of the American Psychoanalytic Association* 4: 56–121.

Erikson, E. (1959) *Identity and the Life Cycle. Psychological Issues Monograph 1*. New York: International Universities Press.

Erikson, F. (1990) 'Social construction of discourse coherence in a family dinner table conversation', in Dorval, B. (ed.) *Conversational Coherence and its Development*. Norwood N J: Ablex, pp. 207–38.

Erikson, K. T. (1966) *Wayward Puritans: A Study into the Sociology of Deviance*. New York: John Wiley.

Evans, G. (2000) *Play like a Man, Win like a Woman*. New York: Broadway Books.

Fairclough, N. (1989) *Language and Power*. London: Longman.

Fairclough, N. (1995a) *Critical Discourse Analysis: The Critical Study of Language*. London: Longman.

Fairclough, N. (1995b) *Media Discourse*. London: Arnold.

Fairclough, N. (1996) 'A reply to Henry Widdowson's discourse analysis: a critical review', *Language and Literature* 5: 1–8.

Fairclough, N. (2003) *Analysing Discourse. Textual Analysis for Social Research*. London: Routledge.

Farrell, R. A. (1972) 'The Argot of the Homosexual Subculture.' *Anthropological Linguistics* 14: 385–91.

Featherstone, M. (1991) *Consumer Culture and Postmodernism*. London: Sage.

Finkelhor, D. (1994) 'The 'backlash' and the future of child protection advocacy: insights from the study of social issues', in Myers, J. E. B. (ed.) *The Backlash: Child Protection under Fire*. California: Sage, pp. 1–16.

Fishman P. M. (1977) 'Interactional shitwork', *Heresies* 2: 99–101.

Fishman, P. M. (1978) 'Interaction: the work women do', *Social Problems* 25: 397–406.

Fishman, P. M. (1980) 'Conversational insecurity', in Giles, H., Robinson, W. P. and Smith, P. M. (eds) *Language: Social Psychological Perspectives*. New York: Pergamon Press, pp. 127–32.

Fishman, P. M. (1983) 'Interaction: the work women do', in Barrie, T., Kramarae, C. and Henley, N. (eds) *Language, Gender and Society*. Rowley, MA: Newbury House, pp. 89–102.

Foucault, M. (1972) *The Archaeology of Knowledge*. London: Tavistock.

Foucault, M. (1976) *The History of Sexuality: An Introduction*. Harmondsworth: Penguin.

Foucault, M. (1984) 'What is enlightenment?' in Rabinow, P. (ed.) *The Foucault Reader*. London: Penguin.

Frankel, L. P. (2004) *Nice Girls Don't Get the Corner Office*. New York: Warner Business Books.

Freud, S. (1905) 'Three essays on the theory of sexuality', in Strachey, J. (ed.) *The Standard Edition of the Complete Psychological Words of Sigmund Freud. Vol. 10*. London: The Hogarth Press, pp. 3–150.

Frosh, S., Phoenix, A. and Pattman, R. (2002) *Young Masculinities*. London: Palgrave.

Gamson, J. (1998) 'Must identity movements self-destruct? A queer dilemma.' In P, Nardi and B. Schneider (eds), *Social Perspectives in Lesbian and Gay Studies*. London: Routledge, pp. 589–604. Reprinted from *Social Problems* 42: 3, (1995), pp. 390–407.

Garber, M. (2000) *Bisexuality and the Eroticism of Everyday Life*. Routledge: New York.

Gates, K. (2000) *Deviant Desires*. New York: Juno Books.

Gaudio, R. P. (1994). 'Sounding gay: pitch properties in the speech of gay and straight men', *American Speech* 69 (1): 30–37.

Gergen, K. (1973) 'Social psychology as history', *Journal of Personality and Social Psychology* 26, 309–320.

Giddens, A. (1991) *Modernity and Self-identity*. Cambridge: Polity Press.

Gilbert, N. and Mackay, M. (1984) *Opening Pandora's Box: A Sociological Analysis of Scientists' Discourse*. Cambridge: Cambridge University Press.

Gilbert, S. (2001) 'New uses for old boys: an interview with Sandra Gilbert', in Hall, D. E. (ed.) *Professions: Conversations on the Future of Literary and Cultural Studies*. Urbana: University of Illinois Press, pp. 244–54.

Gleason, P. (1983). 'Identifying identity: a semantic history', *Journal of American History* 69 (4): 910–31.

Glover, D. and Kaplan, C. (2000) *Genders*. London and New York: Routledge.

Goddard, C. and Saunders, B. J. (2000) 'The gender neglect and textual abuse of children in the print media', *Child Abuse Review* 9: 37–48.

Goffman, E. (1963) *Stigma: Notes on the Management of Spoiled Identity*. Englewood Cliffs. New Jersey: Prentice-Hall. Goldman, R. (1992) *Reading Ads Socially*. London: Routledge.

Goode, E. and Ben-Yehuda, N. (1994) *Moral Panics: The Social Construction of Deviance*. Oxford: Blackwell.

Goodman, S. (1996) 'Market forces speak English' in S. Goodman and D. Graddol (eds) *Redesigning English: new tests, new identities*. London: Routledge, pp. 141–180.

Goodwin, M. H. (1980) 'Directive-response speech sequences in girls' and boy's task activities.' In: S. McConnell-Ginet, R. Broker and N. Forman, N. (eds) *Women and language in literature and society*. Praeger, New York, pp. 157–173.

Goodwin, J. P. (1989) *More Man Than You'll Ever Be: Gay Folklore and Acculturation in Middle America*. Bloomington: Indiana University Press.

Gott, R. (1993) 'The debate about culture: review of Robert Hughes: the culture of complaint', *The Guardian*, June 1: 8.

Graddol, D. (1997) *The Future of English?* London: The British Council.

Graddol, D. and Swann, J. (1989) *Gender voices*. Oxford: Blackwell.

Gramsci A. (1971) *Selections from Prison Notebooks*. London: Lawrence and Wishart. Trans. Q. Hoare and G. Nowell-Smith.

Gramsci, A. (1985) *Selections from the Cultural Writings 1921–1926*. London: Lawrence and Wishart. Ed. D. Forgacs and G. Nowell Smith, trans. W. Boelhower.

Grant, J. (1993) *Fundamental Feminism: Contesting the Core Concepts of Feminist Theory*. New York: Routledge.

Gray, J. (1992) *Men are from Mars, Women are from Venus: A Practical Guide for Improving Communication and Getting What You Want in Your Relationships*. New York: HarperCollins.

Green, J. (1987) 'Polari', *Critical Quarterly* 39 (1): 127–31.

Gumperz, J. J. (1982) *Discourse Strategies*. Cambridge: Cambridge University Press.

Habermas, J. (1979) 'Moral development and ego identity', in *Communication and the Evolution of Society*. Boston: Beacon Press, pp. 69–74.

Hacking, I. (1990) *The Taming of Chance*. Cambridge: Cambridge University Press.

Hajer, M. (1997) *The Politics of Environmental Discourse: Ecological Modernization and the Policy Process*. Oxford: Oxford University Press.

Hall, D. E. (2003) *Queer Theories*. London: Palgrave.

Hall, D. E. and Pramaggiore, M. (eds) (1996) *RePresenting Bisexualities: Subjects and Cultures of Fluid Desire*. New York: New York University Press.

Hall, K. (1995) 'Lip service on the fantasy lines', in Hall, K. and Bucholtz, M. (eds) *Gender Articulated: Language and the Socially Constructed Self.* New York: Routledge, pp. 183–216.

Hall, S. (1994) 'Some 'politically incorrect' pathways through PC', in Dunant, S. (ed.) *The War of the Words: The Political Correctness Debate.* London: Virago, pp. 164–83.

Hall, S. (1997) *Representation: Cultural Representations and Signifying Practices.* London: Sage.

Hall, S. (1997) 'The spectacle of the 'other'', in Hall, S. (ed.) *Representation: Cultural Representations and Signifying Practices.* London: Sage and the Open University, pp. 223–79.

Hall, S., Critcher, C., Jefferson, T., Clarke, J. and Roberts, B. (1978) *Policing the Crisis: Mugging, the State, and Law and Order.* London: Macmillan.

Halliday, M. A. K. (1978) *Language as a Social Semiotic: The Social Interpretation of Language and Meaning.* London: Edward Arnold Ltd.

Halperin, D. (1990) *One Hundred Years of Homosexuality and Other Essays on Greek Love.* Routledge: London.

Halperin. D. (1995) *Saint Foucault: Towards a Gay Hagiography.* New York and Oxford: Oxford University Press.

Hamer, D. H., Hu, S., Magnuson, V. L., Hu, N. and Pattatucci, A. M. L. (1993) 'A linkage between DNA markers on the X chromosome and male sexual orientation', *Science* 261: 321–27.

Hancock, I. (1984) 'Shelta and Polari', in Trudgill, P. (ed.) *The Language of the British Isles.* Cambridge: Cambridge University Press, pp. 384–403.

Harding, S. (1991) *Whose Science? Whose Knowledge? Thinking from Women's Lives.* Ithaca, NY: Cornell University Press.

Harré, R. and Secord, P. F. (1972) *The Explanation of Social Behaviour.* Oxford: Blackwell.

Harrington, K. (2006) '*Perpetuating difference? Corpus linguistics and the gendering of reported dialogue*', paper presented at the Theoretical and Methodological Approaches to Gender and Language Study, BAAL/CUP Seminar. 18–19 November. Birmingham University, UK.

Harris, D. (1997) *The Rise and Fall of Gay Culture.* New York: Ballantine Books.

Harvey, K. (2000) 'Describing camp talk: language/pragmatics/politics', *Language and Literature* 9 (3): 240–60.

Hayes, J. (1976) 'Gayspeak', *The Quarterly Journal of Speech* 62: 256–66. Reprinted in Chesebro, J. W. (ed.) (1981) *Gayspeak: Gay Male and Lesbian Communication.* New York: Pilgrim Press, pp 43–57.

Healey, E. (1996). *Lesbian Sex Wars.* London: Virago.

Hechler, D. (1988) *The Battle and the Backlash: The Child Sexual Abuse War.* Massachusetts: Lexington Books.

Hekman, S. (1999) 'Identity crises: identity, identity politics, and beyond', in Hekman, S. (ed.) *Feminism, Identity and Difference.* London: Frank Cass, pp. 3–26.

Heller, E. (1989) *Wie Farben wirken: Farbpsychologie, Farbsymbolik, krea-
tive Farbgestaltung*. [The Effects of Colours: Colour Psychology, Colour
Symbolism, Creative Colour Design] Reinbek: Rowohlt.

Hemmings, C. (1999) 'Locating bisexual identities.' In M. Storr (ed.) *Bisexuality:
A Critical Reader*. London: Routledge, pp. 193–200.

Herbert, R. K. (1990) 'Sex-based differences in compliment behaviour', *Language
in Society* 19: 201–24.

Herdt, G. H. (1981) *Guardians of the Flutes: Idioms of Masculinity*. New York:
McGraw-Hill.

Hermes, J. (1995) *Reading Women's Magazines* Cambridge: Polity Press.

Jackson, P., Stevenson, N. and Brooks, K. (2001) *Making Sense of Men's
Magazines*. Cambridge: Polity Press.

Herring, S. C. (1993) 'Gender and democracy in computer-mediated communication', *Electronic Journal of Communication* [Online] 3 (2).

Heywood, J. (1997) "The object of desire is the object of contempt': representations of masculinity in *Straight to Hell* magazine', in Meinhof, U. H. and
Johnson, S. (eds) *Language and Masculinity*. Oxford: Basil Blackwell, pp.
188–207.

Hillman, J. S. (1974) 'An analysis of male and female roles in two periods of
children's literature', *Journal of Education Research* 68: 84–88.

Hodge, R. and Kress, G. (1988) *Social Semiotics*. London: Polity Press.

Hoey, M. (1983) *On the Surface of Discourse*. London: Harper-Collins.

Hoey, M. (1986) 'The discourse colony: a preliminary study of a neglected
discourse type', in *Talking about Text*, Discourse Analysis Monograph no. 13,
English Language Research, University of Birmingham, pp. 1–26.

Hoey, M. (1997) 'The organization of narratives of desire. A study of first-person
erotic fantasies', in Meinhof, U. H. and Johnson, S. (eds) *Language and
Masculinity*. Oxford: Basil Blackwell, pp. 85–105.

Holloway, W. (1984) 'Gender difference and the production of subjectivity', in
Henriques, J., Holloway, W., Urwin, C., Venn, C. and Walkerdine, V. (eds)
Changing the Subject: Psychology, Social Regulation and Subjectivity. London:
Methuen, pp. 227–339.

Holmes, J. (1995) *Women, Men and Politeness*. London: Longman.

Holmes, J. and Schnurr, S. (2006) 'Doing femininity and work: More than just
relational practice', *Journal of Sociolinguistics* 10 (1): 31–51.

Houlbrook, M. (2005) *Queer London. Perils and Pleasures in the Sexual
Metropolis, 1918–1957*. Chicago: University of Chicago Press.

Hu, S., Pattatucci, A. M. L., Patterson, C., Li, L., Fulker, D. W., Cherny, S. S.,
Kruglyak, L. and Hamer, D. H. (1995) 'Linkage between sexual orientation
and chromosome Xq28 in males but not in females', *Nature Genetics* 11:
248–56.

Humphreys, L. (1970) *Tearoom Trade*. London: Duckworth.

Hunt, L. (1998) *British Low Culture: From Safari Suits to Sexploitation*. London:
Routledge.

Hutchins, L. and Ka'ahumanu, L. (eds) (1990) *Bi Any Other Name: Bisexual People Speak Out*. Boston: Alyson Publications.

Hyde, J. (2005) 'The gender similiarities hypothesis', *American Psychologist* 60 (6): 581–92.

Innes-Parker, K. (1999) 'Mi bodi henge with thi bodi neiled o rode: the gendering of the Pauline concept of crucifixion with Christ in medieval devotional prose for women', *Studies in Religion* 28 (1): 49–62.

Irigaray, L. (1985) *This Sex Which is Not One*. Ithaca, New York: Cornell University Press. Trans. C. Porter.

Irvine J. T. and Gal, S. (2000) 'Language ideology and linguistic differentiation', in Kroskrity, P. (ed.) *Regimes of Language: Ideologies, Polities and Identities*. Santa Fe, New Mexico: School of American Research Press, pp. 35–83.

Jackson, P., Stevenson, N. and Brooks, K. (2001) *Making Sense of Men's Magazines*. Cambridge: Polity Press.

Jacobs, G, Rogers, H. and Smyth, R. (1999) 'Sounding gay, sounding straight: a search for phonetic correlates', paper presented at *New Ways of Analysing Variation* 28, Toronto.

Jespersen, O. (1922) *Language, Its Nature, Development and Origin*. London: Allen and Unwin.

Johnson, B. '(1993) Economics holds back lesbian ad market', *Advertising Age* 34, January, p. 37.

Johnson, S. and Ensslin, A. (2007) "But her language skills shifted the family dynamics dramatically." Language, gender and the construction of publics in two British newspapers', *Gender and Language*.

Johnson, S. and Meinhof, U. H. (eds) (1997) *Language and Masculinity*. Oxford: Blackwell.

Jule, A. (2001) 'Speaking their sex: linguistic space and gender in a second language classroom', paper presented at the 34th *BAAL Annual Meeting*, Reading University, September.

Kahan, H. and Mulryan, D. (1995) 'Out of the closet', *American Demographics* 17 (4): 40–46.

Katz, J. (1983) *Gay/Lesbian Almanac: A New Documentary*. New York: Harper and Row.

Keller, E. F. (1985) *Reflections on Gender and Science*. New Haven: Yale University Press.

Kelly, A. (1988) 'Gender differences in teacher-pupil interaction: a meta-analytical review', *Research in Education* 39: 1–23.

Kiesling, S. (2002) 'Playing the straight man: displaying and maintaining male heterosexuality in discourse', in Campbell-Kibler, K., Podesva, R. J., Roberts, S. J. and Wong, A. (eds) *Language and Sexuality: Contesting Meaning in Theory and Practice*. Stanford, California: CSLI Publications, pp. 249–66.

Kilgarriff, A. and Tugwell, D. (2001) 'WASP-Bench: an MT lexicographers' workstation supporting state-of-the-art lexical disambiguation', *Proceedings of MT Summit VII*, Santiago de Compostela, pp. 187–90.

Kimmel, M. S. (2000) *The Gendered Society*. Oxford: Oxford University Press.

King, M. and McKeown, E. (2003) *Mental Health and Social Wellbeing of Gay Men, Lesbians and Bisexuals in England and Wales*. London: Mind.

Kinsey, A. C., Pomeroy, B. and Martin, C. E. (1948) *Sexual Behavior in the Human Male*. Philadelphia: W. B. Saunders; Bloomington: Indiana U. Press.

Kinsey, A. C. Pomeroy, W. B., Martin, C. E. and Gebhard, P. H. (1953) *Sexual Behavior in the Human Female*. Philadelphia: W. B. Saunders; Bloomington: Indiana U. Press.

Kitzinger, C. (2005) "Speaking as a heterosexual': (how) does sexuality matter for talk-in-interaction?' *Research on Language and Social Interaction* 38 (3): 221–65.

Kitzinger, J. (1995) 'Qualitative research: introducing focus groups', *British Medical Journal* 311: 299–302.

Kjellmer, G. (1986) "The lesser man': observations on the role of women in modern English writings', in Arts, J. and Meijs, W. (eds) *Corpus Linguistics II*. Amsterdam: Rodopi, pp 163–76.

Klein, F. (1978) *The Bisexual Option: A Concept of One Hundred Percent Intimacy*. Arbor House: New York.

Klein, F. (1980) 'Are you sure you're heterosexual? Or homosexual? Or even bisexual?' *Forum*, December, pp. 41–45.

Klein, F., Sepekoff, B. and Wolf, T. J. (1985) 'Sexual orientation: a multi-variable dynamic process', *Homosex* 11 (1/2): 35–49.

Koller, V. (2006) "Not just a colour': pink as a gender and sexuality marker in visual communication.' http://www.lancs.ac.uk/staff/koller/pink_v3.pdf.

Kortenhaus, C. and Demarest, J. (1993) 'Gender role stereotyping in children's literature: an update', *Sex Roles* 29 (3/4): 219–32.

Kosciw, J. G. (2004) *The 2003 National School Climate Survey: The School-related Experiences of our Nation's Lesbian, Gay, Bisexual and Transgender Youth*. New York: GLSEN.

Kottoff, H. and Wodak, R. (eds) (1997) *Communicating Gender in Context*. Amsterdam: John Benjamins.

Kramarae, C. (1981) *Women and Men Speaking*. Rowley, Mass: Newbury House Publishers, Inc.

Kramarae, C. and Taylor, H. J. (1993) 'Women and men on electronic networks: A conversation or a monologue?' in Taylor, H. J., Kramarae, C. and Ebben, M. (eds) *Women, Information Technology and Scholarship*. Center for Advanced Study, University of Illinois, Urbana-Champaign, pp. 52–61.

Krane, V. (2001) "We can be athletic and feminine,' but do we want to? Challenges to femininity and heterosexuality in women's sport', *Quest* 53: 115–33.

Kress, G. (2006) *Reading Images: the Grammar of Visual Design*. Second ed. London: Routledge.

Kulick, D. (1999) 'Transgender and language', *GLQ* 5: 605–22,

Kulick, D. (2002) 'Queer linguistics?' in Campbell-Kibler, K., Podesva, R. J., Roberts, S. J. and Wong, A. (eds) *Language and Sexuality: Contesting*

Meaning in Theory and Practice. Stanford, California: CSLI Publications, pp. 65–68.

Labov, W. (1966) 'Hypercorrection by the lower middle class as a factor in linguistics change', in Bright, W. (ed.) *Sociolinguistics*. The Hague: Mouton, pp. 84–113.

Lakoff, R. (1975) *Language and Woman's Place*. New York: Harper and Row.

Landry, D. and MacLean, G. (eds) (1996) *The Spivak Reader*. New York and London: Routledge.

Lave, J. and Wenger, E. (1991) *Situated Learning: Legitimate Peripheral Participation*. Cambridge: Cambridge University Press.

Lazar, M. (ed.) (2005) *Feminist Critical Discourse Analysis: Gender, Power and Ideology in Discourse*. Basingstoke: Palgrave.

Leap, W. L. (ed.) (1995) *Beyond the Lavender Lexicon: Authenticity, Imagination and Appropriation in Lesbian and Gay Languages*. New York: Gordon and Breech Press.

Leap, W. L. (1996) *Word's Out: Gay Men's English*. Minneapolis: University of Minnesota Press.

Leap, W. L. and Boellstroff, T. (2003) *Speaking in Queer Tongues: Globalization and Gay Language*. Urbana: University of Illinois Press.

Lee, J. (1988) 'Care to join me in an upwardly mobile tango?' in Gamman, L. and Marshment, M. (eds) *The Female Gaze: Women as Viewers of Popular Culture*. Seattle: Real Comet, pp. 166–72.

Legman, G. (1941) 'The language of homosexuality: an American glossary', in Henry, G. W. (ed.) *Sex Variants. A Study of Homosexual Patterns: Vol. 2*. New York and London: Paul B. Hoeber Inc., pp. 1147–79.

Leidholdt, D. and Raymond, J. (1990) *The Sexual Liberals and the Attack on Feminism*. New York: Pergammon Press.

Le Page, R. B., Christie, P., Jurdant, B., Weekes, A. and Tabouret-Keller, A. (1974) 'Further report on the sociolinguistic survey of multilingual communities', *Language in Society* 3: 1–32.

Le Page, R. B. and Tabouret-Keller, A. (1985) *Acts of Identity: Creole-Based Approaches to Language and Ethnicity*. Cambridge: Cambridge University Press.

Lesch, C. L. (1994) 'Observing theory in practice: sustaining consciousness in a coven', in Frey, L. (ed.) *Group Communication in Context: Studies of Natural Groups*. Hillsdale, NJ: Lawrence Erlbaum, pp. 57–82.

LeVay, S. (1991) 'A difference in hypothalamic structure between heterosexual and homosexual men', *Science* 253: 1034–37.

Levi-Strauss, C. (1970) *The Raw and the Cooked*. London: Cape.

Levorato, A. (2003) *Language and Gender in the Fairy Tale Tradition: A Linguistic Analysis of Old and New Story-Telling*. London: Palgrave.

Levy, A. (2005) *Female Chauvinist Pigs: Women and the Rise of Raunch Culture*. London: Pocket Books.

Lieb, R., Quinsey, V. and Berliner, L. (1998) 'Sexual predators and social policy', in Tonry, M. (ed.) *Crime and Justice*. Chicago: University of Chicago Press, pp. 43–114.

Lippi-Green, R. (1997) *English with an Accent: Language, Ideology and Discrimination in the United States*. New York: Routledge.

Littosseliti, L. (2003) *Using Focus Groups in Research*. London: Continuum.

Litosseliti, L. and Sunderland, J. (eds) (2002) *Gender Identity and Discourse Analysis*. Amsterdam: John Benjamins.

Livia, A. and Hall, K. (eds) (1997) *Queerly Phrased: Language, Gender and Sexuality*. Oxford: Oxford University Press.

Lloyd, M. (1999) 'Performativity, parody, politics', *Theory, Culture and Society* 16 (2): 195–213.

Löbner, S. (2002) *Understanding Semantics*. London: Arnold.

Longino, H. E. (1980) 'Pornography, oppression, and freedom: a closer look' in Lederer, L. (ed.) *Take Back the Night: Women on Pornography*. New York: William Morrow and Co. Inc., pp. 40–45.

Louw, B. (1997) 'The role of corpora in critical literary appreciation', in Wichmann, A., Fligelstone, S., McEnery, T. and Knowles, G. (eds) *Teaching and Language Corpora*. London: Longman, pp. 140–251.

Lucas, I. (1997) 'The color of his eyes: Polari and the Sisters of Perpetual Indulgence', in Livia, A. and Hall, K. (eds) *Queerly Phrased*. Oxford: Oxford Studies in Sociolinguistics, pp. 85–94.

Lumby, M. (1976) 'Code switching and sexual orientation: a test of Bernstein's sociolinguistic theory', *Journal of Homosexuality* 1: (4): 383–99.

Maltz, D. and Borker, R. (1982) 'A cultural approach to male-female miscommunication', in Gumpertz, J. J. (ed.) *Language and Social Identity*. Cambridge: Cambridge University Press, pp. 195–216.

Marcuse, H. (1964) *One-Dimensional Man*. Boston: Beacon Press.

Martin, J. (2004) 'Positive discourse analysis: power, solidarity and change', *Revista* 49: 179–200.

Marwick, A. (1996) *British Social History Since 1945*. London: Penguin.

Masters, W. and Johnson, V. (1982) *Homosexuality in Perspective*. New York: Bantam Books.

Maybin, J. (2002) '"What's the hottest part of the Sun? Page 3!" Children's exploration of adolescent gender identities through informal talk', in Litosseliti, L. and Sunderland, J. (eds) *Gender Identity and Discourse Analysis*. Amsterdam: John Benjamins, pp. 257–73.

McClintock, A. (1995) *Imperial Leather: Race, Gender and Sexuality in the Imperial Context*. London: Routledge.

McCracken, E. (1993) *Decoding Women's Magazines: From Mademoiselle to Ms*. London: Macmillan.

McDonald, B. and Leyland, W. (eds) (1982) *Sex: True Homosexual Experiences from STH Writers Volume 3*. San Francisco: Gay Sunshine Press.

McEnery, T. and Wilson, A. (1996) *Corpus Linguistics*. Edinburgh: Edinburgh University Press.

McIlvenny, P. (2002) 'Critical reflections on performativity and the 'un/doing' of gender and sexuality', in McIlvenny, P. (ed.) *Talking Gender and Sexuality*. Amsterdam: John Benjamins, pp. 111–49.

McLuhan, M. (1964) *Understanding Media*. New York: Mentor.

McNay, L. (1999) 'Subject, Psyche and Agency: The Work of Judith Butler', *Theory, Culture & Society* 16(2): 175–93.

Medhurst, A. (1997) 'Camp', in Medhurst, A. and Munt, S. R. (eds) *Lesbian and Gay Studies: A Critical Introduction*. London: Cassell, pp. 274–93.

Merton, R. K. and Kendall, P. (1946) 'The focused interview', *American Journal of Sociology* 51 (6): 541–57.

Merton, R. K., Fiske, M. and Kendall, P. L. (1956) *The Focused Interview: A Manual of Problems and Procedures*. Glencoe IL: Free Press.

Messerschmidt, J. W. (1993) *Masculinities and Crime: Critique and Reconceptualatization of Theory*. Lanham, Md: Rowan and Littlefield Publishers, Inc.

Meyers, R. A., Brashers, D. E., Winston, L. and Grob, L. (1997) 'Sex differences and group argument: a theoretical framework and empirical investigation', *Communication Studies* 48: 19–41.

Mieli, M. (1980) *Homosexuality and Liberation: Elements of a Gay Critique*. London: Gay Men's Press.

Mills, S. (ed.) (1994) *Gendering the Reader*. Hemel Hempstead: Harvester Wheatsheaf.

Mills, S. (ed.) (1995a) *Language and Gender: Interdisciplinary Perspectives*. London: Longman.

Mills, S. (1995b) *Feminist Stylistics*. London: Routledge.

Mills, S. (1997) *Discourse*. London: Routledge.

Mills, S. (1998) 'Post-feminist text analysis', *Language and Literature* 7(3): 235–53.

Milroy, J. and Milroy, L. (1985) 'Linguistic change, social network and speaker innovation', *Journal of Linguistics* 21: 339–84.

Milroy, L. (1980) *Language and Social Networks*. Oxford: Blackwell.

Money, J. (1955) 'Hermaphroditism, gender and precocity in hyperadreno-corticism: psychologic findings', *Bulletin of the Johns Hopkins Hospital* 96: 253–264.

Moonwomon, B. (1985) 'Toward the study of lesbian speech', in Bremner, S., Caskey, N. and Moonwomon, B. (eds) *Proceedings of the First Berkeley Women and Language Conference*. Berkeley, California: Berkeley Women and Language Group, pp. 96–107.

Moonwomon, B. (1994) 'Lesbian identity, lesbian text', in Bucholtz, M., Liang, A. C., Sutton, L. A. and Hines, C. (eds) *Cultural Performances: Proceedings of the Third Berkeley Women and Language Conference*, 8–10 April. Berkeley: Berkeley Women and Language Group, University of California, pp. 509–24.

Moran, J. (1991) 'Language Use and Social Function in the Gay Community', paper presented at NWAVE (New Ways of Analyzing Variation) 20. October. Georgetown University.

Morgan, R. and Wood, K. (1995) 'Lesbians in the living Room: Collusion, co-construction and co-narration in discourse.' In W. Leap (ed.), *Beyond the Lavender Lexicon: Authenticity, Imagination and Appropriation in Lesbian and Gay Languages*. New York: Gordon and Breach Press, pp. 235–248.

Mort, F. (1996) *Cultures of Consumption: Masculinities and Social Space in Late Twentieth Century Britain*. London: Routledge.

Mulac, A., Wiemann, J. M., Widenmann, S. J. and Gibson, T. W. (1988) 'Male/female language differences in same-sex and mixed-sex dyads: the gender-linked language effect', *Communication Monographs* 55: 315–35.

Murphy, T. F. (1997) *Gay Science: The Ethics of Sexual Orientation Research*. New York: Columbia University Press.

Myers J. E. B. (ed.) (1994) *The Backlash: Child Protection under Fire*. California: Sage.

Nagel, J. (2003) *Race, ethnicity, and sexuality: intimate intersections, forbidden frontiers*. New York: Oxford Univ. Press

Nakamoto, S. (2002) *Men are Like Fish: What Every Woman Needs to Know About Catching a Man*. California: Java Books.

Namaste, V. K. (2000) *Invisible Lives. The Erasure of Transsexual and Transgendered People*. Chicago: University of Chicago Press.

Nair, B. R. (1992) 'Gender, genre and generative grammar: deconstructing the matrimonial column', in Toolan, M. (ed.) *Language, Text and Context: Essays in Stylistics*. London and New York: Routledge, pp. 227–54.

Nixon, S. (1996) *Hard Looks: Masculinities, Spectatorship and Contemporary Consumption*. London: UCI Press.

Noebel, D, Pope, G. and Williams, J. (1977) *The Homosexual Revolution. End Time Abomination*. Colorado: Summit Ministries Press.

Norton, R. (1992) *Mother Clap's Molly House. The Gay Subculture in England 1700–1830*. London: Gay Men's Press.

Nussbaum, M. (1999) 'The professor of parody', *The New Republic Online*. http://www.qwik.ch/the_professor_of_parody. Accessed 10 May 2006.

O'Brien, J. (1999) 'Writing in the body. Gender (re)production in online inter-action', in Smith, M. A. and Kollock, P. (eds) *Communities in Cyberspace*. London: Routledge, pp. 76–104.

Ochs, E. (1991) 'Indexing gender', in Duranti, A. and Goodwin, C. (eds) *Rethinking Context*. Cambridge: Cambridge University Press, pp. 335–58.

Omoniyi, T. (1998) 'The discourse of tourism advertisements: packaging nation and ideology in Singapore', *Working Papers in Applied Linguistics* 4(22): 2–14. London: Thames Valley University.

Orbach, S. (1998) *Fat is a Feminist Issue*. London: Arrow.

Parker, I. (1992) *Discourse Dynamics: Critical Analysis for Social and Individual Psychology*. London: Routledge.

Parker, I. and Burnman, E. (1993) 'Against discursive imperialism, empiricism and constructionism: thirty two problems with discourse analysis.' In E. Burman and I. Parker (eds) *Discourse Analytical Research*. London: Routledge, pp. 155–172.

Parsons. T. (1955) *Family Socialization and Interaction Process*. New York.

Partridge, E. (1950) *Here, There, and Everywhere: Essays Upon Language*. London: Hamish Hamilton.

Pastoureau, M. (2004) *Dictionnaire des Couleurs de Notre Temps*. [Dictionary of the Colours of our Time] Second ed. Paris: Bonneton.

Patthey-Chavez, G. and Youmans, M. (1992) 'The social construction of sexual realities in heterosexual women's and men's erotic texts', in Hall, K., Bucholtz, M. and Moonwomon, B. (eds) *Locating power: Proceedings from the Second Berkeley Women and Language Conference Vol. 2*. Berkeley Women and Language Group: Berkeley, CA. pp. 501–14.

Pearce, M. (2005) 'Informalisation in UK party election broadcasts 1966–97', *Language and Literature* 14 (1): 65–90.

Pearson, S. S. (1981) 'Rhetoric and organizational change: new applications of feminine style', in Forisha, B. L. and Goldman, B. H. (eds) *Outsiders on the inside: Women and Organizations*. Englewood Cliffs, NJ: Prentice-Hall, pp. 55–74.

Pease, B. and Pease, A. (2001) *Why Men Don't Listen and Women Can't Read Maps: How We're Different and What to do about it*. New York: Broadway.

Perry, L. A. M., Turner, L. H. and Sterk, H. M. (eds) (1992) *Constructing and Reconstructing Gender: The Links Among Communication, Language, and Gender*. Albany: SUNY UP.

Petersen, S. B. and Lach, M. A. (1990) 'Gender stereotypes in children's books: their prevalence and influence on cognitive and affective development', *Gender and Education* 2 (2): 185–97.

Philips, S. U. (2003) 'The power of gender ideologies in discourse', in Holmes, J. and Meyerhoff, M. (eds) *The Handbook of Language and Gender*. Oxford: Blackwell, pp. 252–76.

Pinker, S. (1994) *The Language Instinct: How the Mind Creates Language*. London: Penguin.

Pleasance, H. (1991) 'Open or closed: popular magazines and dominant culture', in Franklin, S., Lury, C. and Stacey, J. (eds) *Off Centre: Feminism and Cultural Studies*. London: Harper Collins Academic, pp. 69–84.

Plummer, D. C. (2001) 'The quest for modern manhood: masculine stereotypes, peer culture and the social significance of homophobia', *Journal of Adolescence* 24(1): 15–23.

Podesva, R. J. Roberts, S. J. and Campbell-Kibler, K. (2002) 'Sharing resources and indexing meanings in the production of gay styles', in Campbell-Kibler, K., Podesva, R. J., Roberts, S. J. and Wong, A. (eds) *Language and Sexuality:*

Contesting Meaning in Theory and Practice. Stanford, California: CSLI
Publications, pp. 175–90.

Ponte, M. (1974). 'Life in a parking lot: an ethnography of a homosexual drive-in', in Jacobs, J. (ed.) *Deviance: Field Studies and Self-Disclosure*. Palo Alto, California: National Press Books, pp. 7–29.

Potter, J. and Wetherell, M. (1987) *Discourse and Social Psychology*. London: Sage.

Potter, J. and Wetherell, M. (1995) 'Discourse analysis', in Smith, J., Harré, R. and van Langenhove, L. (eds) *Rethinking Methods in Psychology*. London: Sage, pp. 80–92.

Pratt, M. L. (1987) 'Linguistic Utopias.' In N. Fabb, D. Attridge, A. Durant and C. MacCabe (eds) *The Linguistics of Writing: Arguments between Language and Literature*. Manchester: Manchester University Press, pp. 48–66.

Pujolar, J. C. (1997) 'Masculinities in a multilingual setting', in Johnson, S. and Meinhof, U. (eds) *Language and Masculinity*. London: Blackwell, pp. 88–106.

Queen, R. M. (1997) "I don't speak Spritch'; locating lesbian language', in Livia, A. and Hall, K. (eds) *Queerly Phrased*. Oxford: Oxford Studies in Sociolinguistics, pp. 233–56.

Raban, J. (1973) 'Giggling in code', *Lunch* 20: 16–17.

Rayson, P., Leech, G. and Hodges, M. (1997) 'Social differentiation in the use of English vocabulary: some analyses of the conversational component of the British National Corpus', *International Journal of Corpus Linguistics* 2: 133–50.

Reid, E. (1993) 'Electronic chat: Social issues on Internet Relay Chat.' *Media Information Australia, 67*, 62–70.

Remlinger, K. A. (2005) 'Negotiating the classroom floor: negotiating ideologies of gender and sexuality', in Lazar, M. (ed.) *Feminist Critical Discourse Analysis: Gender, Power and Ideology in Discourse*. London: Palgrave Macmillan, pp. 114–38.

Rice, G., Anderson, C., Risch, N. and Eber, G. (1999) 'Male homosexuality: absence of linkage to microsatellite markers at Xq28', *Science* 284: 665–67.

Ritzer, G. (1998) 'Introduction', in Baudrillard, J. *The Consumer Society: Myth and Structures*. London: Sage, pp. 1–24.

Robins, K. (2000) 'Cyberspace and the world we live in', in Bell, D. and Kennedy, B. (eds) *The Cybercultures Reader*. London: Routledge, pp. 77–80.

Rodgers, B. (1972) *The Queen's Vernacular*. San Francisco: Straight Arrow Books.

Rodino, M. (1997) 'Breaking out of binaries: reconceptualizing gender and its relationship to language in computer-mediated communication', *Journal of Computer Mediated Communication* [Online] 3 (3).

Rogers, H, Smyth, R. and Jacobs, G. (2000) 'Vowel and sibilant duration in gay- and straight-sounding male speech', paper presented at the International Gender and Language Association Conference 1, Stanford.

Romaine, S. (1999) *Communicating Gender*. Mahwah, N.J.: Erlbaum.

Romaine, S. (2001) 'A corpus-based view of gender in British and American English', in Hellinger, M. and Bußmann, H. (eds) *Gender across Languages* Vol. 1. Amsterdam/Philadelphia: John Benjamins, pp. 153–75.

Ross, M-S. (1995) 'Reaching out to the unreachable: an interview with Diane Gobeil from CACTUS Montreal', *Gendertrash* 4: 11–16.

Ross, N. J. (1995) 'Dubbing American in Italy', *English Today* 11: 45–48.

Rowe, C. (2000) *True Gay – Hegemonic Homosexuality? – Representations of Gayness in Conversations between Gay Men*. MA Dissertation. Lancaster University, UK.

Rubin, G. (1975) 'The traffic in women: notes on the 'political economy' of sex', in Reiter, R. R. (ed.) *Toward an Anthropology of Women*. New York: Monthly Review Press, pp. 157–210.

Rubin, G. (1984) 'Thinking sex: notes for a radical theory of the politics of sexuality', in Vance, C. (ed.) *Pleasure and Danger: Exploring Female Sexuality*. London: Pandora, pp. 267–319.

Rudd, D. (2000) *Enid Blyton and the Mystery of Children's Literature*. London: Macmillan.

Rutledge, L. (1989) *The Gay Fireside Companion*. Boston: Alyson.

Sadker, M. and Sadker, D. (1985) 'Sexism in the schoolroom of the '80s', *Pyschology Today*, March: 54–7.

de Saussure, F. (1975) *Course in General Linguistics*. London: Fontana.

Schmid, H.-J. (2003) 'Do women and men really live in different cultures? Evidence from the BNC.' In Lewandowska-Tomaszczyk, B. and Melia, P. J. (eds). *Lodz Studies in Language 8: Corpus Linguistics by the Lune*. Frankfurt: Peter Lang, pp. 185–221.

Schmid, H.-J. and Fauth, J. (2003) 'Women's and men's style: fact or fiction? New grammatical evidence', paper presented at the *Corpus Linguistics Conference*, Lancaster, March 2003.

Schmitt, A. and Sofer, J. (1992) *Sexuality and Eroticism among Males in Moslem Societies*. Binghamton NY: Harrington Park Press.

Schwarz, J. (2006) *'Non-sexist Language' at the Beginning of the 21st Century: Interpretative Repertoires and Evaluation in the Metalinguistic Accounts of Focus Group Participants Representing Differences in Age and Academic Discipline*. PhD thesis. Lancaster University.

Searle, J. R. (1969) *Speech Acts: An Essay in the Philosophy of Language*. Cambridge: Cambridge University Press.

Searle, J. R. (1979) *Expression and Meaning: Studies in the Theory of Speech Acts*. Cambridge: Cambridge University Press.

Searle, J. R. (1983). *Intentionality: An Essay in the Philosophy of Mind*. Cambridge University Press: New York.

Searle, J. R. (1989) 'Consciousness, unconsciousness and intentionality', *Philosophical Topics*, xxxvii (10): 193–209.

Sedgwick, E. K. (1991) *Epistemology of the Closet*. Hemel Hempstead: Harvester Wheatsheaf.

Segal, L. (1994 [1987]) *Is the Future Female? Trouble Thoughts on Contemporary Feminism*. London Virago.

Seidler, J. (1989) *Rediscovering Masculinity: Reason, Language and Sexuality*. New York: Routledge.

Seidman, S. (1993) 'Identity and politics in a 'postmodern' gay culture: some historical and conceptual notes', in Warner, M. (ed.) *Fear of a Queer Planet: Queer Politics and Social Theory*. Minneapolis: University of Minnesota Press, pp. 105–42.

Sheldon, A. (1990) 'Pickle fights: gendered talk in preschool disputes', *Discourse Processes* 13 (1): 5–31.

Shively, C. (1981) 'Introduction', in McDonald, B. (ed.) *Meat*. San Francisco: Gay Sunshine Press, pp. 5–8.

Sigley, R. and Holmes, J. (2002), 'Girl-watching in corpora of English', *Journal of English Linguistics* 30 (2): 138–57.

Simmons, R. (2002) *Odd Girl Out: The Hidden Culture of Aggression in Girls*. New York: Harcourt Trade Publishing.

Sinfield, A. (1994) *The Wilde Century: Effeminacy, Oscar Wilde and the Queer Moment*. London: Cassell.

Skeggs, B. (1997) *Formations of Class and Gender: Becoming Respectable*. London: Sage.

Smith-Rosenberg, C. (1975) 'The female world of love and ritual', *Signs* 1: 1–30.

Soskin, W. F. and John, V. (1963) 'The study of spontaneous talk', in Barker, R. (ed.) *The Stream of Behavior*. New York: Irvington Publishers, Inc., pp. 228–81.

Spargo, T. (1999) *Foucault and Queer Theory*. London: Penguin.

Speer, A. and Potter, J. (2002) 'From performatives to practices: Judith Butler, discursive psychology and the management of heterosexist talk', in McIlvenny, P. (ed.) *Talking Gender and Sexuality*. Amsterdam: John Benjamins, pp. 152–80.

Spencer, C. (1995). *Homosexuality: A History*. London: Fourth Estate.

Spender, D. (1985) 'On feminism and propaganda', in Treichler P. A., Kramarae, C. and Stafford, B. (eds) *Alma Mater: Theory and Practice in Feminist Scholarship*. Urbana: University of Illinois Press, pp. 307–15.

Spender, D. (1980) *Man Made Language*. London: Routledge.

Stallybrass, P. and White, A. (1986) *The Politics and Poetics of Transgression*. London: Metheun.

Stanley, J. P. (1970) 'Homosexual slang', *American Speech* 45: 45–59.

Steinem, G. (1978, November). 'Erotica and pornography: A clear and present difference.' *Ms*. November.

Stephens, J. (1992) *Language and Ideology in Children's Fiction*. London: Longman.

Stone, S. (1991) 'The *empire* strikes back. A posttransexual manifesto', in Epstein, J. and Straub, K. (eds) *Body Guards: The Cultural Politics of Gender Ambiguity*. London: Routledge, pp. 280–304.

Storms, M. S. (1980) 'Theories of sexual orientation', *Journal of Personality and Social Psychology* 38 (5): 738–92.

Storr, M. (1999) *Bisexuality: A Critical Reader*. London: Routledge.

Stubbs, M. (1983) *Discourse Analysis: The Sociolinguistic Analysis of Natural Language*. Chicago: University of Chicago Press.

Stubbs, M. (2001) *Words and Phrases: Corpus Studies of Lexical Semantics*. London: Blackwell.

Sunderland, J. (2004) *Gendered Discourses*. London: Palgrave.

Swacker, M. (1975) 'The sex of the speaker as a sociolinguistic variable', in Thorne, B. and Henley, N. (eds) *Language and Sex: Difference and Dominance*. Massachusetts: Newbury House, pp. 76–83.

Swann, J. (2002) 'Yes, but is it gender?' in Litosseliti, L. and Sunderland, J. (eds) *Gender Identity and Discourse Analysis*. Amsterdam: John Benjamin, pp. 43–67.

Tajfel, H. and Turner, J. (1979) 'An intergrative theory of intergroup conflict', in Austin, W. G. and Worchel, S. (eds) *The Social Psychology of Intergroup Relations*. Monterey CA: Brooks/Cole, pp. 33–47.

Tabben, D. (1990) *You Just Don't Understand: Men and Women in Conversation*. New York: William Morrow.

Talbot, M. M. (1995) *Fictions at Work – Language and Social Practice in Fiction*. London: Longman.

Talbot, M. M. (1997a) "Randy fish boss branded a stinker': coherence and the construction of masculinities in a British tabloid newspaper', in Johnson, S. and Meinhof, U. (eds) *Language and Masculinity*. London: Blackwell, pp. 173–87.

Talbot, M. M. (1997b) "An explosion deep inside her' Women's desire and popular romance fiction', in Harvey, K. and Shalom, C. (eds) *Language and Desire*. London: Routledge, pp. 106–22.

Talbot, M. M. (1998) *Language and Gender. An Introduction*. Cambridge: Polity Press.

Talbot, M. M. (2000) "It's good to talk?' The undermining of feminism in a British Telecom advertisement', *Journal of Sociolinguistics* 4 (1): 108–19.

Tannen, D. (1990) *You Just Don't understand: Women and Men in Conversation*. London: Virago.

Tannen, D. (ed.) (1993) *Gender and Conversational Interaction*. New York: Oxford University Press.

Taub, D. and Leger, R. (1984) 'Argot and the creation of social types in a young gay community', *Human Relations* 37 (3): pp. 181–89.

Thompson, K. (1998) *Moral Panics*. London: Routledge.

Thornborrow, J. (1998) 'Playing hard to get: metaphor and representation in the discourse of car advertisements', *Language and Literature* 7 (3): 254–72.

Thorne, A. and Coupland, J. (1998) 'Articulations of Same-sex Desire: Lesbian and Gay-male Dating Advertisements', *Journal of Sociolinguistics* 2(2): 233–257.

Troemel-Plotz, S. (1991) 'Review essay: selling the apolitical', *Discourse and Society* 2 (4): 489–502.

Trudgill, P. (1972) 'Sex, covert prestige and linguistic change in the urban British English of East Anglia', *Language in Society* 1: 179–95.

Trudgill, P. (1978) *Sociolinguistic Patterns in British English*. London: Edward Arnold.

Trumbach, R. (1991) 'The birth of the queen: sodomy and the emergence of gender equality in modern culture, 1660–1750', in Duberman, M. B., Vicinus, M. and Chauncey, G. (eds) *Hidden From History*. London: Penguin, pp. 129–40.

Tucker, N. (ed.) (1995) *Bisexual Politics: Theories, Queries and Visions*. New York: Harington Park Press.

Turner-Bowker, D. M. (1996) 'Gender stereotyped descriptions in children's future books: does 'Curious Jane' exist in the literature?' *Sex Roles* 35 (7–8): 461–88.

UNICEF (2001) *Early Marriage: Child Spouses*. Florence: UNICEF Innocenti Research Centre.

van Dijk, T. A. (1991) *Racism and the Press. Critical Studies in Racism and Migration*. London and New York: Routledge.

van Dijk, T. A. (1993) 'Principles of Critical Discourse Analysis', *Discourse and Society* 4 (2): 249–83.

Veblen, T. (1899) *Theory of the Leisure Class: An Economic Study in the Evolution of Institutions*. New York: Macmillan.

Ventola, E. (1998) 'Constructing and maintaining sexist ideologies: horses sweat, men perspire, women glow', *Studia Anglica Posnanienisa: International Review of English Studies* 33: 463–74.

von Taschitzki, T. (2006) 'Contemporary pinks: on the individuality of shades', in Nemitz, B. (ed.) *Pink: the Exposed Color in Contemporary Art and Culture*. Ostfildern: Hatje Cantz, pp. 64–77.

Walby, S. and Allen, J. (2004) *Domestic Violence, Sexual Assault and Stalking. Findings from the British Crime Survey. Home Office Research Study 276*. London: Home Office Research.

Warner, M. (ed.) (1993) *Fear of a Queer Planet*. Minneapolis MN: University of Minnesota Press.

Watney, S. (1997) 'Lesbian and gay studies in the age of AIDS' In A. Medhurst and S. Munt (eds) *Lesbian and Gay Studies: A Critical Introduction*. London: Cassell, pp. 368–384.

Webbink, P. (1981) 'Nonverbal behavior and lesbian/gay orientation', in Mayo, C. and Henley, N. (eds) *Gender and Non-Verbal Behavior*. New York: Springer, pp. 253–59.

Weedon, C. (1997) *Feminist Practice and Post-structuralist Theory*. Second edition. Oxford: Blackwell.

Weeks, J. (1977) *Coming Out*. London: Quartet.

Weeks, J. (1985) *The Meaning of Diversity: Sexuality and its Discontents*. London: Routledge.

Weiss, J. T. (2001) 'The gender caste system: identity, privacy, and heteronormativity', *Law and Sexuality* 10: 123–86.

Wellings, K. (2005) 'Lust. Changing sexual behaviour in the UK', in Stewart, I. and Vaitilingam, R. (eds) *Seven Deadly Sins. A New Look at Society through an Old Lens*. Swindon: ESRC, pp. 16–19.

Wernicke (1991) *Promotional Culture*. London: Sage.

West, C. and Zimmerman, D. H. (1985) 'Gender, language and discourse', in van Dijk, T. A. (ed.) *Handbook of Discourse Analysis. Vol. 4: Discourse Analysis in Society*. London: Academic Press, pp. 103–24.

Westwood, G. (1952) Society and the Homosexual. London: Victor Gollancz.

White, E. (1980) 'The political vocabulary of homosexuality', in Michaels, L. and Ricks, P. (eds) *The State of the Language*. Berkeley: University of California Press, pp. 235–46.

Widdowson, H. G. (1995) 'Discourse analysis: a critical view', *Language and Literature* 4 (3): 157–72.

Wilkins, B. M. and Andersen, P. A. (1991) 'Gender differences and similarities in management communication: a meta-analysis', *Management Communication Quarterly* 5: 6–35.

Wilkinson, S. (1996) 'Bisexuality 'à la mode'', *Women's Studies International Forum* 19 (3): 293–301.

Williams, P. and Chrisman, L. (eds) (1993) *Colonial Discourse and Post-colonial Theory: A Reader*. London: Longman.

Wilson, G. and Rahman, Q. (2005) *Born Gay: The Psychobiology of Sexual Orientation*. London: Peter Owen.

Wilton, T. (1997) *Sexualities in Health and Social Care*. Buckingham: Open University Press.

Wiseman, R. (2002) *Queen Bees and Wannabes*. New York: Three Rivers Press.

Wodak, R. (ed.) (1997) *Gender and Discourse*. London: Sage.

Wodak, R. and Meyer, M. (eds) (2001): *Methods of Critical Discourse Analysis*. London: Sage.

Wolf, N. (1991) *The Beauty Myth: How Images of Beauty are used against Women*. London: Vintage.

Yeoman, B. (1999) 'Gay no more?' *Psychology Today*. March/April, pp. 27–29, 68–70.

Zeve, B. (1993) 'The Queen's English: metaphor in gay speech', *English Today* 35 (9.3): 3–9.

Zimmerman, D. and West, C. (1975) 'Sex roles, interruptions and silences in conversation', in Thorne, B. and Henley, N. (eds) *Language and Sex: Difference and Dominance*. Rowley, Massachusetts: Newbury House, pp. 105–29.

Zwicky, A. M. (1997). 'Two lavender issues for linguists', in Livia, A. and Hall, K. (eds) *Queerly Phrased*. Oxford: Oxford Studies in Sociolinguistics, pp. 21–34.

Index

abusive terms 138–140

accommodation 81

action research 16–19

adjective 7, 18, 32, 34, 46, 100, 119, 144, 186, 205, 211, 212, 225, 246 *see empty adjective*

Adler, S. 100

adverb 30, 34, 46, 115, 168, 245

advertising 155–183, 254 *see* personal adverts

African American Vernacular English 66, 83

agency 93, 95, 98, 158, 162, 165, 243, 257, 259, 263

Allen, L. 60

Allen, M. 44–45

America (United States) 5, 34, 43, 48, 50, 53, 54, 55, 56, 66, 83, 87, 103, 122, 125, 127, 137. 146, 147, 148, 154, 168, 169, 203, 198, 220, 224, 228, 230, 243, 246, 254, 261–262

American National Corpus 147

analysis 21–23

Andersen, P. 44

Anderson, B. 65

Angelides, S. 148

Ardil, S. 258

Aries, E. 41

Armistead, N. 17

Austin, J. 73

Babcock, B. 153

bachelor 203–208, 213

Badgett, M. 169

Baker, P. 8, 12, 28, 66–67, 102, 115, 149, 172, 175–176, 183, 188–189, 224, 226, 237, 241–242, 247, 250

Bakhtin, M. 252

banal nationalism 3, 110

Barbie Liberation Organisation 100

Barker, C. 20

Barrett, R. 66, 193, 219

Barthes, R. 72

Baxter, J. 17, 19, 96, 108, 112, 119, 120, 138, 177, 196, 197, 202, 219, 259, 260, 264

Beauvoir, S. 73

Beck, A. 34

Becker, H. 13, 222

Behrendt, G. 42

Bell, S. 73–74

Benwell, B. 135, 157, 179, 180–182, 251, 253, 254

Ben-Yehuda, N. 223

Benyon, J. 156

Berger, J. 113, 162

Berliner, L. 226

Bernstein, B. 20

Betterton, R. 166

bias in research 18

Biber, D. 86, 103

Bible, The 106–107

Billig, M. 3, 100

binary oppositions 3–6, 12–13, 27, 30, 41, 54, 58, 65, 79, 121–122, 145, 152, 167, 170, 186, 208, 248, 255

biological differences: *see essentialist research*

biphobia 149–151

bisexuality 117, 146–151, 188, 255–256

Blachford, G. 183

Blommaert, J. 92

Blumstein, P. 43

Blyton, Enid 101–102

Boellstroff, T. 8, 192

Boltanski, L. 64

Bolton, R. 241

border crossing 174

Bordieu, P. 64

Bordo, S. 137

Borker, R. 33, 41

Bornstein. K. 73–74, 78, 122, 197

Bowker, L. 17–18

boy 104, 199

boys 33, 39, 42, 64, 96–98, 100–101, 110, 112, 134, 138–139, 173, 191

Bright, S. 240

British National Corpus 15, 27, 38, 45–49, 85, 103–105, 139–140, 146–150, 161, 199, 204–213, 224, 229

Brooks, A. 13

Brooks, K. 179

Brown, G. 71

Brown, Penelope, 34

Brown, Phil 17

Brownmiller, S. 240

Bruthiaux, P. 174

Bucholtz, M. 197

Budgeon, S, 252

bulletin board 150–151

Burgess, E. 31

Burman, E. 19

Burr, V. 72, 92

Burroughs, A. 158

but 199, 207–208

Butler, J. 73–78, 84, 93, 94, 118, 157, 186, 187, 196

Caldas-Coulthard, C. 20, 99–100

Cameron, D. 7, 8, 31, 35, 37, 38, 54, 57, 58, 59, 69, 71, 73, 75, 92, 94, 119, 130, 153, 174, 192, 193–4, 197, 251, 261, 262

camp 83–84, 125, 176

Campaign for Homosexual Equality 77, 196

Campbell-Kibler, K. 8, 192, 194

Canary, D. 44–45

capitalism 25, 92, 155–158, 166, 169, 182, 215, 232, 252, 253, 262

Chambers, S. 109

Chasin, A. 170–173, 182

chatline 82

Chesebro, J. 8, 55

Cheshire, J. 64

children 9–11, 13, 25, 41, 49, 96–102, 107–108, 111–113, 122, 127, 144, 178, 200, 202, 203, 206–207, 210, 212, 220–227, 256, 258

children's fiction 100–102

Chilton, P. 92

Chirrey, D. 115

Choi, P. 137

Chrisman, L. 92

Cicourel, I. 17

Cixous, H. 121, 256

Coates, D. 7, 126–127, 130, 136–137

co-construction 68–69

Cohen, S. 222

collocation 20, 28, 95, 96, 119, 144, 161, 172, 204, 208, 224, 229, 263

colloquial language 46, 129, 135, 199, 224, 236, 237

colony text 174

colour terms 33, 48, 172–173

commodity feminism 166–169

communication 14–15

communities of practice 26, 65, 236

complicity 35, 125 127, 130, 134, 135, 139, 140,152, 177, 252

compulsory heterosexuality: *see* heterosexuality

computer mediated communication 78–81, 150–151

Connell, R. 4, 123–125, 138, 146, 153, 176, 185, 242, 252, 259

consumption 25, 156, 158, 160, 164–166, 169, 252–253

context, 21, 48–49, 53, 71, 84

contradiction 40, 93, 130, 135, 137, 166, 168, 172–173, 177, 180, 182, 248, 258–260

conversation analysis 114

co-operative discourse 87

corpus 20, 242

corpus linguistics 45, 103–106

Corrigan, P. 157

Cory, D. 50, 58

Coupland, J. 174, 175, 176, 178–179, 182, 254

Crist, S. 56

critical discourse analysis 102, 119

Cromwell, J. 152

Crosby, F. 34

Crystal, D. 174–175, 261

cyber-identities 78–82

Darsey, J. 53–54

Davies, P. 89

Davis, M. 153

Davy, D. 174–175

deconstruction 18, 26–27, 76–77, 187, 194, 197–198, 215–216, 222, 258

deficit (theory of women's language use) 29–32

Deignan, A. 199

Demarest, J. 101

Derrida, J. 12, 13, 72, 75, 76, 122, 219

desire 9, 25, 192, 199, 216, 221, 240, 247–249, 255–256

discourses 142–144, 226
    female 113, 127, 155, 158
    heterosexual 11, 54, 109, 203
    male 130, 155
    same-sex 10–11, 28, 108, 136, 153, 155, 175, 183, 188, 189, 195, 242, 243, 246

sexual 6–7, 52, 54, 140, 143–144, 146, 155–156, 173, 191, 194–195, 199, 201, 221–222, 227, 237
    tabooed 26, 231, 249, 258–259

difference 12, 16, 41–49, 121, 145, 153, 160

Dindia, K. 44–45

discourse 24–25, 77, 230, 256–257 (*see also gendered discourse*)

definitions 91–2
    specific names of
      'boys will be boys' 97
      'childhood innocence' 103
      'empowering girls' 103
      'gender differences' 2, 96, 112, 162, 167, 261
      'gender equality' 177
      'gender equality now achieved' 162, 259
      '(hetero)sexualizing girls' 113
      'male dominance' 144
      'male firstness' 97
      'male sexual drive' 135, 142, 143
      'nice girls aren't easy' 142
      'romantic love' 156
      'sexual tolerance' 103
      'shame and secrecy' 115
      'vive la différence' 131
      'women as domestic' 101–102
    relationship to language 95
    relationship to sexuality 109
    repetitions 95
    subversion 100–102
    ways of categorizing
      alternative 223
      competing 112, 117, 131–132, 135, 162, 164
      dominant 114, 116, 138, 260, 264
      damaging 93, 102, 112
      instructional 213, 230, 329
      lifeworld 162

moral 229, 230, 249
    over-arching 96
diversity 24, 63,123, 136, 152, 195, 249,
    251
'dogging' 228–230, 249
dominance 247–248 *see* subordination
    theory of women's language use 24,
    32–36
dominant reading 203
double entendre 171
double voicing 251–252
Douglas, M. 121
Dowsett, G. 153
Duggan, L. 240
Dull, D. 162
Dunant, S. 37
Dworkin, A. 241
Dyer, R. 13

Eakins, B, and R. 34
Easlea, B. 17
Easton, D. 140
Eckert, P. 10, 41, 64, 65, 132–135
Edley, N. 59, 93
Ehrenreich, B. 37
Ellece, S. 262
Ellis, H. 189–191
'empty' adjectives 32, 34, 48, 74
English, D. 220
Ensslin, A. 105
Epstein, D. 97
Epstein, S. 11, 13
erasure 104, 148, 150–152, 256
Erfurt, J. 174
Erikson, E. 10, 42, 222
erotic language 79–83
erotica 230, 240–241, 247, 258
essentialism 60–61, 75, 256–257
ethnic identity 83, 170–171, 243
ethnography 55

euphemism 4, 16, 37, 53, 71, 144, 200,
    206, 237, 238, 239, 241
Evans, G. 35, 252
exclamations 86
expectations 2–3, 9
extra-marital relationships 214–216,
    228–229, 249, 256, 263

Fairclough, N. 20, 21, 23, 91, 92, 95, 102,
    119, 162, 174
false needs 157
Farrell, R. 52
fat admirers 231–233
Fauth, J. 46
Featherstone, M. 156
female impersonator 75
femininity 85, 122, 164–165, 172, 252
    emphasised 138, 255
    hegemonic femininity 136–145
feminism 19, 220, 251, 257
    commodity 166–169, 253–254
    liberal 166
    'post-' 13–14, 168–169, 173, 252,
        259–260
    second-wave 14, 32
feminist critical discourse analysis 119
feminist post-structuralist discourse
    analysis 119, 138, 177, 197, 202, 259
fetish 80, 83, 176, 183, 231, 246–248, 258
fictionalising 17
Finkelhor, D. 222
Fishman, P. 34
focus group 38–41, 59, 180–181
foregrounding 98
Foucault, M. 76, 91, 92, 94, 114, 187,
    255, 259
fractal recursivity 150
Frankel, L. 35, 252
frequency 20, 38, 45–49, 59, 103–104,
    139, 146, 148, 150, 204, 208, 241

Freud, S. 76, 146, 223, 255
Frosh, S. 130

Gal, S. 150
Galasinski, D. 20
Gamson, J. 220
Garber, M. 148, 151
Gates, K. 231–233, 237
Gaudio, R. 55
gay 129–130, 153
gay community 195
Gay English 70–71
'gay language' 24, 31–32, 50–58
gay liberation 10, 53, 67, 155, 173, 183,
    189, 196, 216, 243, 246, 251, 255, 257,
    259
Gay Liberation Front 77, 196
gay men 10, 68, 79, 81, 153, 172, 175,
    220, 241, 254, 255
  differences to heterosexual men 60
  erasure or marginalisation 109, 116,
    117, 173, 241, 258
  'ethnic' group 169–170, 182
  fetishisation of heterosexual men 80,
    173, 258
  focus of language studies 8, 29, 50, 68
  language use of 31, 33, 43, 52–58, 60,
    66–67, 70–71, 80, 242
  legal status 67
  negative attitudes towards 52, 125,
    170, 183, 245, 247 (*see* homophobia)
  politics 77
  stereotypes 1, 80, 88, 117, 123, 170,
    177
  stigmatised 36, 249
  subordination 131, 135, 136, 258
gay pride 170
GaySpeak 53–54
'gay voice' 55–57, 87
gaze 55, 73, 113, 162

gender
  change over time 5, 9–10
  definition 3–5, 64, 73, 74, 122
  relationship to sexuality 7–9, 57–58,
    75–76, 80, 88, 109, 145, 176–177,
    256
  relationship to sex 74, 75
gendered discourse 25, 43, 91, 94–110,
    132, 144, 152, 157, 162–165, 175, 206,
    211, 213, 228, 242, 254, 256 (*see* also
    discourse)
gender identity 7, 11, 75, 78–79, 81, 86,
    129–130, 145, 155, 162, 203, 261
gendering 1–2, 262
genderlect 43
gender norms *see norms*
gender performance 72–88, 157, 253,
    256
gender role 4, 9
generic pronoun 40
gender trouble 76, 77
genre 92, 103–104, 128, 174, 207, 217,
    240
Gergen, K. 17
Giddens, A. 155, 156–157, 185
Gilbert, N. 38
Gilbert, S. 19, 257
girl 38–40, 104
girls 4, 33, 42, 64, 96–98, 100, 101,
    110–113, 137–139, 172, 173, 197, 226
Gleason, P. 10
globalisation 261
Glover, D. 77
Goddard, C. 227
Goffman, E. 13
Goldman, R. 155, 166, 168, 253–254
Goode, E. 223
Goodman, S. 174
Goodwin, J. 55, 70
Goodwin, M. 33
Gorski, R. 60

Gott, R. 37
Gough, K. 108
Graddol, D. 7, 261
Gramsci, A. 123
grand narrative 19, 196, 260
Grant, J. 76
Gray, J. 42
Green, J. 66
Gumperz, J. 42

Habermas, J. 11
Hacking, I. 17
Hajer, M. 92
Hall, D. 148, 192, 220–221, 256, 257, 259
Hall, K. 8, 77, 78, 82–83, 156, 192, 194
Hall, S. 12, 37, 223
Halliday, M. 26, 232
Halperin, D. 188, 193
Hamer, D. 60
Hancock, I. 66
Harding, S. 17
Harré, R. 17
Harrington, K. 46, 63
Harris, D. 60, 242–243, 254
Harvey, K. 80, 84, 86
Hause, K. 44–45
Hayes, J. 53, 80
Healey, E. 240
Hechler, D. 222, 226
hedges 32, 48, 179
hegemonic femininity *see* femininity
hegemonic homosexuality *see*
    homosexuality
hegemonic masculinity *see* masculinity
hegemony 123
Hekman, S. 76
Heller, E. 173
Hemmings, C. 150
Henry, G. 31
Herbert, R. 85–86
Herdt, G. 192, 226

Hermes, J. 179
Herring, S. 78–79
he/she 40
heternormativity 8, 25, 109–100, 129,
    155, 166, 169–170 186–187, 215, 261,
    263
heterosexism 151, 191
heterosexuality
    as queer 194–195, 197–201, 216, 228,
        257
    as unstable 186, 242–248
    bias in language 116
    compulsory heterosexuality 107–110,
        112–113, 116, 117, 136
    default status 8, 11, 25, 29, 32, 43, 50,
        56, 57, 58, 59, 69, 107, 117, 121, 144,
        154,
    155, 156, 204
    heterosexual desire 82, 127, 175, 198,
        203, 228, 241
    link to gender 9, 75, 80, 86, 88,
        127–132, 135, 137, 144, 145, 176,
        195, 245–247
    relation to bisexuality 146–151, 185,
        188, 255
    relation to homosexuality 12, 18, 22,
        24, 26, 54, 56, 60–61, 81, 89, 124,
        153, 170, 172, 176, 187–192, 197,
        208, 231, 242–246, 255, 258, 260
heterosexual language use 34, 54, 57,
    82–83, 114–115
heterosexual lifestyle 71, 125
heterosexual matrix 75, 84
heterosexual privilege 150, 185, 255
Heywood, J. 8, 243, 246, 258, 259
hierarchy 13, 18, 123, 137, 140, 145, 185,
    188, 195, 219, 222, 262
    boys 42
    gender 8, 101, 118, 122, 135–136, 150,
        153, 158, 177, 254, 259
    power 27, 137–138, 177

sexuality 75, 118, 187
Hillman, J. 100
Hodge, R. 20
Hoey, M. 161, 174, 241
Holloway, W. 91
Holmes, J. 35–36, 44, 86, 103, 104,
    137–138
homophobia 1, 2, 102, 109, 110, 124,
    130, 131, 132, 149, 151, 153, 191, 224,
    245, 247, 254, 263
homosexuality 121, 124, 129–130,
    169–173, 187–192
    emphasised 176
    hegemonic homosexuality 136, 175
homonyms 129, 204
Houlbrook, M. 188
Hu, S. 60
humour 100–102, 135–136, 253
Humphreys, L. 55
Hunt, L. 156
Hunter, N. 240
husband 208–213
Hutchins, L. 149, 150
Hyde, J. 45
hyper-correct grammar and
    pronunciation 33, 66, 87, 197

iconisation 150
identity 10–13
identity politics 37, 151, 186, 192, 196
ideologies 93, 123–124, 257
imagined communities 65
implicature 127, 161, 168, 207, 212, 238,
    245, 263
inclusive language 116–117
Innes-Parker, K. 107
interactional shitwork 34
International Corpus of English 46
Internet 21, 78–79, 221, 230, 231, 233,
    237, 239, 249, 250, 263
interpretative repertoire 38, 59, 93

interview 21–22, 50, 66, 82, 96, 126,
    131–135, 138–139, 143, 217, 260, 262
introspection 21–2
invitational imperative 238–239
Irigaray, L. 76, 121
irony 136, 201, 253
Irvine, J.150

Jackson, P. 179
Jespersen, O. 29–32, 94
John, V. 34
Johnson, B. 172
Johnson, F. 41
Johnson, S. 8, 105, 123
Johnson, V. 190–191
Jule, A. 98

Ka'ahumanu, L. 149, 150
Kahan, H. 169
Kaplan, C. 77
Katz, J. 187
Keller, E. 17
Kelly, A. 98
Kendall, P. 59
Kiesling, S. 127–128
Kilgarriff, A. 208
Kimmel, M. 4
King, M. 10
Kinsey, A. 6, 31, 146, 255–256
Kitzinger, C. 59, 84, 114–115
Kjellmer, G. 103
Klein, F. 6
Koller,V. 172–173
Kortenhaus, C. 100
Kosciw, J, 10
Kotthoff, H. 76
Kramarae, C. 7, 79
Krane, V. 137
Kress, G. 20, 199
Kulick, D. 8, 31, 35, 54, 57, 69, 71, 73, 75,
    192, 193–4, 197

Labov, W. 32
Lacan, J. 76
Lach, M. 100
Lakoff, R. 32, 36, 41, 74
Landry, D. 197
language 14, 187
  relationship to identities 15–16
late modernity 155
Lave, J. 65
Lazar, M. 19, 76, 91, 119, 151, 169, 260
Leap, W. 8, 68, 70–71, 87, 192
Lee, J. 168
Leger, R. 55
Legman, G. 32
Leidholdt, D. 240
Le Page, R. 66, 81
lesbian continuum 108
lesbians 8, 9, 10, 29, 31–32, 36, 43, 50,
  54, 55, 57, 60, 65, 66, 68, 69, 71, 77, 88,
  109, 116, 117, 125, 147, 151, 169–173,
  182, 220, 242, 250, 254, 255, 258
  language 65, 69–70
  voice 57
Lesch, C. 34
LeVay, S. 60
Levi-Strauss, C. 121
Levorato, A. 101
Levy, A. 140, 168–169, 251, 252
Leyland, W. 242, 246
lexis 115, 161, 229, 232, 237, 263
Lieb,R. 226
linguistics of contact 66
linguistic traces 95
Lippi-Green, R. 84
Litosseliti, L. 8, 59
Livia, A. 8, 77, 78, 192, 194
Lizst, C. 140
Lloyd, M. 75
Löbner, S. 20
log-log algorithm 208
Longino, H. 240

Louw, B.229
Lucas, I. 66
Lumby, M. 55

MacLean, G. 197
magazines 111, 135–136, 140, 166–168,
  171–172, 180–181, 226, 230, 233
male bias 18, 36
Maltz, D. 33, 41
man 103–105, 119
  as a generic term 38
Marcuse, H. 157
marginalisation 125, 127, 195, 215, 219,
  258
marketisation 25, 165, 173, 174, 232,
  253–254, 262
marriage 9, 26, 44, 89, 91, 107, 108, 114,
  115, 117, 188, 192, 201–209, 211–213,
  215, 217, 226, 227–229, 232, 256, 257,
  262
Martin, J. 240, 260
Marwick, A. 9
Marxism 123
masculinity 80, 123–136, 162–164, 176
  hegemonic masculinity 25, 122–136,
    142, 153, 163–164, 175, 181, 197,
    213, 247, 252–255, 261, 263
  protest masculinity 124
Masters, W. 190–191
Mattachine Society 77
Maybin, J. 229
McClintock, A. 8
McConnell-Ginet, S. 10, 41, 64, 65
McCracken, E. 253
McDonald, B. 244, 246
McEnery, T. 20, 45
McIllvenny, P. 8
McKeown, E. 10
McLuhan, M. 261
McNay, L. 76
media discourses 236

Meinhof, U. 8
men's use of language 41–49, 122–137
Merton, R. 59
Messerschmidt, J. 125, 259
metaphor 52
Meyer, M. 21, 119
Meyers, R. 34
Mieli, M. 153
Mills and Boon 140–145, 156
Mills, S. 8, 41, 91, 95, 160–161, 177–178, 197, 259
Milroy, J. 75
Milroy, L. 64, 75
modality 96, 162–163, 209, 210
Money, J. 4
monogamy 9, 26, 213, 227–228, 239, 256–257
Moonwomon, B. 55, 57
moral panic 183, 222–224, 227
Moran, J. 55
Morgan, R. 69–70
MSM identity 81, 89, 175, 176, 189, 242, 245–246
Mulac, A. 34
Mulkay, M. 38
Murlyan, D. 169
Murphy, T. 146
Myers, J. 222, 226

Nagel, J. 109
Nair, B. 174
Nakamoto, S. 42
Namaste, V. 150–151, 152
narratives 126–128, 236–239, 241–248, 258
national identity 3, 87
'nerd' identity 125, 153, 197
Neumark, N. 258
'new man' identity 132–133
news 222
newspapers 115–117, 198–203, 223–227

Nixon, S. 156
Noebel, D. 52
nominalisation 46, 95, 162, 263
non-standard language 46, 64, 80, 87
non-verbal language 14–15, 21, 55, 96,
normality 121–122, 195, 222
norms 118
    gender norms 5, 7, 9, 26, 42, 78, 130, 138, 166, 252
    group norms 59
    language norms 31, 64, 74, 78, 106
    male norms 43, 130, 252
    sexual norms 6, 9, 166, 252
    societal norms 82, 96, 105, 110, 222, 239, 255
    workplace norms 35–36
Norton, R. 188
nursery rhymes 97–99, 119
Nussbaum, M. 76, 77
Nyquist, L. 34
O'Brien, J. 80
Ochs, E. 74
Omoniyi, T. 238
Orbach, S. 232

paedophiles 9, 52, 135, 149, 220, 223–227, 233, 248, 258
Parker, I. 19, 91, 92
Parsons, T. 9
Partridge, E. 66
Pastoreau, M. 172–173
patriarchy 36, 185
Patthey-Chavez, G. 241, 242
Pearce, M. 174
Pearson, S. 34
Pease, B and A. 42
performativity 24, 256 *see gender performance*
Perry, L. 7
personal adverts 174–179
Petersen, S. 100

Philips, S. 251
Pinker, S. 37
'pink pound' 169–173, 262
Pleasance, H. 155
Plummer, D. 10
Podesva, R. 56, 57
Polari 66–68
political correctness 36–41, 102, 253
Ponte, M. 55
pornography 170–171, 220, 240–250, 258
positive discourse analysis 240, 260
post-feminist analysis 177, 197, 202, 259
post-modernism 72, 177, 248, 251, 258–259
post-structuralism 18, 27, 72, 93, 112, 187, 197, 219, 247, 260, 263
Potter, J. 8, 76, 78, 93, 131–132
power 9, 12–14, 17–18, 33, 35, 41, 43, 72, 78, 88, 91–95, 98–101, 105–106, 108, 112–114, 118–119, 121, 122, 123, 131, 219, 240, 247–255, 257–261, 263
Pratt, M. 66
problem-solution pattern 161–162
pronouns 31, 36, 40, 46, 53, 71, 95, 103, 107, 112, 115, 238, 257
Pujolar, J. 125

Queen, R. 65
queens 188
queer 186, 219–222, 245
queer analysis 194, 203, 208, 215–216, 225–226
queer theory 19, 25–26, 27, 78, 152, 178, 186–187, 192–197, 203, 215–216, 219–220, 222, 246, 255, 257–258, 261
Quinsey, V. 226
quotation 168, 229, 238, 246

Raban, J. 67
racism 37, 102

Rahman, Q. 60
rainbow flag 170
Raymond, J. 240
Rayson, P. 45, 49
reception 21, 23, 95, 119, 179, 203, 259
reclaiming 26, 35, 58, 134, 140, 173, 186, 193, 220, 245
Reid, E. 78
religion 106–107
Remlinger, K. 8
research questions 22
Rice, G. 60
Rich, A. 107–108
Ritzer, G. 160
Robins, K. 78
Rodgers, B. 50–53
Rodino, M. 79
Rogers, H. 56
Romaine, S. 8, 103
romantic fiction 140–145, 156
Ross, M-S. 152
Ross, N. 261
Round the Horne 67
Rowe, C. 136, 175
Rubin, G. 4, 108
Rudd, D. 102
Rutledge, L. 88

Sadker, D. and M. 97
Saunders, B. 227
Saussure, F. 72
Schmid, H.-J. 46, 49
Schmitt, A. 191–192, 226
Schnurr, S. 35–36, 137–138
Schwarz, J. 38–40, 257
Schwartz, P. 43
Searle, J. 73
Second Life 79–81, 89
Secord, P. 17
Sedgwick, E. 187
Segal, L. 41

Seidler, J. 41
Seidman, S. 187, 192, 193, 196, 219
semantic prosody 161
sex
  definition 3–4
  sexual activity 79–81, 141–144, 228, 233–247
sex-gender system 4
sexism 102, 167, 251, 259
sexist language 36–41, 103, 138–140, 177
  sexuality 226, 256
  definition 6
  discourses of 109
sexual identity 2, 6–7, 11, 26, 54, 56, 82, 86, 146, 158, 170, 188, 194, 216, 222, 245–246, 250, 260–261
sexual orientation 6, 7, 66, 115, 146, 191, 249
sexual role 144, 183, 188, 243, 245, 250
Shalom, C. 175
Sheldon, A. 42
Shively, C. 246
Sigley, R. 103, 104
sign theory 72
Simmons, R. 137, 139, 177
Sinfield, A. 151, 186
Skeggs, B. 8
slut 134, 137, 139, 140, 177, 202
S/M 247–248, 250, 258
Smith-Rosenberg, C. 187, 188
social class 66, 87, 245, 250
social constructionism 72, 255, 261
social network theory 64
Sofer, J. 191
Soskin, W. 34
Spargo, T. 223
Speer, A. 8, 76, 78, 131–132
Spencer, C. 188
Spender, D. 7, 36, 41, 92
spinster 203–204
Spivak, G. 196

Stallybrass, P. 145
Stanley, J. 50, 188–189
Steinem, G. 240
Stephens, J. 100, 101
stereotype 1, 2, 15, 57
stereotyping 12–13
Stevenson, N. 179
Stokoe, E. 157, 179, 180–182, 253, 254
Stone, S. 152
Stonewall 196
Storms, M. 6
Storr, M. 146, 148
Straight to Hell 243–247
strategic essentialism 196
strategic provisionality 196
structuralist research 17
Stubbs, M. 91, 95, 229
subject positions 181, 202
subordination 124–125, 127, 129, 131, 215, 219, 258
suffragette movement 77
Sunderland, J. 8, 49, 91–93, 95, 100, 101, 109, 119, 162, 232
Swacker, M. 34
Swann, J. 7, 63, 69–70
swearing 47–48, 86
swingers 233–240

taboo 9, 31, 33, 45–46, 48–49, 50, 52, 86, 88, 89, 91, 108, 124, 135, 139, 216, 220, 222–223, 226, 228, 240, 245, 248, 255, 256, 257, 263
Tabouret-Keller, A. 66
tag questions 32, 86
Tajfel, H. 121
Talbot, M. 8, 20, 30, 41, 63, 93, 95, 124, 135, 140, 145, 156, 166–168
Tannen, D. 7, 42–44
Taub, D. 55
Taylor, H. 79

television 20, 65, 101, 129, 158, 168, 169, 174, 214, 224, 228
terms of address 38, 103, 178, 201, 257
text 20, 95, 125, 259, 261
Thompson, K. 222
Thornborrow, J. 157–158
Thorne, A. 175, 176
toys 99–100
trade 188
transgender 151–152, 219
transsexual 73, 151–152
Troemel-Plotz, S. 44
Trudgill, P. 32
Trumbach, R. 188
Tucker, N. 149
Tugwell, D. 208
Turner, J. 122
Turner-Bowker, D. 101

UNICEF 226
USA *see America*

van Dijk, T. 91
van Leeuwen, T. 20, 99–100, 199
Veblen, T. 166
verb 15–16, 46, 80, 95, 119, 143, 162, 171, 186, 209, 229, 237, 245
von Taschitzki, T. 173

Warner, M. 109, 192
warrants 69–70
Watney, S. 220
Webbink, P. 55
Weedon, C. 14
Weeks, J. 155, 156, 187, 220, 221, 247, 258
Weiss, J. 7, 122
Wellings, K. 221, 227–228
Wenger, E. 65
West, C. 34, 42, 162
Westwood, G. 31

Wetherell, M. 93, 132–135, 181
White, A. 145
White, E. 55
Widdowson, H. 102
Wilkins, B. 44
Wilkinson, S. 150
Williams, P. 92
Wilson, A. 20, 45
Wilson, G. 60
Wilton, P. 241
'wimp' 133–134
Wiseman, R. 137–139, 177
Wodak, R. 8, 21, 76, 119
Wolf, N. 232
woman 103–105
women's language 29–36, 41–49, 85–87, 136–140
Wood, K. 69–70
word choice 22 *see lexis*
workplace (women's talk in) 35

Youmans, M. 241, 242
Yule, G. 91

Zeve, B. 55
Zimmerman, D. 34, 42
Zwicky, A. 56, 59–60

rce UK Ltd.
UK
J0

00001B/10

9 78845 530